W9-BAN-739

WITHDRAWN

MARCIA COYLE

THE
ROBERTS
COURT

THE STRUGGLE

FOR THE

CONSTITUTION

SIMON & SCHUSTER

NEW YORK   LONDON   TORONTO   SYDNEY   NEW DELHI

Simon & Schuster
1230 Avenue of the Americas
New York, NY 10020

First Simon & Schuster hardcover edition May 2013

SIMON & SCHUSTER and colophon are registered trademarks of Simon & Schuster, Inc.

For information about special discounts for bulk purchases, please contact
Simon & Schuster Special Sales at 1-866-506-1949 or business@simonandschuster.com.

The Simon & Schuster Speakers Bureau can bring authors to your live event.
For more information or to book an event contact the Simon & Schuster Speakers
Bureau at 1-866-248-3049 or visit our website at www.simonspeakers.com.

Designed by Akasha Archer

Manufactured in the United States of America

10 9 8 7 6 5 4 3 2 1

Library of Congress Cataloging-in-Publication Data
Coyle, Marcia.
    The Roberts court : the struggle for the constitution / Marcia Coyle.
        pages   cm
    Includes bibliographical references and index.
    1. United States. Supreme Court—History—21st century.   2. Political questions
and judicial power—United States—History—21st century.   3. Roberts, John G.,
1955–   I. Title.
    KF8742.C69 2013
    347.73'26—dc23   2012051637

ISBN 978-1-4516-2751-0
ISBN 978-1-4516-2753-4 (ebook)

For Ray, Robbie, and Kat

CONTENTS

PART 4: HEALTH CARE

INTRODUCTION

A bell rings through the chambers of the nine justices of the Supreme Court just five minutes before they take their seats in the courtroom to hear arguments in the day's cases. The sound reminds them that it is time to go to the robing room, an oak-paneled room, containing nine closets, each with a brass nameplate of the justice whose robes are inside. As soon as more than one justice enters, the traditional handshake in which each justice shakes hands with each of the other eight begins. If someone is missed there, the next opportunity is the next stop: the main conference room off of the chief justice's chambers. Chief Justice John Roberts Jr. likes to be the first justice into the conference room in order to greet his colleagues as they enter.

The handshake is done before arguments and before each conference in which the justices discuss petitions for review and vote on cases. Chief Justice Melvin Fuller started the tradition in the late nineteenth century as a reminder that although they may differ—sometimes passionately—in their opinions, they can find harmony in their common purpose.

When the justices leave the conference room on argument days, they wait in a small area behind the heavy maroon drapes that separate them from the courtroom for the buzzer announcing the 10 am start of court. On some days, the waiting public may hear muffled voices or laughter behind those drapes. On June 28, 2012, the day on which the Roberts Court would issue its most important decision in seven years, a decision with the potential to shape a presidential election and to alter the constitutional structure of government, no sound came from behind the curtains, and silence quickly descended upon a courtroom whose atmosphere was electric with anticipation.

All of the justices did shake hands that morning before the fate of the nation's new health care law was revealed, confirmed one justice, but the harmony of a shared purpose was harder for some to grasp. This was a bitterly divided Court.

In one sense, the Roberts Court had come full circle. The last day of the 2006–07 term (ironically also June 28), had been the high-water mark for intense emotion and disagreement on the Court. A 5–4 conservative majority, led by Roberts, rejected two school districts' attempts to maintain racial diversity in their public schools. The Court's four moderate-liberal justices, in passionate dissent, accused Roberts and the majority of distorting the meaning of the landmark *Brown v. Board of Education*, which ended school segregation, and of abandoning other important precedents on issues ranging from abortion to antitrust law. On the final day of the 2011–12 term, Roberts and the four moderate-liberal justices found common ground to save the linchpin of the new health care law—the individual mandate—while the four remaining conservatives, in angry dissent, skewered the majority for rewriting the law, they claimed, to make it constitutional. That day, one justice later said, was as intensely emotional for all of them as the day of the school race decision five years earlier.

Disparagingly dubbed "Obamacare" by its opponents, the Patient Protection and Affordable Care Act became the centerpiece of the latest struggle for ownership of the true meaning and scope of some of the U.S. Constitution's most significant grants of power. It is a struggle as old as the Constitution itself, and it engages public passions particularly when the nation faces pressing social or economic questions.

The struggle is not between one president and one chief justice, or between the Congress and the Supreme Court. It is a struggle within the Supreme Court itself and it reflects differing visions as well within the other branches of government, the political parties, and the American people themselves.

"However counterintuitive it may seem, the integrity and coherence of constitutional law are to be found in, not apart from, controversy," wrote one constitutional law scholar a decade ago.[1]

Four signature decisions of the Roberts Court expose the fault lines among the justices as they engage in this ongoing struggle. They reveal a confident conservative majority with a muscular sense of power, a notable disdain for Congress, and a willingness to act aggressively and in distinctly unconservative ways by:

Boldly raising questions not asked or not necessary to resolve, as in the 2010 campaign finance blockbuster, *Citizens United v. Federal Election Commission*;

Refusing to defer to decisions by elected and accountable local or national officials, as in the 2008 Second Amendment gun ruling—*District of Columbia v. Heller*—the 2007 Seattle-Louisville public school integration decision, and the 2012 landmark health care ruling,

And overruling precedents, both old and recent, as in *Citizens United*, *Heller*, and the Seattle-Louisville cases.

In each of the four decisions, the justices do battle and ultimately divide 5–4 over the meaning of parts of the Constitution: the Fourteenth Amendment's guarantee of equal protection in the school race cases; the Second Amendment's right of the people to keep and bear arms in the gun challenge; the First Amendment's guarantee of free speech in the campaign finance case; and Article I's grant of power to Congress to regulate commerce and to tax and spend for the general welfare in the health care challenge.

Cases usually get to the Supreme Court after an expensive, hard slog through the lower courts. Some begin, as the Seattle-Louisville cases did, with mothers upset that their children did not get into their first choice of a public school. Others, like the *Heller* gun case, start with two lawyers deciding, over drinks, to manufacture a Second Amendment case.

All four landmark Roberts Court decisions had at their inception very smart and talented conservative or libertarian lawyers who, when necessary, handpicked the most sympathetic clients for their lawsuits, strategized over the best courts in which to file, and, with an eye toward their ultimate target—an increasingly friendly and conservative Supreme Court—framed the winning arguments.

In fact, the same scenario is unfolding in the 2012–13 term in the Court's most important challenge to affirmative action in almost a decade. *Fisher v. University of Texas* is a challenge by a white student rejected for admission to the university. She claims that the consideration of race as one of many factors in the admissions policy violates the Constitution. The driving force behind the *Fisher* lawsuit was not the student, Abigail Fisher, but Edward Blum, head of the conservative one-man, anti–affirmative action organization, the Project on Fair Representation.

As he said in a *Texas Tribune* interview: "I find the plaintiff, I find the lawyer, and I put them together, and then I worry about it for four years."[2] Blum, who opposes all race-based classifications, is also behind a key challenge in the Supreme Court to the Voting Rights Act of 1965, the most successful civil rights law in history.

More than 50 percent of the Court's cases each term are decided unanimously or nearly unanimously by 8–1 or 7–2 votes. That fairly consistent rate of agreement is a reflection of the remarkable ability of the Court to achieve consensus on widely varying questions of law. So why focus on 5–4 decisions and these four rulings in particular? First, the four cases are defining—landmark—rulings of the Roberts Court and deserve close scrutiny. Second, it is from the Court's 5–4 decisions that we learn the most about the justices themselves. The most closely divided rulings of the Roberts Court reveal sharply divergent views of history, approaches to interpreting the Constitution, the role of government in American lives, and what makes a just society.

Those decisions also are a reminder of the importance of presidential elections to the future direction of the Court. As a new presidential term unfolds this year, four justices are in their seventies, two on the Court's conservative wing—Antonin Scalia and Anthony Kennedy—and two on the moderate-liberal wing—Ruth Bader Ginsburg (who turned eighty on March 15, 2013) and Stephen Breyer. Although none shows any inclination to step down, the replacement of just one of the four has implications for the outcomes on issues that narrowly divide them.

Consider the four decisions whose stories are told here. Each has left the door open to future efforts to push the envelope in those controversial areas of the law. Gun rights activists are filing challenges to state bans on assault weapons and the open carrying of guns and to guns on campuses. State public finance systems for election campaigns are under attack post–*Citizens United*. The affirmative action challenge to the University of Texas's admissions policy, now before the Supreme Court, is being pursued in the name of the "color-blind Constitution" endorsed by four conservative justices in the Seattle-Louisville ruling. And after the health care decision, new suits attacking parts of the law on religious and other grounds have been filed. Supreme Court decisions matter, and so too do presidential elections.

The health care challenge, perhaps the most important of the four cases here, arrived at the U.S. Supreme Court at a particularly sensitive time for the Roberts Court. In what one presidential and Supreme Court scholar has called an "unprecedented" phenomenon, the ideologies of the nine justices are aligned with the politics of the presidents who appointed them.[3] The Court's five conservative justices were appointed by Republican presidents, and the four liberal justices by Democratic presidents. That was not the case when recently retired Justices John Paul Stevens and David Souter sat on the Court. Both were Republican appointees, but they sided most often with the Court's Democratic appointees, and so blurred the ideological and political lines.

As if sensing the coming political tornado embodied by the health care challenge, Justice Ruth Bader Ginsburg, in an interview in the summer of 2011, said: "What I care most about, and I think most of my colleagues do, too, is that we want this institution to maintain the position that it has had in this system, where it is not considered a political branch of government."[4]

The Supreme Court, however, sits atop a political branch of government, one of three branches whose powers and duties are enshrined in the Constitution. Federal judges and justices get their jobs through a political process: political recommendations to the president, appointment by the president, and confirmation by the Senate. Ginsburg's real concern and fervent hope were that the Court not be considered a partisan institution.

"The Court survived one great danger—*Bush v. Gore*," said one justice, referring to charges that politics drove the outcome in the 2000 ruling by the Rehnquist Court that decided the presidential election. "At least to me that seemed highly political."

However, *Bush v. Gore* triggered an enduring cynicism about the Court among many Americans. That cynicism deepened with the Roberts Court's 2010 decision in *Citizens United v. Federal Election Commission*, which eliminated legal bans on the use of general treasury funds by corporations and unions for making independent expenditures in elections. "It's the most hated of any recent Supreme Court decision, even more than *Bush v. Gore*," said the lawyer who won both cases, Theodore Olson.[5] And this cynicism was reflected in a number of public opinion polls taken shortly before the 2012 health care ruling in which a majority of voters said politics would influence the outcome of the challenge to the new law.

Whether the justices are practicing law or politics in their most controversial cases is a profoundly difficult question, but one that scholars and others have tried to define, measure, or answer in various ways. "Judicial activism" is by now an overused and mostly unsatisfactory way of answering the question and implying a political agenda. For many people, a charge of judicial activism today has come to mean a decision with which those making the charge disagree.

Yale Law School's Jack Balkin and others have written about "high politics" and "low politics" on the Supreme Court.

"It is ok for judges and Justices to have constitutional politics, to have larger visions of what the Constitution means or should mean and what rights Americans have or should have," explains Balkin. "That is what I mean by 'high politics,' and there's nothing wrong with judges having such views." Judges pursue "high politics," he adds, through their legal arguments.[6]

On the other hand, judges should not pursue "low politics"—the manipulation of doctrine to give an advantage or power to a particular group or political party. For Balkin, the decision in *Bush v. Gore* was "low politics," and others would point to the *Citizens United* decision.

The justices themselves vehemently deny that politics, especially of the "low" kind, ever enters their deliberations.

"I don't think the Court is political at all," Justice Scalia said during a television interview a month after the health care decision. "People say that because at least in the recent couple of years since John Paul Stevens and David Souter have left the Court, the breakout is often 5 to 4, with 5 [Republican-appointed judges] and 4 by Democrats on the other side. Why should they be surprised that after assiduously trying to get people with these philosophies, [presidents] end up with people with these philosophies?"[7]

Politics is what happens "across the street," Justice Clarence Thomas has said, referring to Congress, which meets across the street from the U.S. Supreme Court Building.

Another justice, speaking only on background, explained, "I think when Justice *X* sits down and starts working on a case, that justice doesn't think, 'This is the result I want to reach because I'm a [liberal Democrat or a conservative Republican].' That justice does what I do: reads the briefs, reads the statute, reads the cases. And even if nine times out of ten looking back you see it in a certain way, we all know that's just not how the process works."

Justice Stephen Breyer too has chafed at what he considers to be the media's portrayal of the justices at times as "junior league politicians." Breyer has written that "[p]olitics in our decision-making process does not exist. By politics, I mean . . . will it help certain individuals be elected? Personal ideology or philosophy is a different matter. Judges have had different life experiences and different kinds of training, and they come from different backgrounds. Judges appointed by different presidents of different political parties may have different views about the interpretation of the law and its relation to the world."[8]

When the Roberts Court split 5–4 along ideological lines in the four cases at the center of this book, or when it divides that way in any of its cases, the media covering the Court, often short of time and space, may find it simpler to speak in terms of the conservative or liberal wings of the Court in explaining those votes. However, as the four decisions here show, those wings or blocks are not monolithic.

In the Seattle-Louisville school cases, Justice Anthony Kennedy refused to join Roberts, Scalia, Samuel Alito Jr., and Thomas in their view that the Constitution is color-blind even though he agreed that the school plans were unconstitutional. A color-blind Constitution, said Kennedy, is still an aspiration.

Although they divided 5–4 in *Citizens United* in striking down the ban on the use of treasury funds for corporate independent expenditures, eight justices agreed that the federal law's reporting and disclosure requirements on those expenditures were constitutional. Thomas did not agree.

And four conservative justices in the health care ruling—Kennedy, Scalia, Thomas, and Alito—disagreed with Roberts that the penalty for not having minimum health insurance was a constitutional tax.

The Court's liberal justices also do not always stand as one. Justices Breyer and Elena Kagan disagreed with Ginsburg and Sonia Sotomayor on the constitutionality of the health care law's expansion of Medicaid for the poor and disabled. Ginsburg and Breyer part company with each other over Scalia's view of the Sixth Amendment's confrontation clause and on certain sentencing issues.

"It's always troubling, and I know it's an easy way to get a hook on things, to say that there are however many conservatives or liberals on one side or another, but that's not the way we approach any individual case," insisted another justice. "The results are what the results are, but this idea that there's one bloc or two blocs is just not the way we do it."

Each of the justices is the product of his or her experiences in life and in law, and each brings those experiences to bear when deciding cases. The justices' personal biases are constrained by certain doctrines, such as *stare decisis* (respect for precedents), and some justices adhere to those doctrines more strongly than others do.

"Justice Scalia has a fixed view of what is good for the country and of the Constitution," said one justice, adding, "I have my own view."

So what is the public to make of the Roberts Court and its signature decisions? Few who closely watch the Court doubt that it is the most conservative Supreme Court in decades, despite the ruling upholding the health care reform law. It is more conservative than its predecessor, the Rehnquist Court, primarily because Samuel Alito Jr. replaced Sandra Day O'Connor, formerly the center of the Court, and Alito is more conservative than O'Connor was. And because Alito replaced O'Connor, Anthony Kennedy moved into the current center of the Court—its crucial swing vote—and he votes more often with his conservative colleagues in cases closely dividing the Court than O'Connor did.

However, that is the easiest way to tell the story of the Roberts Court and the ongoing struggle for the Constitution. There is a more difficult way.

In a recent public conversation about civics and the Supreme Court, retired Justice David Souter spoke of the range of language in the Constitution. Some language is specific, such as the age of eligibility to be president is thirty-five years old. Other language, he said, has "extraordinary breadth," for example, "unreasonable searches and seizures," or even "freedom of speech."

Those general terms, he said, are best understood as a "listing or a menu of approved values, the application of which has got to be worked out over time." A great deal of what the Supreme Court does is to attempt to figure out the application of those values.

Sometimes the values compete. In *Citizens United*, he said, the liberty model of free expression says corporations can spend all the money they want independent of candidates. However, an equality approach would say there must be some limitation on corporations so they do not drown out other speech. The Constitution does not contain a provision telling the justices how to resolve the tension between those values.

How then does the public judge the justices? The public, said Souter, has to read the Court's decisions.

"A principled decision is one in which the Court candidly and convincingly explains why this principle prevailed over that principle," he said. "It is the choice of principles that is the tough part. The public judgment has got to be a judgment on whether they believe what the Court says, whether they believe what the Court says is convincing in making that choice between principles."[9]

In the four rulings on schools and racial diversity, gun rights, campaign finance, and health care reform, the justices confront and choose between principles amidst a modern-day tsunami of special interests trying to sway the final choice. In the end, however, the public's judgment remains the key to the Court's most important and only institutional power: its legitimacy in the eyes of the American people.

PART 1

—◆—

RACE

CHAPTER 1

——————

"What kind of justice will John Roberts be? Will you be a truly modest, temperate, careful judge in the tradition of Harlan, Jackson, Frankfurter and Friendly?"

—Senator Charles Schumer (D-NY), 2005

On October 3, 2005—the first Monday in October of that year—the Roberts Court, named after its newly sworn chief justice, John Roberts Jr., officially began its first Supreme Court term and a new era in the Court's history. But that was not the true beginning of the Roberts Court.

The real start of the Roberts Court would take place some eight months later in a conference room just off of the chief justice's chambers. A vote would be cast to hear and decide two cases exposing one of the deepest and most enduring divides among the justices. The cases concerned a question of race. They also would cast doubt on the new chief justice's public commitment during his Senate confirmation hearings to so-called minimalism—narrow decision making—and respect for the Court's prior decisions.

On that warm October day in 2005, the Roberts Court was not yet fully formed. Earlier that summer, Justice Sandra Day O'Connor had announced her plans to leave the Court as soon as her successor was confirmed. By the time the first Monday in October arrived, she was still on the Court awaiting the nomination and confirmation of that successor. O'Connor would keep her seat for nearly four more months.

It was a period of major transition for the Court. Roberts was the first new justice in eleven years—the longest time in which the Court had gone without a change in modern history. Roberts's predecessor, William H. Rehnquist, had died and was buried just three weeks before the new chief was sworn into office. And although O'Connor's departure date was unknown, everyone inside the Court keenly felt the impending end to her presence in the building and to her remarkable contribution to the Court's work.

"These were not only two, very long tenured justices; they were beloved," said James Ho, former clerk to Justice Clarence Thomas in the 2005–06 term. "Rehnquist's passing—it's not possible to overstate the emotional impact that had on the Court. And O'Connor, she was not just a Court institution but an American institution because of her biography. When you lose two people like that, it has a big impact."[1]

Rehnquist's style as chief was dramatically different from the style of his predecessor—Warren Burger. Rehnquist was fair in his assigning of opinions to his colleagues, did not hold grudges, and had a self-deprecating and sometimes mischievous sense of humor. For example, his favorite Gilbert and Sullivan operetta, *Iolanthe*, was the inspiration for the four gold stripes that appeared on the sleeves of the black robe that he wore into court one morning and thereafter—stripes modeled after the costume worn by the Lord Chancellor in an *Iolanthe* production.[2]

"A plain speaker without airs or affectations, the Chief fostered a spirit of collegiality among the nine of us perhaps unparalleled in the Court's history," said Justice Ruth Bader Ginsburg in a statement issued after his death.

And that spirit was felt by more people than just the nine justices. Inside the Supreme Court's majestic building, there is a strong sense of family among all who work there, from the police officers to the justices' secretaries, many of whom spend their entire careers at the Court. While tourists crowd the lower level, inspecting justices' portraits, the gift shop, and other exhibits, a quiet calmness pervades the carpeted upper hallways, signaling the seriousness and respect with which the work is done within the justices' chambers. Not surprisingly, then, nearly everyone inside the Court felt the impact of the first major changes there in eleven years.

But it also was a time of excitement and some anxiety, Ho and others recalled. Two new justices were coming on board. "Every year at the Court is historic, but this transition made it especially so," said Ho.

No one knew at the time that this transition would not end with the new chief justice and the successor to O'Connor. In 2009 and 2010, two more of the Court's members—David Souter and John Paul Stevens—retired. In just five short years, roughly half of the Supreme Court had changed.

Ask a justice what it means for the Court when one justice departs and a new one arrives and the most common answer is to repeat the late Justice Byron White's well-worn comment that it is a new Court with each new justice. But what does that really mean?

"Old alliances, people you could rely on for certain positions in prior cases aren't there anymore," said a relaxed Justice Antonin Scalia in his chambers on a hot summer afternoon in 2011. "That's always the principal effect of a new justice."[3]

Scalia himself is a perfect example of what a change in the Court's membership can mean to an individual justice and his or her work in certain areas of the law. Ask him of what decision he is proudest in his high court tenure and he will say his 2004 ruling in *Crawford v. Washington*, which involved the confrontation clause in the Sixth Amendment to the Constitution. That clause guarantees that "in all criminal prosecutions, the accused shall enjoy the right . . . to be confronted with the witnesses against him."

In the *Crawford* case, Michael Crawford was accused of stabbing a man who, Crawford claimed, tried to rape his wife. During the jury trial, prosecutors played the wife's tape-recorded statement to police in which she described the stabbing. Her statement conflicted with

Crawford's defense. He had no opportunity for cross-examination and he argued that admitting the wife's statement would violate his Sixth Amendment right to be confronted with the witnesses against him.

A 1980 Supreme Court decision, however, held that the Sixth Amendment right does not prohibit the admission of a statement by a witness who is not available if the statement has "adequate 'indicia of reliability.' " The trial court found, and the later appellate court agreed, that the wife's statement against Crawford was trustworthy. His conviction for assault was upheld.

The Supreme Court, in an opinion by Scalia, reversed. Scalia, a leading proponent of interpreting the Constitution according to its "original public meaning," traced the Founding Fathers' concept of the right to confront one's accusers to English common law. He said the key question is whether the evidence the government seeks to introduce is testimonial; if it is testimonial, the defendant must be given an opportunity to cross-examine the person who made the statement or created the evidence.

The unanimous opinion overruled the 1980 decision, and during the next decade, the Court—and Scalia in particular—has been applying what is a surprisingly defendant-friendly view of the confrontation clause to a variety of circumstances in which the prosecution seeks to present testimonial evidence without the person who made the statement or created the evidence.

But the rulings in this area of the law stopped being unanimous as new questions arose about who must testify at trial in order to satisfy the confrontation right. Does the state laboratory analyst who prepared a certificate stating what drug was seized by police have to testify or is the certificate enough? And what about a statement to police by a wounded crime victim identifying who shot him when the victim later dies?

Scalia's drive to restore the confrontation clause to its original meaning depended on his unlikely alliance with Justices John Paul Stevens, David Souter, and Ruth Bader Ginsburg as the rulings split 5–4. With

Stevens and Souter gone, Scalia's success is fragile in the face of staunch disagreement by Roberts and Justices Anthony Kennedy, Stephen Breyer, and Samuel Alito Jr. While Justices Sonia Sotomayor and Elena Kagan have sometimes joined with the Scalia view, the strength of their commitment in this area is yet unknown. Neither is an "originalist" like Scalia, and perhaps not even "originalists for a day" in the context of the confrontation clause.

A transition also affects the dynamic within the justices' private conference where they meet to discuss and vote on which cases to hear and to decide the cases already argued and ready for decision. On cases ready for decision, the chief justice speaks first, presenting the issue in the case and his vote. The discussion and vote then proceed around the rectangular conference table in order of seniority. With Stevens's retirement, Scalia is the senior associate justice and he speaks after Roberts. The last justice to speak and vote—sometimes casting the decisive vote—is now Kagan, the most junior justice. Before Kagan, it was Sotomayor, for only one term, and before her, Alito held the junior justice seat.

The junior justice also takes notes on what happens in the conference and reports results to the clerk of the Court.

And a transition obviously affects relationships among the justices.[4]

"Just think of any other organization where you have twenty percent turnover," described one justice. "It's going to be different. You develop not only a relationship with the Court but individual relationships as well. I miss David Souter very, very much. Like anything else, you suddenly get a new member of the family and you try to get to know them, to establish a relationship with them, how they like to deal with colleagues, be it a close personal relationship or to maintain a more distant one. It adds a new element, and then you do it again a year later. It reshuffles the deck. I don't know that I would go as far as Justice White's comment."

For Roberts, Sotomayor, and Kagan—all in their fifties—the probability of working together for twenty or more years can be daunting. "That's a marriage, right?" said another justice. "And different people have different ways of dealing with marriage. One way is whatever little things you don't like, you may as well raise them because they'll be annoying for how many years, or do you wait and only raise the big things? It's an interesting dynamic."

But on that first Monday in October 2005, the dynamic was just beginning to take shape.

Less than an hour before Roberts was to be formally invested in his new role, President George W. Bush, with White House counsel Harriet Miers at his side, announced that he was nominating Miers to the seat held by O'Connor. After the stunning announcement, Bush left the White House and headed to the Supreme Court for Roberts's investiture. The Miers nomination would implode before the month's end. Although Miers was criticized across the political spectrum for her close personal ties to Bush and for having an inadequate grasp of constitutional and statutory issues, the most conservative elements of the Republican Party who doubted her fealty to their legal causes ultimately torpedoed her nomination.[5]

But no one could have foreseen that outcome when at roughly 9:15 am, about an hour before the new term officially began, Roberts entered the courtroom in his black robe and took a seat in front of the press section, a row of wooden pews to the left of the bench as he faced it. He sat in the black leather-bound chair first used by Chief Justice John Marshall two centuries earlier as he waited to take the ceremonial oath of office before a courtroom packed with visiting friends, family, dignitaries, and officials. The other justices stepped out from behind the maroon velvet curtain that separates them from the courtroom and the formal investiture ceremony began.

Attorney General Alberto Gonzales, wearing a formal morning coat with tails, stepped to the lectern in front of the bench and presented and read Roberts's commission—an ivory-colored document that President Bush had signed stating his intent to nominate Roberts as chief justice.

Roberts then walked up to the bench and faced Justice John Paul Stevens, the senior associate justice, who would administer the oath.

The contrast between the two men was striking: Roberts, youthful and serious; Stevens, relaxed and white-haired, his trademark bow tie poking out of his black robe. After taking the oath, Roberts sat down in the chair which last had been occupied by Rehnquist for nineteen of his thirty-three years on the Court. At age fifty, Roberts was likely to have just as long a tenure.

Stevens noted that flags outside of the building were flying at half-mast in honor of Rehnquist, whom he called "truly first among equals." He then welcomed Roberts, saying the justices knew him well. Roberts had argued thirty-nine cases before the Court, as a former principal deputy solicitor general during the George H. W. Bush administration and as one of the most respected Supreme Court practitioners in private practice. The thirty-nine cases, added Stevens with a smile, "exceeds the combined experience of the rest of us."

Roberts then formally closed the October 2004–05 term and opened the 2005–06 term. As is traditional, he welcomed attorneys sworn in as new members of the bar of the Supreme Court and announced arguments in the first case of the new term.

When the new chief justice assumed the center seat on the bench, the press and other observers that day agreed that his new role seemed to fit like a pair of old slippers. But it was not as easy as it seemed.

A protégé of Chief Justice William H. Rehnquist, Roberts had helped to bury his predecessor, who had lost his battle with thyroid cancer, just weeks before the opening of the new term. Roberts had been confirmed the Thursday before the first Monday in October, and he was superstitious enough about his confirmation chances that he had done nothing to prepare for the first cases to be argued—no reading of the briefs, nothing.

However, he was no stranger to the rhythm of the Court's life. He had clerked for Rehnquist, and, as Stevens had told the audience that morning, Roberts had represented the United States in the Supreme Court as a principal deputy solicitor general, and had been one of the premier advocates before the Court as a lawyer in private practice.

Like many aspects of life at the Court, there was a well-known script to follow. Roberts knew it and used it to ease himself through a very difficult time.

Experience also had helped Roberts get through the political endurance test of his confirmation hearings. He had previously faced the Senate Judiciary Committee. President George W. Bush nominated him in 2001 for a seat on the District of Columbia federal appellate court, but his nomination was never voted on by the Democratic-controlled Senate Judiciary Committee. He had proven his partisan bona fides when, in the legal battles over the Florida presidential balloting in 2000, he played a role on the legal team defending candidate George W. Bush. And Bush and his top aides remembered him. Bush renominated him in 2003 and Roberts was confirmed by a voice vote in the Republican-controlled Senate.

In his memoir, *Decision Points*, Bush described Roberts as a "genuine man with a gentle soul." The president wrote: "I believed Roberts would be a natural leader. I didn't worry about him drifting away from his principles over time. He described his philosophy of judicial modesty with a baseball analogy that stuck with me: 'A good judge is like an umpire—and no umpire thinks he is the most important person on the field.' "[6]

Bush's concern about a justice "drifting" from his principles stemmed, he wrote, from his father's disappointment with the appointment of Justice David Souter who, in his second term, began to move to the Court's left and remained there until his retirement in 2009.

Roberts was one of five finalists, and not the top choice of some of Bush's staff. White House counsel Harriet Miers preferred Samuel Alito Jr., a judge on the U.S. Court of Appeals for the Third Circuit. Attorney General Alberto Gonzales and Vice President Dick Cheney wanted Michael Luttig, a judge on the U.S. Court of Appeals for the Fourth Circuit. In the end, however, the "tiebreaker" question, according to Bush, was who would be the most effective leader on the Court, and the answer was, he believed, Roberts.

Hearings on Supreme Court nominations today appear to be more about the political agendas of the individual senators than about what is in the mind of the nominee. There was little in Roberts's only forty-nine opinions as an appellate judge for skeptical Democrats on the Senate Judiciary Committee to use to show him as an ultra or radical conservative. But he had been a foot soldier in the Reagan administration, where he had worked as a young lawyer in the Department of Justice, first as a special assistant to Attorney General William French Smith, and afterward as associate counsel to President Reagan in the Office of White House Counsel. Roberts's memos on a variety of controversial legal issues during those years as well as his legal briefs when he served as deputy solicitor general in the George H. W. Bush administration provided a paper trail for those who sought to derail his nomination or who, accepting that he was a conservative, honestly wondered, or feared, how far to the right he might lead the Court.

The hearings revisited the Reagan legal revolution of the 1980s in which the administration strategically sought to remake the judiciary with young conservative appointees. Top advisers, such as William French Smith and Edwin Meese, accused the federal courts—and the Supreme Court in particular—of straying from the Constitution's text by finding a right to an abortion, approving affirmative action, and enforcing anti-discrimination laws too aggressively. Democrats also revisited Rehnquist Court rulings restricting abortion, affirmative action, voting rights, and civil rights laws involving disabilities and sex discrimination, among other issues. Roberts's memos and legal briefs reflected a keen commitment to the goals of the administration in which he worked at the time.

When the hearings opened, the public saw a youthful nominee, leaning forward in his chair at the witness table in front of the Judiciary panel, earnest and yet relaxed, much as he is today during Supreme Court arguments. He quickly displayed a broad and deep knowledge of a range of constitutional areas and gave his answers to questions with a polish developed during years of appellate arguments in the federal courts. He also deflected more probing questions about positions taken in his memos—positions largely rejected by Congress—by saying he was acting as a lawyer for his client, the president, and advocating for his client's positions.

"John Roberts is a master at the sort of gentle, persuasive answers that don't go to the nub of what they want to know," said one supporter at the time.

Central to all Supreme Court confirmation hearings is an attempt by senators to define the nominee's judicial philosophy and faithfulness to *stare decisis* (respect for previously decided cases). The latter was hugely important to those who wanted to preserve or overturn such rulings as the landmark abortion case, *Roe v. Wade*.

Senator Orrin Hatch, Republican from Utah, pressed Roberts during the hearings on his judicial philosophy. Hatch noted that he had recently read a book in which the author, legal scholar Cass Sunstein, discussed various judicial philosophies. "Some of the philosophies he discussed were whether a judge should be an originalist, a strict constructionist, a fundamentalist, a perfectionist, a majoritarian or a minimalist. Which of those categories do you fit in?" he asked Roberts.

As he has ever since, Roberts resisted a label. "I have told people when pressed that I prefer to be known as a modest judge, and to me that means some of the things that you talked about in those other labels," he told Hatch. "It means an appreciation that the role of the judge is limited, that a judge is to decide the cases before them, they're not to legislate, they're not to execute the laws.

"Another part of that humility has to do with respect for precedent that forms part of the rule of law that the judge is obligated to apply under principles of stare decisis. Part of that modesty has to do with being open to the considered views of your colleagues on the bench. They've looked at the same cases. And if they're seeing things in a very different way, you need to be open to that and try to take another look at your view and make sure that you're on solid ground.

"Now, I think that general approach results in a modest approach to judging which is good for the legal system as a whole. I don't think the courts should have a dominant role in society and redressing society's problems. It is their job to say what the law is."

And in perhaps one of his most memorable comments in those hearings, Roberts compared the job of a judge to that of a baseball umpire— the analogy that had stuck with Bush: "Judges are like umpires. Umpires don't make the rules, they apply them. The role of an umpire and a judge is critical to make sure everybody plays by the rules. But it is a limited role. Nobody ever went to a ball game to see the umpire. . . . And I will remember that it's my job to call balls and strikes, and not pitch or bat."[7]

Senator Arlen Specter, committee chair and Republican from Pennsylvania, took up the question of Roberts's view of *stare decisis*. Specter, a moderate Republican and longtime supporter of *Roe v. Wade*, probed Roberts as hard as he could, in the context of that abortion ruling, on his faithfulness to precedents of the Court. Specter and other defenders of *Roe* had reason to be suspicious of Roberts's view of the *Roe* decision. As a lawyer in the Reagan administration, Roberts had written legal memos defending the administration's anti-abortion policies. And as deputy solicitor general in the George H. W. Bush administration, he had signed a brief urging the Supreme Court to overturn *Roe*.

To Specter's questions on *stare decisis*, Roberts said, "I do think that it is a jolt to the legal system when you overrule a precedent. Precedent plays an important role in promoting stability and evenhandedness. It is not enough—and the Court has emphasized this on several occasions— it is not enough that you may think the prior decision was wrongly decided. That really doesn't answer the question. It just poses the question. And you do look at these other factors, like settled expectations, like the legitimacy of the Court, like whether a particular precedent is workable or not, whether a precedent has been eroded by subsequent developments. All of those factors go into the determination of whether to revisit a precedent under the principles of stare decisis."[8]

But as to *Roe v. Wade*, Roberts would only say that the decision is "settled as a precedent of the court, entitled to respect under principles of stare decisis."

In his last round of questions, Democratic senator Charles Schumer of New York said the "fundamental question" facing the Senate and the public was: "What kind of justice will John Roberts be? Will you be a truly modest, temperate, careful judge in the tradition of Harlan, Jackson, Frankfurter and Friendly? Will you be a very conservative judge who will impede congressional prerogatives but does not use the bench to remake society, like Justice Rehnquist? Or will you use your enormous talents to use the Court to turn back a near century of progress and create the majority that Justices Scalia and Thomas could not achieve?"[9]

That question was very much on the minds of the justices and their clerks on that first Monday of Roberts's first day as chief justice of the United States. As the coming years and cases would show, the answer to the question would be: Roberts shares some of the qualities of all of those justices, and he is unafraid to deliver a major "jolt" to the system if he disagrees with the law's direction.

During his confirmation hearings, Roberts had said he admired Chief Justice John Marshall, the nation's fourth chief justice and considered its greatest. He spoke of Marshall's ability to achieve consensus among his colleagues. From 1801 until 1835 when Marshall died, the Court generally did speak with one voice and often in Marshall's own voice. Of some 1,000 opinions during that period, Marshall wrote more than 500.

Some senators pressed Roberts about the large number of 5–4 decisions and separate concurring and dissenting opinions being issued in recent years. By the end of his hearings, Roberts had made clear two goals as chief justice: greater consensus on the Court and minimalism— a preference for narrow decision making.

As he would explain in a speech in the spring of his first term, "If it is not necessary to decide more to a case, then in my view it is necessary not to decide more to a case. Division should not be artificially suppressed, but the rule of law benefits from a broader agreement. The broader the agreement among the justices, the more likely it is a decision on the narrowest possible grounds."[10]

Consensus, minimalist decision making, respect for prior precedents—Roberts had laid down the markers of his tenure on the Supreme Court.

As the first term of the Roberts Court got underway, the docket offered a trove of potential blockbuster cases that could test Roberts's triple goals. Awaiting arguments were cases involving a minor's access to abortion, disabled prisoners' right to sue states under the nation's law against disability discrimination, a clash between the federal government and Oregon's assisted suicide law, and religious use of a hallucinogenic tea containing a drug banned by federal law. And waiting in the wings was a case likely to define the term: an appeal questioning the legality of the Bush administration's military commissions for trials of Guantánamo Bay detainees.

The justices had moved only through their first session of oral arguments when news broke that White House counsel Harriet Miers, nominated to replace retiring Justice Sandra Day O'Connor, had asked that her nomination be withdrawn. President Bush wasted no time in naming a successor, and on October 31, he turned to a contemporary of Roberts for the nomination: Samuel Alito Jr., fifty-five, a judge on the U.S. Court of Appeals for the Third Circuit. In 1981, the same year Roberts joined the Reagan Justice Department, Alito, a former federal prosecutor, began work there as an assistant to the solicitor general and later, in a promotion, as deputy assistant attorney general in the Office of Legal Counsel—the same office in which Chief Justice Rehnquist and Justice Antonin Scalia once had served as Nixon appointees.

The Alito confirmation, however, was months away, and the Court had a high-stakes docket to confront. O'Connor and the rest of her colleagues were in an unusual position that fall. Neither knew when she would be leaving the bench. And her votes in cases would be effective only if the decisions were issued while she was still sitting.

As the term unfolded, the new chief justice appeared to be making considerable headway on his goals. From October 3, 2005, until O'Connor left the Court at the end of January 2006, the justices issued nineteen decisions; twelve were unanimous and only two were by 5–4 votes. The 5–4 decisions involved a death penalty case, in which the majority, consisting of Roberts, O'Connor, Scalia, Kennedy, and Thomas, ruled against the prisoner; and a bankruptcy case, in which the majority, with Stevens, O'Connor, Souter, Ginsburg, and Breyer voting, rejected a state's claim of sovereign immunity from suit. Both decisions reflected the importance of O'Connor as the longtime "swing" vote.

The unanimous decisions included what many observers thought would be one of the term's most controversial issues: its first abortion case in five years. The case—*Ayotte v. Planned Parenthood of Northern New England*—began as a challenge to a New Hampshire law barring doctors from performing abortions for teenagers under the age of eighteen until forty-eight hours after a parent has been notified. Contrary to past Supreme Court decisions, the law had no exception for medical emergencies when necessary to protect a pregnant teen's health, only the teen's life. The lower courts had struck down the law because of that omission.

But O'Connor, writing for the Court, said the lower courts acted too broadly by striking down the entire law. "When a statute restricting access to abortion may be applied in a manner that harms women's health, what is the appropriate relief?" she asked. "Generally speaking, when confronting a constitutional flaw in a statute, we try to limit the solution to the problem. We prefer, for example, to enjoin only the unconstitutional applications of a statute while leaving other applications in force, or to sever its problematic portions while leaving the remainder intact."

She said the lower court should find a solution short of invalidating the entire law. The case was sent back to the lower court with instructions to craft a narrower remedy and to determine if that remedy would be consistent with what the state legislature had intended.

O'Connor read a summary of her decision from the bench on January 18, 2006. It was her last decision as a justice. Thirteen days later, on January 31, she officially retired from the Court. That same day, Samuel Alito Jr. was confirmed by the Senate as O'Connor's successor and took his seat as an associate justice.

Alito's replacement of Sandra Day O'Connor would be as critical a change on the Roberts Court as that of Clarence Thomas for Thurgood Marshall on the Rehnquist Court. Combined with the arrival that month of two cases challenging the race-based assignments of public school students, the stage was set for the true unfolding of the Roberts Court era.

CHAPTER 2

━━━◆━━━

"I said this before I even knew who Sarah Palin was, 'I'm a momma bear just protecting her cubs.' I said, 'This race tiebreaker, this just isn't right.'"

—Kathleen Brose, head of Parents Involved
in Community Schools, 2011

On a crisp morning the following December, a chill wind cut unforgivingly across the wide plaza in front of the Supreme Court and through the crowd of several thousand amassing at the plaza's steps. The mostly high school and college-aged demonstrators waved signs urging the justices inside to "Save *Brown v. Board of Education*" and "Fight for Equality" as they chanted: "Jim Crow? Hell, no! We won't go!"

As they prepared to march down Capitol Hill toward the Lincoln Memorial, the line of people hoping to get seats in the courtroom that day continued to grow on the Supreme Court's plaza under the watchful eyes of the Supreme Court police.

At 10 am sharp, the courtroom buzzer signaled those inside to stand as the justices stepped from behind the maroon velvet curtain and prepared to hear the first arguments of the day. On the calendar that morning were two cases that embodied the nation's long and divisive struggle with racial discrimination. By the end of the Supreme Court term, the opinions in the two cases would reflect shattered hopes for greater consensus among the justices and bitter feelings of betrayal on both sides of what had emerged as the deepest divide on the fledgling Roberts Court.

The justices were being asked to judge the constitutionality of attempts by local, elected school boards in Seattle, Washington, and Louisville, Kentucky, to maintain racial diversity in their primary and secondary schools.

A group of Seattle parents whose children did not get into their top choices of high schools challenged the constitutionality of the district's use of race as one factor in its student assignment plan. And a Louisville mother whose son could not attend the kindergarten program closest to his home initiated the lawsuit attacking that district's diversity plan.

These were not the first race-related cases to come before the new Roberts Court. In its first term, the 2005–06 term, the Roberts Court, which by then included Justice Samuel Alito Jr., took up a challenge to a congressional redistricting plan drafted by the Texas state legislature mainly to protect and enhance the chances of Republican candidates. In highly splintered opinions, the Court largely upheld the Texas plan but struck down one congressional district because it diluted the voting power of Latinos in violation of the federal 1965 Voting Rights Act.

It was in the Texas case—*LULAC v. Perry*—that Chief Justice Roberts, who dissented from the decision's holding on the constitutionality of a Latino district, wrote a line that was, at once, both striking and ominous to civil rights groups: "It is a sordid business, this divvying us up by race."

A redistricting case—complex, highly partisan, and, in the end, local—was unlikely to capture the attention and emotions of many Americans, not like a school case could. Most parents either had or soon would have to deal with finding the best possible schools for their children and with their districts' plans for assigning students. The Seattle and Louisville cases had an additional element: they put in play the meaning and continuing import of the revered Warren Court 1954 landmark ruling that struck down school segregation: *Brown v. Board of Education*.

From *Brown* going forward, the Supreme Court and lower federal courts had struck down laws and policies that used race to separate children in public schools. The Supreme Court had never ruled in a case where the challenge was to the voluntary use of race to achieve the benefits of diversity and to end racial isolation of students.

The Seattle and Louisville cases would offer the first close-up look at the views of Roberts and Alito on whether racial diversity was a compelling interest in elementary and secondary education.

David Engle stood in the line on the Court's plaza that morning and tried to keep warm. He had arrived early to increase his chances of getting into the arguments, but not as early as a group in front of him who had camped out Sunday night, braving freezing temperatures, to be first in line.[1]

Engle had not planned to attend. The trip from Seattle was long and expensive. And besides, he had moved on. Four years earlier, he had resigned as principal of Ballard High School in Seattle in protest of the district's decision to drop the so-called race tiebreaker in the district's "open choice" assignment plan even as it continued to defend it in the courts. A student's race was one of three considerations used by the district to fill slots at oversubscribed high schools whose student populations deviated more than 15 points from the districtwide racial demographic of 40 percent white and 60 percent non-white.

Before becoming Ballard's principal, the silver-haired, soft-spoken Engle had been a high school principal in a district across the lake from Seattle. He was drawn to Seattle by Superintendent John Stanford's vision for the school district and its growing success in increasing diversity in the predominantly white schools in north Seattle without the heavy hand of forced busing.

Ballard was his dream job. Engle lived in the Ballard neighborhood, could walk to the high school, and was given the opportunity to create a world-class academic program in a brand-new facility. The old high school had been torn down and rebuilt into a state-of-the-art facility, and its popularity among parents was on the rise.

"I felt, as a principal, the race tiebreaker allowed me to bring into play a dynamic that I was told by my students over and over again was a real positive," he said. "When I moved the [student] wait list into the school, I looked at that. I thought it was an asset. I had just created an international program where I didn't have the kind of diversity that would have made the program really rich. I wanted to create a school that didn't give lip service to the notion of diversity."

When Engle became principal in 2000, the school's racial composition was about 70–30 white. When he left, he had moved the composition to about 57–43 white.

"The first week I was on the job I had a visit from parents who ended up being in the group behind the lawsuit. They lived outside of the Ballard neighborhood and wanted me to move the wait list so their kids could come to Ballard. I said it couldn't happen. I had full capacity. I knew there would be issues around that."

Two years later, after the parents' group, known as PICS (Parents Involved in Community Schools), won its first court victory, Engle felt he personally needed to do something concrete to show his commitment to diversity and to the use of the race tiebreaker as a tool that principals should have available to them. He announced his resignation to his students in the high school auditorium and explained why. His action stunned parents and colleagues, some of whom applauded him while others criticized him.

Finding another principal's job after his resignation was "a little tough" for a while, he recalled, describing himself as somewhat "politically radioactive" because of his action. But the district offered him a position advising its high schools and he accepted.

"I worked with all ten of the high schools at some point," he said. "The inequities in the high schools were shameful. The poorest quality academic programs were reserved for predominantly schools of color, across the board. For me, that was the larger shame. Seattleites could be pretty smug about that, saying, 'Those kids want to go to neighborhood schools.'"

After about two years working with the district's high schools on a variety of problems, Engle moved to Bellingham, Washington, to take a position as a high school principal.

He found himself standing on the Supreme Court plaza that December 2006 morning because of a phone call from a Ballard parent who asked Engle if he was going to the arguments. "I said no, and this parent said, 'I'm going to buy you a plane ticket and you're going.' It was the right thing to do," he admitted. "Ballard was at the heart of this controversy."

Kathleen Brose was also at the Supreme Court that morning with another parent, Jill Kurfirst, but they did not have to wait in line for a seat. Brose, a determined, down-to-earth mother of two daughters, had been the face, voice, and driving force of Parents Involved in Community Schools for the last six years. She had attended every court hearing on the lawsuit during those years with the group's main lawyer, Harry Korrell of Seattle's Davis Wright Tremaine. She and Kurfirst had arrived a day early at the Supreme Court.[2]

Brose, who teaches piano in her home, became involved in the school district's high school assignment plan in 1999 as her older daughter prepared to enter her freshman year in 2000. Under the plan, known as "open choice," students and parents ranked their choices of the city's ten public high schools. The district used three tiebreakers to assign students to schools that could not accommodate all of those seeking admission: whether the applicant had a sibling in the school; how the applicant would affect the racial composition of the school; and the applicant's distance from the school.

Brose's daughter, who is white, did not get into any of her top three choices, all in majority-white north Seattle: the brand-new Ballard, which was closest; Nathan Hale, a little farther north; and Roosevelt, also north of Ballard. She was assigned to her fourth choice, Franklin, in predominantly minority south Seattle, but because it had no orchestra program (she played the cello), she transferred to Ingraham, in northeast Seattle. Ingraham was one of the least popular schools and was located at the city limits, far from her home. As a result of its location, Ingraham should have been an elite white high school, but it had lagged behind in educational quality for years. Brose's daughter stayed there only a year because the district in the meantime had opened a smaller high school closer to where the family lived, and their daughter graduated from that school. But during her three years at Seattle Center High School, she had to rely on her mother to drive her to and from Ballard, where she played in that school's orchestra.

Jill Kurfirst's son, also white, had qualified for admission to Ballard's biotechnology program, but he was not assigned to Ballard—his first choice—nor to his second and third choices. He was assigned to Ingraham.

In 2000, when Brose and her group were fighting with the school board over the assignment plan, the most popular choices for incoming ninth graders were Ballard, Roosevelt, Franklin, and Hale.

As Brose prepared to enter the Supreme Court for arguments in the school challenges, she believed that many people still misunderstood what was at the core of the two cases. The day before, she had faced "some rather aggressive" media interviews, she recalled.

"A lot of people thought we were racists and we wanted our kids to stay in these lily-white schools and our schools aren't that way if you look at the statistics," she said. "I said we like diversity but we like neighborhood schools. I tried to hammer that over and over. I didn't want parents to go through this. I've been told I am as tenacious as a bulldog and I am. I said this before I even knew who Sarah Palin was, 'I'm a momma bear just protecting her cubs.' I said, 'This race tiebreaker, this just isn't right.' "

The Brose family lived in Seattle's Magnolia neighborhood, and Kurfirst, the other mother with Brose at the Supreme Court, lived in nearby Queen Anne neighborhood. Seattle is shaped like an imperfect hourglass. The Ship Canal, a narrow waterway, cuts the city in half from Lake Washington to the east, through Lake Union, and on to the Puget Sound to the west. The canal has been described by some as Seattle's "Mason-Dixon line" because the city's predominantly white neighborhoods are north of the waterway, and to the south are the ethnically and racially diverse central district and south end. Magnolia, the city's second largest neighborhood, sits on a hilly peninsula northwest of the city's downtown area. It is home to some of the city's wealthiest residents, whose houses command sweeping waterfront views. By and large, however, it is an upper-middle-class community of about 22,000, with median income of about $69,000 and median house values of $534,000. The neighborhood's racial composition is 87.4 percent white; 5.8 percent Asian; 1.6 percent African American; 0.6 percent Native American; 0.3 percent Pacific Islander; 1 percent other races, and the remainder from two or more races.[3]

Magnolia is isolated geographically from the rest of Seattle and its residents get into the city by crossing one of three bridges. Queen Anne, to the southeast of Magnolia, borders the north end of the center and covers the city's highest hill. The community has a population of about 32,000, including a large number of young single adults. The median income is $49,000 and the racial composition is similar to Magnolia's.

Unlike Jefferson County School District in Kentucky—the target of the second school challenge in the Supreme Court that December morning—Seattle had never been under a federal court order to desegregate its schools, but that did not mean there was no problem in the schools.

Although *Brown v. Board of Education* outlawed segregated schools in 1954, the hard work of desegregation did not begin until almost a decade later and then often under orders by federal courts. In 1962, Garfield High School, located in Seattle's central district, became the first predominantly black high school in the state, with more than 51 percent black students. More than half of the city's other high schools had no more than five black students. That grim picture triggered a lawsuit against the school district by the Seattle chapter of the NAACP. The district, settling the suit out of court, appointed a committee to address "gross racial imbalance" in certain city schools. That imbalance mirrored Seattle's long history of housing segregation.[4]

A voluntary student transfer program was launched, and at its peak nearly ten years later 2,604 students participated, of whom 2,200 were black. There were additional attempts to promote voluntary integration—magnet programs at certain schools, for example. But by 1977, the district claimed that twenty-six schools remained racially imbalanced.

In that year, the NAACP filed a complaint with the U.S. Office of Civil Rights, and the American Civil Liberties Union and the Church Council of Greater Seattle threatened to file a lawsuit. By the end of that year, the school board had approved a mandatory busing plan, and the city became the first in the nation to adopt a comprehensive school desegregation plan without the sledgehammer of a federal court order.

Two months after the plan took effect, 61 percent of Seattle voters and 66 percent of voters statewide approved an anti-busing initiative sponsored by the Citizens for Voluntary Integration Committee. The U.S. Supreme Court in 1982 found the state initiative unconstitutional.

The city's efforts to address the racial problems in its schools without intervention by a federal court ironically would work against it when the Roberts Court, two decades later, on that December morning, heard arguments in the case against the city's school district.

With busing came white and middle-class flight from the public schools. By the 1980s, the baby boom had peaked, which contributed to declining public school enrollments. Seattle closed ten elementary schools, two middle schools, and two high schools. One of the two high schools was Queen Anne High School, and therein was the root of the problem for parents like Kathleen Brose and Jill Kurfirst. Queen Anne High School was considered the neighborhood school for Magnolia and Queen Anne residents—and it no longer existed.

Throughout the 1980s and the 1990s, the school district tinkered with its busing plan, introducing and expanding a "controlled choice" plan in which parents could choose from a cluster of schools and applicants who could contribute to a school's racial diversity were given priority.

In 1995, the man whose vision drew David Engle across the lake to Ballard High School became superintendent. As superintendent, John Stanford, an African American, decided to end mandatory busing. He had two goals: achieve diversity in the public schools and bring back middle-class families.

Stanford ended mandatory busing and moved the district to the "open choice" plan. He and Joseph Olchefske, who was the district's chief financial officer under Stanford and who succeeded Stanford after Stanford's death from cancer, knew that minority and low-income parents wanted the same thing as white parents—schools near home— and that kids who had been bused to the north were likely to choose schools in the city's south, concentrating the highest needs populations in schools with no offset for the change in quality and resources for their education. They devised a new form of budgeting—backpack budgeting—where the district's money is attached to the student.

"Sure enough, exactly according to plan, there was this big migration of kids, of enrollment, from north to south," recalled Olchefske. "They took their money with them. And schools in the south started swelling in enrollments and schools in the north started shrinking in enrollments."[5]

Under the new policy, ninth graders could choose any high school in the district and as many as possible were given their first choice. If more students chose a particular school than the school had capacity, the tiebreakers were applied.

While Seattle's school district was working through its new policy, opponents of affirmative action were making headway in the courts and at the polls. Ward Connerly, leader of the successful anti–affirmative action movement in California, was supporting a similar effort in Washington State. On the day the Seattle School District implemented its open choice policy, Washington voters approved Initiative 200, prohibiting racial preferences in public employment, education, and contracts.

That initiative would become one of the bases of the lawsuit by Parents Involved in Community Schools.

Once Seattle students could choose their schools, an open market existed and schools, particularly those in the northern part of the city with excess capacity, began competing for enrollment in order to survive. The northern schools became home to some of the district's most creative programs, such as biotechnology and theater programs. Non-public school parents began taking notice. Over a period of five to six years, the district increased the percentage of parents choosing public schools by about 10 percent.

"As soon as you go to open choice, you have to confront the fact that some schools are more popular than others and you don't know year to year which ones," said Olchefske, referring to variations in programs offered. "In a choice system, you must have criteria for deciding what to do when you have an oversubscribed school. It all would come down to these tiebreakers."

The tiebreakers—do you have a sibling in the school; do you live in the neighborhood; do you help diversify the school; and what is your distance from the school—worked well for elementary and middle schools. With sixty-five elementary schools, each had a neighborhood. The ten middle schools were put into five regions, with two schools in each, so a student was guaranteed to go to one of the two. But the high schools had to draw from such large areas that there were no "neighborhoods," and so diversity became the second tiebreaker.

Kathleen Brose had the "elementary and middle school view of the world," which did not exist for high schools, said Olchefske. The year in which Brose's daughter was to start high school, parts of Magnolia fell outside of the circle for Ballard High School's draw area. Pick a street in Magnolia and on one side, parents were happy because they fell within the circle's boundaries, and people on the other side of the street were unhappy. Any other year, it may not have been a problem.

"Every year there was a different set of angry white moms who would come to my office, and whatever supply-demand imbalance occurred, they advocated very strongly in lots of different ways to change the outcomes of the assignment process," he recalled. "They'd say, 'Draw the boundaries differently,' or, 'You said only three hundred kids could go to X school, make it three hundred fifty,' or, 'Change the tiebreakers a little bit.' As soon as you get into the business of making one exception, it's a slippery slope. I was going to enforce the policy as written. It was up to the school board to make any changes."

And to the school board was exactly where Brose and similarly situated parents—mostly mothers—went.

"We knew a year or so before the assignment implosion that this was going to happen," recalled Brose. "The Ballard high school had just been remodeled. Everyone was excited about going to a brand-new school. Not only did you have a lot of public school kids who wanted access to the school, you had a lot of private school kids. The school district didn't understand what the numbers were. We went to the school board and said, 'Look, there's too many kids trying to get into this school. And we know you are using the racial tiebreaker,' and they also had the sibling tiebreaker and the distance tiebreaker. We went to a lot of school board meetings. Kids went and got up. A few of us cried. We were pretty vocal and newspapers covered it quite a bit. And they just basically said, 'Oh don't worry about it.' They were very patronizing."

Brose had a "legitimate beef," conceded Olchefske, but, he added, "We could rightfully say to her and others, 'What do you mean, you don't get a school?' We were giving them schools. I do not believe Kathleen Brose was waiting around for a race issue. She just wanted her kid to get into the school she wanted, period."

Before it was rebuilt, Ballard, ironically, was not a school that anyone in Magnolia or Queen Anne would have sought out. It was considered a terrible school. Although located in a white neighborhood, it was predominantly minority. It also was viewed as unsafe because there had been a drive-by shooting that resulted in the death of a student.

In fact, as one Ballard neighborhood resident and parent, critical of the lawsuit, blogged on a "save seattle schools" blog: "If the principle of attending one's neighborhood school is so important, why weren't people suing to get into Ballard High School when the ceiling tiles were falling on people's heads?"

With a new building, a biotech program, and a creative new principal, Ballard became the rising superstar.

For the 2000–01 school year, about 82 percent of students selected an oversubscribed high school as their first choice, and only 18 percent picked one of the undersubscribed high schools as a first choice.

The school district estimated that without using the race tiebreaker, the non-white composition of the ninth-grade class that year at Franklin, a south end high school, would have been 79.2 percent, and in north end Hale, 30.5 percent; Ballard, 33 percent, and Roosevelt, 41.1 percent. But with the tiebreaker, the actual non-white populations at the same schools, respectively, were 59.5 percent, 40.6 percent, 54.2 percent, and 55.3 percent.[6]

The tiebreaker actually was race-neutral, according to Olchefske and others. There were schools in Seattle that were minority-dominated that white students wanted to attend, such as Franklin, which had an advanced placement program, and there were white-dominated schools that minority students wanted to attend. "This wasn't like people tried to paint it—affirmative action, get minority kids in the best schools," insisted Olchefske.

Before it was abandoned in 2002, the race tiebreaker had been used in only a few schools and it accounted for an estimated 300 students out of 3,000 assignments to the ninth grade in 2000–01, the year that Brose's daughter entered high school. The small number of students affected also would weigh against the district in the Roberts Court.

The school board knew that by going to open choice, there would be a decrease in diversity, given the residential patterns of the city. However, unlike some cities at the time, race was not simply black and white in Seattle. A port city, the residents were white, African American, Latino, Asian, Native American, and combinations thereof.

In certain neighborhoods, without the race tiebreaker, students were going to be in racially concentrated schools. "The promise was not to require that, but to give students options," said Olchefske. "I think that was an important principle to defend. The race-based tiebreaker was a clear, practical provision that addressed those concerns."

But despite the melting pot race and ethnicity of Seattle residents, the school board created a very blunt instrument for implementing the diversity tiebreaker: students were classified as "white or non-white." That too would create serious problems for the district when the Roberts Court took up the Seattle lawsuit.

It was too blunt an instrument for Kathleen Brose and her group. "In Magnolia, we had a group of kids who had been together since kindergarten," said Brose. "It was diverse, not a lot, but we had kids who came from Eastern Europe. These kids played together, were on sports teams together. We didn't look at these kids and give them hyphenated names. And these kids weren't looking at skin colors; they were just friends. When the school district said, 'You are going to the right and you to the left,' all of a sudden these kids are asking, 'Why does it matter?' That was really tough on these kids. I think that's a lesson they will take with them for the rest of their lives."

While the Seattle school board held its ground on its choice and diversity plan, a school district clear across the country and whose fate would become entwined with the Seattle plan in the U.S. Supreme Court, also held firm to the success of its school integration efforts.

Unlike in Seattle, litigation in the early 1970s led to a federal court ruling that schools in Louisville, Kentucky, were segregated by law— so-called de jure segregation. In July 1975, a federal appeals court ordered a desegregation plan for the Jefferson County School District, which includes Louisville, "to the end that all remaining vestiges of the state imposed segregation shall be removed from the said school district."

In the 1975–76 school year, 22,600 students (half black, half white) out of 130,000 were bused. The plan was resisted by groups of parents, unions, and the Ku Klux Klan, but supported by some churches, citizen groups, and government. There were boycotts, blockades, and riots.

Like Seattle, the school district modified and adjusted its integration plans over the years, moving from busing to programmatic options, including magnet schools in the inner city, but with court approval. After twenty-five years under judicial supervision, the district in 2000 was found to be "unitary," that is, it had achieved integration, and the court desegregation order was dissolved.

By 2000, community support for integrated schools had grown strong. The district was considered a model for the rest of the country, and business, parents, and community groups shared a belief in the value of diversity in education.

Carole Haddad, a white parent, lived through the turmoil that followed the court-imposed desegregation order. "There were fires in the streets," she recalled in a National Public Radio interview. "We had to put monitors and police on buses because bricks were being thrown at students going into certain areas. Over at the school behind my home, they brought in the National Guard, and used it for a bomb squad."

Upset and furious, Haddad decided to run for election to the school board to oppose the plan. But more than two decades later, she had become a supporter. "I've come a long way and taken a big turn since then," she explained. "The parents really like it."[7]

However, without a court-ordered plan in place, there was concern that resegregation was likely.

As the school district later explained to the Roberts Court, "Jefferson County housing is substantially segregated along racial lines." The assignment of district students to "neighborhood schools"—the same goal being sought by Seattle's PICS organization—would lead to a substantial number of racially segregated schools, according to the Kentucky district.[8]

As Kathleen Brose prepared to go to court to challenge the Seattle diversity tiebreaker, the Jefferson County school board voted to maintain the essential outlines of its integration plan and to implement a complex system of "managed choice" in student assignments. The plan provided that each school (except preschools, kindergartens, alternative and special education schools, and self-contained special education units) was to have not less than 15 percent and not more than 50 percent black students. The affected student population was 34 percent "black" and 66 percent "other" (terms used in the court desegregation decree, but which still reflected the community's racial composition).

Crystal Meredith and her five-year-old son, Joshua, moved into the school district in August 2002. She tried to enroll her son in kindergarten at a school about a mile from their home, but she was late—classes in that school had been underway for seven weeks. The district informed her that the school was full. She then sought to enroll him in another nearby school which was not in the designated "cluster" of ten schools for her area. Her request was rejected because, she was told, his assignment would upset the school's racial balance. Her son was assigned to another school, within her cluster, which was about ten miles from home.

Ironically, the district's rejection letter was a mistake. The diversity plan did not apply to kindergartens. However, the wheels of litigation were about to roll quickly.

"I was not told my son could not go to Bloom," Meredith said referring to the school she wanted. "I was told he could not leave Young—to go anywhere. I was told by the school board that my son's education was not as important as their plan. I was told I should sacrifice his learning in order to maintain the status quo. I was told by the school board appeal committee that the only way my son could go to another school that was a better fit for him was for us to move—to another county!"[9]

(The school board challenged Meredith's version of her experiences. In its brief in the U.S. Supreme Court, it said Meredith never appealed the denial of her transfer request and did not indicate early in 2003 a choice other than Young for her son's enrollment in 2003–04. She had testified in the lower court that it took her son twenty minutes to get to

Young and she had to drive him, but the school board said it made bus transportation available to Joshua.)

By the time Brose and Meredith were fighting with their school boards, the legal and political landscapes surrounding school desegregation and affirmative action had shifted dramatically from the days when both were considered critical remedies for discrimination.

Despite the Supreme Court's epic *Brown v. Board of Education* decision of 1954 invalidating state laws mandating school segregation, the Court did little in the following decade to make clear what steps could be taken to remedy prior segregation, remaining mostly silent until 1968. In that year, the Warren Court, named for Chief Justice Earl Warren, decided *Green v. County School Board,* a case from rural eastern Virginia. Frustrated with the slow pace of desegregation, the Court emphasized: "School boards, such as the respondent, then operating state-compelled dual systems were nevertheless clearly charged with the affirmative duty to take whatever steps might be necessary to convert to a unitary system in which racial discrimination would be eliminated root and branch."

Writing for the unanimous Court in *Green*, Justice William Brennan Jr., referring to the command in *Brown v. Board of Education* and *Brown II*, added, in a footnote, "We bear in mind that the court has not merely the power, but the duty, to render a decree which will, so far as possible, eliminate the discriminatory effects of the past, as well as bar like discrimination in the future." (*Brown II* was the Court's follow-up decision to the 1954 landmark ruling. The justices held that localities should act "with all deliberate speed" to comply with the mandate to desegregate schools.)

Three years later, in 1971, the Burger Court followed the *Green* decision with *Swann v. Charlotte-Mecklenberg Board of Education,* which, recognizing that "white flight" to private schools and the suburbs made school integration impossible in many segregated districts, approved busing students across cities and city-county boundaries. Busing triggered a huge white backlash and strengthened a growing conservative political movement.

In 1973, *Brown*'s command to eliminate discrimination "root and branch" was heard not just in the South but in the North and West as well when the justices decided *Keyes v. School District No. 1,* a case out of Denver, Colorado. The Denver school system had never operated under a constitutional or statutory provision that mandated or permitted racial segregation in the public schools. However, a group of parents charged that the school board, through a variety of techniques and policies, created or maintained racially and ethnically segregated schools. The Burger Court, in an opinion by Brennan, with Associate Justice William Rehnquist dissenting, held that such intentional policies may constitute unconstitutional de jure segregation.

This period coincided with the presidency of Richard Nixon, who had campaigned on law-and-order and anti-busing platforms. Nixon was determined to try to reverse the activism of the Warren Court in criminal justice and procedure. He made four appointments to the Supreme Court during his first term: Burger; Rehnquist; Lewis F. Powell Jr.; and Harry Blackmun. Those appointments would change the course of the Court's belated school desegregation efforts.

As the school desegregation scholar James E. Ryan has explained: "There were two problems with the Court's new commitment to integration: it came late, and it was short-lived. By the time the Court became serious about integration in *Green, Swann,* and *Keyes,* many urban school districts in and outside of the South had become predominantly black, which obviously made integration harder if not impossible to achieve. In many metropolitan areas, meaningful integration would have required that suburban schools participate in desegregation plans."[10]

But the Supreme Court was not going to allow that to occur. The Burger Court's 1974 decision in *Milliken v. Bradley* was the start of a conservative shift in its desegregation rulings. The *Milliken* ruling prohibited cross-district busing without proof of district gerrymandering. The lower federal court had found that a Detroit-only desegregation order would not effectively desegregate Detroit city schools and ordered cross-district busing because there simply were not enough white students in the city school district who could be shifted around within it to accomplish desegregation. As Ryan explained, proof that the school board was consciously gerrymandering attendance zones "was hard to come by, in part because housing discrimination kept most African-Americans out of the suburbs, so there was no need to play around with school district boundaries in order to keep suburban schools mostly white. *Milliken* effectively halted the progress of desegregation just a few short years after the Court became serious about it."[11]

Chief Justice Burger wrote the majority opinion in *Milliken* and was joined by the three Nixon appointees—Justices Blackmun, Powell, and Rehnquist—and Potter Stewart, nominated by President Dwight Eisenhower.

"The constitutional right of the Negro respondents residing in Detroit is to attend a unitary school system in that district," wrote Burger. "Unless petitioners drew the district lines in a discriminatory fashion, or arranged for white students residing in the Detroit District to attend schools in Oakland and Macomb Counties, they were under no constitutional duty to make provisions for Negro students to do so."

Ironically for what was to come later in the Seattle and Louisville cases in the Roberts Court, Burger also spoke directly to the power of local school boards to manage education within their districts. He wrote:

"Boundary lines may be bridged where there has been a constitutional violation calling for interdistrict relief, but the notion that school district lines may be casually ignored or treated as a mere administrative convenience is contrary to the history of public education in our country. No single tradition in public education is more deeply rooted than local control over the operation of schools; local autonomy has long been thought essential both to the maintenance of community concern and support for public schools and to quality of the educational process."

Justice Thurgood Marshall, one of four dissenters, called the decision "an emasculation" of the constitutional guarantee of equal protection. "Our Nation, I fear, will be ill-served by the Court's refusal to remedy separate and unequal education, for unless our children begin to learn together, there is little hope that our people will ever learn to live together."

Six years later, in 1980, a young Harvard Law School graduate named John Roberts Jr. walked into the Supreme Court to begin his clerkship with Associate Justice William Rehnquist, who, after he became chief justice in 1986, would lead the Court's withdrawal from the school desegregation effort as well as a retreat from affirmative action.

The Court did little with school desegregation in the 1980s, explains Ryan, but the Rehnquist Court took up three cases in the early nineties that would get federal courts out of the business of overseeing school districts' integration plans: *Board of Education v. Dowell* in 1991 (a 5–3 decision by Rehnquist); *Freeman v. Pitts* in 1992 (8–0 decision by Justice Anthony Kennedy); and *Missouri v. Jenkins* in 1995 (5–4 decision by Rehnquist).

Between 1969 and 2006, the year the Seattle and Louisville lawsuits reached the Supreme Court, presidents made fourteen appointments to the Court, twelve of which came from Republican presidents. Many of the later desegregation and affirmative action rulings were the work of the Court's conservative majorities, more often than not by 5–4 margins.

"Constitutional interpretation involves judicial discretion; judicial discretion reflects political ideology; and conservative justices tend, unsurprisingly, to subscribe to the conservative racial ideology of the party that appointed them," wrote the Harvard legal historian and constitutional law scholar Michael Klarman, author of *From Jim Crow to Civil Rights,* after the Seattle-Louisville decisions in 2007. "That ideology embraces a narrow, formalist conception of what counts as race discrimination; abhors the use of racial preferences, whether benignly motivated or not; and deems this nation's ugly history of white supremacy as something more to be repudiated than remedied."[12]

With court orders to desegregate schools slowly being withdrawn, a second wave of legal challenges arose, challenges to *voluntary* school plans designed to prevent racial isolation or resegregation. The newly formed Roberts Court now would be asked to step back onto the battlefield of school integration to answer whether race could be used in this context. And this time, those asking would not be parents seeking to force recalcitrant school and state officials vested in a discriminatory educational system, but parents who themselves felt discriminated against by the good faith efforts of school officials to maintain racial diversity in their schools.

CHAPTER 3

———— • ————

"In order to get beyond racism, we must first take account of race."
—Justice Harry A. Blackmun, 1978

B y the time her daughter graduated from middle school in June 2000, Kathleen Brose and the other parents in her group knew that despite their intense lobbying efforts, the Seattle school board was not going to change the assignment plan.

"When we started talking about a lawsuit, a lot of people got scared," remembered Brose. "That's a pejorative term, a real negative. But we just didn't know what else to do. Nobody wants to go into a lawsuit. We weren't thinking national at all; we were just thinking local. It was just about our city." [1]

But a lawsuit meant finding a lawyer, and for this particular type of lawsuit, that could be a difficult task in one of the most liberal and Democratic cities in the country.

Conservative libertarian lawyers in Washington, D.C., like to joke that because their numbers are so small, they can meet in a phone booth. Conservative Republican lawyers in Seattle, chuckled one member, need a little more space—perhaps a closet.

Word went out through the right channels, however, that the PICS group was thinking about a lawsuit. Dick Deran, a well-known advocate of conservative political causes and a retired attorney from Seattle's Davis Wright Tremaine, contacted a young, energetic fellow believer, Harry Korrell III, a Davis Wright partner who focused on litigation and employment law. At about the same time, Sharon Browne of the conservative Pacific Legal Foundation in Sacramento, California, also was approached by some of the parents.

Korrell eventually took the lead, along with Davis Wright partner Dan Ritter, on the Seattle lawsuit, with Browne and her foundation providing support at each stage of the case. Browne also would become deeply involved in the Louisville litigation.

The Pacific Legal Foundation, the oldest conservative public interest litigating organization, was established in 1973 and describes itself as "devoted to a vision of individual freedom, responsible government, and color-blind justice." Its founders, Ronald Zumbrun and Raymond Momboisse, had been advisers to California governor Ronald Reagan during Reagan's campaign in the state legislature for welfare reforms. They looked for a way to counter liberal public interest groups who challenged those reforms in the courts.[2]

With advice from another Reagan adviser at the time—Edwin Meese, who would become attorney general of the United States after Reagan's election as president—and with funding from the California Chamber of Commerce and other groups, Zumbrun and Momboisse launched the foundation. Today, it has four offices and nearly twenty attorneys on staff who work in three main areas: defending private property rights, challenging environmental and governmental regulations, and fighting racial preferences.

Browne, a senior attorney skilled in trial and appellate work, joined in 1985. She made her reputation in California defending Proposition 209 (the California Civil Rights Initiative), which state voters approved in November 1996. The initiative amended the state constitution to prohibit race- and gender-based preferences in public contracting, public employment, and public education. The initiative was funded by the California Civil Rights Initiative Campaign, led by the University of California regent at the time, Ward Connerly. Connerly subsequently took his successful anti–affirmative action campaign to Washington State, which approved Initiative 200 in 1998, and to Michigan.

Fifteen years after the adoption of Proposition 209, it is still the subject of litigation in state and federal courts, as is the Michigan initiative adopted in the same year.

Korrell's conservative bona fides were firmly established before the Seattle lawsuit reached the U.S. Supreme Court. Although his law practice focused on employment law, he became known to Seattleites through election law activities. He was volunteer lead counsel in Washington State's Lawyers for Bush-Cheney 2004, a national network of Republican lawyers ready to go to court if the presidential race became contested in any state, as it was in Florida in 2000. He also was one of the lead attorneys for the state Republican Party when it unsuccessfully challenged the outcome of the 2004 governor's race, in which Democrat Christine Gregoire defeated Republican Dino Rossi by 129 votes.

Today, Korrell sits on the Federalist Society's national and Seattle executive boards. The society was founded in 1982 by law students who wanted to challenge the liberal orthodoxy on law school faculties and in the judiciary as well as the legacies of the Warren and Burger Supreme Courts.

The society, supported financially by conservative foundations such as the John M. Olin and Sarah Scaife foundations, experienced phenomenal growth in its first decade, and its influence spread primarily through its network of outstanding conservative litigators, such as Theodore Olson, who successfully argued *Bush v. Gore,* and politically connected lawyers, such as former Reagan attorney general Ed Meese. Many of the top positions within the George W. Bush administration were filled with society members.

Whether Chief Justice John Roberts Jr. was ever a society member provoked a mini-controversy during his Supreme Court nomination hearings in 2005. *The Washington Post* obtained a copy of the society's *Lawyers' Division Leadership Directory* for 1997–98, which listed Roberts, who was then in private practice, as a member of the steering committee of the Washington chapter. The Bush White House, at the time, said

Roberts had no memory of being a member of the society or its steering committee, although he did participate in some society activities.

Korrell was a newly minted partner in Davis Wright and barely into his thirties when he attended his first meeting of the PICS group at the home of John Miller, one of Seattle's former—and rare—Republican congressmen. The controversy over school assignments had not been on Korrell's radar screen previously; his own children were not yet of school age. But when the call came from Dick Deran telling him that some parents wanted to meet with him, Korrell was interested.[3]

Notices for student assignments for the 2000 academic year already had been sent out by the school district. A court order halting the assignments was the only way to undo them, and Korrell considered it unlikely that a court would issue such an order.

During the meeting at Miller's home, Korrell laid out what the parents would have to do and the basis of a lawsuit.

"This was all new to us," recalled Brose, who was there with six or seven other parents. "This small group decided we wanted to go forward."

Korrell thought the law was clear and that the dispute would end quickly—either the school district would change the assignments or a court would rule for the parents.

On the law, Korrell looked to Washington voters' approval of the anti–affirmative action Initiative 200 in 1998, prohibiting preferential treatment on the basis of race and gender in public contracting, employment, and education. Initiative 200 was "spot on" for the school dispute, he thought. And Korrell examined the Rehnquist Court's race rulings, which—although involving affirmative action, not school integration, and generally sharply divided rulings—"did not acknowledge some kind of diversity exception to the equal protection clause," he concluded.

"This seems pretty straightforward," he told the parents. "We'll make a demand, and if the district won't either change its policy or make some sort of accommodation for these particular parents, we will proceed in district court and get a decision pretty early on."

Korrell thought the school district would recognize it had made a mistake, and so he sent a demand letter containing a deadline for a response. When the district didn't meet the deadline, Korrell filed the lawsuit in federal court on July 18, 2000.

Korrell agreed with Superintendent Joseph Olchefske's assessment that before the lawsuit was filed, there was little controversy on the whole over the school's open choice plan.

"As a general matter, people were able to get into the schools they wanted to go to," recalled Korrell. "[The district] shuffled a couple of hundred students around out of twelve thousand. You're not making any material change in the diversity composition of the schools. But the price you pay is subjecting several hundred students to the indignity of being told you can't go into this program because you have the wrong skin color. That's too high a price to pay for what you get, which is almost nothing."

As soon as the lawsuit was filed, the community reaction was divided. Korrell felt that "polite opinion" in Seattle was against the suit. Editorial writers, education reporters, law professors, judges, and major law firms opposed it. Korrell's own law firm was somewhat reluctant to get involved but agreed to take on the lawsuit as a pro bono matter.

With Korrell taking the lead on the lawsuit, Sharon Browne and the Pacific Legal Foundation moved into a key supporting role. At each significant step going forward, she and the foundation would file a brief backing up the parents' arguments. "Whenever there was a dispositive motion being filed, we would file an amicus curiae brief and argue that this choice program was really just racial balancing," she said, adding that the Supreme Court in earlier school desegregation decisions had made clear that racial balancing was unconstitutional.[4]

Although not everyone on the school board supported the race tiebreaker, the board believed its use was constitutional and should be defended.

"The School Board clearly has said that to prepare kids for the world they're going to enter they need exposure to a diverse environment," said Superintendent Olchefske on the day the lawsuit was filed. "That doesn't happen by accident."[5]

The board's confidence rested partly on the fact that it had looked into the legality of using race-conscious measures shortly after Washington's Initiative 200 was adopted by voters. The board turned to Michael Madden of Seattle's Bennett Bigelow & Leedom who, at the time, had been defending the use of race as a factor in the admissions policy of the University of Washington School of Law—the actual target of the Initiative 200 campaign.

The school board was doing its periodic review and update of the school assignment plan and wanted to know if Initiative 200 required it to abandon any race-based plan. It wondered if it had accomplished as much as it could with race-based measures or if there was room and a need for something more.

"I think the majority view of the board at that time was they were sufficiently concerned about disparities in opportunities between the north end and the south end that they weren't willing to completely let go of race-based assignments," said Madden, a big man with a broad, friendly face topped by a shock of white hair. "They were going to use race as a tiebreaker."[6]

The board was confident it could continue to use race because of the U.S. Supreme Court's 1982 decision finding unconstitutional a state-wide initiative mandating a neighborhood school policy. The initiative was intended to halt Seattle's mandatory busing plan.

Madden advised the school board that the terms in Initiative 200, such as racial preferences and discrimination, would not apply to the school assignment plan. If they did, he added, there was a credible argument that if the initiative prohibited assignments for the purpose of desegregation, it would be unconstitutional under the Washington State constitution.

"Having made that bold prediction, when the PICS lawsuit came along, at least a year and a half later, we were asked to defend against it," he said. "We told the school district we could defend this and we turned out to be right."

Was the lawsuit at heart only about the parents' desire for neighborhood schools? "Yeah, now that I like my neighborhood school," added Madden. "When I didn't like my neighborhood school, it was all about going to some other school. That's the one piece of hypocrisy in their pitch. You ask those parents if any of them went to Ballard High School. None of Harry's clients was a Ballard alum. None of them could say, 'That's been our neighborhood school for years.' "

After the lawsuit was filed, the school board and the parents tried mediation with another federal judge in an effort to settle the lawsuit. After several hours of the judge shuttling back and forth between the parents and the school board members, the judge told them it was "highly likely" the case would go to the U.S. Supreme Court.

"When he said that, I had some chills go up my spine," said Brose. "I believed it right then and I believed we would win."

As the lawsuit moved forward, some of the parents in the group grew tired of it and moved on, she recalled, adding, "I told Harry, 'We're just going to take this as far as we can.' He said okay, and we did. We had nothing to lose. It wasn't just for my kids, it was for this whole city."

The next five years were a roller-coaster ride through the state and federal court systems for both sides. The first decision in the lawsuit came in April 2001 by U.S. District Judge Barbara Rothstein, who ruled for the school district on both the state claim involving Initiative 200's application and the federal claim involving the Fourteenth Amendment's equal protection clause.

The district's policy, she wrote, is a "deck-shuffle," and as such "does not, strictly speaking, prefer one race over any other. All children in the district are subject to the plan, and children of all races may attend at least one of the district's popular schools. At the same time, the plan maximizes the effect students' choices have on their assignments. These

facts render the open choice policy in stark contrast to the court-sanc-
tioned mandatory busing plans of earlier decades."

Korrell and his partner, Dan Ritter, appealed to the U.S. Court of
Appeals for the Ninth Circuit, and in April 2002, a three-judge panel
reversed the trial court's decision. It issued an injunction preventing the
use of the race tiebreaker in assigning ninth graders for the 2002–03
school year. But two months later, the panel withdrew its decision and
injunction. The federal court asked the Washington Supreme Court
whether the race tiebreaker violated the state law implementing Initiative 200.

At that point, the school district decided to "deactivate" the race tiebreaker, and David Engle, the excited new principal of bright and shiny
Ballard High School, decided to resign in protest.

"We never knew when rulings were coming down," explained Superintendent Olchefske. "If a ruling came down that de-authorized the
use of the tiebreaker, we would have to redo the entire choice process,
which would have driven the district into chaos. So we said we will
deactivate that tiebreaker. In the overall scope of things, it is a technical
change not very difficult to implement—just change the code on the
computer."

The PICS's lawyers and the school district's lawyers faced off again
that fall in the Washington Supreme Court. They would have an eight-
month wait for that court's ruling.

Three days before the Seattle arguments in the Washington Supreme
Court, Crystal Meredith, the Louisville, Kentucky, mother who could
not get her son Joshua into the kindergarten of her choice, joined three
other parents in filing a lawsuit challenging the Jefferson County school
board's assignment plan. Meredith claimed her son was denied admit-
tance to his "neighborhood" school; the other parents said their children
had been denied entry into countywide magnet traditional schools.

The two main lawyers for the parents and the school board were as different as Kentucky moonshine and Booker's bourbon whiskey.

Meredith's attorney, Teddy Gordon, a native of Louisville, was a sole practitioner—outspoken, some would say, bombastic, and emotional, but passionately dedicated to the lawsuit. He first became involved in the school assignment plan in 1998 when a group of African American teachers approached him and said they believed the plan discriminated against minority students who were denied admission to the Central High School magnet program. He won a federal court ruling that race could not be used in determining admission to magnet schools. That high-profile victory made him the logical choice of counsel for future unhappy parents.[7]

Francis Mellen and his law firm started representing the county board of education in the late 1970s. A quiet, deliberate-spoken attorney, Mellen had been advising the board on the student assignment plan and its revisions for a number of years. His firm's Louisville office—one of eight—employed about one hundred attorneys.

Both lawyers had children who had attended the Louisville public schools. Gordon earned his law degree at night at the University of Louisville Law School; Mellen graduated from Harvard Law.

At a pretrial conference on Gordon's lawsuit, U.S. District Judge John Heyburn II asked both sides to delay a trial, and both agreed to his request. Judge Heyburn sought the delay because he wanted to wait for the U.S. Supreme Court's decision in one of the most closely watched cases of the 2002–03 term, one that could be key to answering the question raised by the Louisville and Seattle lawsuits. The Rehnquist Court had agreed to decide whether race-conscious admissions policies at the University of Michigan Law School and undergraduate program violated the Constitution's equal protection clause.

The Center for Individual Rights, a non-profit, libertarian public interest law firm, had challenged the Michigan policies. It also had taken the lead in challenging the use of a race-conscious admissions policy at the University of Washington—the same case that Michael Madden, lawyer for the Seattle School District, was defending when the school district turned to him for advice on its school assignment plan. To this day, the center concentrates its efforts on getting "the government out of the business of classifying citizens by race," among other goals.

The Michigan cases—*Grutter v. Bollinger* and *Gratz v. Bollinger*—were not the first time the Supreme Court had examined affirmative action in higher education enrollment. The Burger Court, in a highly fractured ruling in 1978, struck down what a majority found to be racial quotas in the admissions policy at the University of California, Davis, medical school. Allan Bakke, a white applicant who was twice denied admission to the medical school despite better grades and test scores than successful minority applicants, charged the school with reverse discrimination. The medical school reserved sixteen spots for minority students out of a total limited enrollment of one hundred annually.

Justice Lewis F. Powell Jr., the courtly, southern lawyer appointed to the Court by Richard Nixon, who was considered the center or swing vote on the Court, wrote what is known as the controlling opinion in *Regents of the University of California v. Bakke*. Racial and ethnic classifications of any sort, he said, are inherently suspect and call for the most exacting judicial scrutiny. The goal of achieving a diverse student body is sufficiently compelling to justify consideration of race in admissions decisions under some circumstances, he explained, but this special admissions program, which foreclosed consideration to persons like Bakke, was unnecessary to achieve that compelling goal.

Crucial to the pending Michigan cases was Powell's view of a university's compelling interest in a diverse student body. "This clearly is a constitutionally permissible goal for an institution of higher education," he wrote. "Academic freedom, though not a specifically enumerated constitutional right, long has been viewed as a special concern of the First Amendment. The freedom of a university to make its own judgments as to education includes the selection of its student body."

And as a concurring justice, Harry Blackmun, wrote: "In order to get beyond racism, we must first take account of race."

The high stakes in the *Bakke* case were reflected in the blizzard of amicus—friend of the court—briefs filed by civil rights, educational, medical, business, ethnic, law enforcement, and political organizations. Twenty-five years later, a similar blizzard engulfed the two Michigan cases in which the university and law school defended their admissions policies as narrowly tailored to achieve their compelling interest in a diverse student body.

On June 23, 2003, three days before the Washington Supreme Court ruled in favor of the Seattle School District, the decisions in the Michigan cases came down.

In the law school case, a 5–4 majority, led by Justice Sandra Day O'Connor, held that a diverse student body was a compelling government interest and that the law school admissions program was narrowly tailored to achieve that goal. The program used race as one of many factors, not the dominant factor, in an individualized review of each applicant.

O'Connor wrote: "In the context of its individualized inquiry into the possible diversity contributions of all applicants, the Law School's race-conscious admissions program does not unduly harm nonminority applicants."

But a 6–3 majority, led by Chief Justice William Rehnquist, held that the university's undergraduate admissions program failed the narrow tailoring test because it automatically assigned a number of points to a candidate based on the person's race, which could determine admission, and the university did not give an individualized assessment of each applicant.

Anti–affirmative action activists viewed the Michigan decisions as a "total defeat," and some in the movement said it would take a future and different Supreme Court to put teeth into the scrutiny of race-conscious programs that the Constitution demanded.

With the Michigan cases decided, the Louisville and Seattle lawsuits moved forward in the federal courts. In December 2003, federal Judge Heyburn held the trial in the Louisville lawsuit. That same month, the

PICS parents, having lost in the Washington Supreme Court, went back to the same three-judge, federal appellate panel that had ruled in their favor more than a year earlier.

Judge Heyburn, relying on the Michigan decisions, ruled against Crystal Meredith in late June 2004. The school board, he said, "meets the compelling interest requirement because it has articulated some of the same reasons for integrated public schools that the Supreme Court upheld in *Grutter*." The board, he added, also identified other compelling interests and benefits of integrated schools, such as improved student education and community support for public schools. The student assignment plan also was mostly narrowly tailored, wrote the judge. "Its broad racial guidelines do not constitute a quota. The Board avoids the use of race in predominant and unnecessary ways that unduly harm members of a particular racial group."

Meredith's attorney, Teddy Gordon, promptly filed an appeal with the U.S. Court of Appeals for the Sixth Circuit in Cincinnati, Ohio.

Over on the west coast, a month later, the three-judge panel in the Seattle lawsuit again ruled 2–1 against the school district, holding that use of the race tiebreaker violated the equal protection clause of the Fourteenth Amendment because it was not narrowly tailored to achieve the benefits of diversity. The school district sought review by the full Ninth Circuit and eleven judges on that court agreed to hear the case.

Both the Louisville and Seattle challenges were now on parallel tracks, and rapidly closing in on the Roberts Court, which itself was about to undergo dramatic change.

In June 2005, the two federal appellate courts, separated by roughly 2,000 miles, heard arguments in the Louisville and Seattle appeals. As all parties waited for the decisions, Justice O'Connor made the announcement that rocked the legal and political worlds. On July 1, she said she would retire from the Supreme Court.

Gordon, representing Crystal Meredith, recalled in a later interview how thrilled he was by the O'Connor announcement. He told the *Louisville Magazine* in 2009, "I have this cliché that I say: Never underestimate the power of divine intervention."[8]

His elation at the news was based on two assumptions held by many at the time: one, that O'Connor, who had upheld the race-conscious admissions policy at the University of Michigan Law School, would be sympathetic to the school district's assignment policy if the Louisville case went to the Supreme Court, as seemed likely; and two, that President George W. Bush probably would nominate someone more solidly and reliably conservative than O'Connor, who had disappointed and frustrated the most conservative elements of the Republican Party.

One thing was true: O'Connor, through her position as the Court's center, had been the critical fifth vote for the victories—few though they were—of the moderate-liberal wing of the Court in abortion, church-state, campaign finance, race, and death penalty issues.

Justice Anthony Kennedy would assume the center position in most of the closely decided cases. More conservative than O'Connor, he would swing to the left less often. The real question, however, was who would replace O'Connor.

President Bush answered that question by nominating John Roberts. Two days later, the federal appellate court considering the Louisville school case ruled in favor of the school district in a brief, unsigned opinion affirming Judge Heyburn's decision. Gordon filed a motion for a rehearing.

Louisville's counterparts in Seattle still had no word on their case from the Ninth Circuit.

Throughout the summer of 2005, the White House, Senate Judiciary Committee Democrats and Republicans, and special interest groups across the political spectrum geared up for hearings on Roberts's nomination. On August 29, Hurricane Katrina struck the Gulf Coast—the deadliest hurricane since 1928 and one of the five most destructive in American history. And on September 3, Chief Justice William H. Rehnquist died.

President Bush withdrew Roberts's nomination as O'Connor's successor and nominated him as chief justice. The Senate Judiciary Committee held hearings the week of September 12, and the Senate voted to confirm Roberts, 50, as the seventeenth chief justice of the United States on September 29, by a vote of 78–22. He was the youngest chief justice since John Marshall took the bench in 1801 at the age of forty-five.

CHAPTER 4

"I didn't factor in Alito."
—Michael Madden, attorney for the Seattle School District, 2011

A challenge to a school district's integration plan already was waiting for the justices' first look when the 2005–06 term opened, but it was not the Seattle or Louisville plan.

Over the past two decades, the city of Lynn, Massachusetts, had experienced a dramatic demographic shift. The city's white population declined from 93 percent to 63 percent. That increased residential segregation. By the late 1980s, nearly half of the city's eighteen elementary schools had greater than 90 percent non-white enrollment, and racial tension in the city was rising.[1]

The Lynn School Committee developed a voluntary, neighborhood-centered school choice plan with two goals: desegregation and diversity. The committee defined an elementary school as "racially balanced" if it had between 43 percent and 73 percent non-white students and between 48 percent and 68 percent for all other public schools. A school was "racially imbalanced" if the non-white student population was above those ranges; and if below, the school was considered "racially isolated."

Students initially were assigned to schools in their neighborhoods. Race came into play when students or parents asked for a transfer from their local school. Any student could transfer between racially balanced schools. A student could transfer to or from a racially imbalanced or isolated school if the transfer would have a "desegregative" effect, but not if the transfer further segregated the racially imbalanced or isolated school.

In 1999, the same year that Seattle's Kathleen Brose and her group were fighting with their school board, a group of parents sued the Lynn School Committee. They charged that the race-based transfer system violated the Fourteenth Amendment's equal protection clause.

A federal district judge upheld the transfer policy, ruling: "The value of a diverse classroom setting at these ages does not inhere in the range of perspectives and experience that students can offer in discussions; rather, diversity is valuable because it enables students to learn racial tolerance by building cross-racial relationships." The parent group appealed and the full U.S. Court of Appeals for the First Circuit affirmed the district judge's decision, holding that racial diversity was as compelling an interest in grades K–12 as the U.S. Supreme Court had found viewpoint diversity to be in higher education in the Michigan University cases. The court explained that in higher education, the emphasis is on the exchange of ideas, while the emphasis in primary education is on fostering interracial cooperation.

Chief Judge Michael Boudin, concurring in the decision, said that race-based classifications are usually unconstitutional, but, he added, the "Lynn plan is far from the original evils at which the Fourteenth Amendment was addressed." A dissenting judge, however, said the use of race in the school plan was more mechanical and less flexible than the admissions policy that the Supreme Court struck down in one of the two Michigan cases.

The losing parent group filed a petition for certiorari (a petition seeking review of the appellate court's ruling) in the Supreme Court on September 12, 2005. Sharon Browne of the Pacific Legal Foundation, who was also aiding the challengers to the Seattle and Louisville plans, filed an amicus brief supporting the group's appeal to the justices.

The justices scheduled their first discussion of the Massachusetts petition at their Friday, December 2 conference. Three days later, they denied review, without comment.

The votes of four justices are required in order to grant review of a petition. For unstated reasons, the Court, which included Justice O'Connor, author of the *Grutter* decision upholding the race-conscious admissions policy at the University of Michigan Law School, did not have four votes. Or, the Court may have had four votes to hear the Lynn challenge, but not the five votes ultimately needed for a majority decision in the case.

"When you don't have all the votes to overturn a race-based plan, maybe it was just as well Lynn wasn't the case to take," said Sharon Browne, who believed the Lynn plan was unconstitutional.[2] The Court's decision not to take a case is no reflection on the merits of the appeal. It simply leaves the lower court's decision in place.

A little more than a month before the Court acted on the Lynn petition, the wait for final word from the appellate courts in the Louisville and Seattle cases ended. The Sixth Circuit rejected Crystal Meredith's motion for a rehearing and left in place its rather perfunctory approval of the Louisville school assignment plan. The Ninth Circuit handed the Seattle School District a hard-fought victory. Unlike the Sixth Circuit, the eleven judges on the Ninth Circuit, voting 7–4, issued lengthy majority and dissenting opinions.

The Ninth Circuit majority, applying the Supreme Court's *Grutter* decision involving the race-conscious admissions policy at the University of Michigan Law School, concluded that the Seattle School District had a compelling interest in "securing the educational and social benefits of racial (and ethnic) diversity, and in ameliorating racial isolation or concentration in its high schools by ensuring its assignments do not simply replicate Seattle's segregated housing patterns."

The plan also was narrowly tailored to achieve its goal, according to the court. "In sum, because (1) the District is entitled to assign all students to any of its schools, (2) no student is entitled to attend any specific school and (3) the tiebreaker does not uniformly benefit any race or group of individuals to the detriment of another, the tiebreaker does not unduly harm any students in the District."

One of the court's most conservative judges, Alex Kozinski, surprisingly agreed that the plan was constitutional. He would not even have subjected the plan to strict scrutiny—the most searching examination under the Constitution—as the majority did. He said the plan did not suffer from any of the defects that other racial classifications by the government suffered.

"Through their elected officials, the people of Seattle have adopted a plan that emphasizes school choice, yet tempers such choice somewhat in order to ensure that the schools reflect the city's population," he wrote. "Such stirring of the melting pot strikes me as eminently sensible."

Kozinski wrote that he hoped when the Supreme Court reviewed the Seattle plan or one like it, the justices would seriously consider not applying strict—"and almost deadly"—scrutiny. "Not only does a plan that promotes the mixing of the races deserve support rather than suspicion and hostility from the judiciary, but there is much to be said for returning primacy on matters of educational policy to local officials."

Judge Carlos Bea was not convinced. In his dissent, he called the Seattle plan "simple racial balancing, which the Equal Protection Clause forbids."

The only option remaining for the challengers to the Seattle and Louisville plans was to file a petition for review with the Supreme Court.

But when the Supreme Court in early December rejected the Lynn, Massachusetts, appeal, Michael Madden, attorney for the Seattle School District, thought, "naively," that his opponents might not file a petition.

"I thought, hmmm, Lynn was a better Supreme Court case because it came up after a trial. It had a more complete record than ours," he said later. "Our case was very stale and had an obvious mootness issue—the tiebreaker wasn't being implemented." He also remembered that the justices had declined to hear a Texas case involving a race-conscious admissions policy because the university had abandoned the policy.

"I naively thought Harry [Korrell, his opponent] might not waste his money [filing a petition]; or if he did, there was no reason to believe a different result. I didn't factor in Alito."[3]

As the lawyers in the Seattle and Louisville school cases pondered their next moves, Samuel Alito Jr. prepared for the Senate Judiciary Committee hearing on his nomination to succeed Justice Sandra Day O'Connor on the Supreme Court.

While the Court, with O'Connor, worked through its docket that fall, the Senate hearings on Alito's nomination were getting closer. Although President Bush had nominated Alito at the end of October 2005, Senate Judiciary chairman Arlen Specter said his committee needed time to comb through the large volume of work produced by Alito while on the federal appellate court. Unlike Roberts, who had written forty-nine opinions as an appellate judge during just two years on the District of Columbia Circuit court, Alito had spent fifteen years on the Third Circuit court and had written more than three hundred opinions.

Less than four months after the confirmation of John Roberts, the Judiciary Committee on January 9, 2006, opened its hearings into the nomination of Samuel Alito Jr. This time, however, Alito would endure more contentious questioning than Roberts did. This time the stakes were higher.

Senator Richard Durbin, Democrat from Illinois, described those high stakes before Alito even had the opportunity to make the traditional opening statement to the committee:

"You have heard time and again from my colleagues why this seat on the Supreme Court means so much. They have quoted the statistics of 193 5–4 decisions, where Sandra Day O'Connor was the deciding vote in 148 of those instances. She was a critical vote in issues of civil rights, human rights, workers' rights, women's rights, restraining the power of an overreaching President.

"If you look at the record, the enviable record which Sandra Day O'Connor has written, you find she was the fifth and decisive vote to safeguard Americans' right to privacy, to require courtrooms to grant access to the disabled, to allow the Federal Government to pass laws to protect the environment, to preserve the right of universities to use affirmative action, to ban the execution of children in America. And Justice O'Connor was the fifth vote to uphold the time-honored principle, which bears repeating, of separation of church and state. . . . We believe, many of us, that the decision on filling this vacancy is going to tip the scales of justice on the Supreme Court one way or the other."[4]

The physical contrast between Roberts, the private school–educated son of a midwestern steel executive, and Alito, the New Jersey public school–educated son of an Italian immigrant, could not have been greater. At his hearings, Roberts had looked trim, rested, youthful, and well dressed, and was polished in his delivery of answers to the questions—evidence of his experience as one of the preeminent appellate lawyers before the Supreme Court when he was in private practice. Alito appeared somewhat rumpled and he slouched slightly in his chair at the witness table. He answered often pointed questions in a dispassionate manner, never flustered or impatient. Despite the visible differences, he showed the same command of the law as Roberts did. Both men were products of Ivy League law schools: Roberts of Harvard; Alito of Yale.

By the end of three days and nearly eighteen hours of questioning, the committee's Republican staff had compiled an informal tally of the questions: senators asked more than a hundred questions about abortion and one hundred twenty about presidential powers. There were also questions—but fewer—about race, women, disability rights, and voting rights. In all, Alito fielded more than seven hundred questions over the three days.

The focus on abortion stemmed not only from fears by Democrats and liberal groups that, with O'Connor off the Court, the landmark *Roe v. Wade* would be in even greater peril of being overruled. It also arose because of statements made by Alito in memos when he was a young lawyer in the Reagan administration—like Roberts—as well as in some of his judicial opinions.

In a job application to Attorney General Edwin Meese in 1985, when Alito was an assistant to the solicitor general in the Department of Justice, Alito, who was seeking a promotion at the time, wrote that he was "particularly proud" of efforts he had made in cases before the Supreme Court in which the administration argued that racial and ethnic quotas were unconstitutional, and that "the Constitution does not protect a right to an abortion." He said those were positions "I personally believe very strongly."

As an appellate judge, he had dissented in a case in which his colleagues struck down Pennsylvania abortion restrictions, including one requiring married women to notify their husbands before getting an abortion. But in two other cases, he voted to strike down abortion restrictions.

During committee questioning, Alito repeatedly said *Roe v. Wade* was entitled to respect as a precedent of the Supreme Court, but, unlike Roberts, he refused to call it "settled law." He conceded only that when a precedent is reaffirmed, "that strengthens the precedent," and "special justification" would be required to overrule a precedent.

He also had written in his application to Meese that his interest in constitutional law was motivated largely by his disagreement with rulings by the Supreme Court under Chief Justice Earl Warren, particularly rulings dealing with "criminal procedure, the establishment clause and reapportionment." That too triggered alarm bells for Democratic senators and liberal special interest groups. The Warren Court produced key rulings that, among others, required *Miranda* warnings before police questioned suspects, adopted the exclusionary rule for evidence illegally obtained by police, recognized a right to counsel for indigent criminal defendants, established the one-man, one-vote principle, and prohibited organized prayer in the public schools.

Alito did not disavow any of his early statements; but, again like Roberts, he explained them away as the views of a young lawyer in the Reagan administration, and, he added, "a great deal has happened in the case law since then."

In his final day at the witness table, Alito faced a series of tough questions from Democratic senators about his views on executive power. Just a month before Alito's hearings, President George W. Bush encountered a firestorm of criticism following disclosures by the press that he had authorized the National Security Agency, without seeking court permission, to intercept international phone calls and other communications of people in the United States with known links to terrorists. Domestic electronic surveillance without a court warrant was made illegal by Congress in 1978.

In response to questions from Senator Russell Feingold, Democrat of Wisconsin, Alito said there could be times when a president violates a law because he believes, for example, that his powers as commander in chief trump the law; but, he added, "It would be a rare instance in which it would be justifiable for the president or any member of the executive branch not to abide by a statute passed by Congress."

The one emotional moment in the hearings came not from Alito but from his wife, Martha-Ann. Some Democratic senators pressed Alito hard on his membership in Concerned Alumni of Princeton, an organization that opposed the admission of women and minorities to Princeton, Alito's undergraduate alma mater. Alito had listed that membership—thirteen years after he left the university—on his 1985 job application in the Reagan Justice Department. The nominee repeatedly said he had no memory of membership in the group and he disavowed the group's purpose.

When his round of questioning arrived, Senator Lindsey Graham, Republican of South Carolina, told Alito that he was sorry that the nominee was being treated so harshly by Democratic committee members. To settle the question of whether Alito was biased against women and minorities, Graham sympathetically asked, "Are you a bigot?" Alito answered, "I'm not any kind of bigot." His wife, who was sitting behind her husband, began to cry and walked out of the hearing room.

In the end, what had the committee learned? Not much more than what Roberts was willing to reveal—knowledge of the Constitution, statutes, and Supreme Court rulings, but nothing of their own personal views.

Alito appeared to be much as everyone expected from his judicial opinions and answers: a reliably conservative judge who, like Roberts, eschewed labels as to his judicial philosophy but made clear he would not call himself an originalist, like Justices Antonin Scalia and Clarence Thomas, in his approach to interpreting the Constitution.

That Alito and Roberts were so alike in their approaches and answers in the hearings should be no surprise given their coming of age as lawyers in the Reagan administration, said Professor John Yoo, a deputy assistant attorney general in the Department of Justice during the George W. Bush administration and author of the now infamous memo on the legality of torture in the interrogation of suspected terrorists.

"It shows the fruition of the Reagan-Meese approach of grooming young lawyers in the 1980s who could do well at hearings 20 years later," he said in a *New York Times* interview in 2006.[5]

On January 13, 2006, the hearings wrapped up with testimony by special interest groups, former clerks and associates of Alito, and legal scholars who supported or opposed his nomination. Alito emerged relatively unscathed and appeared headed for confirmation.

Five days later, on January 18, the parents who had lost their challenges to the Seattle and Louisville school assignment plans took their legal battle to the U.S. Supreme Court by filing separate petitions for review.

Although the Supreme Court generally finishes its work in each term by the end of June, the first term of the Roberts Court was coming to a close in a sense by the end of that January because of the confirmation of Alito and the departure of O'Connor.

After a failed attempt by some Democratic senators to filibuster his nomination, Alito was confirmed by a vote of 58–42 on January 31—the closest confirmation vote since the 52–48 vote for Clarence Thomas in 1991. Alito watched the Senate vote on his nomination with his wife and President Bush in the Roosevelt Room of the White House. Of the Senate's fifty-five Republicans, only Senator Lincoln Chafee of Rhode Island, a moderate in a largely Democratic state, voted against Alito's confirmation. Four Democrats, representing states that President Bush carried in 2000 and 2004, crossed over party lines to support the nominee: West Virginia's Robert Byrd, North Dakota's Kent Conrad, South Dakota's Tim Johnson, and Nebraska's Ben Nelson.

Alito was sworn into office at the Supreme Court just hours after the vote. President Bush, in his memoirs, writes that later at the White House, he told Alito: "Sam, you ought to thank Harriet Miers for making this possible," a reference to her withdrawal of her own nomination and her support of Alito. Alito responded: "Mr. President, you're exactly right."[6]

After the executive branch's inept response to the devastating Hurricane Katrina and the outrage surrounding the National Security Agency's secret surveillance program, Bush had achieved a major victory in placing two solidly conservative and extremely intelligent jurists on the Supreme Court—and given their likely long tenure on that Court, he also had achieved perhaps his most important presidential legacy.

Justice Kennedy now clearly occupied the Court's center. More conservative than O'Connor in certain areas of the law, Kennedy held the key to major shifts or to moderating views. But for all of the focus on Kennedy's influential position in the coming terms, the real game-changer was the switch of Alito for O'Connor.

"The dramatic change came when Sandra left," said one justice. "Every five-to-four decision the term after she left, I think would have been five-to-four the other way if she had stayed. That was the big shift in the Court. Every justice was sorry Justice [John Paul] Stevens decided to step down [in 2010], but in terms of outcomes, the big change came with Sandra leaving the Court."

Walter Dellinger, acting solicitor general during the Clinton administration and a constitutional law scholar, agreed, saying, "People said if Anthony Kennedy were to step down it would be the mother of all confirmation battles. But actually the great shifting point on the Court came when Alito replaced O'Connor. I think the fact we had just been through a chief justice confirmation and the fact we had just been through the nomination of Harriet Miers, it was like nomination fatigue had set in by the time Alito came along. But that was the very dramatic shift, and it has had extraordinary consequences in moving the Court."[7]

Samuel Alito on the bench and Samuel Alito in chambers or in private seem to be almost two different people. On the bench, the public sees a justice who appears rather humorless, even dour. He often sits leaning forward with his chin in the palm of his hand, or "he looks like he's watching something crawling up the wall," noted one clerk. On the rare occasion when he does attempt some humor, it seems to have an edge. In 2010, when the justices were hearing arguments in a First Amendment challenge to a California law banning the sale of violent video games to minors, Justice Scalia was questioning one of the lawyers about the Framers' view of the First Amendment. Alito tartly interjected, "What Justice Scalia wants to know is what James Madison thought about violent video games. Did he enjoy them?" Scalia, rarely trumped, shot back, "No, I want to know what Madison thought about violence." Alito does not ask as many questions as some of his colleagues, but his questions are direct and incisive.

In private, however, he is awkward at first, but with a dry and hilarious sense of humor when he opens up, according to former clerks and associates; somewhat nerdy, kind and generous, someone who loves law and legal history, a judge's judge, they say.

Despite jumping in midterm, the newest justice got up to speed quickly. It would not take long either for his colleagues to discover how Alito viewed the law. The impact of O'Connor's departure was seen in at least two of three cases scheduled for reargument after she left. The Court had the option of ordering reargument in any case in which the justices had divided 4–4 before Alito's arrival and also in a case where there was a majority decision but the opinion was not issued before O'Connor retired.

Based on the pattern of assignments of majority opinions, Alito's vote appeared to have changed the prevailing majority from the Court's more liberal wing to its more conservative bloc in *Hudson v. Michigan* and *Garcetti v. Ceballos.* Scalia, joined by Roberts, Kennedy, Thomas, and Alito, held in *Hudson* that the Fourth Amendment's exclusionary rule—which blocks the admission into court of illegally obtained evidence—does not apply to evidence seized by police who violate the requirement that they "knock and announce" their presence when executing a search warrant. All but Kennedy expressed obvious hostility to the exclusionary rule itself. And in *Garcetti*, Kennedy led the same justices in limiting the First Amendment protection of speech by government employees. The majority ruled that the amendment does not protect a public employee from being disciplined for speech in the course of his official duties—here a memo by an assistant prosecutor about inaccuracies in an affidavit used to obtain a search warrant in a pending criminal case.

The third reargued case was a death penalty challenge. *Kansas v. Marsh* may have originally resulted in a 4–4 split. After reargument, Thomas, joined by Roberts, Kennedy, Scalia, and Alito, upheld the constitutionality of Kansas's law allowing the imposition of the death penalty when jurors found that factors weighing in favor of and against a death sentence were of equal weight. The Kansas Supreme Court had ruled that the state law violated the Eighth Amendment bar against cruel and unusual punishments.

The Court rarely begins a term with a full docket of cases to be argued. From October until about mid-January of each term, the justices examine petitions for review filed in the Court and add deserving cases until all of the argument slots are filled. In November 2005, the Roberts Court added what was to become the defining case of that term: *Hamdan v. Rumsfeld*—a challenge to military commissions set up by President Bush to try enemy combatants detained at Guantánamo Bay.

The justices do not grant review in cases that simply intrigue or interest them. The rules of the Supreme Court set out factors for review that are "neither controlling nor fully measuring the Court's discretion." There are basically three reasons. One, a federal appellate court has issued a decision that conflicts with the decision of another federal appellate court on the same important issue, or conflicts with a decision by a state court of last resort. Two, a state court of last resort has decided an important question of federal law in a way that conflicts with another state court of last resort or a federal appellate court. And third, a state or federal appellate court has decided an important federal question that should be settled by the Supreme Court, or the decision conflicts with Supreme Court precedents.

So review basically comes down to conflicts in the lower courts on an important federal question, and issues of national importance. Winning Supreme Court review is a daunting task. The grant rate is less than 1 percent of petitions filed. During the October 2010 term, more than 8,000 cases were filed with the Court.

And the justices are not the first persons to look at the cases filed. Since 1973, the justices have used what is called the cert pool to handle newly filed petitions. The incoming petitions are divided among their chambers. Within each chamber, one law clerk is assigned to those petitions and writes a memo that summarizes and makes a recommendation on whether to grant or deny review. That memo is shared with the justices participating in the pool. The recommendation carries considerable weight and there is a tendency among the clerks to recommend denial of review.

"The clerks have it drilled into them that you want to recommend to deny cert in ninety-nine percent of the cases," said one former clerk.

The concern that the clerks might recommend against reviewing a case that had merit motivated Justice John Paul Stevens to stay out of the pool until his retirement in 2010. In Stevens's chambers, his four clerks would divide the 8,000 or so petitions among themselves. Stevens only wanted a memo if his clerk thought a petition might generate interest in him or another justice. If the clerk thought the petition was a possible grant, then the memo was to be one or two pages because Stevens wanted to look at the petition for himself.

The pool is particularly helpful to a new justice adjusting to the

Court's workload. Alito joined the pool shortly after joining the Court but dropped out of the pool in 2008. The Court's newest justices—Sonia Sotomayor, who joined the Court in 2009, and Elena Kagan, who joined in 2010—participate in the pool. With Stevens's retirement, Alito is the only justice whose clerks review every petition.

If a petition beats the odds and review is granted, that also does not mean that review will come quickly. After a petition is filed, the opposing party has thirty days in which to file a brief in opposition to the request for review. There may be requests for extensions which sometimes are granted. And the petitioner may file a reply to the brief in opposition.

Except in May and June when the justices are no longer hearing arguments, they meet on Fridays during the term to consider the petitions. At this point, a chief justice has a certain amount of agenda-setting influence. Roberts creates the "discuss list," a list of potential cert grants that is distributed before the conference to each of the justices who, in turn, may add to the list. The justices' decisions on whether to grant or deny review are often released on an orders list the Monday after the Friday conference in which they have considered a particular petition.

When they filed their petitions on January 18, 2005, the parents challenging the Seattle and Louisville school assignment plans had no idea how long the process would take until the justices decided to grant or deny their requests for review.

Harry Korrell, the lawyer for the Seattle parents, was optimistic the justices would take both cases despite having quickly turned away the Lynn, Massachusetts, school challenge just a month earlier. With the two cases, the justices, he thought, could answer the constitutional question about the use of race in student assignments across a broader set of circumstances. Louisville had once been under a court order to desegregate its schools; Seattle had not.

The justices scheduled the Louisville case for their March 24 conference. The Seattle case was slightly behind because an extension of time was given for the filing of the brief in opposition. There was no word on the Louisville case after the March 24 conference. Both cases next were taken up by the justices at their April 21 conference, but with no action on the petitions.

After that conference, there began an extraordinary relisting of the two cases for additional conferences week after week after week. The media, civil rights organizations, anti–affirmative action groups, school associations—all were watching and waiting to see what the Court would do.

"My heart was in my throat," recalled Korrell. "I was checking the [Court's] Web site regularly."

The Seattle school board's lawyer, Michael Madden, turned to Eric Schnapper, an experienced and successful civil rights advocate before the Supreme Court and a professor at the University of Washington School of Law.

"I remember calling Schnapper and saying, 'You've got more experience than anyone I know. What's going on?' Eric's take was, 'I'm aware of this happening only when a justice is writing a dissent from a denial of cert.' "[8]

And that was exactly what was happening. At least two justices felt strongly that the Court should take the cases and pushed hard for review, but they did not have the necessary four votes. The Court decided to deny review, but the announcement was delayed because one justice wanted to write a dissent from the denial of review.

Justice Thomas relisted the cases multiple times in order to write that dissent. His dissent, said one justice, was powerful and, ultimately, after nearly six months of behind-the-scenes efforts, it was persuasive in capturing a third and then a critical fourth vote for taking the two cases: Justice Alito.

The Louisville case had been listed for conference seven times, and the Seattle case a total of six times. On June 5, 2006, the Court announced it would hear both cases in its October 2006 term.

While time seemed to stand still for the Seattle and Louisville parties as they waited nearly six months for the Supreme Court to act on the petitions for review, it had moved backward in a sense in the Seattle high schools.

At predominantly white, north end Ballard High School—the over-subscribed first choice of Kathleen Brose—43.2 percent of students were minority in 2001–02 when the district dropped the race tiebreaker. By 2004–05, that number had dropped to 37 percent. And at south end Franklin High School, where 79 percent of the students were minority in 2001–02, that number had grown to 87 percent by 2004–05.[9]

To Brose, the numbers were not necessarily bad because, she explained, they meant more students were able to attend their neighborhood schools. To the school board, however, the numbers were sadly anticipated. They reflected what was predicted with the loss of the tiebreaker—less diversity and greater racial isolation in some schools.

The conservative justices' votes to hear the two school cases rattled the civil rights community. There was no obvious reason for the grants of review. There was no clear conflict in the lower circuit courts; in fact, the two appellate courts in the Seattle and Louisville litigation had approved the school plans and a third appellate court approved a similar plan in the Lynn, Massachusetts, case. The school boards were acting voluntarily, not under the mandate of a law or court order, and with broad community support. And voluntary school integration efforts were not a burning issue on the nation's agenda.

If the civil rights community was alarmed, the conservative organizations that had been fighting race-conscious actions by the government in higher education, contracting, employment, and other areas were energized and cautiously optimistic about the Court's review. Their optimism was tempered by what they considered the "total defeat" in the University of Michigan affirmative action cases.

At 7:33 am the morning after the Court's announcement in the Seattle and Louisville cases, Roger Clegg, president of the Center for Equal Opportunity, a non-profit, conservative organization that "promotes a color-blind society," had posted a plan of action on National Review Online. Clegg had filed a friend of the court brief urging review in the school cases as had Sharon Browne of the conservative Pacific Legal Foundation. He now urged supporters to do the following: marshal amicus briefs by conservative educators and businesses to counter anticipated briefs from the left supporting race-based assignments; have the Republican base make clear to the Bush administration that any brief it files must be better than the "lackluster" briefs it filed in the Michigan cases; counter expected social science claims of benefits from diversity in education; and demonstrate that "discrimination like Seattle's and Louisville's" is not the rule by urging briefs from school officials "who reject this nonsense."

Clegg wrote that a majority of justices was inclined "to do the right thing." However, he added, "because they are conservatives, they will be worried if they are striking down a policy that everyone else—education officials at the federal, state, and local levels; social science and education experts; and parents—apparently likes. So the case has to be made to these conservatives that, if they do the right thing, they will not be all alone." [10]

The battle over the legacy and meaning of *Brown v. Board of Education* had begun. The two school cases would create a chasm over race on the Roberts Court in a term dramatically different from the one rapidly drawing to a close.

After the June 5 announcement on the two school cases, the justices headed into the final three weeks of the 2005–06 term.

Regardless of when a case is scheduled for argument in October through April, the toughest, most divisive decisions are issued most often in June, usually the last month in which the justices meet. In the seven terms of the Roberts Court, the justices have not completed their work in only two cases by their June departure: in 2009, what would become the highly controversial, campaign finance blockbuster *Citizens United v. Federal Election Commission*, in which they ordered reargument for the following September; and in 2012, reargument the next term in a case asking whether corporations could be sued for human rights violations committed abroad.

The justices get their work done through a combination of tradition and peer pressure, according to Justice Ginsburg.

"Each year, in mid-May, the Chief sends around a notice reminding us that all majority opinions are due June 1, or if June 1 is on a Sunday, then June 2, and all dissents, by June 15," recounted Ginsburg in a 2009 interview. "In all the years that I've been a member of the Court, no justice has ever missed those deadlines no matter how much dillydallying goes on during the term. When it comes to the end of the line, June 1, all majorities [majority opinions] are in circulation. It's great that we have that system, otherwise we'd never get away for the summer. The number of petitions goes up and up." [11]

Justice Kennedy is the unofficial opinion tracker. He lets the chief know if the Court is on pace to leave at the end of June.

After a remarkable run, the Court's unanimity in the Roberts Court's first term broke down with the June decisions, as happens traditionally. Seven of the term's eleven cases decided by 5–4 votes were issued in the last two weeks, including two that had to be reheard after O'Connor's departure: the Kansas death penalty case and the Fourth Amendment "knock and announce" case. Another four cases were decided by votes of 5–3, and one by a vote of 5–2, because one or more justices did not participate.

Of the sixteen cases decided by five-vote majorities, Kennedy was in the majority in eleven of them, more than any other justice. And in half of the sixteen where the justices divided along traditional ideological fault lines, Kennedy voted in four with the Court's liberal wing and in four with the conservative wing—a sign of his clear emergence as the Court's swing vote, replacing O'Connor in that influential position.

Kennedy resists and dislikes being characterized as the Court's "swing" vote. He is not the "swing" or decisive vote in every five-vote majority in which he appears. He actually leads the Court in certain areas of the law, such as in the First Amendment and voting rights law.

One of the 5–4 votes in which Kennedy led the Court came in the last two days of the Roberts Court's first term. *League of United Latin American Citizens v. Perry* was a complicated congressional redistricting challenge that involved the state of Texas.

After the 2000 Census, a divided Texas legislature was unable to approve a new redistricting plan in 2001. Because of that failure, a federal court imposed a plan. In the next election, Republicans took control of the legislature and the governor's office. They replaced the court plan in 2003, but only after three attempts. Democrats in the legislature captured national attention by fleeing the state twice, to New Mexico and Oklahoma. The new plan was the masterwork of Tom DeLay, then majority leader of the U.S. House of Representatives. DeLay's undisputed goal was to replace all ten incumbent Democratic congressmen and add seven Republicans to the state delegation. He also sought to protect Republican incumbent Henry Bonilla by moving 100,000 Hispanic voters out of Bonilla's District 23 into a new district and replacing them with white voters. Latino voters had been voting in increasing numbers against Bonilla.

The DeLay plan worked: in the next election, the Texas delegation shifted from a 17–15 Democratic majority to a 21–11 Republican majority.

The 2003 plan was challenged by the League of United Latin American Citizens and others on the grounds that the plan was a partisan gerrymander that violated the equal protection clause and the Voting Rights Act. Seven justices, led by Kennedy, upheld most of the plan, but the Roberts Court split 5–4 in finding that the plan's treatment of Hispanic voters in the Bonilla district violated the Voting Rights Act.

"The changes to District 23 undermined the progress of a racial group that has been subject to significant voting-related discrimination and that was becoming increasingly politically active and cohesive," explained Kennedy for the 5–4 majority. "The Latinos' diminishing electoral support for Bonilla indicates their belief he was 'unresponsive to the particularized needs of the members of the minority group.' In essence the State took away the Latinos' opportunity because Latinos were about to exercise it. This bears the mark of intentional discrimination that could give rise to an equal protection violation."

Chief Justice Roberts disagreed with Kennedy's analysis that because the new district joined together two Hispanic communities of different geographic and socioeconomic status, it could not compensate for dilution of the Hispanic vote in the old district. He believed the new district created by the plan for the displaced Hispanic voters was an effective Latino majority district. Kennedy, he said, simply did not like the fact that the new district was created by drawing voters from two different areas of Texas—the Rio Grande and Austin areas.

"I do not believe it is our role to make judgments about which mixes of minority voters should count for purposes of forming a majority in an electoral district, in the face of factual findings that the district is an effective majority-minority district," wrote Roberts. "It is a sordid business, this divvying us up by race." Justice Alito joined his dissent.

His catchy turn of phrase about the "sordid business" of "divvying us up by race" resounded across the political spectrum and was repeated in news stories, opinion pieces, and blog posts. Just that one sentence offered the first hint of where he—and possibly Alito—stood in the looming battle over the Seattle and Louisville school challenges.

The next day, Thursday, June 29, was the final day of the term. On most final days, the justices emerge from behind their maroon velvet curtain with smiles and nods to those in the courtroom. There is almost a palpable sense of relief that a term has ended. But there were no smiles on June 29 and perhaps it was not entirely due to the enormity of the decision about to be announced.

This Court looked tired, and with good reason. They had buried a chief with whom many of them had worked for decades. They had bid farewell to another highly respected colleague, a key vote in their most difficult cases and a behind-the-scenes force among them. They had welcomed two new justices—one in the middle of the term—onto a bench that had seen no changes in eleven years. And then there was *Hamdan*.

The Court issued the defining decision of the Roberts Court's first term, a decision in which Kennedy did cast the decisive vote: *Hamdan v. Rumsfeld*. Roberts did not participate in the case because in his previous position as a judge on the District of Columbia circuit court, he had considered and voted on this challenge to the Bush administration's military commissions for trials of Guantánamo Bay detainees. He had voted to uphold the administration's authority to create the commissions.

Salim Ahmed Hamdan, a Yemeni citizen and onetime driver for Osama bin Laden, challenged the legality of the military commissions. The government contended that the president's inherent executive powers and the Authorization for Use of Military Force, passed by Congress in the wake of the September 11 terrorist attacks, allowed him to establish the military commissions.

In a 5–3 opinion by Justice John Paul Stevens, the majority disagreed with the Bush administration. Reading a summary of the decision from the bench in his even, calm manner, Stevens—joined by Kennedy, Souter, Breyer, and Ginsburg—first said that the Court had jurisdiction to review Hamdan's case despite a law passed by Congress to block court review of detainees' federal habeas petitions. That law did not apply to petitions pending at the time it was enacted, according to the majority. The Stevens majority then held that the commissions lacked authority to proceed because their structure and procedures violated the Uniform Code of Military Justice and four Geneva Conventions signed in 1949.

As Justice Kennedy detailed in a concurring opinion: "These structural differences between the military commissions and courts-martial—the concentration of functions, including legal decisionmaking, in a single executive official; the less rigorous standards for composition of the tribunal; and the creation of special review procedures in place of institutions created and regulated by Congress—remove safeguards that are important to the fairness of the proceedings and the independence of the court. Congress has prescribed these guarantees for courts-martial; and no evident practical need explains the departures here. For these reasons the commission cannot be considered regularly constituted under United States law and thus does not satisfy Congress' requirement that military commissions conform to the law of war."

Stevens stressed that the decision was narrow and pointed to a concurring opinion by Breyer in which that justice had said, "Nothing prevents the President from returning to Congress to seek the authority he believes necessary."

Justices Scalia, Thomas, and Alito dissented in separate opinions. Scalia, also reading a summary from the bench, focused on the jurisdiction issue and argued that the Detainee Treatment Act of 2005 stripped all courts of jurisdiction to consider petitions filed by Guantánamo detainees. Thomas, who summarized his dissent as well, argued that a "heavy measure of deference" was owed the president when he exercised his power as commander in chief and that power was reinforced by congressional action—the Authorization for Use of Military Force. He warned that the decision would "sorely hamper the President's ability to confront and defeat a new and deadly enemy."

With *Hamdan* announced, the first term of the Roberts Court ended. Within days, scholars, litigators, and others offered identical assessments clothed in varying clichés. The first term of the new Roberts Court was marking time, treading water, in a calm before the storm, and in a pause.

The term had shaped early as a potential legal blockbuster with cases involving abortions for minors, assisted suicide, religious expression, voting rights, wetland regulation, and the death penalty. Many of the key cases were disposed of narrowly or in splintered rulings. Kennedy's vote kept his conservative colleagues from dramatically restricting the authority of federal regulators under the Clean Water Act of 1972, and he deserted them in a key part of the Texas voting rights decision.

In the end, it was really only *Hamdan* that broke major ground.

But two things were clear by term's end. First, this was a more conservative Court than the one headed by Rehnquist, and the reason was Alito.

According to one Court watcher's statistical analysis of the justices' voting patterns, Alito voted with his four conservative colleagues an average of 15 percent more often than O'Connor had, and he agreed with the four liberals an average of 16 percent less often.[12] The number of unanimous decisions and 5–4 splits were on a par with the average number over the previous decade.

Second, the new term that would begin just three months later promised to test Chief Justice Roberts's commitment, in particular, to what he had emphasized during his confirmation hearings: narrow rulings and respect for precedents. Besides the Louisville and Seattle school race cases, already on the docket were challenges involving the federal ban on so-called partial birth abortions and the authority of the Environmental Protection Agency to regulate gases contributing to global warming. Waiting in the wings were cases concerning campaign finance, student speech rights, pay discrimination, and capital punishment of the mentally ill.

The real first term of the new Roberts Court was about to begin.

CHAPTER 5

———•———

"There is no such thing [as a strategic leader of the Court or of a wing of the Court]. It may depend on a particular case. You have to listen to people and try to put it together."

—Associate Justice Stephen Breyer, 2011

B
y the time the Supreme Court had decided to hear the Seattle and Louisville school cases, six years had passed since Kathleen Brose and her organization, Parents Involved in Community Schools, had begun their odyssey through the state and federal court systems.

Brose's eldest daughter had graduated from high school in Seattle. Crystal Meredith's son, Joshua, no longer a kindergartner, was completing the third grade in Louisville.

Brose had kept her commitment "to take this [challenge] as far as we can." And so had the Seattle School District. At this point, the city had a whole new school board and a new superintendent, but the prevailing sentiment had not changed: school boards should have the race tiebreaker available as a tool and the Constitution permits the use of race to integrate schools without a court order.

Brose and Meredith and their lawyers had reason to be optimistic, despite having lost their lawsuits in the lower courts. The Supreme Court generally does not take cases to affirm lower court decisions. The justices reverse the lower courts' rulings in about 70–75 percent of the cases in which they have granted review. The fact that review here was granted even in the absence of any genuine confusion or conflict among the circuit courts over race-conscious school assignment plans also indicated intense interest on the part of some justices.

And because of those reasons, the Seattle School District's attorney, Michael Madden, believed Seattle's case was lost. "The day cert was granted I knew it was done. It was just how bad we would lose," he recalled.[1]

But neither side was ready at this stage to cede ground in a fight that journalists, scholars, and others were calling potentially the most important school desegregation challenge since the landmark *Brown v. Board of Education* of 1954.

Both school cases had now entered the stratosphere of Supreme Court litigation. Arguments before the justices were six months away. In the meantime, the lawyers had to write their briefs, organize an amicus effort (briefs written by supporters), and prepare for the oral arguments.

The "script" that helped Chief Justice Roberts get through his first days on the Court kicks in for lawyers handling cases as well. The school assignment challengers had forty-five days to write and submit their briefs on the merits of their challenge. The school districts had thirty days after those submissions to respond with their counterarguments. The challengers would get a final comment thirty days after the districts responded.

Although oral arguments in a Supreme Court case are often the most dramatic part of the case, many of the justices have emphasized that the most important part to them are the parties' briefs. A well-written brief, some have said, can win a weak case, while a poorly written brief may lose a strong one.

"The oral argument is the tip of the iceberg—the most visible part of the process—but the briefs are more important," said Chief Justice Roberts in a 2007 interview.[2]

Justice Ginsburg agrees, saying, "Of the two components of the presentation of a case, the brief is ever so much more important. It's what we start with; it's what we go back to. The oral argument is fleeting and very concentrated, just a half hour per side. It is a conversation between the Court and counsel. It gives counsel an opportunity to face the decision-makers, to try to answer the questions that trouble the judges. So oral argument is important, but far less important than the brief."[3]

The merits briefs, as they are known, lay out the facts of the case for the justices: how and why the lawsuit began; what happened to the lawsuit in the lower courts and the reasoning of the lower court judges; and finally, in the bulk of the briefs, the legal arguments as to why the Supreme Court should rule in a certain way.

Korrell and his partner Dan Ritter, who were representing the Seattle parents' group, soon discovered that even the most obscure case, once the Supreme Court has granted review, is catapulted to the attention of special interest organizations and lawyers who specialize in handling Supreme Court cases.

"Until the Supreme Court, we did everything, with help from some terrific associates at my firm," said Korrell. "There wasn't a lot of [outside] interest. We couldn't even get an expert to help us for free. The parents had to go out and raise money to have an expert rebut the school district. When we got to the Supreme Court, people started paying attention and were full of suggestions about what we should say."[4]

But Korrell and Ritter shouldered the brief-writing chores, turning for advice, when needed, to their earliest supporters: Sharon Browne of the conservative Pacific Legal Foundation and Roger Clegg of the conservative Center for Equal Opportunity.

Browne knew that Korrell had an excellent grasp of the legal analysis and so she offered, as additional help, her foundation's communications department. She had learned from experience that there soon would be a media onslaught, particularly in a case dealing with race and schools. Her department would coach Kathleen Brose—the parent face of the case—on how to handle media questions. And Browne herself took on the task of coordinating groups and individuals who wanted to submit amicus briefs supporting the Seattle challengers.

One of the "trickiest" legal questions facing Korrell was what to tell the Court about its most recent decision on race in education—the 2003 University of Michigan Law School admissions case: *Grutter v. Bollinger*. A number of groups believed *Grutter* was ripe to be overruled and were eager to have the cases push for that result.

Justice O'Connor had authored the 5–4 *Grutter* decision, finding that the law school had a compelling educational interest in maintaining a diverse student body. But O'Connor was no longer on the Court, and her successor, Alito, was proving to be more conservative in his voting than she was. Kennedy had dissented in the *Grutter* case because he felt the majority had failed to apply strict scrutiny—the most exacting judicial examination—to the law school's use of race which, in his view, looked more like unconstitutional quotas. Chief Justice Roberts's views, like Alito's, were unknown, but, after all, both men had been foot soldiers in the anti–affirmative action Reagan administration, according to conventional wisdom. The stars seemed to be aligning in favor of dumping the *Grutter* precedent.

The Supreme Court does not have to be asked to overrule a precedent. The validity of a particular precedent in a case is always before the Court. Asking the justices to overturn a prior decision is generally considered a fairly aggressive act.

Korrell decided not to attack the *Grutter* decision. "Better to say you win under the controlling case than to say the controlling case is wrong," he explained. "I wanted to win for my clients. We didn't have an agenda to undo *Grutter*."

But others obviously did have that agenda. Of the fourteen amicus briefs supporting the Seattle parent group, three urged the Court to overrule *Grutter*. Those briefs came from Florida governor Jeb Bush, the conservative Mountain States Legal Foundation, and the Project on Fair Representation. The last organization has been, and continues to be, at the forefront of litigation challenging the constitutionality of not only affirmative action but also the most important part of the landmark Voting Rights Act of 1965.

"I was never convinced these cases were the appropriate vehicle to overturn *Grutter*," said Browne in an interview. "What we could do is make sure it was very much contained. That's what I wanted to do: contain *Grutter* to the very limited purpose to which it was actually being used—for prestigious law schools where race is going to be used as only one factor for diversity. And then there is the First Amendment factor—universities have academic freedom, the right to decide how to comprise their student bodies. All of these factors are completely missing from elementary and secondary education."[5]

Korrell's counterpart challenging the Louisville school plan, Teddy Gordon, appeared to have asked the Court to overrule the *Grutter* decision in his petition for review. Gordon's petition posed one of the most convoluted questions in recent memory, but on a close reading actually did not ask the justices to undo *Grutter*. The eccentric Gordon's ultimate brief on the merits also was memorable. He shocked those inside and outside of the Court by using just eight of his allotted fifty pages to make his legal arguments against the Louisville school plan.

As she did for Korrell in Seattle, Browne worked to garner amicus support for Gordon. He had hired his own communications firm to deal with media and Browne worked with that firm "to the best of our ability." She also used her own amicus brief to flesh out the legal arguments against the Louisville school plan.

"Teddy was a little difficult to deal with, but for some reason he trusted me," she recalled. In fact, he trusted her to such a degree that he asked her to sit with him at the counsel table when the Louisville case was argued.

However, inside the Court, justices and clerks were shocked and chagrined at the quality of Gordon's briefs and his later oral argument. "The quality of advocacy wasn't what it could have been," said one former clerk from the term. "It was the same with the oral argument. It's interesting that such an important case would have that level of advocacy."

But sometimes even poor briefs and oral arguments win in spite of themselves in the Supreme Court.

As Korrell and Gordon worked on their merits briefs, the Bush administration was weighing its own position in the school cases. The legal territory was not exactly virgin.

Only three years had passed since the Court had decided the constitutionality of the race-conscious admissions plans in the University of Michigan cases. At the time of those cases, then Solicitor General Theodore Olson, who had successfully argued *Bush v. Gore*, had gone to the White House with his principal deputy, Paul Clement, and Attorney General John Ashcroft, to urge that the administration should oppose any use of race in the admissions policies and seek to overturn the 1978 *Regents of the University of California v. Bakke*. The *Bakke* decision was the foundation for the Court's later decisions in the two University of Michigan cases. But the Bush administration did not want to go that far. Instead, the government supported diversity in higher education but opposed the Michigan University and Law School race-conscious admissions plans because they were not narrowly tailored— there were race-neutral alternatives to achieving diversity, argued the administration.

"I wanted to take a stronger position in *Grutter* and *Gratz*," said Olson. "As it turned out, it wasn't terribly helpful to take a mushy position on narrow tailoring. It produced decisions coming out one way with the law school [admissions plan upheld] and another way with the campus generally [admissions plan struck down]."[6]

Olson's deputy, Clement, now was solicitor general and faced once again the question of whether racial diversity could be a compelling government interest, but this time in the context of elementary and secondary education.

The solicitor general of the United States—the fourth-ranking official within the Department of Justice—supervises government litigation in the Supreme Court and also reviews all cases in the lower courts in which the government has lost to determine whether to appeal those losses. Often called the tenth justice, the solicitor general has a special relationship with the Supreme Court. Former Solicitor General Seth Waxman once described that relationship as being "to respect and honor the principle of stare decisis, to exercise restraint in invoking the Court's jurisdiction, and to be absolutely scrupulous in every representation made."[7] Because of that relationship, the solicitor general is given a certain amount of independence not accorded other offices within the Justice Department.

Clement, a Wisconsin native and Harvard Law graduate, became acting solicitor general in July 2004 at the age of thirty-eight, when Olson resigned. A former Scalia clerk, he was confirmed as solicitor general by the Senate in June 2005. He is considered one of the best Supreme Court advocates in the nation. Even in the most complex case, he stands at the lectern before the justices' bench without notes or briefs and with total recall of facts and legal precedents down to page numbers and footnotes. In private practice now, he handles some of the most high profile, conservative litigation in the courts today, including a challenge to the Obama administration's health care law and the defense of the federal Defense of Marriage Act and Arizona's tough anti-immigration law.

There is a procedure within the solicitor general's office for determining, first, whether to get involved in a Supreme Court case in which the government is not a party, and then what the government's position should be if it does get involved. The office reaches out to all components of the executive branch that could be affected by the case and asks for their views. If a case involves a particularly controversial issue, there also may be communication with the attorney general and the White House.

A "big case" atmosphere surrounded the Seattle and Louisville school challenges in the solicitor general's office, and the White House was following the cases. But the Michigan case experience was still fresh; only some of the government players had changed in the ensuing years.[8]

"In that kind of a case, the important view you want to get is the Department of Education," said a lawyer close to the process. Secretary of Education Margaret Spellings had advocated for the elimination of race as a criterion for public school assignments, but like President Bush, she supported the concept of diverse public schools.

As the solicitor general considered the government's position, the lawyers in the Seattle case sought meetings with Clement to seek the government's support. It is fairly common for lawyers in Supreme Court cases to either seek that support or urge the government to stay out of the case.

"We thought the only possible way that the solicitor general would stay out of the case was on standing grounds," said Madden, the Seattle School District's lawyer. He was referring to the requirement that a party who is suing must have suffered a direct, concrete injury such that there is a real case or controversy for a federal court to resolve.

"We said, 'This is really not an issue the Court can provide any redress for because the race tiebreaker is not being implemented and all [our opponents] want to do is use this as a lever to force what they call neighborhood schools,' " explained Madden, adding, "It was a lost cause."[9]

Madden's opponent, Harry Korrell, would have more success. Clement had decided the government would support the challengers, although not as aggressively as Korrell would have liked, but consistent with its positions in the *Grutter* and *Gratz* cases. Clement also attended a moot court arranged for Korrell by the Heritage Foundation, the conservative think tank in Washington, D.C., in preparation for the upcoming arguments, and he invited Korrell and his partner, Dan Ritter, to observe his own moot court put on by the Justice Department.

By the second week of the October 2006 term, all of the briefs in the two school cases had been lodged with the Court. Roughly a dozen briefs supported the Seattle parent challengers and nearly fifty lined up behind the school districts. Key among parents' supporters was a brief by social scientists contending that research on the relationship between attendance at racially diverse or integrated schools and student achievement was not "uniform, consistent or sufficiently conclusive" to support finding that achieving racial diversity was a compelling government interest.

Countering the challengers' social science brief was a brief representing the views of fifty-five social scientists. This brief argued that "racially integrated schools prepare students to be effective citizens in our pluralistic society, further social cohesion, and reinforce democratic values. They promote cross-racial understanding, reduce prejudice, improve critical thinking skills and academic achievement, and enhance life opportunities for students of all races."

At this point Michael Madden had a core group of lawyers assisting on the case, including Eric Schnapper of the University of Washington School of Law and Maree Snead, John Borkowski, and Audrey Anderson of Hogan & Hartson, a Washington law firm where, ironically, John Roberts had headed the appellate practice before becoming a federal judge. Snead and Schnapper coordinated the amicus effort.

The school districts' supporting briefs came from civil rights organizations, historians, social scientists, retired military officers, and Fortune 500 officers, among others. The outpouring was remarkably similar to the amicus effort on behalf of the University of Michigan's race-conscious admissions policies.

Even though Justice Kennedy had voted against the Michigan plans, the school district lawyers believed his vote could determine the outcome in their cases. And they hoped that even just one of their many supporting briefs might be the one to persuade Kennedy to see the landscape of urban public schools as they did.

"People were struck by the impact of the [military] service academies' briefs in the Michigan cases," said Madden. "We were thinking maybe lightning would strike twice and someone would care about an amicus brief other than the solicitor general's."

As everyone settled into the new term, two questions lingered inside the Court: Would Chief Justice Roberts be able, as he said in a speech that spring, to achieve more consensus on the Court through narrow—minimalist—opinions? And what about Justice Alito? He had shown himself to be reliably conservative, but in what ways would he differ, if at all, from the Court's other conservative justices, Scalia and Thomas?

Because of Roberts's speech, there was a sense among some justices and the new class of clerks that there would be more room for compromise in individual cases. And compromise in the Court is not horse trading.

"I was very, very surprised there was no horse trading of any kind," said one clerk of his experience that term, a view echoed by others. "I was a little surprised at how pure that was. But as far as a justice saying, 'I can join [an opinion] if this or that word is changed or this happens,' that's the nature of compromise."

It was more of that kind of compromise that justices on the Court's left wing were hoping to see. Perhaps more than any of the justices, Justice Stephen Breyer would look for a willingness to give a little if a little were offered. That had been part of Sandra Day O'Connor's strategic successes.

Breyer and O'Connor had a close relationship on the Court. Although they did not always end up in the same place in case decisions, he believed they both approached cases pragmatically. They also shared an understanding of the art of compromise—O'Connor from her days as an elected state legislator, and Breyer from his time as legal counsel to the U.S. Senate Judiciary Committee and later as a member of the U.S. Sentencing Commission, which developed mandatory guidelines used by judges to impose punishments for criminal offenses.

"Much more than Justice Stevens, he has a certain faith in the ability to be strategic," said another former clerk.

But Breyer undoubtedly sensed where the Court was heading at the end of the 2005–06 term. In the last full term in which O'Connor served—the 2004–05 term—Breyer had cast only 10 dissenting votes and O'Connor 11, the fewest of all the justices. In the term that had just ended, Breyer cast 15 dissenting votes, only 2 fewer than Stevens, who cast the largest number.

Even after the 2006 term had turned into a rout for Breyer and his colleagues on the left, the justice from Massachusetts would continue to look for that willingness to give a little in subsequent Court terms, and would be disappointed more often than not.

The justices reject the notion that any one among them acts as a strategic leader of the left or the right or in any particular area of the law. John Paul Stevens was often dubbed by the media as the strategic leader of the Court's left wing. He served as the senior associate justice from 1994, when Harry Blackmun retired, until his own retirement in June 2010. As senior associate justice, he had the power to assign opinions whenever he and the chief justice were on different sides. He would assign the majority opinion when the chief was in dissent, and the lead dissent when the chief was in the majority.

Roberts himself has said that using the assigning power is like solving a Rubik's Cube. There are numerous factors to weigh in deciding who should write a majority opinion, such as evenness of workload among the justices and which justice is most likely to write in a way that holds the majority together.

One Court observer wrote that Stevens used the assigning power "to build coalitions and has become the undisputed leader of the resistance against the conservatives on the Court."[10] Not everyone agrees.

"I think it's a misperception," said one justice. "In giving out assignments, he took most of them himself, although he was very fair. I don't see him as a leader."

"There is no such thing [as a strategic leader]," insisted Breyer. "It may depend on a particular case. You have to listen to people and try to put it together."

Another justice explained, "I think it's neither there are leaders in camps now nor nine separate stovepipes. If you think hard about what people are saying, why they are where they are, that gives opportunities. It would not be right to say it's in every case. There are just some cases where there are four saying one thing and four saying another, and we sit around and wonder where the ninth is coming out. Or, it will be clear where he is, and we walk in and everybody knows this is going to be a five-to-four case. Of course at that point, you can have all the strategic leadership in the world and it won't get you anywhere. On the cases where there is play in the joints, I think it happens a little bit more sort of organically. Sometimes it might be one person who has the good idea to get something done; sometimes it might be another person." [11]

Stevens did not think of himself as playing the leader role, corralling other justices into joining an opinion, said some of his former clerks. His voice did carry weight with his colleagues, particularly because of his long tenure on the Court. "He had seen everything before and the other justices responded to that," noted one former clerk. And Stevens had a remarkable memory.

"I think it was more circumstance than active leadership," said another. "He wasn't the kind of justice who would go and have a long conversation with another justice, in part because he thought it was so important for each justice to come to his or her own conclusion."

Antonin Scalia became the senior associate justice after Stevens's retirement. Since he is not often in disagreement with Roberts, he does not often get the opportunity to use the assigning power. "All it does for me is I get introduced as the senior associate justice. I feel I ought to come in with a walker. No good otherwise," he said. [12]

But in October 2006, it was still Stevens as the senior associate justice and the most frequent voice in counterpoint to the Court's conservatives. Alito was beginning his first full term. And Kennedy was about to occupy—to a degree he had never done—the center of the Court and, with that position, the power to determine the outcome in its closest cases.

· · ·

From October through April, the Court each month sits in argument sessions for two weeks and then is in non-argument session for the remaining two weeks, during which the justices are reading briefs and writing opinions. During argument weeks, the justices hear cases on Monday, Tuesday, and Wednesday, usually allotting one hour (thirty minutes per side) for each case. The number of cases heard each term has decreased dramatically over the years—from about one hundred fifty per term before 1990 to about eighty since then. As a result, arguments rarely go beyond the noon hour today. Once arguments are finished in late April, the justices spend May and June completing their decisions, the bulk of which are issued in June.

The October 2006 term began on the traditional first Monday—October 2—but no arguments were heard that day because it was the Jewish holyday, Yom Kippur, and the justices only released an "orders list"—a listing of cases from the summer granted and denied review.

The next morning, the October argument session began. Nine cases were argued in the two-week session, none of which offered a hint of what was to come. Beginning with the November argument session and each month thereafter, the justices heard one or more cases that continuously upped the stakes in the term.

In November, it was *Gonzales v. Carhart*—the Bush administration's appeal of a decision by a lower federal appellate court striking down the Partial-Birth Abortion Ban Act of 2003. The lower court held that the act imposed an undue burden on a woman's right to choose an abortion because it lacked an exception to protect a woman's health, as required by earlier Supreme Court abortion precedents. That court found the act was overbroad in that its language banned more procedures than the targeted "intact dilation and evacuation" abortion method.

In December, the Seattle and Louisville school cases were on the argument calendar along with the Court's first global warming case, which galvanized the business and environmental communities. The justices also would hear the now famous Lilly Ledbetter pay discrimination challenge and the first in a series of procedural cases that would become the basis of later charges that the Roberts Court is a pro-business or pro-corporate court.

Still to come in the new year were cases involving capital punishment and the mentally ill; the ability of taxpayers to challenge federal programs that may violate separation of church and state; and regulation of campaign advertising by corporations—a prelude to *Citizens United*.

By the end of the term, pundits and analysts would be calling the Court the "Kennedy Court" because of Anthony Kennedy's decisive role in so many of the key cases. The fragile attempt at consensus, which succeeded to a certain degree in the previous term, would fall apart. And it would be clear that a new sheriff was in charge and he and his team were eliminating or "disarming" precedents with which they disagreed.

But none of that was yet apparent to the lawyers and crowds gathered outside the Court on that bracing, clear December day for arguments in the Seattle and Louisville school cases.

Kathleen Brose and her friend Jill Kurfirst were among the lucky few with reservations. They thought they would get special seats, but reservations only guarantee seats in the pews in the public viewing section. The courtroom holds about 250 people and, like most visitors, they were surprised by the intimate nature of the room. Unlike most appellate courtrooms, where the judges sit on elevated benches quite distant from the lawyers and audience, the justices are near to both. A tall lawyer at the lectern before the bench would be almost on eye-level with the chief justice, who occupies the center seat.

Between the public seats and the Supreme Court bench are rows of chairs for lawyer members of the Supreme Court bar. To the right of the bench, from the public's view, are several pews reserved for the justices' families and special guests. To the left are pews reserved for the press.

The courtroom was packed that morning. An undercurrent of excitement flows through the building and the courtroom in particular when a "big case" is being argued. Extra rows of chairs were placed behind the press rows to accommodate an overflow of reporters. Korrell, representing the Seattle parents' group, and Madden, the school district's lawyer, sat at the lawyers' table directly in front of the justices' bench and were separated by the lectern. The Seattle case was first on the calendar. Korrell shared table space with Solicitor General Paul Clement, whom the Court had given ten minutes out of Korrell's thirty minutes to make the government's argument—a not unusual practice. Madden sat with Hogan & Hartson attorney Audrey Anderson and watched as the courtroom filled.

Madden saw the widow of Justice Thurgood Marshall being escorted to a seat in the special guest section. "I leaned over to Audrey and said, 'I guess this is a pretty big deal.' She said, 'Nah, the last case she came for was Anna Nicole Smith.' It was a nice moment to break the tension."

Korrell felt invigorated, not nervous. His wife recently had been undergoing cancer treatments and that put the Supreme Court experience into perspective for him. "I wasn't the nervous wreck I might have been," he said.

Both lawyers knew they would be lucky to get out three or four sentences before the justices pounced with questions.

Senator Ted Kennedy of Massachusetts and the trial judges in the Seattle and Louisville cases also took seats in the courtroom.

The Louisville lawyers—Teddy Gordon for Crystal Meredith and Frank Mellen for the school district—sat at separate tables behind the Seattle contingent. The Court also had given Clement fifteen minutes of Gordon's time because, it was speculated, the justices feared Gordon's argument might be inadequate given his astoundingly short eight-page brief on the merits of his case.

At one minute past 10 am, the chief justice opened arguments in the school cases. The next two hours revealed clear divisions among the justices: Madden's prediction—six months earlier—that the only question was how badly the school districts would lose appeared to be right on target.

Anthony Kennedy, whom many believed held the key to the outcome, accepted that the school boards in the cases were acting in good faith to maintain integrated schools. But, he said to Madden, "The problem is that unlike strategic siting [of new schools], magnet schools, special resources, special programs in some schools, you're characterizing each student by reason of the color of his or her skin. And it seems to me that that should only be, if ever allowed, allowed as a last resort."

Justice Kennedy, however, also did not seem entirely satisfied by the challengers' arguments. He probed Korrell on whether it was permissible for a school district, dealing with the effects of segregated housing patterns, to have a race-conscious objective, for example, in selecting among sites for a new school the one that would create racial diversity or balance. Korrell responded that if the sole goal were to achieve racial balance, that would be unconstitutional absent past discrimination.

Korrell's core argument was that the Fourteenth Amendment's equal protection clause commands that government treat people as individuals, not simply as members of a racial class. The school district here was not remedying past discrimination but trying to achieve a white/ non-white racial balance. Louisville's Gordon took a similar position. Although the Louisville School District, unlike Seattle, had been under a court order to desegregate its schools, when that order was lifted, race-based remedies were no longer allowed by the Fourteenth Amendment, he argued. The school assignment plan, which required each school to have from 15 percent to 50 percent black students, was an unconstitutional quota system, he said.

Solicitor General Clement, although opposing the two school plans, conceded more of a role for race than did the challengers. The government argued that school districts have an "unquestioned interest" in reducing minority isolation but must use race-neutral means. He told Kennedy that his strategic school siting hypothetical would be permissible. Broad measures with a racial objective are constitutional; simply classifying individuals by race is not.

As the school district lawyers struggled to persuade skeptical conservative justices that diversity was a compelling interest and their use of race a narrowly tailored means to achieve that goal, they received help from Justices Breyer, Souter, and Ginsburg.

Breyer repeatedly brought up long-standing desegregation decisions by the Court, such as *Swann v. Charlotte-Mecklenburg Board of Education*, which approved busing and racial balancing to achieve desegregation—far more radical methods than what was at issue in the Seattle and Louisville cases, he said.

Madden emphasized that the Seattle school board was trying to distribute, to sort out seats that were available at popular high schools. Every student, he said, had the opportunity to be assigned to at least one of those popular schools. Unlike affirmative action programs, he said, "This is not a selective or merit-based system where we adjudge one student to be better than the other. We do consider individual factors before we get to race, starting with choice and family connection, and how close you live to the school."

Roberts asked the one question that simultaneously shocked civil rights advocates in the audience and foreshadowed where he might be headed in his thinking about the two cases and a venerable landmark decision.

"Everyone got a seat in *Brown* as well, but because they were assigned to those seats on the basis of race, it violated equal protection," he said. "How is your argument that there's no problem here because everybody gets a seat distinguishable?"

Madden paused, taken aback that the chief justice seemed to suggest that segregation before *Brown v. Board of Education* was equal to Seattle's attempt to integrate. He then replied, "Because segregation is harmful. Integration, the Court has recognized in *Swann*, in the first Seattle school case, has benefits."

Justice Ginsburg could not let the implications of Roberts's question go without comment. Shortly after Madden's response, she said, "And the question of whether any use of a racial criterion in integration is the same as segregation, it seems to me, is pretty far from the kind of headlines that attended the *Brown* decision. There were, at last, white and black children together on the same school bench. That seems to be worlds apart from saying we'll separate them."

Madden later recalled that when Roberts asked the "everyone got a seat" question, his colleague, Audrey Anderson, who had clerked for Chief Justice William Rehnquist and had worked with Roberts in private practice, let out an audible gasp in surprise and jerked in her chair. "I could hear Audrey and I knew he could, too."

As the arguments drew to a close, Justice Thomas, who very rarely asked questions during any arguments, moved in a way that suggested this time he would. He leaned forward and raised his arm. "You could hear a pin drop," recalled Kathleen Brose later. Reporters in the press section also quickly had pens ready. (Thomas asked his last question during a Supreme Court argument on February 26, 2006.)

But Thomas then reached for the drinking goblet each justice has and sat back. "What I could see then is he leaned over to Justice Kennedy next to him, and I can read his lips perfectly well, and he said, 'Got 'em,' " chuckled Madden. "The justices were so hot and at each other. I wondered if it was an attempt at an icebreaker."

When Roberts gaveled the arguments to a close, it was clear to all in the courtroom that there would be no quick decisions in the two cases. But even if the public has not been told an outcome, the justices know it shortly after the arguments. For Monday and Tuesday arguments, they meet that Wednesday to vote on the outcomes. For Wednesday cases, they vote in their Friday conferences. Within a day or two of the conference, the chief justice, if he is in the majority, sends the opinion assignments to the other justices. When he and the senior associate justice are on opposite sides, they confer so he is better able to make the other assignments and equalize the workload.

The end of the December argument session marked the beginning of one of two long breaks on the Court's argument calendar. The second is in February. During those breaks, the justices are not idle. They prepare for arguments, draft and exchange opinions, handle emergency matters—almost always requests for execution delays—and review in-coming petitions.

A clearer picture of the 2006–07 term would not begin to emerge publicly until April—four months after arguments in the school cases. But inside the justices' chambers, the image became clearer at a faster pace, and it was neither happy nor pretty.

CHAPTER 6

"The way to stop discrimination on the basis of race is to stop discriminating on the basis of race."

—Chief Justice John Roberts Jr., 2007

As the term moved into 2007, more than one former clerk used the same words to describe the feelings inside the Court: "very fractured," "heated," and "tense." The feelings were reflected primarily in the justices' draft opinions and in "a lot of serious conversations" among the clerks as well.

The justices generally allow their clerks to decide how to divide up the merits cases they will be working on in the term. In some chambers, the clerks draw straws. In Kennedy's chambers one term, a mock NFL draft was done each month. In Stevens's chambers, the clerks in one term also separated the term's biggest merits cases and divided those as well to ensure that each of them had a chance to work on one of the big cases.

A clerk then becomes the expert or "point clerk" on his or her selected cases. In Roberts's chambers, if the chief had an opinion to write, the point clerk did the first draft. It was not unusual for Roberts, who writes his opinions in longhand, to work through ten to thirty drafts. At some point, all of his clerks would get a chance to weigh in on the opinion. At the end, 80–100 percent of the words were Roberts's words, "and every good line is his handwritten work," said one former clerk.

Justice Scalia also uses his clerks for first drafts, sometimes providing very detailed guidance and sometimes less so, but always after discussion. Justice Stevens "always wrote the first draft—a framework of what he wants to hold," said one of his former clerks. "Sometimes it would be a rough idea of what he wanted to say; sometimes it would be more full and reference key cases. The clerk would transform what he said into what resembled a full opinion and then there would be back-and-forth."

Justice Thomas has a much more structured approach, which partly reflects how little value he puts on oral arguments. In a 2007 interview for *The Scribes Journal of Legal Writing*, he said that before he goes on the bench for arguments in a case, "We [he and his clerks] have an outline form of the disposition of the case that we've discussed. So when we go on the bench, we already have an outline, if we get the opinion, of how we would do it. That's when we go on the bench for oral argument. Then after, when we go in conference, we have the final-disposition memorandum. We have further discussions about the case. So when we get a draft, when we get an opinion draft, we're already three-quarters down the road—which is just a matter of putting it on paper."

If their justice is not writing an opinion, their clerks monitor the other justices' draft opinions and write memos to their justice or advise their justice on whether to join, not join, or suggest particular changes in those opinions. The clerks also talk with each other. "We tried to pay attention to who was working on what and where their bosses were coming out," said one former clerk. "Every justice wants to get a sense of what is nine to zero or five to four."

The fractured nature of the term would be seen at the end in the number of decisions decided by five-vote majorities: twenty-four compared to sixteen in Roberts's first term (eleven with 5–4 majorities). Nearly every high-profile case fell into that category. The Court's liberal wing (Stevens, Souter, Breyer, Ginsburg) prevailed in only one major case. The Court's conservative wing dominated thirteen of the twenty-four most closely divided decisions, while the liberal wing prevailed in six. Kennedy remarkably was in the majority in all twenty-four—a sign of his critical role—and he dissented only twice all term.

In early April 2007, the Court announced the liberal wing's only major victory—the justices' first brush with global warming. In *Massachusetts v. Environmental Protection Agency*, the majority, led by Stevens, held, first, that states had special standing to bring a lawsuit challenging the EPA's refusal to regulate greenhouse gas emissions from new motor vehicles; and second, that the Clean Air Act provided the authority for regulation by the EPA.

It was, in a sense, downhill from there for the four to the left of the Court's center. Two weeks later, Kennedy led a 5–4 majority in *Gonzales v. Carhart* to uphold the federal Partial-Birth Abortion Ban Act of 2003, even though the banned abortion procedure lacked an exception to protect a woman's health when necessary. Alito, who did not ask a single question during arguments in the case, joined the majority. Breyer, just seven years earlier, had led a different 5–4 majority—which included O'Connor—in striking down a similar Nebraska statute because it lacked the health exception. Kennedy had authored a bitter dissent in that case.

Kennedy attempted in his analysis to distinguish the Nebraska case, but the dissenters viewed it as having been overruled. Kennedy's opinion contained some of the most paternalistic language about women in modern Supreme Court opinions and he clearly had adopted the language and arguments of the anti-abortion movement. He also revealed his own personal feelings by referring to obstetrician-gynecologists as "abortion doctors" and the fetus as the "unborn child" throughout his opinion.

Ginsburg was not shy in her response, which she summarized for the dissenters from the bench after Kennedy announced the decision:

"The Court invokes an antiabortion shibboleth for which it concededly has no reliable evidence: Women who have abortions come to regret their choices, and consequently suffer from '[s]evere depression and loss of esteem.' Because of women's fragile emotional state and because of

the 'bond of love the mother has for her child,' the Court worries, doctors may withhold information about the nature of the intact D&E procedure. . . . This way of thinking reflects ancient notions about women's
place in the family and under the Constitution—ideas that have long
since been discredited."

Reading a dissent from the bench is still rare and a sign of intense
disagreement. More was to come. Four weeks later, Alito led the same
majority in *Ledbetter v. Goodyear Tire & Rubber Co.* in holding that the
nation's job bias law required workers with pay discrimination claims to
file their claim with the Equal Employment Opportunity Commission
(EEOC) within 180 days of receiving the first allegedly unlawful paycheck. Rejecting the EEOC's long-standing policy, Alito said Lilly Ledbetter's claim was untimely. Ginsburg, again reading from the bench,
took the majority to task, this time for ignoring, she said, the reality of
workplace practices. She called on Congress to respond, which it did
with legislation President Barack Obama signed into law in 2009 shortly
after becoming president.

In quick succession, six more decisions were announced in which the
justices divided and debated whether older precedents had been overruled either outright or by stealth. The decisions crossed diverse areas
of the law, including antitrust, campaign finance, juries and the death
penalty, and standing to challenge government-supported, faith-based
agencies.

Alito, too, was emerging as a strongly reliable conservative vote. By
the term's end, Alito and Roberts would have the highest rates of vote
agreement. Roberts's confidence in Alito was reflected in his assigning
him the majority opinions in three major cases—remarkable for so new
a justice, even a veteran judge like Alito—and notably better assignments overall than given in the term to his more veteran conservative
colleagues, Scalia and Thomas.[1]

The tensions among the justices were almost palpable in their opinions. Roberts was being criticized across the bench. For example, Scalia, although he agreed with the outcome, charged that the decision in

Hein v. Freedom From Religion Foundation, written by Alito, "beat to a pulp" a 1968 precedent that, he believed, should have been abandoned. "Minimalism is an admirable judicial trait, but not when it comes at the cost of meaningless and disingenuous distinctions that hold the sure promise of engendering further meaningless and disingenuous distinctions in the future," he wrote. And Scalia, again agreeing only with the result, accused Roberts of "faux judicial minimalism" and "judicial obfuscation" in *Federal Election Commission v. Wisconsin Right to Life* for failing to overrule outright the Court's 2003 decision upholding the McCain-Feingold Bipartisan Campaign Reform Act of 2002. (Roberts and fellow conservatives would deal a near-lethal blow to that law in 2010 in *Citizens United v. FEC*.)

Roberts and Alito refused to follow Scalia and Thomas in three other cases in which those two justices wanted to push the law further to the right. One case involved a school district's authority to prohibit and discipline a student for waving a sign with the message BONG HITS FOR JESUS outside the school during an Olympic torch relay in Alaska. Roberts wrote that the student's First Amendment speech rights were not violated when the principal suspended him. But neither Roberts nor Alito adopted Thomas's concurring argument that students had no First Amendment speech rights at all and the Court should overrule a 1969 decision recognizing such rights.[2]

And Roberts and Alito did not sign on to a Scalia concurrence in which that justice argued that limiting a jury's discretion to consider all mitigating evidence in a death penalty case does not violate the Eighth Amendment.[3]

"There was frustration on each side," recalled a former clerk. "I think everybody was sensible about it, but there was definitely some open, serious disagreement."

For the four justices most often in dissent—Stevens, Souter, Ginsburg, Breyer—the dominant feeling was "depression," added another clerk. "That wing of the Court would lose over and over again."

The "crowning moment of disappointment" for that wing came on

June 28, the term's final day. The school cases remained, and two others: an antitrust case in which the Court's conservatives, ruling 5–4, overturned a precedent dating back almost a century; and the death case involving a mentally ill prisoner in which the Court's liberal wing actually prevailed.

The school cases were the last to be announced, and although the outcome was expected given the tenor of the December arguments, the courtroom atmosphere was tense. The next roughly thirty minutes offered those gathered before the bench a rare glimpse of high drama in the Supreme Court.

Two successors to Thurgood Marshall's leadership of the NAACP Legal Defense Fund—one current and one future—sat together with one of the nation's most recognized scholars on *Brown v. Board of Education*. They watched intently as Roberts began his summary of the Court's decision by reciting the facts in both cases. But as he moved through the decision, his delivery was flat, not his usual forceful reading.

When the government uses racial classifications, he said, its actions are reviewed under strict scrutiny (the Constitution's most exacting review). To satisfy strict scrutiny, the districts must show the classifications are narrowly tailored to achieve a compelling interest.

The Court, he explained, has recognized two compelling interests in the school context: remedying the effects of past intentional discrimination (which neither Seattle nor Louisville were doing with their plans), and diversity in higher education, not focused on race alone but on all factors that might contribute to student body diversity.

The Seattle and Louisville plans, he said, use a limited notion of diversity, viewing race exclusively in white/non-white terms in Seattle and black/other terms in Louisville.

"In design and operation, the plans are directed only to racial balance, pure and simple, an objective the Court has repeatedly condemned as illegitimate," wrote Roberts. The minimal impact of the school plans on enrollment, he added, cast doubt on the need to use racial classifications. And the districts failed to show they considered methods other than racial classifications. "Narrow tailoring requires serious, good faith consideration of workable race-neutral alternatives."

As he did in his opinion in the Texas redistricting cases with his clever and memorable comment, "It's a sordid business, this divvying us up by race," Roberts ended his opinion with another statement certain to capture public and media attention: "The way to stop discrimination on the basis of race is to stop discriminating on the basis of race." (It was actually a paraphrase of a comment by Judge Carlos Bea, who dissented in the lower court decision upholding the Seattle school plan.)

When Roberts finished, Kennedy briefly summarized his concurring opinion. He agreed the school plans were unconstitutional, but he said he could not fully join Roberts's opinion because it implied "an unyielding insistence" that race can never be a factor because the Constitution is "color-blind." Diversity, said Kennedy, is a compelling educational goal that a school district may pursue.

Because Kennedy would not join parts of Roberts's opinion endorsing the color-blind principle, Roberts's opinion only had four votes—a plurality, not a majority of the Court. In that situation, the narrower opinion—here Kennedy's—became the controlling opinion.

"To the extent the plurality opinion suggests the Constitution mandates that state and local authorities must accept the status quo of racial isolation in schools, it is, in my view, profoundly mistaken," Justice Kennedy said. The "color-blind Constitution" that those justices relied on, he wrote, is an aspiration.

In pursuing diversity or avoiding racial isolation in schools, he said, race may be a factor—not alone but along with demographic factors, plus special talents and needs. Kennedy suggested the use of alternative, race-neutral methods, such as strategic site selection, recruiting students and faculty in a targeted fashion, allocating resources for special programs, and strategic drawing of attendance zones.

However, he also accused the dissenting justices of misinterpreting the Court's precedents and warned that accepting their reasoning would result in government racial classifications beyond education.

After Kennedy spoke, Stephen Breyer, in a remarkable counterpoint to Roberts's dispassionate delivery, announced a passionate dissent. His summary lasted twenty-two minutes and he told the courtroom that his written dissent—77 pages—was twice as long as any dissent he had ever written. But the length was necessary, he explained, because it was important to tell the history of the Court's desegregation jurisprudence, to show how the Court now was departing from it wrongly, and to recount the voluntary efforts of the two locally elected school boards to prevent resegregation of their schools.

Breyer, who often strives to bridge gulfs, legal and otherwise, barely controlled his outrage as he bluntly announced to the courtroom: "The majority is wrong." The school decision seemed to embody all of Breyer's anguish over the direction taken by the Court's conservative majority that term and what he believed was the wrongful overruling of precedents in eight other cases that same term.

In his written dissent in the school cases, Breyer said the Court's precedents had recognized that the interests at stake in cases like the Louisville and Seattle school cases are compelling. "We have approved of 'narrowly tailored' plans that are no less race-conscious than the plans before us," he wrote. "And we have understood that the Constitution permits local communities to adopt desegregation plans even where it does not require them to do so." The words "compelling" interests and "narrowly tailored" are the language of the Court's toughest test for determining the constitutionality of government actions. Known as "strict scrutiny," the test asks whether there is a compelling governmental interest for the action and is that action narrowly tailored to achieve it.

Roberts's opinion, he said, "distorts precedent, it misapplies the relevant constitutional principles, it announces legal rules that will obstruct efforts by state and local governments to deal effectively with the growing resegregation of public schools, it threatens to substitute for present calm a disruptive round of race-related litigation, and it undermines Brown's promise of integrated primary and secondary education that local communities have sought to make a reality. This cannot be justified in the name of the Equal Protection Clause."

He plaintively asked from the bench, "And what about stare decisis?" Breyer recited a long list of prior Supreme Court decisions that he said supported what the Seattle and Louisville school districts were attempting to achieve and which the Court's majority was ignoring. The Court, he said, had long held that the Constitution gives school districts considerable leeway when it is using race in an inclusive manner.

As Roberts stared straight ahead with a visibly clenched jaw, Breyer concluded his oral summary with a comment found nowhere in his written dissent: "It is not often in the law that so few have so quickly changed so much."

There were other opinions. Thomas, writing only for himself in an intensely personal way, as he often does in race-related cases, emphasized that the Constitution was color-blind and compared Breyer's arguments to arguments made by segregationists who also had relied heavily on Court precedents—an especially stinging comparison for Breyer, who had so eloquently described the Court's march against segregation.

"In place of the color-blind Constitution, the dissent would permit measures to keep the races together and proscribe measures to keep the races apart," Thomas wrote. "Although no such distinction is apparent in the Fourteenth Amendment, the dissent would constitutionalize today's faddish social theories that embrace that distinction. The Constitution is not that malleable. Even if current social theories favor classroom racial engineering as necessary to 'solve the problems at hand,' the Constitution enshrines principles independent of social theories."

His view of the color-blind Constitution, he said, was the view of dissenting Justice John Marshall Harlan in *Plessy v. Ferguson*. "And my view was the rallying cry for the lawyers who litigated *Brown*," he wrote.

Thurgood Marshall, who litigated *Brown v. Board of Education* and argued it in the Supreme Court, would not have agreed with Thomas's characterization of the *Brown* lawyers, Marshall's colleagues in *Brown* said later that day.

In 1978, when the Court considered its first affirmative action case in the education area—*Regents of the University of California v. Bakke*—the justices, in highly splintered opinions, decided that race classifications crafted to remedy discrimination should be judged by the same strict standard as those designed to harm minorities. Justice Marshall, in a bitter dissent, traced the history of race discrimination in America. He concluded: "It must be remembered that, during most of the past 200 years, the Constitution, as interpreted by this Court, did not prohibit the most ingenious and pervasive forms of discrimination against the Negro. Now, when a State acts to remedy the effects of that legacy of discrimination, I cannot believe that this same Constitution stands as a barrier."

Surprisingly, neither Thomas nor Scalia—the Court's most committed proponents of interpreting the Constitution according to its original meaning—referred to the original meaning of the Fourteenth Amendment to support their view in the school cases. An amicus brief submitted by sixty scholars who had devoted their careers to the study of Reconstruction-era history, abolitionism, race relations, and civil rights, said the school assignment plans were "fully consistent with the original purpose of the Fourteenth Amendment. Indeed, the same Congress that passed the Fourteenth Amendment enacted a wide range of race-conscious programs and funded deliberate efforts to integrate schools." The brief was filed on their behalf by one of the lawyers who helped to litigate *Brown*—Jack Greenberg of Columbia University Law School.

For civil rights advocates, historians, and others who had supported the two school plans, to have lost in the Supreme Court was painful enough; but particularly upsetting, even "abominable," said John Payton, then president of the NAACP Legal Defense Fund, was to see how Roberts, in a brief portion of his opinion, "twisted" the meaning of *Brown*, the landmark decision ending school segregation.[4]

After Roberts had completed his analysis and conclusion in the school cases, he wrote, almost as an afterword in three brief paragraphs, about the debate between the two sides in the cases as to who was more

faithful to the heritage of *Brown*. To support his view of *Brown*—
that it prohibited classifications on the basis of race or color—Roberts
quoted from the briefs of the lawyers representing the schoolchildren
in *Brown* and from the oral argument of one of those lawyers, (the
late senior federal judge) Robert Carter of the NAACP Legal Defense
Fund.

Roberts cited Carter, who said in 1952: "We have one fundamental
contention which we will seek to develop in the course of this argument,
and that contention is that no State has any authority under the equal-
protection clause of the Fourteenth Amendment to use race as a factor in affording educational opportunities among its citizens." Roberts
then wrote, "What do the racial classifications do in these cases, if not
determine admission to a public school on a racial basis? Before *Brown*,
schoolchildren were told where they could and could not go to school
based on the color of their skin. The school districts in these cases have
not carried the heavy burden of demonstrating that we should allow this
once again—even for very different reasons."

Justice Stevens wrote a short dissent directed at Roberts's use of
Brown: "There is a cruel irony in the Chief Justice's reliance on our decision in *Brown v. Board of Education*. The first sentence in the conclud-
ing paragraph of his opinion states: 'Before *Brown*, schoolchildren were
told where they could and could not go to school based on the color
of their skin.' This sentence reminds me of Anatole France's observa-
tion: '[T]he majestic equality of the la[w], forbid[s] rich and poor alike
to sleep under bridges, to beg in the streets, and to steal their bread.'
The Chief Justice fails to note that it was only black schoolchildren who
were so ordered; indeed, the history books do not tell stories of white
children struggling to attend black schools. In this and other ways, the
Chief Justice rewrites the history of one of this Court's most important
decisions."

Stevens ended his dissent by stating: "It is my firm conviction that
no Member of the Court that I joined in 1975 would have agreed with

today's decision." Sitting on the Court back then was William Rehnquist, for whom Roberts would clerk five years later.

Shortly after the decision was issued, three of the lawyers in *Brown*, including Carter, were interviewed, and they accused Roberts of misinterpreting their arguments and the meaning of *Brown*.

The *Brown* lawyers explained that they and the *Brown* decision did not take the position that the Constitution prohibited all racial classifications. Instead, they had argued that the Constitution prohibited the use of racial classifications to subjugate blacks, which was the position and interpretation of *Brown* taken by Breyer and the dissenters in the two school cases.

"All that race was used for at that point in time was to deny equal opportunity to black people," Carter told *The New York Times*. "It's to stand that argument on its head to use race the way they use it now." And Jack Greenberg of Columbia Law School added, "The plaintiffs in *Brown* were concerned with the marginalization and subjugation of black people. They said you can't consider race, but that's how race was being used."[5]

And while it was not a cruel irony, it was certainly ironical and highly unusual for a justice to quote and rely on the lawyers who argued a case for the meaning of a Court precedent. Both Roberts and Alito had emphasized during their Senate confirmation hearings that when they had advocated certain often controversial legal positions as lawyers, they were only representing their client, the government, not their own personal views.

The Seattle and Louisville cases exposed a great divide among the justices over race under the Fourteenth Amendment's equal protection clause. Four justices—Roberts, Scalia, Alito, and Thomas—adopted the view that the Constitution is color-blind and prohibits almost all use of racial classifications. Four justices—Stevens, Souter, Breyer, and Ginsburg—saw a constitutional distinction between the use of race that seeks to exclude and that which seeks to include members of minority races. Breyer wrote: "I can find no case in which this Court has followed Justice Thomas' 'colorblind' approach."

In the middle was Kennedy. "The statement by Justice Harlan that 'Our Constitution is color-blind' was most certainly justified in the context of his dissent in *Plessy v. Ferguson* [the 1896 decision upholding "separate but equal"]. . . . and, as an aspiration, Justice Harlan's axiom must command our assent. In the real world, it is regrettable to say, it cannot be a universal constitutional principle," he wrote. The enduring hope, he added, is that race should not matter; but "the reality is that too often it does."

Kennedy has written forcefully against the use of racial classifications in cases involving affirmative action, voting rights, and reverse discrimination. In fact, he has never voted to uphold an affirmative action plan. But Kennedy, say his former clerks and others, is an idealist, and his somewhat more moderate views in the school cases may reflect his hope that schools will not just educate but will foster interracial and interethnic relationships.

"He said school boards may pursue the goal of bringing the races together," emphasized Payton of the NAACP Legal Defense Fund, shortly before his death. "He embraced this as a compelling interest. It has a democracy component."

Whether Kennedy would be a moderating force in other contexts concerning race remained to be seen, and another clue could come very soon.

During the Court's deliberations in the school cases, the outcome was not a foregone conclusion, according to some former clerks. "I remember there being discussions about Kennedy and how he might be persuaded," said one.

Kennedy had been fairly specific about what troubled him in Roberts's draft opinion, said another clerk, and yet Roberts, who could have had a majority if he had moderated his draft, would not change it. "There was pretty extreme language in the plurality opinion that indicated to me that perhaps at least as to race, there was a certain recalcitrance that didn't look like the person who sat before the Senate Judiciary Committee," another clerk added.

Roberts, joined by Alito, now had made clear his view of racial classifications, and that view was remarkably similar to his view during his foot soldier days in the Reagan administration. He did not repudiate the Court's affirmative action decision in the Michigan case that O'Connor had written, but he limited it to the circumstances of that particular university case. He and the rest of the Court would fight another day over the vitality of O'Connor's ruling. And that day was coming fast. On February 21, 2012, the Court agreed to once again consider the role of race in a university's admission policy by granting review in a case involving the University of Texas.[6]

Given the strong views expressed by Chief Justice Roberts and those who joined him in the school cases and those who did not, the Court's divide on race is likely to continue even with the recent additions of Justices Sonia Sotomayor and Elena Kagan. Kagan's views are unknown, but Sotomayor, who succeeded Souter in 2009, gave a brief insight into her thinking during a January 2011 speech at the University of Chicago Law School. She called "too simple" Roberts's statement that "the way to stop discrimination on the basis of race is to stop discriminating on the basis of race."

"I don't borrow Chief Justice Roberts's description of what colorblindness is," she said. "Our society is too complex to use that kind of analysis."

The bitterness at the end of the first full term of the newly constituted Roberts Court stemmed primarily from feelings—justified or not—among justices to the left of center that Roberts's publicly stated commitment to greater consensus through narrow decisions and, in particular, to respect for precedents, had dissolved in the face of result-driven judging.

To conservative Court watchers, the Court's sharper turn to the right was "quite predictable," but did not accomplish all that was necessary, according to former Reagan Justice Department official Michael Carvin, partner in Jones Day. Carvin, who in the summer of 2012 lodged a major challenge to the nation's premier civil rights law—the Voting Rights Act—described the Court's conservative justices as being in a "holding pattern." They will need one more vote "to complete the sweep and a return to the rule of law," he said. Carvin left unsaid that one more vote was needed because of the unreliability of Kennedy.[7]

Regardless, the Court on that final day of the 2006 term appeared exactly as Roberts had hoped then, and continues to hope, it would never seem to be: an ideologically riven, political institution.

The Seattle school contingent—Korrell and his client Kathleen Brose, and the school district's lawyer, Madden—knew the last day was decision day in their case. Korrell and Brose were at home when the decision was announced, and Madden was in his office despite the three-hour difference between the east and west coasts.

"The phone started ringing at seven and didn't stop the whole day," recalled Korrell. The lawyer liked Roberts's opinion but found Kennedy's opinion "frustrating" because, he said, "it's obtuse in an area where we all benefit from clarity. Both sides are parsing Kennedy's opinion as to what they are allowed to do and aren't."

The truth is there are some schools in Seattle that are very good and some that are hard to improve, he added, and there is political pressure to do something—pressure from minority communities not being well served by these schools. "The something the school district was doing was letting them bump kids out of schools. It's politically expedient but leaves the problem. Having that device [the race tiebreaker] taken away was appropriate."

The Court's decision meant to Brose a return to neighborhood schools, even though her community still did not have one to call its own.

"Something people don't understand about this school choice issue is when you give parents the choice to pick a school, and it's not necessarily your neighborhood school, people will pick schools that have all these special programs," she said. "If a school is perceived not to do well, people who can will abandon it. So you create these schools with issues, and this is what happened. But when you have a neighborhood school in Seattle, you actually have better diversity because you get a mixture of kids and parents like me get in to volunteer. Neighborhood schools work."

Madden had been resigned to losing the case but the decision still stung, particularly Roberts's claim that the school plan imposed a huge individual burden for little benefit.

"If you looked at the open choice program, there was really only two years' worth of information in the court record and you could say that," he said. "If you looked at open choice as the end or nearly the end of desegregation measures that started in the 1960s, that peaked with the 1978 mandatory busing plan and then were reduced in intensity and frequency over the ensuing twenty years, then I don't think you could readily say it did little."

Seattle, he added, was "ripe for plucking as a de jure segregation" case in the seventies, which was why it was threatened with a lawsuit, why the Carter administration threatened to withhold federal funds, and why the school district turned to mandatory busing. "And Roberts says, 'Well, Seattle never operated a segregated school system.' It depends on who you ask."

Still, the "abiding thing" Madden said he learned from the case was no matter what side parents are on, it is all about what they think is the best for their kids. "The interest groups and the academics all have their respective points of view. But the universal thing for the parents is they're there trying to achieve what they think is best for their kids at a particular point in time, and doctrine isn't all that important to them.

"If Harry's clients could have used race to get them into the school they wanted, they would have been fine with it."

Chief Justice John G. Roberts Jr.

Senior Associate Justice Antonin Scalia

Associate Justice Anthony Kennedy

Associate Justice Clarence Thomas

Associate Justice Ruth Bader Ginsburg

6

Associate Justice Stephen Breyer

Associate Justice Samuel Alito Jr.

7

8

Associate Justice Sonia Sotomayor enjoyed a moment during her 2009 Senate confirmation hearing.

9

Associate Justice Elena Kagan listened to senators' questions during her 2010 confirmation hearing on her nomination.

Associate Justice Sandra Day O'Connor left the Court in 2006 to care for her ailing husband. Justice Samuel Alito Jr. took her seat on the bench.

10

Associate Justice David Souter retired in 2009 and was succeeded by Justice Sonia Sotomayor.

11

Senior Associate Justice John Paul Stevens stepped down from the Court in 2010. Justice Elena Kagan assumed his seat.

12

Kathleen Brose, head of Parents Involved in Community Schools, led the organization's legal fight against the Seattle School District. Harry Korrell, center, handled the lawsuit and argued in the Supreme Court; Brian Hodges, right, of the Pacific Legal Foundation assisted.

13

Students at Ballard High, considered the preferred public high school by many parents, funnel into a hallway between classes.

14

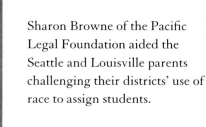

Sharon Browne of the Pacific Legal Foundation aided the Seattle and Louisville parents challenging their districts' use of race to assign students.

15

Clark Neily of the
libertarian Institute for
Justice and a colleague
decided over drinks one
evening that the time
was right for a Second
Amendment challenge.

16

17

Robert Levy, a self-made millionaire and libertarian, agreed to finance the
Second Amendment challenge to the District of Columbia's gun ban.

Richard Heller, a private security guard, became the lead plaintiff in the challenge to the gun ban.

18

Alan Gura was brought on board by Clark Neily and Robert Levy to lead the lawsuit against the District of Columbia and to argue in the Supreme Court that the Second Amendment guaranteed an individual right to possess a gun.

19

Alan Morrison developed the District of Columbia's defense of its gun ban in the Supreme Court until D.C. Attorney General Peter Nickles replaced him with Walter Dellinger.

20

21

After Supreme Court arguments in the gun case, D.C. Attorney General Peter Nickles (l), Walter Dellinger (c) and D.C. mayor Anthony Fenty (r) walked down the Court steps to meet the press.

22

Gun rights demonstrators rallied outside the Supreme Court.

David Bossie, president of Citizens United, created *Hillary: The Movie* and challenged federal campaign finance restrictions.

Senators Russell Feingold (l) and John McCain (r) authored the Bipartisan Campaign Finance Reform Act at the center of the battle in *Citizens United v. FEC*.

Prominent conservative
lawyer James Bopp Jr. was
hired by Bossie to take
Citizens United's challenge
to the Supreme Court.

25

Former Bush solicitor
general Theodore Olson
successfully argued in
Citizens United that
federal campaign finance
restrictions violated the
Constitution.

26

Washington lawyer David Rivkin laid the early legal groundwork for the state attorneys general's challenge to the federal healthcare law.

27

Florida attorney general Bill McCollum took the lead in organizing the state attorneys general in their challenge to the healthcare law.

28

Acting Solicitor General Neal Katyal led the Obama administration's defense of the healthcare law in the lower appellate courts.

29

Law professor Randy Barnett crafted a key legal argument against the consti- tutionality of the healthcare law.

30

Healthcare law supporters dem- onstrated outside the Supreme Court during arguments.

31

Former Bush solicitor general Paul Clement was hired to represent the twenty-six state attorneys general challenging the fed- eral healthcare law in the Supreme Court.

32

33

Washington lawyer Michael Carvin argued against the healthcare law in the Supreme Court on behalf of the National Federation of Independent Business.

34

Obama solicitor general Donald Verrilli Jr. defended the constitutionality of the healthcare law in the Supreme Court.

35

Supporters and opponents of the healthcare law awaited the Supreme Court decision.

PART 2

GUNS

CHAPTER 7

—•—

*"For most Americans, they always assumed they had a right to defend
themselves with a firearm in the home."*
—David Lehman, general counsel, National Rifle Association, 2011

Whatever the justices' plans were immediately after the term
of their discontent, guns and the Second Amendment were
not on their summer reading lists.

But that would change quickly. In just two months, one of the longest running political, social, and legal debates in the country's history would arrive at the Roberts Court, which, as it had demonstrated in the school assignment cases, would be willing to step into the shoes of local elected officials, whatever their judgments, to provide the final answer.

The words of the Second Amendment, ratified in 1791 with the nine other amendments known as the Bill of Rights, seem deceptively simple: "A well regulated Militia, being necessary to the security of a free State, the right of the people to keep and bear Arms, shall not be infringed." And yet those twenty-seven words had inspired a staggering number of competing interpretations in law reviews, books, and opinion pieces over the last three decades.

The debate essentially boiled down to two views. One view held that the amendment's first clause—the preamble—makes clear that the right is a collective right tied to service in and preservation of a militia. The other view relied on the second clause—the operative clause—as creating an individual right to possess firearms not tethered to militia service.

There was little controversy over the meaning of the Second Amendment for most of the last century. Historians, courts, legal scholars, and others either accepted or endorsed the militia-based interpretation. But beginning in the 1980s and blossoming in the 1990s, a series of law review articles—primarily by conservative legal scholars—aggressively pushed the individual right interpretation. Some of the research was funded by the National Rifle Association (NRA). Many historians of the Founding era challenged the research and criticized it as "law office history." With harsh words for the NRA, even former Chief Justice Warren Burger, in a 1991 interview on public television, said that the Second Amendment was "the subject of one of the greatest pieces of fraud, I repeat the word 'fraud,' on the American public by special interest groups that I have ever seen in my lifetime."

But the individual right view gained considerable traction over time with the public and even with some well-known, liberal constitutional law scholars. By the time the question of the amendment's meaning reached the Supreme Court, the justices would find scholarship on its meaning deeply divided.

If the justices were not thinking about the meaning of the Second Amendment that summer of 2007, three determined, conservative libertarian lawyers were, and had been for the previous five years. During that period, they manufactured the near-perfect lawsuit designed with one ultimate objective: a Supreme Court ruling that the Second Amendment guaranteed an individual right to possess firearms—not a collective right connected to service in a militia.

Happy Hours and guns can be a potentially lethal combination, but during one evening in 2002, they marked the beginning of a winning combination.

Clark Neily, intense and aggressively articulate, of average height and build, and Steve Simpson, tall, thin, soft-spoken, with a professorial look, are young, senior attorneys with the Institute for Justice, a libertarian public interest law firm in Arlington, Virginia, just outside Washington, D.C. The institute was set up in 1991 by two Reagan administration veterans: William "Chip" Mellor and Clint Bolick, who had worked with Clarence Thomas when Thomas headed the Equal Employment Opportunity Commission. The institute's lawyers litigate on behalf of private property rights, free speech, and school choice, and against government regulation of business. With remarkably sympathetic plaintiffs and smart lawyering, the institute has scored a number of victories in state and federal courts, including the U.S. Supreme Court.

But on that June evening in 2002, Neily and Simpson discussed over drinks a legal case not on the institute's agenda. A federal appellate court, in a dramatic break with all other federal appellate courts to consider the question, had ruled in a criminal case that the Second Amendment protected an individual right to keep and bear arms.

The case—*United States v. Emerson*—stemmed from charges against Dr. Timothy Emerson for violating a section of a federal firearms law that prohibited the subject of a domestic restraining order from possessing a gun, here a Beretta pistol purchased by Emerson. The Texas doctor, in the process of a messy divorce, had threatened his wife and daughter with the pistol. He argued the federal provision banning his possession of a gun violated his rights under the Second Amendment and the due process clause of the Fifth Amendment.

Although a three-judge panel of the U.S. Court of Appeals for the Fifth Circuit, which includes Texas, Louisiana, and Mississippi, ruled 2–1 that the Second Amendment's text and history supported the individual right interpretation, the panel unanimously held that the federal firearms provision was constitutional as it applied to Emerson. The panel explained that the individual right protected by the Second Amendment "does not mean that those rights may never be made subject to any limited, narrowly tailored specific exceptions or restrictions for particular cases that are reasonable and not inconsistent with the right of Americans generally to individually keep and bear their private arms as historically understood in this country."[1]

The two judges in the majority rejected the federal government's steadfast position—advanced by the Clinton administration—that the

Supreme Court's decision in a 1939 case (*United States v. Miller*)[2] was binding precedent for the militia-based interpretation of the amendment.

The one judge who refused to join the Second Amendment finding called the majority's eighty-four pages of analysis "dicta," or non-binding, extraneous material not necessary to resolve the case. "Unfortunately, however, the majority's exposition pertains to one of the most hotly-contested issues of the day," he wrote. "By overreaching in the area of Second Amendment law, the majority stirs this controversy without necessity when prudence and respect for stare decisis calls for it to say nothing at all."

The decision did, indeed, heat the controversy to a boil. Gun rights groups immediately hailed it as the most important Second Amendment decision in history.

While the *Emerson* case was pending before the appellate court, presidential administrations had changed. George W. Bush assumed the presidency and his administration dramatically shifted the government's position on the Second Amendment. Just five months before the appellate court issued its opinion, Attorney General John Ashcroft, responding to a letter from the executive director of the National Rifle Association, wrote back on Department of Justice stationery:

"While I cannot comment on any pending litigation, let me state unequivocally my view that the text and the original intent of the Second Amendment clearly protect the right of individuals to keep and bear firearms. While some have argued that the Second Amendment guarantees only a 'collective' right of the States to maintain militias, I believe the Amendment's plain meaning and original intent prove otherwise."[3]

Of course, the "some" who had argued for the collective rights interpretation included the federal government in court cases for almost seventy years. Gun rights and gun control groups as well as numerous media outlets broadcast the Ashcroft letter, its change in the government's view of the Second Amendment, and what the future implications for gun law and gun litigation might be.

The appellate court in the *Emerson* case, however, did not address the Ashcroft position, only what the Department of Justice had advocated throughout the case—the collective rights position.

After the appellate court ruled in October 2001, Ashcroft, himself a member of the National Rifle Association, sent a memo the next month to all U.S. attorneys in which he told them, "In my view, the *Emerson* opinion, and the balance it strikes, generally reflect the correct understanding of the Second Amendment."[4]

Emerson sought review in the U.S. Supreme Court, which was then headed by Chief Justice William Rehnquist. In opposing review, the Bush administration's solicitor general, Theodore Olson, informed the justices of the government's new position on the Second Amendment. In a footnote in his brief, Olson wrote:

"In its brief to the court of appeals, the government argued that the Second Amendment protects only such acts of firearm possession as are reasonably related to the preservation or efficiency of the militia. The current position of the United States, however, is that the Second Amendment more broadly protects the rights of individuals, including persons who are not members of any militia or engaged in active military service or training, to possess and bear their own firearms, subject to reasonable restrictions designed to prevent possession by unfit persons or to restrict the possession of types of firearms that are particularly suited to criminal misuse."

The "subject to reasonable restrictions" caveat was of particular importance to the Justice Department because it is charged with defending and enforcing federal firearms laws and it did not want those laws undermined. The Supreme Court, without comment, denied review of Emerson's petition in June 2002.

The two libertarian lawyers, Neily and Simpson, sensed opportunity in the combination of the *Emerson* decision and the Ashcroft memo as they chatted over their drinks. The issue for them as libertarians was less about guns per se and more about individual liberty, even though neither man was a stranger to guns. Simpson had an extensive gun collection. Neily's father, who had grown up in Maine where he hunted, taught Neily and his sister how to shoot. "I think just on the premise if there are going to be guns in the house, then it's important you know how to use them, but also to respect them," Neily recalled.[5]

As the two lawyers talked that evening, they agreed now that at least one federal circuit court had ruled in favor of the individual right theory, someone should challenge the District of Columbia's gun law, considered the most restrictive law in the country—"In fact, the most sweeping law ever, I guess, with the exception maybe of slavery and the disarmament of blacks," added Neily.

"Then there's almost this comical moment, this brief pause when we both realize we're public interest lawyers, libertarian public interest lawyers who like guns, and one of us looks at the other and says, 'We ought to challenge that,' " said Neily.

The D.C. gun law, which required that all guns be registered, essentially had prohibited handguns from being registered for more than thirty years. If a resident had a legally registered handgun dating from 1976 or earlier, the gun could not be moved from room to room within one's home without a special permit, and permits were not available.

The law also required that all firearms, including pre-ban handguns and lawfully registered rifles and shotguns, had to be unloaded and either disassembled or bound by a trigger lock at all times while kept at home. The city council had voted 12–1 in 1976 to enact the regulations in an attempt to stem the tide of gun violence in the city.

Neily and Simpson swiftly moved from talk to action when they approached Bob Levy in late June 2002 at a social gathering following a meeting of the conservative Federalist Society in Georgetown. Levy, quiet, small in stature, with a mischievous twinkle in his eyes, is chairman of the board of directors of the Cato Institute, the libertarian think tank in Washington, D.C. He also sits on the boards of the Institute for Justice, where Neily and Simpson worked, the Federalist Society, and George Mason University School of Law. A self-made millionaire who sold his investment information and software company and enrolled in law school in 1991 at age forty-nine, Levy had little interest in guns but an intense interest in the Constitution.

Neily and Levy were close personal friends, having served together as law clerks on the federal district court in Washington, D.C. Levy subsequently clerked on the federal appeals court in D.C. for Judge Douglas Ginsburg, who, some might remember, was nominated to the U.S. Supreme Court by Ronald Reagan after the failed Robert Bork nomination, but who withdrew after news accounts revealed that he had used marijuana as a student and a professor at Harvard. When Simpson and Neily presented Levy with their idea of a Second Amendment challenge to the District of Columbia's gun regulations, he essentially told them: great idea, what do you need from me, and make it happen.

"They convinced me the time was right," recalled Levy. "It was a confluence of factors."[6] Those factors, he said, were: the draconian nature of the District's regulations; horrible crime statistics since the handgun ban was implemented; the *Emerson* decision; the Ashcroft announcement that the Second Amendment secured an individual right; and finally, the outpouring of recent scholarship that took the individual right position, including by some liberal constitutional law scholars.

Levy agreed to bankroll the litigation out of his own funds, and although the Cato Institute blessed the project, it was not to be a Cato or Institute for Justice project. He did not seek or want funds from any outside source because his interest was not to advance the gun rights agenda, he claimed, but to "vindicate the Constitution." Chip Mellor, head of the Institute for Justice, gave the green light to Neily's working on the litigation on his own time, but he wanted Simpson, who had only been with the institute less than a year, to do only institute work.

As the parents and school districts in the Seattle and Louisville cases were discovering around the same time, litigation in the federal courts with an eye toward the Supreme Court is not for the fainthearted. Levy and Neily took their first step in what would be their own five-year odyssey by searching for sympathetic clients in the lawsuit that they were planning.

They knew exactly the type of person they wanted: six District residents who were diverse in race, age, gender, and social backgrounds, and who sincerely believed their personal safety was at risk by living in the District. "I think probably most importantly, people who first and foremost were equally committed to the goal of vindicating the Second Amendment as an individual right, not people who thought it would be fun to be along for the ride but people with a personal reason for wanting to be involved," said Neily.

He and Levy sent word through the "conservative-libertarian grapevine" that they were seeking clients for a Second Amendment challenge. They scoured newspapers in the District for stories about and letters by people who might fit their criteria. With the help of a Cato lawyer, they found and interviewed nearly three dozen people before settling on six: three men and three women, four of them white and two black, and ranging in age from their twenties to their early sixties.

Two of the six had stories that struck a strong chord in Neily. Tom Palmer was harassed by a skinhead gang in California and believed he would have been murdered but for the gun he had in his backpack. "The reason he had that pistol is his mother gave it to him and basically said, 'Tom, if you're going to be openly gay, you may need this one day.' He didn't shoot anybody; he pulled it out of his backpack and said, 'If you don't stop, I'll kill you.' "

And there was Dick Heller, a security guard who was allowed to carry a gun on his job at the Thurgood Marshall Building, housing the Administrative Office of the U.S. Courts, and who lived in a high-crime neighborhood in the District. "What I felt and I know what Dick felt about the situation was it reflected this incredible government hypocrisy. It was perfectly fine for Dick Heller to carry a gun if he's protecting the lives of government officials, but it's not okay for Dick Heller to take that gun home or to protect his own life or the life of his family," said Neily.

Heller would eventually become a key figure in the legal challenge.

"It's remarkable the effect just telling the story of any one of our clients has on an audience," added Neily. "It doesn't make people agree with you, but it makes clear this is a subject on which reasonable people can have different views. That's important because so many people otherwise would just write you off as a gun nut. But you tell a story about an openly gay man, almost murdered by skinheads, who saved his own life with a gun, or Shelly Parker, who wanted to be able to fend off drug dealers in her neighborhood who threatened her in her home—it's very hard to dismiss those people and their experiences. You either have to say they're lying or just tell them to call 911 and everything will be fine. Nobody who lives in the city believes the latter."

Levy viewed the Second Amendment project from the beginning as having three phases: first, a lawsuit to determine the meaning of the Second Amendment; second, if successful in proving an individual right, litigation to get the Second Amendment applied to all of the states (the District of Columbia is not a state but a federal enclave); and third, litigation to determine the scope of the individual right—what gun restrictions would or would not pass constitutional muster.

"We sought to make incremental progress as Thurgood Marshall had done," said Levy, referring to Marshall's litigation strategy to end segregation. "He bit off a little at a time and we thought that was the right approach as well. D.C. seemed like the perfect place to start—we had the timing, the location, and the plaintiffs."

It was also important to the two men that their case was not one in which a criminal defendant was fighting a gun charge or conviction on the basis of an individual right to own the gun under the Second Amendment. At the time, Second Amendment claims were being raised mostly in criminal cases and the claims often were frivolous, the two lawyers believed. Because they were frivolous, the courts did not take the Second Amendment arguments seriously, which had led to sloppy collective rights decisions, they said.

"Look at the mountain of bad precedent predating the *Emerson* decision," said Neily. "Most of it is 'United States versus somebody,' mostly criminal cases. The last thing in the world you want, if you think the

Second Amendment protects an individual right and you want to vindicate that right, is to see that get litigated in the Supreme Court in the guise of a criminal case. We were mindful of that." In other words, who would they rather have as the poster boy for the Second Amendment: a criminal or a law-abiding citizen?

That summer as the lawsuit came together, Levy received a call from Nelson Lund, who holds the NRA-endowed chair of Constitutional Law and the Second Amendment at George Mason University School of Law. Lund suggested a meeting with Levy and Washington lawyer Charles Cooper, a longtime NRA litigator and former Reagan Justice Department official who is now heading the defense of California's Proposition 8, the ban on same-sex marriages. Levy and Neily met the two men at the Cato Institute, but the meeting did not go well.

"They were not pleased," recalled Levy. "They said we might achieve victory in the lower courts, but the Supreme Court was not hospitable. They didn't say this, but there also may have been a turf issue." Levy did not buy their Supreme Court argument. "Looking at the Supreme Court at the time, Bush was in office. The next folks likely to go off the Court seemed to be O'Connor or one of the liberals. We thought we had a very powerful case and it was likely the Court was as good or better than its current posture."

But David Lehman, the NRA's deputy executive director and general counsel, downplayed the disagreement at that time, saying, "When you get a number of lawyers together, you'll have a variety of different strategies. We all had the same goal but took different paths to get there. We all had the same goal of the Court finding an individual right. We also were working on the legislative side of things as well."[7]

Undeterred by the NRA's apparent lack of enthusiasm, Levy and Neily moved forward. For the rest of the summer of 2002, Neily worked on drafting the lawsuit. But he also was being drawn more and more into another case that the Institute for Justice was handling. The net result of those demands prevented Neily from pushing the gun complaint "across the finish line." Levy, although a very knowledgeable constitutional lawyer, was not and had never been a litigator. He suggested, and Neily agreed, that they bring in a third lawyer.

Levy started looking for a "hard-charging, hungry young lawyer" to take on the litigating responsibility for the lawsuit, and found Alan Gura. He knew Gura through the libertarian circles in which they both moved—a notably small community in the nation's capital.

"If you show any kind of interest in some of these ideas in the community, then your path might cross with Bob's," said Gura. "He's a very prolific writer and commentator, a good guy."[8]

Like Levy, Gura had not thought much about the Second Amendment before being approached about the lawsuit in December 2002. He had started his own law firm in the center of historic Old Town Alexandria, Virginia, just a little over a year before getting Levy's call. Before that, he had left the big firm environment of Sidley Austin to spend a year as counsel to the U.S. Senate Judiciary Committee's subcommittee on criminal justice oversight. He also had worked as a deputy attorney general for the state of California.

"One of the reasons I think Bob called me is I did have a civil rights practice," said Gura. "I had always litigated civil rights throughout my career. It was logical that someone with my background would be involved, just as it was logical for Clark Neily and Steve Simpson to get involved because they did civil rights work at the Institute for Justice. It sounded like a great case; it sounded like a lot of fun. It made sense, and I figured, 'Why not?' "

Levy offered what he called "subsistence wages" to Gura, and even though he wanted to pay him more as the lawsuit became increasingly complex, Gura stuck to the original agreement, saying, "A deal is a deal."

Once on board, Gura, who has a hurried, almost impatient air about him, burrowed into the history of the Second Amendment and put the final touches on the lawsuit with the skill and confidence of a lawyer well beyond his years. "When Alan gets moving, he gets moving fast," chuckled Neily.

Besides deciding to bring a civil, not a criminal, legal challenge, all three men agreed on another critical element in their strategy of getting the case to the Supreme Court. "We were in agreement it would be a very clean case, just one claim and the narrowest relief we could ask for," said Neily. "We were not going to get into concealed carry and other issues, just having a gun at home. I don't think you have to be too deeply knowledgeable about Supreme Court practice and history to know that if you're asking them to tread on fresh ground, it's best to ask them to take the smallest step they can."

Keeping it simple and straightforward, the trio of lawyers filed their soon-to-be historic challenge to the District of Columbia's gun laws in federal district court in Washington on February 10, 2003. Shelly Parker, the scourge of neighborhood drug dealers, was the first name on the lawsuit. It also named as defendants the District of Columbia and its mayor at the time, Anthony Fenty. In their complaint, they told the court: "At a minimum, the Second Amendment guarantees individuals a fundamental right to possess a functional, personal firearm, such as a handgun or ordinary long gun [shotgun or rifle] within the home. Defendants currently maintain and actively enforce a set of laws, customs, practices, and policies which operate to deprive individuals, including the plaintiffs, of this important right."

To the surprise of the three lawyers, resistance to the filing of the lawsuit was immediate, especially from conservative and libertarian groups. Gun rights advocates voiced concerns similar to those expressed by the NRA: the timing was not right; the chance of a bad decision was too risky.

"We had a frank discussion with a couple of folks from the NRA," recalled Neily. "They weren't nasty. I think they were taken aback that we weren't willing to get with the program. I think it's fair to say from their perspective, not every challenge that had come before us was a credible challenge. I can see how some could be concerned about whether these three guys are credible lawyers, and can they get this done. That's a reasonable concern."

But less than two months after they filed their lawsuit, another Second Amendment lawsuit landed on the district court's doorstep: a suit funded by the NRA. That action created tension and hard feelings between the NRA and Levy's legal team during the next two years. The libertarian lawyers viewed what they called the "copycat" lawsuit as, at best, an attempt to delay their own lawsuit, and, at worst, an effort to derail it.

Stephen Halbrook, a longtime legal consultant to the NRA, represented five D.C. residents in *Seegars v. [Attorney General John] Ashcroft*, the second lawsuit. Halbrook has written extensively about the Second Amendment—books and law review articles—for more than three decades. He had argued and won three cases in the Supreme Court, including *Printz v. United States*, a 1997 decision striking down a temporary provision in the Brady Handgun Violence Prevention Act requiring state and local law enforcement officials to perform background checks on handgun buyers until a national background check system was developed.

Halbrook grew up in a small farming community and hunted as a youth. In summers, he went to a camp which had a junior NRA program teaching gun safety. He continued his NRA membership in college and began studying the Bill of Rights. "I quickly found there was no literature on the Second Amendment, maybe about three law review articles," he recalled. "The other amendments had an enormous amount of literature. This was in the late sixties. It was a fertile field, and it became my primary interest."[9]

Although the NRA was providing financial support, the Seegars lawsuit was not the NRA's case, he insisted, adding, "My clients are my clients and not the NRA's." But, he said, "I know it to be a fact, the reason the NRA supported the *Seegars* case was they wanted to get the best result. It was unclear what the Supreme Court would do. It was very risky. But if there was going to be a case, they wanted to encourage any input to try to get the right result."

The two cases were in front of different federal trial judges. Filing a copycat lawsuit was bad enough from the perspective of the Levy team, but Halbrook's motion to consolidate the two cases before one judge infuriated them, particularly Gura, the chief litigator.

The problem was that Halbrook's suit was not identical to the other case and those differences presented real problems for the three libertarian lawyers. The first problem was that Halbrook had sued the U.S. attorney general, John Ashcroft, while Gura had sued only the District of Columbia. The D.C. gun provisions targeted by Gura, if violated, were misdemeanor crimes that would be prosecuted by the D.C. Office of Corporation Counsel. The U.S. Department of Justice only prosecuted felonies.

"We did not believe Ashcroft was the proper defendant," said Gura. "Also, we didn't want to include Ashcroft because we did not wish to take on the Department of Justice. It's just another set of very excellent lawyers who are going to be tenacious and creative in thinking of ways to get rid of the case."

Gura was prescient. In fact, it was Justice Department lawyers and not D.C. government lawyers who argued a legal theory that subsequently knocked Halbrook's case out of court and nearly did the same to Gura's case—that their clients had no standing to bring the lawsuits.

The second problem that Gura and his colleagues had with Halbrook's lawsuit was that it did not present a simple, straightforward Second Amendment challenge. Halbrook also charged that the gun laws violated due process, equal protection, and the Civil Rights Act of 1866, which, after the Civil War, overturned the so-called Black Codes, enacted by some states, including the ban on African Americans' possession of firearms. That sort of kitchen sink approach, they believed, had failed in the past.

All of the lawyers met to discuss Halbrook's motion to consolidate the cases. "We told him this was a terrible idea," said Gura. But Halbrook was not convinced. "Based on the uniqueness of this kind of challenge, there was a good likelihood the court would see these as related cases and the court would consolidate them anyway," explained Halbrook, adding, "They had inexperienced attorneys. None had done work on the Second Amendment, either academic or litigation. There had been many cases brought that resulted in adverse decisions. Our idea was if we were all before the same judge, we could present what would hopefully make the best possible case."

But Gura continued to see it differently. "The NRA filed a copycat case with the express mission of inserting themselves into the process. The NRA is amazingly territorial. They fight very hard to protect their turf. They're still like that. It is what it is."

From April to July 2003, the lawyers sparred over the motion to consolidate and Halbrook's role in the litigation. In July, the federal judge in Halbrook's case rejected his motion to join the two cases. The real delay in Gura's case was not caused so much by Halbrook as by Gura's opponent, the District of Columbia, whose lawyers missed a key deadline and then sought and received a two-month extension. But by the end of the summer, the judges in both cases had scheduled them for October hearings.

While the litigation dance continued throughout that summer, gun control groups were watching closely. A group of lawyers at the Brady Center to Prevent Gun Violence flagged Gura's case early in the legal process. "We try to monitor potentially significant cases involving attacks on gun laws and cases that have potential to produce important legal precedents," said Dennis Henigan, vice president. "We spotted this one as being potentially troublesome."[10]

Troublesome for the same reasons that Clark Neily and Steve Simpson saw opportunity a year earlier. "You had the *Emerson* case in the Fifth Circuit which was kind of the first crack in the dam for gun rights litigators, even though it wasn't brought as a gun rights case but a criminal defense case," explained Henigan. "It did in fact produce the first federal court ruling that the Second Amendment was broader than simply a militia-related right. You also had the Bush Justice Department entering the fray with John Ashcroft writing the NRA and saying he agreed."

Henigan's organization had even filed an ethics complaint against

Ashcroft, charging that by writing the NRA letter, he had violated his duty to his client—the United States—which, at the same time, was making the militia argument in the *Emerson* case.

The Brady Center had litigated against Halbrook for many years because he brought most of the major Second Amendment challenges, primarily for the NRA or its affiliates. Halbrook was a known quantity. "Gura was this young upstart, but supported by Bob Levy. We took both cases seriously," Henigan added. "Our primary worry was the D.C. Circuit [the federal appellate court], which had gotten so conservative, and, of course, our worries were validated."

The Brady Center, he said, does not favor a handgun ban as a matter of policy. "We basically think local jurisdictions should be allowed to make their own gun laws," he explained. "As a matter of policy, we're kind of moderates on this. We think carefully designed gun restrictions could still allow law-abiding citizens to have guns in the home and still reduce the risk of them being in the hands of dangerous people.

"It's certainly understandable that Mayor Fenty would want to defend his law, which was very popular. Whether it was controversial at the time, D.C.-elected officials in the community clearly supported it for its entire history. There never was any effort to repeal it. Every mayor, police chief, and city council supported it."

In January 2004, Halbrook's case—*Seegars v. Ashcroft*—was dismissed by the federal district judge. Two months later, Gura's case—*Parker v. District of Columbia*—met the same fate at the hands of its judge.

In *Seegars*, as Gura predicted, government lawyers successfully argued that all but one of Halbrook's clients lacked standing to bring their lawsuit. Standing is the key to the federal courthouse door. Federal courts can only decide actual cases and controversies, so someone bringing a lawsuit must show he or she has suffered a "concrete and particularized" injury, actual or imminent, for which a court can provide relief. But there also are times when federal courts will hear so-called pre-enforcement challenges. For example, a person wants to engage in a course of conduct that a law forbids and he believes that law violates a constitutional right. The Supreme Court has said that person does not have to wait to be prosecuted to seek relief. He or she can bring the challenge as long as there is a credible threat of prosecution.

Despite the Supreme Court's rule, the U.S. Court of Appeals for the District of Columbia has a tougher standard for pre-enforcement challenges, like those brought by Halbrook and Gura. It requires more than a general threat of prosecution; the threat must be imminent to the person suing.

The district court judge found that Halbrook's clients were neither prosecuted nor threatened with prosecution under the District's gun laws, and except for one, they did not own a gun and never applied to register one. As for the one client who did have standing, the court rejected the individual right agument.

Had Halbrook not sued the Department of Justice, believed Gura, the standing question would never have arisen.

Gura, however, lost his case on the merits of the Second Amendment issue. The judge in his case concluded: "While plaintiffs extol many thought-provoking and historically interesting arguments for finding an individual right, this Court would be in error to overlook sixty-five years of unchanged Supreme Court precedent and the deluge of circuit case law rejecting an individual right to bear arms not in conjunction with service in the Militia."[11]

Both lawyers filed appeals with the federal appellate court. By then, the cases had attracted national attention. Halbrook's case was heard first and he went into the appellate courtroom with support from sixteen state attorneys general. The Brady Center supported the United States and the District of Columbia in urging that the lower court decision be upheld. Thirteen months after the trial judge's ruling, a three-judge appellate panel, voting 2–1, agreed that Halbrook's clients lacked standing. Four months after that, in June 2005, Halbrook's request for a rehearing before the full appellate court was rejected. Three of the court's ten judges had voted to rehear Halbrook's appeal, one of whom was Judge John Roberts Jr., by then just four weeks away from being nominated by President Bush to the U.S. Supreme Court.

Gura, meanwhile, had been waiting impatiently for his appeal, which he had filed in April 2004, to be heard. It had been put on hold by the appellate court pending the decision in Halbrook's appeal.

Argument day in *Parker v. District of Columbia* finally came on December 7, 2006, more than two years after Gura filed his notice of appeal. As he headed into the appellate court, he was backed by supporting briefs from thirteen state attorneys general, and conservative and gun rights groups, including the Second Amendment Foundation, the Congress of Racial Equality, the American Civil Rights Union, and his earlier nemesis—the NRA.

The District's in-house attorney, Todd Kim, also had supporters on appeal—three states and the cities of San Francisco, New York, Chicago, and Los Angeles, as well as the Brady Center to Prevent Gun Violence, which had taken an active role in helping to prepare the District's lawyers.

With Halbrook's case defeated and a lower court ruling against his own case, Gura might have felt on the defensive as he faced the three-judge appellate panel. But the young lawyer had a reservoir of confidence that stopped just short of arrogance. He knew his clients faced the same legal obstacle that knocked out Halbrook's clients—standing to sue—but he believed, despite the trial court decision, that he had shown more than enough evidence that the District was prepared to prosecute his clients and so the threat to them was more than a general one.

The three-judge panel, however, disagreed. On March 9, 2007, now four years after Gura filed the lawsuit, the appellate panel issued its decision. None of Gura's clients had standing, ruled the court, except one, the private security guard—Dick Heller—and one was all the court needed to get to the merits of the Second Amendment challenge.

On the merits, the panel, voting 2–1, held that the Second Amendment protects an individual right to keep and bear arms. "That right existed prior to the formation of the new government under the Constitution and was premised on the private use of arms for activities such as hunting and self-defense, the latter being understood as resistance to either private lawlessness or the depredations of a tyrannical government (or a threat from abroad)," wrote a conservative icon and Reagan appointee, Judge Laurence Silberman, for himself and Judge Thomas Griffith, a George W. Bush appointee, in a 58-page opinion. "In addition, the right to keep and bear arms had the important and salutary civic purpose of helping to preserve the citizen militia."[12]

The dissenting judge, Karen LeCraft Henderson, appointed by President George H. W. Bush, said the only twentieth-century Supreme Court decision to analyze the amendment's scope—*United States v. Miller* in 1939—was clear in stating that the amendment's "obvious purpose" was to assure a continued and effective militia. Until the Supreme Court itself overrules *Miller*, she said, lower courts are bound by it. And second, the dissenting judge said the amendment was drafted to protect the states from a perceived threat posed by a national standing army. The District, she said, was not a state but a federal entity, with no need to protect itself from the federal government, and so the amendment did not apply.

One simple step by a security guard had kept the Levy team's case in the game, positioning it for the game clincher. The step? During the summer of 2003, when the lawyers were preparing for the hearing in their case, their client Dick Heller, at the urging of his close friend Dane Von Breichenruchardt, actually applied for and was denied a registration certificate to own a handgun. That routine process of application and denial, according to the appellate court, was an injury sufficiently "concrete and particular" to give him standing to sue the District, and it was something the other five plaintiffs never had done.

Von Breichenruchardt, stocky, with a white handlebar mustache and comb-over, and the silver-haired Heller, taller, wiry, and with a perpetual ball cap perched atop his head, had been discussing a Second Amendment lawsuit against the District for years.

Heller, who had served in the U.S. Army, moved into the District in

1975, before the gun law was passed. He had bought a nine-inch barrel cowboy pistol "like I had seen on *Gunsmoke*." Although he was grandfathered into the new gun law, he never registered the pistol or two rifles. He lived on the east side of Capitol Hill, near a housing project that gradually was taken over by drug dealers. Bullets had soared through the front window and door of his house from random shootings.

In 1993, Von Breichenruchardt and Heller met when the former rented a room from Heller in connection with a short-term job project. "I had been on the U.S. shooting team and had been competitively shooting my entire life," said Von Breichenruchardt. "When I moved in, I had my guns with me and asked where I could put them. He informed me there was a ban and I could not keep them in the District at all. I was absolutely incensed about that."[13]

The two men began discussing how to challenge the gun regulations. Von Breichenruchardt stayed in the District after his project ended, formed the U.S. Bill of Rights Foundation, and plugged into the libertarian-conservative network by attending functions at the Heritage Foundation and the Cato Institute. He also took some law courses and plunged into the history of the Second Amendment. At Cato, he met Bob Levy and took every opportunity to bend his ear about challenging the District's gun laws. Levy always listened carefully, but was noncommittal.

When Von Breichenruchardt heard in 2002 that Levy was backing a Second Amendment lawsuit, he called him and offered Heller as a plaintiff, an offer accepted by the lawyers. The following summer, he talked to Levy again because, he said, he was worried about a possible problem with standing in the lawsuit. Levy, he said, told him to contact Alan Gura.

"Gura said the city always has prosecuted these cases; that's sufficient, and clearly [Heller] has been chilled from registering. I said, 'You better send [Heller] down' " to register his gun, he recalled, explaining that once Heller was turned away, that was actual harm, which was the requirement for standing. "He said no."

Von Breichenruchardt then told Heller to do it anyway. "I said, 'Go down [to city hall], bring back the paperwork, and we're going to fill out the forms, and when they turn you down, [the lawyers] will have standing.' Dick went down the next day, picked up the information, and we filled it out. He went back down and they told him, 'No, you have to be a sworn officer; we don't consider officers for hire to be sworn officers.' I told him to get something in his hand—application denied, or a police officer's name. They stamped it 'Denied' and the police officer cited the regulation.

"It's the simplest thing in the world—Law 101, standing."

Levy and Neily agree that Von Breichenruchardt did get Heller to fill out the forms, "and it turned out to be incredibly important," said Neily.

Incredibly important and incredible, thought Dennis Henigan of the Brady Center, which had backed the District in the federal appellate court. "How ridiculous is it that the fact that Heller applied to register knowing he would be denied gives him standing?" said a chagrined Henigan. "Conservative judges on the D.C. Circuit have made a career of slamming the door on consumer and environmental plaintiffs, and then they find an artificial way of making sure this case goes forward."

Gura, Levy, and Neily were elated by the decision, of course, and held a celebration with their clients four days later at the Cato Institute. Mayor Fenty and city officials were not in a celebratory mood. Adrian Fenty said he was "deeply disappointed and frankly outraged" by the decision. The laws, he said, had helped to decrease gun violence in the District. He vowed to "do everything in our power to work to get the decision overturned, and we will vigorously enforce our handgun laws during that time."[14]

But despite the victory in the appellate court, the Levy team soon faced another obstacle on their road to the Supreme Court. Senator Kay Bailey Hutchison (R-TX) introduced her perennial, NRA-backed bill to repeal the District's gun laws. Levy, Gura, and Neily believed the bill was another effort by the NRA to stop their case.

"The effect of that effort, had it succeeded, would have been not only to moot the case and thus prevent Supreme Court review, but also to vacate the D.C. Circuit's favorable decision—the first and only time a federal court ever struck down a gun law on Second Amendment grounds," said Neily. "In the weeks after the D.C. Circuit's favorable ruling, it appeared very possible to us that the NRA would in fact succeed in getting the repeal law passed, thus mooting the case."

Levy found himself in the odd position of testifying against the legislation. He told the committee considering the bill that the best way to proceed was in the courts, not in Congress, because a future Congress could repeal whatever the current one did.

And then, on April 16, 2007, a Virginia Tech student shot and killed thirty-two people before turning his gun on himself and ending the deadliest mass shooting in American history. Fifteen others were wounded during the campus rampage.[15]

"The tragedy at Virginia Tech spelled an end to any legislative repeal effort, at least in the near term, which meant that the NRA's effort—if in fact it was a serious effort, which they have consistently, though not plausibly, in my view, denied—to moot the *Heller* case itself became moot," said Neily.

The District's Mayor Fenty, in the meantime, had asked the full federal appellate court to review the three-judge panel's ruling against the District. But about two weeks after the Virginia Tech shootings, the D.C. Circuit declined to review the decision. Fenty then was faced with deciding whether to appeal to the Supreme Court.

Most lawyers who win their case in a federal appellate court do not want their defeated opponents to appeal to the Supreme Court. They have nothing to gain, only a victory to lose. But after that evening over drinks more than five years earlier, the Supreme Court had always been the ultimate target of Levy, Neily, and Gura.

And now the fate of the Levy team's carefully manufactured test case on the meaning of the Second Amendment was in the hands of its opponents: Mayor Fenty and his legal advisers.

CHAPTER 8

"What kind of message are you sending? This is not Dodge City in the 1800s."

— Kenny Barnes, whose son was shot to death on a D.C. street in 2001, reacting to the 2007 D.C. Circuit decision

The National Rifle Association and its frequent legal counsel, Stephen Halbrook, kept a scorecard over the years on how justices of the Supreme Court might vote on whether the Second Amendment protected an individual right to keep and bear arms.

Justice Antonin Scalia, they believed, tipped his hand in his commentary in his book *A Matter of Interpretation* (1997). He wrote then that he interpreted the amendment "as a guarantee that the federal government will not interfere with the individual's right to bear arms for self-defense." Scalia added later in the essay, "Of course, properly understood, it is no limitation upon arms control by the states."[1]

"I said to myself, 'Justice Scalia looks safe,'" recalled Halbrook.

Justice Clarence Thomas, in a concurring opinion in *Printz v. United States*, a 1997 decision involving background checks on handgun applicants, had noted: "Marshaling an impressive array of historical evidence, a growing body of scholarly commentary indicates that the 'right to keep and bear arms' is, as the Amendment's text suggests, a personal right."

"I thought, okay, Justice Thomas might be favorable," said Halbrook. And Justice Ruth Bader Ginsburg, in a dissent in *Muscarello v.*

United States (1998), had argued that the phrase "carries a firearm" in a federal criminal law means to carry it so it is ready to use. In reaching that interpretation, she referred to the Second Amendment's "keep and bear arms" language as an example of the ordinary meaning of carrying a firearm. "She was considered someone who might vote favorably," added Halbrook.

Justice Stephen Breyer was not viewed as a favorable vote, and the other justices were difficult to predict.

A petition to the Supreme Court in the District of Columbia gun case was "certainly risky" for gun rights groups, thought Halbrook, but the appellate court's decision was an excellent one, a very serious look at the question.

Too risky, however, for some gun control groups, who urged Mayor Fenty not to file a petition.

"If it had been up to us, we would not have taken it up [to the Supreme Court]," said Henigan of the Brady Center. "We weren't real willing to throw the dice because of the potential impact on gun laws nationally. We thought the District of Columbia laws could be rewritten in a way that still made them very, very strong."

Although there were serious discussions, there was never any serious doubt in the Fenty administration about appealing the decision striking down the District's gun laws to the Supreme Court. Every mayoral administration since its enactment had supported the regulations and every city council as well. The District's police and fire chiefs also backed the gun laws. And while there was ongoing debate in the country about the Second Amendment and gun regulations, there was no evident public controversy within the District itself over its own gun regulations.

"Certainly any time you lose a case you have to think about whether you're going to file for cert or not, and what the upsides and downsides are," said Alan Morrison, who was special counsel to the District at the time. "The arguments we heard were, 'Look, the D.C. law is the harshest law; you don't want this case to go to the Supreme Court.' To which my answer was, 'Well, suppose some other case gets up there?' At this point, we have no gun law in the District. We have sort of a fiduciary responsibility to the city council which enacted it, to the mayor who wants it enforced, and to the police chief who desperately wants it enforced. It had to be a very good reason, it seemed to me, to lay down, take it easy, and let some other case come up."

And there was also something to be said, thought Morrison, for taking "the most in-your-face law" to the Supreme Court, because "we didn't want wishy-washy laws. Everyone wanted this law because they thought it was important,"[2] he said.

Morrison is a passionate public interest lawyer. With Ralph Nader, he co-founded and directed for more than twenty-five years the Public Citizen Litigation Group, a division within the non-profit consumer organization Public Citizen. The bearded, energetic Morrison, who currently teaches at George Washington University School of Law, has argued twenty cases in the Supreme Court on issues ranging from the First Amendment to separation of powers.

He was finishing up a temporary teaching stint at Stanford Law School in California when D.C. Attorney General Linda Singer, newly appointed to that post by newly elected Mayor Fenty, invited him to return east to work with her. He did not want to be a line attorney or have a caseload with court deadlines, so Morrison suggested becoming a special counsel with responsibility for special legal projects within Singer's office. Singer agreed, and before Morrison had even hired movers for the trip home to D.C., the first project arrived: the lawsuit against the District's gun regulations.

"I had never done a case with the Second Amendment," said Morrison. "I had never written about it. We used to joke about it: the right to bear arms is the right to arm bears. While I didn't agree with Warren Burger on many things, he said a great fraud that's been committed on the American public is that the Second Amendment has anything to do with personal rights. Burger was wrong about a lot of things and apparently he was wrong about this one too," he added ruefully.

Singer also sought outside advice about an appeal to the Supreme Court from former acting Solicitor General Walter Dellinger, a highly respected constitutional law scholar who was in private practice at O'Melveny & Myers law firm in D.C., and from high court litigator Thomas Goldstein, who at the time headed the appellate practice at D.C.'s Akin Gump Strauss Hauer & Feld. But she wanted the case to be a District case because these were District laws. She wanted it handled by District lawyers, and Morrison was integral to that identity.

Once the decision was made to go to the Supreme Court, everyone was united. Throughout the summer of 2007, Morrison and the District's lawyers worked on the petition for review even though Morrison was still in California. At some point that summer, he approached Singer about making an early decision on who would argue the case if the Supreme Court granted review.

"I said I think we should decide this early because it's going to affect how we're going to staff it, who is going to do what when, and we wanted to send a message that we were ready," he recalled.

There were three possibilities. Todd Kim, an able chief of the appeals section who had never argued in the Supreme Court and whose pregnant wife was due near the time an argument might be scheduled; an "outsider," like Dellinger or Goldstein; and Morrison.

"I told her, 'I can get up to speed and I will find the time to devote as much time as I need to this,' " he recalled. Singer asked about his other projects for her, and Morrison promised to do those as well. After a few days, Singer told Morrison that he would argue the case and write the briefs with the help of the District's other lawyers.

On September 4, 2007, the Tuesday after Labor Day, Mayor Fenty held a press conference on the steps of the old city hall to announce the filing of the District's petition in the Supreme Court. All petitions to the Supreme Court must present a question for the justices at the outset. The District's question was: Whether the Second Amendment forbids the District of Columbia from banning private possession of handguns while allowing possession of rifles and shotguns.[3]

The District's opponents—Gura, Levy, and Neily—had been on pins and needles all summer awaiting the petition. When they saw how the District had framed the question for the justices to decide, they were not happy. The question was disingenuous, they believed, because it ignored the fact that the District's gun laws required that all firearms (rifles, shotguns, and pre-ban handguns) be "unloaded and disassembled or bound by a trigger-lock or similar device unless such firearm is kept at [a] place of business, or [is] being used for lawful recreational purposes within the District of Columbia."

To Gura, the District's question was like saying *Time* magazine could be banned as long as the District allowed residents to read *Newsweek*. "This case was about whether handguns are protected under the Second Amendment and also could the city ban all functional firearms," Gura explained, adding, "We took issue with the suggestion the city actually lets you have rifles and shotguns. They allowed you to have things that looked like rifles and shotguns but you could never render them operable, so what good is that? We argued the right to bear arms is the right to have arms that actually work. There's no point in having a gun if you can't ever fire it at someone breaking into your home."

In their response to the District's petition, the Levy team said the question for the justices was: Whether the Second Amendment guarantees law-abiding, adult individuals a right to keep ordinary, functional firearms, including handguns, in their homes.

And because the whole point of their five-year litigation battle had been to get an answer from the Supreme Court, they did not oppose review by the justices but told them the case presented a "unique opportunity to correct a persistent misconception that the people do not actually enjoy a right that is specifically enumerated in the Constitution. 'The people'—individuals in our country—retain the right to keep and bear arms."[4]

In November, the justices announced they would hear arguments in *District of Columbia v. Heller*, now named after Gura's only client to have had standing to sue, Dick Heller. And the justices rewrote the question that they would decide to include the long gun provisions in the laws: whether three District gun regulations "violate the Second Amendment rights of individuals who are not affiliated with any state-regulated militia, but who wish to keep handguns and other firearms for private use in their homes."

Arguments in the Court's first substantive Second Amendment case in nearly a century were just four months away.

Based on its own criteria for granting review, did the Court have a strong reason for taking the District's appeal? And what would have happened if it had denied review?

A federal appellate court, of course, had struck down the District's gun restrictions—the first decision to invalidate a law on Second Amendment grounds—but there was no burning conflict among the federal appellate courts to resolve, a key criterion for Supreme Court review. There certainly was no burning controversy within the District itself since the regulations had been overwhelmingly approved by the elected city council in 1976 and there was no populist movement to repeal them. The appellate court also had said the individual right, like other rights, was not absolute and could be subject to reasonable regulation. If the Supreme Court had not gotten involved, the District conceivably could have tried to write new regulations that met constitutional concerns. There was substantial consensus throughout the country on the existence of an individual right to possess firearms: forty-two states had provisions in their state constitutions protecting that right. And those protections were not at risk. There was little appetite in Congress for national gun control legislation so there was no realistic risk that any individual right, if it did exist, was in danger.

With a Supreme Court precedent on the books for nearly seventy years that courts had accepted as settling the question in favor of a militia–collective rights interpretation, and with no great national problem vexing elected officials, it was an aggressive conservative Court taking on a long-sought objective on the conservative political agenda.

The October 2007 term was underway for more than a month when the justices made their announcement to hear the District's gun appeal. The term had opened quietly, relative to the prior term, with two potential landmark rulings on the docket.

The justices had decided to step back into legal fallout from the nation's war on terror. Since 2004, the Court had considered five challenges to the Bush administration's approach to detaining enemy combatants—both citizens and aliens.[5]

The cases in the 2007 term—*Boumediene v. Bush* and *Al Odah v. United States*, which were consolidated for argument—involved Congress's response to *Hamdan v. Rumsfeld*, in which the Court in 2006 struck down military commissions authorized by President Bush because they violated the Uniform Code of Military Justice and the Geneva Conventions.

Congress subsequently enacted the Military Commissions Act of 2006. The six *Boumediene* and *Al Odah* detainees at Guantánamo Bay were asking the justices, among other questions, whether the 2006 act's prohibition on their seeking federal court review of their detentions through the use of habeas corpus petitions violated the Constitution's suspension clause. The clause, in Article I, Section 9, states: "The Privilege of the Writ of Habeas Corpus shall not be suspended, unless when in Cases of Rebellion or Invasion the Public Safety may require it."

The Bush administration and Congress had suffered one setback after another in the Supreme Court in terrorism-related challenges and their latest efforts struck at the heart of the judiciary's role in the separation of powers. All eyes were trained on the two cases, all eyes, that is, until the District's gun case competed for top billing in the new term.

The District's Alan Morrison and his colleagues had started working on their merits brief (brief in which all arguments are fleshed out) for the Court before review was granted in order to avoid the time crunch between a grant of review and oral arguments. They sent a draft out to Dellinger and Goldstein for input. Morrison faced a moot court of about fifteen lawyers based on the draft brief to uncover any holes in the legal arguments.

"I was willing to do that because this was not an issue I knew a lot about and I had to feel comfortable with our arguments," he said. "Nobody thought we had missed any issues. That was quite comforting actually."

At the same time, the District's legal team and their opponents—the Levy team—both sought support from the solicitor general of the United States. A supporting brief by the solicitor general, whose office is highly respected and trusted by the justices for its honesty and clarity of legal analysis, is a boon to any party's effort in the Court. The United States had not been sued by the Levy team, so it was not a party to the case, but it did have an important government interest and was expected to file a brief. Congress had passed numerous laws regulating firearms and the Department of Justice was responsible for enforcing them and prosecuting violators. The sweeping and categorical nature of the lower appellate court's ruling cast doubt, for example, on the constitutionality of existing federal laws prohibiting the possession of certain firearms, such as machine guns.

Attorney General John Ashcroft, in keeping with the Bush administration's position, had reversed the department's policy on the Second Amendment in 2001. Because of that policy, both sides in the *Heller* case knew that the department would argue that the Second Amendment protected an individual right to possess firearms unrelated to militia operations. But they did not know what the government's position would be on a standard or test that the justices should announce for judging the constitutionality of gun regulations going forward.

The Court has devised basically three tests, or standards, when it reviews the constitutionality of government actions. The toughest review—strict scrutiny—requires that the government have a compelling interest or objective and that the means chosen to achieve it are narrowly tailored and the least restrictive possible. A middle-level standard—heightened scrutiny—demands an important government objective and means that are substantially related to achieving the objective. The third test—rational basis—is the easiest review for the government to pass and requires a legitimate government objective and means that are rationally related to the objective.

Morrison, Linda Singer (the district's attorney general), and Todd Kim (the district's chief of appeals) headed to the Justice Department in December for a meeting with Solicitor General Paul Clement. The conference room in which they met was filled with department lawyers: Clement; his principal deputy, Gregory Garre; Assistant to the Solicitor General Malcolm Stewart; and members of the department's criminal appeals division, among others.

"We knew there was no point in saying to them, 'Change Ashcroft's opinion,' " said Morrison. "We told them, 'We need you very much because we can live with a private basis for the Second Amendment so long as there's appropriate deference given to government regulations.' We had a long discussion. We told them, 'Look, there's a very important issue here as to the standard of review and you have just as much at stake in this as the District.' "

They left the discussion without knowing what the solicitor general would tell the Supreme Court.

On December 14, 2007, it was their opponents' turn. Once again the conference room was packed. The discussion was cordial as the Levy team argued that the government should urge the justices to adopt strict scrutiny as the standard of review for gun regulations. But no one with the department tipped his or her hand, and there was no strong expression of support.

The three lawyers left the department and took a cab to Tony

Cheng's restaurant in nearby Chinatown for a Federalist Society lunch. In the cab, Clark Neily shared his misgivings about the tenor of the meeting.

"Given what would have been reasonable to expect because you've got a president who throughout his career was strong on the Second Amendment and there was the Ashcroft memo—it was sort of like the dog that didn't bark," he said. "At the same time, I'm not naive. I recognized the challenge the solicitor general's office was facing in the sense there's a lot of federal laws on the books involving guns, and once this door is opened, where does it go?"

Gura's assessment was harsher. "Clearly these are government lawyers who are very jealous of their authority and they don't need any more constitutional rights out there restricting their freedom of operation. Institutionally, these people are statist and are not interested in any more tools for individuals to challenge their authority. That was made very clear."

The solicitor general operates with a certain degree of independence within the Justice Department, but reports to the attorney general, who, in turn, is an appointee of the president. Inside the solicitor general's office, the *Heller* challenge was considered a huge and tricky case—politically and legally—not one the office was particularly eager to confront.

"It's one thing to say it's an individual right and another thing to flesh out where that leads," explained a department lawyer. "This was something the department had been struggling with since the Ashcroft memo. The Department of Justice and the solicitor general in particular have responsibility for defending the constitutionality of statutes. There are a whole lot of firearm-related restrictions. It would be very difficult to take a position that would have led to the Court holding unconstitutional a number of these laws. At the same time, there was a president and vice president who had been very outspoken on this, and ultimately the president gets to set the policy for his administration."

There also was a new attorney general—Michael Mukasey—who

became increasingly involved when communications from the White House on what the government's brief would say stepped up as the filing deadline approached. Although there was no huge showdown, discussions and rewriting of the brief continued up to the final hour. Mukasey ultimately told Clement to file the brief that he—Clement—thought the department should file and nothing else.

Going down to the wire, the solicitor general filed the government's brief on a Friday evening and, as expected, urged the Court to rule that the Second Amendment protected an individual right to possess firearms. But he told the justices that the lower appellate court did not apply the correct standard for evaluating *Heller*'s Second Amendment claims.

"Like other provisions of the Constitution that secure individual rights, the Second Amendment's protection of individual rights does not render all laws limiting gun ownership automatically invalid," wrote Clement. The correct standard of review, he said, was "heightened scrutiny," the intermediate standard. Under that standard, he wrote, "the 'rigorousness' of the inquiry depends on the degree of the burden on protected conduct, and important regulatory interests are typically sufficient to justify reasonable restrictions."

Because the lower court used the wrong standard of review, Clement urged the Court to send the case back to the lower court to apply the proper standard to *Heller*'s claims. The brief was not labeled as supporting either side in the case.

Reaction from gun rights groups was rapid and furious. The head of the Second Amendment Foundation posted on his Web site that the brief was "a transparent exercise of political pandering." A conservative group said that the Bush administration had "blundered in catastrophic fashion." Clement was singled out for criticism in a *Wall Street Journal* editorial.[6]

In an unprecedented act, Vice President Dick Cheney subsequently broke with the government's position and signed on to an amicus brief filed by members of Congress that supported in full the lower court's decision. In his 2011 memoir *In My Time*, Cheney recalled the episode and explained that the government's brief "seemed inconsistent with the president's previous position on the Second Amendment and it was certainly inconsistent with my view." He also wrote that Justice Antonin Scalia, who would author the *Heller* decision and was Cheney's friend, later joked the Court was uncertain about how to rule until "the vice president's brief showed up."[7]

Neily thought the government's reasoning was "shoddy," and it had offered a brief at war with itself. "What it ultimately asked was to send the case back to the district court where it could conveniently be smothered." Levy agreed, saying, "We failed miserably with Paul Clement. The administration had been good on gun rights, and Clement was a conservative. Their concern with federal gun laws—nobody was even thinking of challenging those laws."

Senator Kay Bailey Hutchison was "livid" when she saw the government's brief, said Stephen Halbrook, the Second Amendment litigator. She contacted him about writing an amicus brief for members of Congress, the brief that Cheney eventually signed. "Congress in reports and elsewhere interpreted the Second Amendment as an individual right," recalled Halbrook. "I thought a brief would be good for the Court not only on original understanding but how it had been interpreted by another branch over the years. Hutchison's office rounded up a whole other bunch of members. The vice president's joining our brief was orchestrated by Hutchison's office."

But gun control advocates saw the government's brief as something of a gift, given the administration's position on the individual right. The door would still be open to reasonable gun regulation under the government's approach.

"We thought we had gotten about as much out of them as we could," recalled Morrison. "It was very unclear what test they were applying. Asking for a remand to the lower court was as much as we could hope."

But Morrison had bigger problems at hand. The ground was shifting under his feet in the District's legal office.

The District's attorney general, Linda Singer, was increasingly frustrated by the growing involvement of the mayor's general counsel, Peter Nickles, in her office's work. The attorney general is appointed by the mayor and confirmed by the city council as the city's chief legal officer. The mayor's general counsel is appointed by the mayor and tasked with handling legal issues particular to that office. Nickles, a longtime friend of the mayor's father, had known the mayor since he was a child. An aggressive, veteran big firm litigator, Nickles had the mayor's trust and saw few boundaries to his duties.

Their clashes had become frequent enough that Singer, just eleven months on the job, decided in December 2007 that she would resign, but she wanted to wait until the District's merits brief in the gun appeal was ready to be filed with the Supreme Court. She had been heavily involved in the case's briefing and felt responsibility for it. In her resignation letter to the mayor, she took the high road and said nothing about her frustrations with Nickles.

Nickles, who was named acting attorney general, called Morrison into his office on December 21, just after Singer resigned, for what Morrison described as a "very unpleasant conversation." He asked if Morrison had talked to the press about Singer's resignation, which by then had been reported with Nickles portrayed as the "heavy." Morrison said he denied speaking to the press. Nickles also said he had not decided what to do about who would argue the gun case. Morrison made a strong pitch for himself, saying he had worked on the merits brief, had started to prepare for the argument, and had time to write the reply brief which would come after the Levy team filed its own merits brief. Nickles was noncommittal.

Morrison continued to put final touches on the District's merits brief. "The only thing I was really insistent upon was [that] one word would not appear in our brief, and that word was 'clear' because the history [of the Second Amendment] wasn't clear. To say it was clear would have denigrated the thousands of trees that had been killed in the name of Second Amendment scholarship in the last thirty years," he said. "What we said every time was 'the better view, taking into account both the history and everything else.' "

But Nickles felt that Morrison was not making the strongest argument on behalf of the District. "When I got into review of the final drafts of the brief, the argument not being made was as long as the District reasonably regulated the use, possession of guns, that would not violate the Second Amendment no matter what the Court thought the Second Amendment meant," Nickles said. "I thought that was a very important point and I was not making a lot of progress. I always think it's better to win something than to lose everything."[8]

Less than a week after his meeting with Nickles, Morrison received an e-mail from the District's deputy attorney general informing him that Nickles had decided Morrison would not argue the case and was to clear out his office by the end of the following week—the day on which the District's merits brief was to be filed. No decision had been made on who would argue the gun case, arguments which were now a little over two months away in perhaps the most important case in the city's history.

"I thought I was not inherently the best person to argue this case, but given where we were in January, it was a bad idea to have somebody else," said Morrison.

Nickles turned to Walter Dellinger, a constitutional law scholar on leave from Duke University School of Law and head of the Supreme Court and appellate practice at O'Melveny & Myers. The silver-haired Dellinger speaks with a soft southern drawl and is an unabashed liberal who most recently has been a highly visible, outspoken defender of the constitutionality of the Obama administration's Affordable Care Act. He served as legal adviser to President Bill Clinton before being nominated by Clinton to head the Office of Legal Counsel in the Department of Justice. He oversaw that office from 1993 until 1996, when he was appointed acting solicitor general of the United States. He argued nine cases as acting solicitor general in the 1996–97 Supreme Court term.

Dellinger was reluctant to take on the District's gun appeal, but not because he thought it was a losing proposition. He told Nickles that he already had two arguments scheduled in the Court in February 2008. He was representing Morgan Stanley Capital Group in a complex electric energy contract dispute in arguments on February 19. A week later, on February 27, Dellinger was making Exxon's arguments in its high-stakes battle to reverse a $5 billion punitive damages award for the 1989 oil spill by the *Exxon Valdez* tanker in Prince William Sound. And the gun arguments were scheduled less than three weeks after the *Exxon* case.

Nickles was not concerned, and persuaded Dellinger to step into the vacuum that he had created. "I got a guy who I think is one of the finest, most experienced presenter of arguments in the Supreme Court," said Nickles. "I didn't really know Morrison and I have nothing but good things to say about him. When I talked to Walter, I said, 'Can you do it?' He said yes. That's all I needed to know. The busy people very generally are the best people because everybody prizes their talent. I also discussed with him the argument I thought we were neglecting. It became a sharper argument in the reply brief than it had been in our opening argument."

Stepping into the gun arguments "was the single hardest thing I'd done since getting out of law school," recalled Dellinger. "They were all three major, half-hour arguments. The problem was once Alan Morrison was no longer working on the case, it was hard to figure out who else could argue it. Alan was like a scholar in residence for the District's legal office. He was there to do something exactly like this if it came along. At least I had been involved in the briefing, though not in the way I'm involved in a case I'm planning to argue. I told [Nickles] that."[9]

On the other side, Alan Gura's partner, Bob Levy, also was not immune to pressures surrounding who would argue the case for Dick Heller. "I was under considerable pressure from the gun rights movement to get Ted Olson, Ken Starr, Miguel Estrada [leading conservative lawyers], or some other Supreme Court expert and squeeze Alan out of the picture," he said. "It actually was less the gun rights community than pressure from the legal community. I had to consider the prospect of victory with an experienced Supreme Court litigator. The other side of the argument was I had promised Alan if this became a big case, it would be his big case. Secondly, he had done a good job. I became convinced that faced with the choice of an experienced litigator who hadn't immersed himself in the issue and one who had, I was better off with Alan."

The stage was set for the eventual face-off between the Supreme Court veteran, Walter Dellinger, and the Supreme Court novice, Alan Gura.

As the drama within the District's legal office played out, supporters on both sides of the gun case engaged in what was one of the largest amicus efforts in the Court's history. By the time the deadline for filing all briefs in the case passed, sixty-seven green-covered friend of the court briefs—forty-seven supporting Heller, twenty backing the District—lined up like toy soldiers on shelves in the Court's public information office and other offices in the Supreme Court Building.

Many of the briefs represented the views of multiple organizations or individuals. There were dueling briefs by former Department of Justice officials, district attorneys, members of Congress, state attorneys general, criminologists, academics, and historians. And arguments were made as well by organizations against domestic violence, conservative legal foundations, health associations, numerous rifle and pistol clubs, libertarian think tanks, and religious organizations. Besides legal and historical analysis, the briefs discussed policy issues, such as racial discrimination and the safety of children, and offered statistical evidence on gun-related crimes.

The sheer number of groups and organizations involved reflected not only the high stakes in the gun case but also, more generally, the modern explosion of interest group participation in Supreme Court cases. In the 1960s, amicus briefs were filed in about 41 percent of the justices' cases, with an average of one per case, according to a scholarly study. From the 1990s to 2008 (when the gun briefs were filed), the number jumped to 90 percent of the cases, with an average of six per case.[10]

Do those briefs really matter? There have been rare occasions when an argument in an amicus brief became the basis for the Court's majority opinion. For example, a brief filed by twenty-nine high-ranking former U.S. military leaders had a direct impact on the outcome of the University of Michigan Law School's affirmative action case in 2003. Their arguments on the importance of a diverse officer corps were cited by Justice Sandra Day O'Connor during oral arguments in the case, in her majority opinion, and in the summary of her decision which she read from the bench.

In the gun case, Levy, Gura, and Neily drew up a list of issues that they hoped amicus briefs would address, such as empirical data on the ineffectiveness of gun control in preventing violence and the actual meaning of "well regulated Militia." They then attempted to match that list to organizations and attorneys most suited to deal with the issues.

Of the forty-seven briefs supporting their side, Neily believed one signed by fifty-five U.S. senators, two hundred fifty U.S. representatives, and Vice President Dick Cheney, and another by thirty-one state attorneys general both were crucial. The congressional brief was authored by Stephen Halbrook, who, along with the NRA, had been the Levy team's earlier nemesis but now were committed supporters. Besides filing its own amicus brief, the NRA helped "immeasurably" with the congressional brief, according to Levy, whose team lacked the NRA's resources and influence.

The congressional and states' briefs were important not so much for their legal analysis but because they gave the Court "the assurance that what we were asking them to do represented the mainstream position, contrary to what you might think if you were insulated in an ivory tower or went to work every day in a building protected by armed guards and lived in a pretty nice part of town," said Neily. "It might not occur to you there actually are people in the country who do need a gun to defend themselves. Having those briefs was a way of letting the Court know that despite the fact we were asking it to reject the position of nine circuit courts at that time, we were taking the less radical position."

The fewer number on the District's side did not mean less outside support for its position. Dellinger, based on years of experience, knew that justices and their clerks, faced daily with a barrage of reading material, valued brevity. Key among his amicus briefs was one by Founding-era scholars, including the Pulitzer Prize–winning historian Jack Rakove. Dellinger's instinct told him that less was more and that this historic battle would become a battle over history.

CHAPTER 9

"I am a textualist. I am an originalist. I am not a nut."
                                    —Antonin Scalia, 2008

When he joined the Supreme Court in 1986, Associate Justice Antonin Scalia was the lone clarion for a particular way of interpreting the U.S. Constitution.

Sitting in his chambers in July 2011, shortly after the end of the October 2010 term, Scalia, relaxed yet somewhat formal, took a break from working on his second book with Bryan Garner, *Reading Law: The Interpretation of Legal Texts*. He recalled: "When I first came on this Court, I was the only originalist. Counsel would not even allude to original meaning. They would just cite the last Supreme Court case. All of the research into what [a provision] was originally understood to mean I had to do myself and my law clerks."[1]

But the gun case—*District of Columbia v. Heller*—showed just how much that situation had changed in two decades. The final decision, he said, was the greatest "vindication of originalism."

A year before Scalia became a justice, President Reagan's attorney general, Edwin Meese, jump-started nationally what had been largely a closely held debate within law schools and law reviews. In a 1985 speech to the American Bar Association, he criticized Supreme Court justices for seeming to "roam at large in a veritable constitutional forest." The courts, he said, needed jurists who would "judge policies in light of principles, rather than remold principles in light of policies." He called for a "jurisprudence of original intention," in which judges interpreted the Constitution by determining the intent of its framers. It was the first in a series of speeches by Meese about originalism and represented the continuation of attacks on the Warren Court's decisions aggressively pursued by President Richard Nixon.

Later that same year, Justice William Brennan Jr.—whom Scalia called the most influential justice of the twentieth century—offered a competing vision of constitutional interpretation. "The genius of the Constitution rests not in any static meaning it might have had in a world that is dead and gone, but in the adaptability of its great principles to cope with current times and current needs," said Brennan in a speech at Georgetown University.

The great debate over the two approaches—"originalism" versus what its proponents called derisively "living constitutionalism"—was revitalized, and it rages on today.

Originalism became the darling of many conservative legal scholars, as did its most high profile advocate, Scalia, but even they agreed with critics that there were some problems with discerning the various intentions of the numerous Framers of the Constitution. In 1988, Scalia gave a lecture in Cincinnati entitled "Originalism: The Lesser Evil." Scholars on both sides of the debate credit him with shifting the emphasis in constitutional interpretation away from divining the Framers' intentions toward basing it, instead, on the original public meaning of the text at the time of its enactment.

Scalia conceded in his speech that originalism had "warts." He explained: "Its greatest defect, in my view, is the difficulty of applying it correctly. . . . What is true is that it is often exceedingly difficult to plumb the original understanding of an ancient text. Properly done, the task requires the consideration of an enormous mass of material. . . . It is, in short, a task sometimes better suited to the historian than the lawyer."

And, he added, the second most serious objection to originalism is that, "In its undiluted form, at least, it is medicine that seems too strong to swallow. Thus, almost every originalist would adulterate it with the doctrine of stare decisis. . . ." He meant that carried to its logical end, an originalist approach could result in different outcomes to such landmark decisions as *Marbury v. Madison* (establishing judicial review of laws) and *Brown v. Board of Education* (striking down school segregation). But originalism is more of a restraint on a judge's preferences than the non-originalist approach of applying "fundamental values" underlying the Constitution to current times, he said. And it more often leads to a moderate instead of an extreme result. So originalism for Scalia is the "lesser evil."

But then Scalia confessed that "in a crunch I may prove a fainthearted originalist." He could not imagine upholding a statute imposing flogging as a punishment even if the public's original understanding of cruel and unusual punishment at the time the Eighth Amendment was ratified included flogging.

In his chambers that late summer afternoon in 2011, Scalia said he has "recanted" being a "faint-hearted originalist." "I think I would vote to uphold it if there were a state law providing for notching of ears. I think I would say it's a stupid idea but it's not unconstitutional. You have to be principled, and I try to be. The only other thoroughgoing originalist is Clarence." Indeed, Thomas does not "adulterate" his originalism with *stare decisis* (respect for precedents). He views *stare decisis* as no obstacle to achieving what, in his opinion, is the correct reading of the Constitution.

Some of Scalia's fans question whether he has truly recanted. True believers in original public meaning originalism call him out for not joining originalist opinions by Thomas or, at the very least, for failing to explain why he did not join Thomas in those opinions. In some of those cases, Thomas's originalism had led him to conclude that students have no First Amendment speech rights; that the establishment clause does not restrain the states from favoring particular religions; the commerce clause does not allow the Congress to regulate economic activity that substantially affects interstate commerce, such as the intrastate production of marijuana; the First Amendment protects corporations from laws requiring disclosure and reporting of campaign contributions; and that the Second Amendment applies to the states through the privileges and immunities clause, not the due process clause, of the Fourteenth Amendment.

Thomas has developed a coherent, if often unorthodox, body of constitutional interpretations. He has said he is quite comfortable expressing those views in dissents or concurrences that no other justice will join and generally will not respond to as well. And although he is admired by some for the purity and originality of his vision, his uncompromising positions and willingness to cast aside *stare decisis* tend to limit his influence within the Court.

"One way of dividing up the world of judges are the judges who care more about being right versus being judges who just want to win," said a former Thomas clerk. "Some judges work very hard to get a majority— they want their views to prevail. If that means I have to dilute it a bit, I'm willing to do that. If you really care about getting a majority judgment, you behave in a certain way.

"Another person would say, 'My views are my views and if there's not a majority, that's fine. I'm going to express them.' Thomas is clearly in the second camp. He doesn't mind winning, but I don't think that's what's most important to him. He is playing a longer-term game. It has been said by folks across the spectrum that a dissent today can be a majority opinion tomorrow. I think he sees the world that way and he is ready to accept the consequences of his originalism."

One committed originalist scholar, Randy Barnett of Georgetown University Law Center, questioned in a 2006 lecture whether Scalia was really an originalist based on an evaluation of Scalia's decisions and public statements. "Whatever virtues he attributes to originalism, he leaves himself not one but three different routes by which to escape adhering to the original meaning of the text," wrote Barnett. "These are more than enough to allow him, or any judge, to reach any result he wishes. Where originalism gives him the results he wants, he can embrace originalism. Where it does not, he can embrace precedent that will. Where friendly precedent is unavailing, he can assert the nonjusticiability of clauses that yield results to which he is opposed. And where all else fails, he can simply punt, perhaps citing the history of traditionally-accepted practices of which he approves."[2]

Originalism is a subset of textualism, said Scalia. And a textualist, he explained, is someone who believes that the meaning of a statute is to be derived exclusively from the text enacted by Congress and signed by the president, or else re-passed over his veto. It is the sole source that the judge ought to be using in making his judgment.

Scalia's most frequent sparring partner on and off the Court on how to interpret the Constitution and statutes has been Justice Stephen Breyer, appointed to the Court by President Bill Clinton in 1994. The two men could not be more different, and the difference is not just in judicial philosophies. On the bench, Scalia rarely indulges in complicated hypotheticals. Leaning forward as if ready to pounce on an unsuspecting lawyer, he directs quick and punchy questions and interjects comments that can be funny or cuttingly sarcastic. He has open disdain for Congress and the legislative history surrounding its enactment of laws.

On the other hand, Breyer, with arms and hands gesticulating, is the master of the lengthy, complex, sometimes humorous, hypothetical question. He often will wait until almost the end of a lawyer's argument to summarize that argument, state his problems with it, and say to the lawyer, "Now tell me why I'm wrong." Perhaps because of his early experience as a Senate committee counsel, he voices more faith in, or respect for, the legislative branch of government.

During the past decade, Scalia and Breyer have engaged together in a remarkable series of public appearances in which they discuss their contrasting approaches. As counterpoint to Scalia's search for the original public meaning of constitutional provisions at issue in cases, Breyer emphasizes a pragmatic approach and has written two books explaining that approach and its importance. In his most recent book, *Making Our Democracy Work*, Breyer said modern pragmatic judges seeking to interpret an ambiguous text in the Constitution look to the text's language, history, context, traditions, precedent, purposes, and consequences.

"But when faced with open-ended language and a difficult interpretive question, they rely heavily on purposes and related consequences," he wrote.[3] Breyer views the latter two tools as particularly important to public acceptance of the Supreme Court's work which, in turn, requires a Constitution that works well for the public today. It will work well if regarded as having "unwavering values" that are applied flexibly to changing circumstances, he contends, and if courts consider the roles of the other government institutions and the relationships among them.

But as Scalia countered in one public debate with Breyer, "The problem is purposes and consequences involve subjective judgment. I've sat with three colleagues who believed the death penalty is unconstitutional. Nothing has changed. Yet the living constitutionalist could one day say, 'We feel differently about it than we used to, therefore I am going to prescribe from the bench it is unconstitutional.' If you want to change things, you don't have to use the Constitution to do it. Use the legislature. The issue is whether the judge can say the living constitution has morphed and what used to be okay is bad."

Breyer believes the originalist judge is more likely to impose his or her subjective views. History often fails to provide the answer to a legal question, and historians often disagree on the meaning of historical materials. And if history does point in one direction, should it be followed if the values and thinking at the time of the drafting of a provision conflict with today's values and understanding? For example, racially segregated schools in the District of Columbia existed at the time of the framing of the Fourteenth Amendment's equal protection clause, he noted. The Court in *Brown v. Board of Education* in 1954 did not follow what the clause's authors might have thought about segregated schools in the 1860s.

The pragmatic judge's subjective views are constrained and the judge is held accountable, he counters Scalia, by transparency—writing out legally defensible reasoning in a publicly accessible way. "Emphasizing [purposes and consequences] is more likely to keep you in touch with the legislature which is more in touch with the people," he said in one debate.

The approaches taken by Scalia of the wickedly incisive pen, on the right, and by Breyer of the step-by-step, written-for-the-masses pen, on the left, inevitably would collide in the District of Columbia gun case. And another justice, John Paul Stevens, also would attempt to meet Scalia on his own playing field.

The justices learn for the first time what their colleagues are thinking about a case during oral arguments in that case. No memos are exchanged beforehand; no secret meetings between two or more justices take place. It is a tradition intended to prevent lobbying and secret alliances. They formally announce their positions in a closed-door conference after each week's arguments. The chief justice speaks first, summarizing the case and stating his view, and then the other justices take turns by seniority—most senior to junior—stating their views. No justice speaks twice until each justice has spoken once. Each justice is listening carefully and taking notes on the various views in the event he or she is assigned an opinion. The junior justice tallies the vote. Afterwards, they communicate about the case through memos and draft opinions.

The justices have voiced varying opinions about the value of oral arguments and how persuasive they may be, but most of them have had their minds changed or made up on occasion by the arguments of one side or the other.

As part of a series of interviews for *The Scribes Journal of Legal Writing*, Chief Justice Roberts noted, "Even when you're tentatively leaning, you have issues that you want to raise that give the other side a chance to sway you. Some cases, you go in and you don't have a clue. And you're really looking forward to the argument because you want a little greater degree of certainty." Justice John Paul Stevens explained that "most of the time, by the time the argument's over I'm fairly well persuaded one way or the other. But as I said, I've changed my mind not only after argument but after conference and after starting to write an opinion. So there's a lot of flexibility and variation from case to case." And Justice Scalia offered, "To begin with, you should know that oral advocacy is important, that judges don't often have their minds changed by oral advocacy, but very often have their minds made up. I often go into a case right on the knife's edge, and persuasive counsel can persuade me that I ought to flip to this side rather than the other side." But Justice Thomas said his view of a case is "almost never" changed by oral arguments, and his colleagues' minds, he suggested, are changed "in 5 or 10% of the cases, maybe, and I'm being generous there." Justice Anthony Kennedy confessed to loving oral arguments, and added, "And I think it's cruelly short. We need that help, and I didn't realize before I went on the bench how much the judges really want help from the advocate. It's not pretend."[4]

The only "pretend" part of the process are the moot (mock) courts that the lawyers who will argue the cases undergo to prepare for their actual arguments. Alan Gura, who was representing Dick Heller, did five moot court arguments in which conservative Second Amendment legal scholars, such as Stephen Halbrook, Don Kates, and Joseph Olson, and conservative and libertarian lawyers, such as Ted Cruz, Ed Meese, and Ilya Shapiro, tested him on every conceivable question he might encounter.

Gura and Neily were confident they would get five votes to win, and believed they might get even more than five. Two justices had more than a passing interest and familiarity with guns: Scalia, they knew, was an avid hunter. And Alito, as revealed by his wife at the time of his appointment to the Court, was a "great marksman—he can do double clays," his wife proudly said.[5]

At the time the case was filed, Gura and Neily saw two wild cards: Sandra Day O'Connor and Anthony Kennedy. O'Connor would soon leave. "I don't think there's any question about the conventional wisdom that trading Justice O'Connor for Justice Alito was a good change for an individual right reading of the Second Amendment," said Neily. "That just left Kennedy."

"People are obsessed with Justice Kennedy and wonder how he's going to vote in any particular case," added Gura. "I had no particular reason to think he would be any more of a swing vote than anybody else in this case. I based that just on the fact he tends to be very open-minded to claims of individual rights. He is not a statist, just somebody who doesn't mind enjoining unconstitutional laws."

From their perspective, it was hard to imagine that a Supreme Court justice who thinks of himself as to the right of the divide on the Court would be the fifth vote to "neuter" the Second Amendment. "You don't get on the Supreme Court if you're apolitical. You just don't because you don't move in the circles that would result in you being appointed," insisted Neily. "The idea somebody would want to be the fifth vote in what is going to be a landmark case and have as one of their legacies that they went against not only the political views of the party that nominated them but the majority of people in this country seemed unlikely to me. The other thing great about it too is they had so much cover. Some of the most well known luminaries of constitutional law had said if you take a frank look at this stuff, it's pretty clear."

And, he added, every Democratic candidate for president in 2008, with perhaps the exception of Dennis Kucinich, had voiced support of the individual right interpretation. "I don't know how many of them were sincere, but they knew they had to say it."

The District's Walter Dellinger knew heading into the argument the decision would be very close. He did not think Kennedy's vote was easy to predict. He also hoped the Court would be thinking about Congress's authority to regulate for the District, which is a national security zone. "I honestly believe not a single person involved in adopting the Second Amendment would have remotely thought it would have limited what Congress could do in the ten-square-mile area set aside for the national government," he said. "It's not that D.C. residents don't have the same rights set aside for everybody else—they do. But nobody when they come into the District, whether they live here or come from outside, possesses any more right to possess a gun than if they lived at Fort Bragg." Dellinger soon would discover that no one on the Court was interested in a D.C.-only ruling.

Dellinger also kept coming back to *United States v. Miller*, the last time the Supreme Court had addressed the substance of the Second Amendment. The 1939 decision was the precedent on which all of the federal appellate courts had relied for the militia–collective rights view until the 2001 opinion by the Fifth Circuit in *United States v. Emerson*, which adopted the individual right interpretation.

Jack Miller and Frank Layton were Oklahoma bank robbers who were stopped by Oklahoma and Arkansas state police in 1938. They had with them an unregistered, double-barrel, 12-gauge sawed-off shotgun. They were arrested for violating the National Firearms Act of 1934. The trial court found that the act violated the Second Amendment. The United States appealed to the Supreme Court. Miller's attorney never participated in the case. An eight-member Supreme Court reversed the trial court.

Although both gun rights and gun control advocates agree the *Miller* decision was poorly written, both claim support in it for their views. Gun rights groups argue the decision was limited to the type of weapon at issue—a sawed-off shotgun—because Justice James Clark McReynolds wrote: "In the absence of any evidence tending to show that possession or use of a 'shotgun having a barrel of less than eighteen inches in length' at this time has some reasonable relationship to the preservation or efficiency of a well regulated militia, we cannot say that the Second Amendment guarantees the right to keep and bear such an instrument. Certainly it is not within judicial notice that this weapon is any part of the ordinary military equipment or that its use could contribute to the common defense."

But gun control groups contend that McReynolds's opinion supported the militia-based right because the justice also wrote: "With obvious purpose to assure the continuation and render possible the effectiveness of such [militia] forces the declaration and guarantee of the Second Amendment were made. It must be interpreted and applied with that end in view."

In the *Heller* gun challenge, the District of Columbia federal appellate court concluded that Miller meant that the Second Amendment protects an individual right to possess and use weapons "of the kind in common use at the time," including handguns. Dellinger was not convinced.

"There had been a campaign for decades in this sort of public Second Amendment debate to delegitimize *Miller*," he said. "Everybody who advised me said it had been so successful I was just going to get into a lot of trouble by raising *Miller*. It seemed to me this issue was resolved in *Miller* and the Court was going to have to overrule *Miller* to find an individual right. I was very tempted to begin my argument by saying the issue in this case is whether *United States v. Miller* should be overruled."

The Court had scheduled the argument for March 18, 2008, a Tuesday morning, at 10 am. The usual argument time—sixty minutes, with thirty minutes per side—had been lengthened to seventy-five minutes, including time allotted to Solicitor General Paul Clement for the government's position. During the arguments, Chief Justice Roberts would extend the time an additional twenty-two minutes to accommodate the justices' intense questioning.

On the Sunday before the argument, Dellinger was in his firm's downtown office preparing when he turned on the television at 6 pm to get the sports scores. "The local news was live from the steps of the Supreme Court where people were lined up out to the street on Sunday night for the Tuesday morning argument," he recalled. "It made my knees buckle. I immediately turned off the television and went back to work without getting the sports scores."

The night before the argument was a normal one for Gura, who had dinner with his family, went to bed, and slept "okay." He, Neily, and Levy got to the Court early the next morning. The line of people that had begun to form two nights before to get into the courtroom now snaked across the plaza and down around the block. The trio had given a fourth seat at counsel's table to Dave Kopel, research director of the Independence Institute in Golden, Colorado, who has written extensively about the Second Amendment and was instrumental in coordinating the amicus briefs. The men met in the lawyers' lounge off of the courtroom and had coffee.

Despite the chilly morning, Dellinger, as was his practice, biked to the Court, a practice that helped him "clear his head." Paul Clement, the solicitor general, waited in his own office at the Court. That office is a symbol of how important the solicitor general is to the institution: the solicitor general is the only federal official with an office in both the judicial and the executive branches of government.

No empty seats could be found in the courtroom that morning. Extra rows of chairs to accommodate the overflow press filled the aisle behind the marble pillars that marked off the regular press pews. The same sense of anticipation that had electrified the room on the morning of the Seattle-Louisville school arguments a year earlier charged the atmosphere once again. But everyone would have to wait just a few more minutes. After the justices took their seats at 10 am, Chief Justice Roberts announced that Justice Thomas had the Court's opinion in *Washington State Grange v. Washington State Republican Party.*

Because Thomas's voice is so rarely heard in the courtroom, the audience was rapt as he explained the issue in the case. Washington voters had approved an initiative requiring that candidates for office must be identified on the primary ballot by their self-designated party preference; that voters may vote for any candidate; and that the two top vote-getters for each office, regardless of party preference, advance to the general election. The states' political parties charged that the new law, on its face, violated a party's First Amendment association rights by usurping their right to nominate their own candidates and by forcing them to associate with candidates they did not endorse. Thomas, in a 7–2 decision, said the initiative, on its face, did not impose a severe burden on the parties' association rights. Justices Scalia and Kennedy dissented.

The 2007 term, up to this point, had been relatively uneventful, particularly compared to the prior term's menu of hot-button cases triggering high emotions. The Court in December had heard arguments in another potential headliner case—the Guantánamo Bay detainee challenge, *Boumediene v. Bush*—but no decision had been issued. And another closely watched case involving a challenge to Louisiana's imposition of the death penalty for the rape of a child was not being argued until mid-April.

The emotional thermometer inside the Court was lower as well from the prior term. "People calm down; they move on," explained one justice.

After Thomas finished his summary of the election decision, Roberts announced argument in *District of Columbia v. Heller*.

Dellinger, representing the District, rose and pressed his main argument that the Second Amendment was a reaction to the militia clauses in Article I of the Constitution, which gave the new national Congress "the surprising, perhaps even shocking, power to organize, arm, and presumably disarm the state militias," he said. The individual right protected by the amendment, he argued, was the right to participate in the common defense and to go to court if a federal law or regulation interfered with that right.

Minutes into Dellinger's argument, Kennedy tipped his hand. It was a moment when all of the lawyers, including those in the audience who had followed the long debate over the amendment's meaning, knew that the gun rights arguments had won. Kennedy told Dellinger that he saw a way to conform the amendment's two clauses and, in effect, delink them. He was referring to the preamble (A well-regulated Militia, being necessary to the security of a free State) and the second clause (the right of the people to keep and bear Arms, shall not be infringed).

"The first clause, I submit, can be read consistently with the purpose I've indicated of simply reaffirming the existence and importance of the militia clauses," said Kennedy, referring to Article I, Section 8 of the Constitution, which gives Congress the power to call "forth the Militia to execute the Laws of the Union, suppress Insurrections and repel Invasions."

"And so in effect the [Second] amendment says we reaffirm the right to have a militia, we've established it [in another part of the Constitution], but in addition, there is a right to bear arms," suggested Kennedy.

Dellinger countered there was nothing at the time in the debates over the Second Amendment that referred to the use of weapons for personal purposes.

Kennedy was not deterred, asking, "It had nothing to do with the concern of the remote settler to defend himself and his family against hostile Indian tribes and outlaws, wolves and bears and grizzlies and things like that?"

No, responded Dellinger, that was not part of the Second Amendment discourse.

Kennedy's suggestion was so inconsistent with the historical record, Dellinger thought, there was no hope of reaching him. Kennedy was saying that the first clause of the Second Amendment was written simply to emphasize the importance of another section of the Constitution, the so-called militia clause in Article I, Section 8, outlining the powers of Congress.

Kennedy's interpretation was "exactly totally backward," Dellinger said later. "The Second Amendment arose out of hostility to the militia clause, deep hostility to it, when it gave Congress control over the state militias. Everything about it was a reaction to that hostility. The idea [the Framers] wanted to reemphasize the value of the militia clause turns the history of this amendment literally upside down and backwards."

Dellinger knew at that moment that he was going to lose, as did Peter Nickles, the District's attorney general, sitting at the counsel table.

Gura and Neily, sitting next to each other at the counsel's table on the other side of the lectern, tried mightily not to look at each other after Kennedy's comments. "That was an electric moment," said Neily. "I remember it vividly, and essentially trying to keep my face pointed forward and looking over with my eyes, making eye contact with Alan, and both of us knowing at that moment we had Kennedy. We had won."

The moment and its significance were not lost on some in the audience as well. Gun rights litigator Stephen Halbrook remembered, "The big wild card for us was Kennedy. We're on the edge of our seats and Kennedy opens his mouth and he comes out with colonists and frontiersmen and they have to protect themselves from grizzly bears— grizzly bears in the East!" He laughed. "That suggested the individual right interpretation."

His frequent opponent, Dennis Henigan of the Brady Center, had waited in the cold from four thirty that morning for a seat inside. "There was nothing but anxiety going into it. It was clearly up to Kennedy," said Henigan. "Once he spoke and started talking about the need for guns to confront bears and cougars . . . I have spent a good part of my professional career writing and talking about the Second Amendment and essentially arguing against the individual right view in every way I know how. There was the U.S. Supreme Court going to endorse this view I thought was total bunk. I just closed my eyes."

Scalia also showed his hand when, reacting to Kennedy's suggested reading of the amendment's two clauses, he said, "I don't see how there's any contradiction between reading the second clause as a personal guarantee and reading the first one as assuring the existence of a militia. The two clauses go together beautifully: Since we need a militia, the right of the people to keep and bear arms shall not be infringed." He also referred to William Blackstone, the great eighteenth-century English jurist whose commentaries on the laws of England were highly influential with the Framers. Blackstone thought the right of self-defense was inherent, said Scalia.

And Roberts asked Dellinger, "What is reasonable about a total ban on possession?" Dellinger answered, "What is reasonable about a total ban on possession is that it's a ban only on the possession of one kind of weapon, of handguns, that has been considered especially, especially dangerous."

When his turn came, Solicitor General Paul Clement held steadfastly to the government's argument that the amendment protected an individual right to possess a gun in the home, but the right was subject to government regulation that should not have to undergo the toughest constitutional scrutiny, but some lesser standard. Roberts pushed back, saying, "I wonder why in this case we have to articulate an all-encompassing standard. Isn't it enough to determine the scope of the existing right that the amendment refers to, look at the various regulations that were available at the time . . . and determine how this restriction and the scope of this right look in relation to those?"

Scalia asked Clement what he was worried about—machine guns, armored bullets? And Clement responded that the lower federal appellate court's language in the *Heller* decision seemed to say that once something is defined as a firearm, the District could not ban it, and that raised concerns about certain provisions in federal firearm laws.

Alan Gura faced his most aggressive questioning from Justices Breyer, Stevens, and Ginsburg. Breyer asked, assuming the nature of the right is to maintain a citizen army and for people to understand weapons—which they can do with the rifles that the District allows—why is it unreasonable "for a city with a very high crime rate to say no handguns here?" Because, answered Gura, proficiency in use and familiarity with the handgun at issue would further a militia purpose.

Stevens asked if the amendment limits the kinds of arms appropriate to a militia, "Why does it not also limit the kind of people who may have arms?" And Gura replied, "It would certainly be an odd right that we would have against the Congress, if Congress could then redefine people out of that right." Stevens also pressed him on the fact that only two state constitutions at the time of the Second Amendment's framing referred to keeping and bearing arms for self-defense; the others referred to the common defense.

In a concession that angered many in the gun rights community, Gura told the Court that the government could ban arms not appropriate for civilian use, such as machine guns, or plastic, undetectable handguns.

Dellinger returned to the lectern for rebuttal and immediately ran into trouble from the chief justice, who focused on the District's requirement that all firearms (rifles, shotguns, and pre-ban handguns) be "unloaded and disassembled or bound by a trigger-lock or similar device."

Roberts asked how many minutes it takes to remove a trigger lock and load a rifle.

Dellinger said a gun with a numerical code would take about three seconds.

Scalia interjected, "You turn on the lamp next to your bed so you can turn the knob at 3-22-95 . . ."

And Roberts, to laughter in the courtroom, added, "So then you turn on the lamp, you pick up your reading glasses . . ."

Dellinger said, "The District believes that what is important here is the ban on handguns. And it also believes that you're entitled to have a functional usable weapon for self-defense in the home, and that's why this is a very proportionate law."

By the end of the arguments, the Court appeared divided along ideological lines, with the five conservatives supporting the individual right interpretation and the four liberals siding with the militia-based collective rights view.

After the argument, the lawyers and their clients followed the tradition in high-profile cases of walking down the building's front steps to the television cameras awaiting their recap of the arguments inside. Gura and Levy then headed over to the Cato Institute to handle press calls. Neily stayed with Dick Heller to help him navigate the media. Henigan of the Brady Center stood with a team of his center's lawyers. "It was basically a wake," he said. "A lot of head-shaking."

The justices would not discuss the case until their conference that week. They would vote during their conference, and opinion assignments would be given soon afterwards. But work on the case actually had begun much earlier and in depth in one justice's chambers.

"I had felt very strongly that *Miller* had been law for nearly a hundred years," said Justice Stevens. "You don't upset cases like that except for an awfully good reason. I remember asking my clerk when the case was coming up to tell me if there had been any major changes in the scholarship that differed. She started to work on that very early in the case and did a very thorough study for me about state constitutional provisions bearing on gun control, some of which expansively covered hunting and personal defense. We found out [James] Madison's draft definitely differed from those state constitutions and we thought that was powerful evidence that the preamble meant what it said."

Only two states had provisions that addressed self-defense and hunting. The others, like James Madison's draft of the amendment, addressed the need to preserve militias. The combination of the *Miller* decision, even though poorly drafted, Madison's draft, state constitutional provisions, and the Framers' overriding concern for the maintenance of the militia convinced Stevens that the Second Amendment was adopted to protect the right of the people to preserve a well-regulated militia.

After the conference vote on the *Heller* case, Chief Justice Roberts assigned the majority opinion to Justice Scalia. Stevens, the most senior justice in the minority, chose not to assign the lead dissent to Souter, Ginsburg, or Breyer, who also were in the minority, but to keep the dissent for himself; Breyer decided to write a separate dissent.

Scalia was thrilled with the assignment—his most important opinion since joining the Court and one that would be a major "vindication of originalism."

As chief justice, Roberts has shown himself to be fair in his use of what he calls his only real power—the assigning of opinions—as was his predecessor, William H. Rehnquist, agree the justices. And that fairness has been an important contribution to the Court's well-known collegiality under both men.

Recalling Roberts's assignment of *Heller*, Scalia commented, "He assigned it to me, for which I was very grateful because he knew I would care a lot about it. And he knew it would be a big, big opinion, which he could have kept for himself. I was very grateful for that."

After receiving the assignment of the majority opinion, Scalia had one of his clerks take on the research into the history of the Second Amendment. "It was an enormous effort. My law clerk working on that case was just a bear. He was fantastic." What also helped—and what showed how much had changed since his early years on the Court, when he and his clerks labored to do historical research without assistance— were the amicus briefs filed in *Heller*, according to Scalia.

"There was a huge amount of historical assistance from legal historians and others," he said. "That has made the practice of originalism a lot easier. When there are two people on the Court who are going to be affected by that argument, of course counsel will try to get those two votes by giving any historical evidence they can gin up."

Scalia said he likes historians for their raw material, but he does not think they are impartial. "They're just as causey as anybody else. They won't gather to submit a brief on one side or the other unless they care which way it comes out." So the mere fact that academics file doesn't carry much weight, and it shouldn't, according to Scalia. "When I was an academic, I never once signed on to an amicus brief," he added. "You can sign on whether you know the area or not. I never thought that was a proper role for the academic." Proper or not, amicus briefs by academic scholars of every stripe are now a common feature in Supreme Court cases.

Despite the vote in *Heller*, the dissenters, based on their own exhaustive historical research, still were hopeful that a fair and thorough analysis of the amendment's history would persuade possibly Kennedy or Thomas to join them instead of Scalia. Thomas, in particular, had a keen interest in history, thought one justice, and might be reachable. They were wrong.

The Supreme Court rarely writes on a clean slate. In most cases, earlier decisions offer guidance or a rule that may be applied to help resolve the issue before the justices. The *Heller* gun case was that rare and, for the justices, exciting exception where the Court had said little of substance about the Second Amendment. The gun case, however, was not the only major case that term to thrust the justices into the role of amateur historians.

Before the *Heller* decision came down, the Court on June 12, 2008, issued its decision in the Guantánamo Bay detainee case: *Boumediene v. Bush*. The case brought by six Algerian detainees asked whether the Military Commissions Act of 2006 had stripped the federal courts of jurisdiction over federal habeas petitions filed by detainees challenging the legality of their detentions. If the act did divest the courts of jurisdiction, the case also asked whether that was a violation of the suspension clause of the Constitution. That clause, in Article I, Section 9, states that "The privilege of the Writ of Habeas Corpus shall not be suspended, unless when in Cases of Rebellion or Invasion the Public Safety may require it."

The Framers knew the writ was indispensable to individual liberty. They had experienced being jailed without charge. The writ, which has its foundation in English common law, compels the government to state a legitimate reason for detention. To answer the questions in *Boumediene*, the justices delved into the history and scope of the common law writ, examining sources such as the Habeas Corpus Act of 1679; the Magna Carta, the English Bill of Rights; and the text and drafting history of the Constitution's suspension clause. And they looked to competing arguments in amicus briefs filed by legal historians.

In a 5–4 decision by Kennedy, the Court held that the Military Commissions Act did strip the federal courts of their habeas jurisdiction, and because procedures set out in a companion law—the Detainee Treatment Act—were not adequate substitutes for the habeas writ, the 2006 act violated the suspension clause. The justices split along ideological lines in their view of the writ's history, whether the writ may be used by aliens abroad, and how much deference should be paid to Congress's decisions in this area.

"Within the Constitution's separation-of-powers structure, few exercises of judicial power are as legitimate or as necessary as the responsibility to hear challenges to the authority of the Executive to imprison a person," wrote Kennedy for the Court's liberal wing. "Some of these petitioners have been in custody for six years with no definitive judicial determination as to the legality of their detention. Their access to the writ is a necessity to determine the lawfulness of their status, even if, in the end, they do not obtain the relief they seek."

Scalia's interpretation of the text and history of the suspension clause did not prevail. In a fiery dissent joined by Roberts, Thomas, and Alito, he argued that the writ did not apply to the detainees and that the Court had no business interfering with an ongoing military matter.

"What drives today's decision is neither the meaning of the Suspension Clause, nor the principles of our precedents, but rather an inflated notion of judicial supremacy," he charged. He ended his dissent with the memorable, and what some critics labeled hyperbolic, statement: "The Nation will live to regret what the Court has done today."

Scalia was answered by Souter in a concurring opinion joined by Breyer and Ginsburg. Souter essentially said there was nothing radical about the decision because four years earlier in *Rasul v. Bush*, which involved detainees and their rights under the federal habeas corpus statute, not the constitutional writ, five justices had said that "[a]pplication of the habeas statute to persons detained at [Guantánamo] is consistent with the historical reach of the writ of habeas corpus." He also noted, as did Kennedy in the majority opinion, that the Algerian detainees had been held for six years thus far without any review. "After six years of sustained executive detentions in Guantánamo, subject to habeas jurisdiction but without any actual habeas scrutiny, today's decision is no judicial victory, but an act of perseverance in trying to make habeas review, and the obligation of the courts to provide it, mean something of value both to prisoners and to the Nation," wrote Souter.

Boumediene was the first time that the Court had found an act of Congress violated the suspension clause, and it was a rebuke not just to Congress but to the Bush administration as well.

Twelve days after *Boumediene* was issued, Kennedy led the same five-justice majority in *Kennedy v. Louisiana* (this Kennedy was no relation to the justice). The majority held that the Eighth Amendment's prohibition against cruel and unusual punishment barred Louisiana from imposing the death penalty for the rape of a child where death did not result, and was not intended to result, in the child's death.

The decision was the third in just six years to narrow the category of people eligible for the death penalty. Kennedy explained that the Court has said that capital punishment must "be limited to those offenders who commit 'a narrow category of the most serious crimes' and whose extreme culpability makes them 'the most deserving of execution.' " That principle had been applied in 2002 in *Atkins v. Virginia* to bar the execution of mentally retarded persons, and in 2005 in *Roper v. Simmons* to prohibit capital punishment for murderers under age eighteen. In those two cases, both types of offenders, wrote Kennedy, had diminished personal responsibility for the crime. Particularly relevant to the question of imposing the death penalty for child rape, Kennedy indicated, were the Court's prior decisions finding that the death penalty can be disproportionate to the crime itself, and thus unconstitutional, where death did not result or was not the intended result.

In analyzing whether a punishment is cruel and unusual under the Eighth Amendment, the Court also looks to "the evolving standards of decency that mark the progress of a maturing society."

In this case, Kennedy said, the perpetrator's crime "was one that cannot be recounted in these pages in a way sufficient to capture in full the hurt and horror inflicted on his victim or to convey the revulsion society, and the jury that represents it, sought to express by sentencing petitioner to death."

However, he and justices Stevens, Souter, Breyer, and Ginsburg, agreed there was a national consensus against the death penalty for child rapes. Only six states have enacted that penalty, noted Kennedy. No individual had been executed for the rape of an adult or child since 1964, and no execution for any other nonhomicide offense has been conducted since 1963.

And in determining whether the death penalty is excessive, Kennedy wrote, "There is a distinction between intentional first-degree murder on the one hand and nonhomicide crimes against individual persons, even including child rape, on the other. The latter crimes may be devastating in their harm, as here, but 'in terms of moral depravity and of the injury to the person and to the public,' they cannot be compared to murder in their 'severity and irrevocability.' "

Alito, writing for Chief Justice Roberts and justices Scalia and Thomas, dissented, saying the decision was not supported by the original meaning of the Eighth Amendment or any precedent of the Court. There were no "objective indicia" of a national consensus in support of the Court's position, he added, and the Court previously had held the Eighth Amendment is not "a one-way ratchet that prohibits legislatures from adopting new capital punishment statutes to meet new problems.

"The worst child rapists exhibit the epitome of moral depravity," he wrote, "and child rape inflicts grievous injury on victims and on society in general."

Alito is not an originalist of the same commitment as Scalia. The latter justice railed against the majority's approach to the Eighth Amendment in the 2005 decision striking down the death penalty for juveniles under age eighteen and noted that the Court had found the opposite just fifteen years earlier. Noting Alexander Hamilton's vision of a judiciary "bound down by strict rules and precedents" (The Federalist No. 78, p. 465 (C. Rossiter ed. 1961)), Scalia wrote in 2005: "What a mockery today's opinion makes of Hamilton's expectation, announcing the Court's conclusion that the meaning of our Constitution has changed over the past 15 years—not, mind you, that this Court's decision 15 years ago was *wrong*, but that the Constitution *has changed*."

The Kennedy-Alito debate about how to interpret the Eighth

Amendment in particular, and the Constitution in general, mirrored the forthcoming debate over the Second Amendment: original public meaning versus application of values in the Constitution to changing times.

With the announcement of the decision in the child rape death penalty case, the Court was only one day away from the end of the 2007–08 term, and what a difference one term can make. Supreme Court terms are defined as much by what is not on the docket as by what is. Unlike the highly divisive preceding term, the current session had no major race, abortion, speech, or religion cases. Fewer cases were ending in 5–4 splits (17 percent of all decisions as opposed to 33 percent in the prior term). And the 5–4 splits were not the lopsided victories for the Court's conservatives of a year ago.

But on June 26, the term's final day, only one decision of the Roberts Court was foremost on the minds of a full and intensely focused audience. Three cases were outstanding. The justices read summaries of their decisions in order of seniority, from the least senior to the most senior. Roberts announced that Justice Alito, the Court's junior justice, had the decision in *Davis v. Federal Election Commission*.

Davis was a challenge to the so-called millionaire's amendment in the McCain-Feingold campaign finance reform act, more formally known as the Bipartisan Campaign Reform Act of 2002. When a self-financing candidate for Congress spent personal funds in excess of $350,000, the amendment permitted the non-self-financing opponent to receive triple the amount of personal contributions allowed by law and to accept coordinated party contributions. The self-financing candidate still had to abide by the law's contribution limits. Jack Davis intended to spend $1 million of his own money on his congressional campaign in New York and sued to stop the FEC from enforcing the millionaire's amendment, claiming a violation of the First Amendment.

Alito, joined by Roberts, Scalia, Kennedy, and Thomas, agreed with Davis.

Davis is one of the stepping stones laid by the Roberts Court in its movement toward campaign finance deregulation. The conservative majority had taken its first step in the previous term in *Wisconsin Right to Life v. Federal Election Commission*. The great divide within the Court over the First Amendment and campaign financing would explode into the public's consciousness with the Court's 2010 decision in *Citizens United*.

The soft outlines of the still-young Roberts Court were beginning to come into focus with the latest rulings. The Roberts Court's conservative majority, in a fundamental disagreement with the liberal justices on the Fourteenth Amendment's equal protection clause, had shown impatience with and a desire to end racial classifications, whether in redistricting by legislatures or in public school efforts to preserve or create diversity in their classrooms. On the scope of the First Amendment's speech protections, it was moving to end or restrict campaign finance regulations at the federal and state levels—a movement that would culminate in the blockbuster *Citizens United* decision.

Roberts announced that Justice Scalia had the second of three final cases in the term, a complicated energy contract dispute between utility companies and wholesale energy suppliers. And finally, Roberts said that Scalia also had the Court's opinion in *District of Columbia v. Heller*.

Alan Gura, counsel to Dick Heller, was not taking any chance on missing the announcement. He had been going to the courtroom on decision days for the past week. "I got to listen to some great decisions about ERISA [pension law] and Indian trusts," he chuckled. He and his colleagues, Clark Neily and Bob Levy, were sitting in the front row of the lawyers' section in the courtroom, which is directly behind the main table for lawyers arguing cases. Solicitor General Clement and lawyers from his office, as is traditional, were seated at the main counsel table.

"When Chief Justice Roberts said Justice Scalia has the opinion in No. 08-290, we knew," said Neily. "If you were confident we were going to win, which we were, and you had to pick which justice was most likely to write it, it seemed likely it would be the chief justice because it would be his to assign and maybe he would have assigned it to himself because it seems like a pretty plum opinion, or maybe Justice Scalia because it's maybe the single greatest opportunity to roll out his version of originalism in the context of a really meaningful constitutional case that there has ever been."

Scalia, summarizing his 64-page majority opinion, said the Second Amendment protects an individual right to possess a firearm unconnected to service in a militia, and to use that firearm for lawful purposes, such as self-defense in the home. The preamble—"A well regulated Militia, being necessary to the security of a free State"—states a purpose but does not limit or expand the scope of the operative clause, and that clause's text and history demonstrate that it connotes an individual right to keep and bear arms. Read together, he said, the two clauses essentially say, "Since we need a people's militia, the people will not be deprived of the right to keep and bear arms."

The majority's interpretation, he said, is confirmed by analogous arms-bearing provisions in state constitutions adopted before and after the Second Amendment, and by legal scholars, courts, and legislators from ratification of the amendment through the late nineteenth century. The Court's 1939 decision in *United States v. Miller* is not to the contrary, he insisted, but stands only for the type of weapon not eligible for Second Amendment protection.

Scalia emphasized that the Second Amendment was not unlimited. "Nothing in our opinion should be taken to cast doubt on longstanding prohibitions on the possession of firearms by felons and the mentally ill, or laws forbidding the carrying of firearms in sensitive places such as schools and government buildings, or laws imposing conditions and qualifications on the commercial sale of arms," he said. As the *Miller* decision stated, the sort of weapons protected, he added, were those in "common use at the time." That limitation, he said, is fairly supported by the historical tradition of prohibiting the carrying of "dangerous and unusual weapons."

And yet, turning to the District's handgun ban, Scalia said, "Under any of the standards of scrutiny that we have applied to enumerated constitutional rights, banning from the home the most preferred firearm in the nation to 'keep and use for protection of one's home and family' would fail constitutional muster." And the District's regulation that firearms in the home be kept inoperable, he added, "makes it impossible for citizens to use them for the core lawful purpose of self-defense and is hence unconstitutional."

Stevens read from the bench summaries of his 46-page dissent and also Breyer's 44-page dissent. Stevens went toe-to-toe with Scalia on the meaning of the words in the two clauses. He focused primarily on the immediate history surrounding the drafting and ratification of the amendment and analyzed sources contemporaneous with the amendment.

Scalia had presumed a preexisting right, and his historical analysis focused primarily on sources in periods much earlier and later than the events surrounding the amendment's drafting, debate, and ratification.

Scalia's written opinion for the majority was odd in one important respect. He actually began his analysis of the Second Amendment with the amendment's second clause—the operative clause—and not the opening clause—the preamble. He explained that he would come back later in the opinion to show how the preamble worked with his interpretation of the operative clause. That approach, which was the opposite of the general approach of the Court to interpreting the text, seemed to suggest that he did not have a strong argument for reconciling the two clauses.

But Scalia's odd approach also may have stemmed from a highly unusual step taken by the dissenters in the drafting process. So confident were the dissenters of their view of the history of the Second Amendment that Stevens, hoping to persuade someone in the majority to change his vote, circulated his draft dissent before Scalia circulated his draft majority opinion.

That effort, of course, failed. However, Scalia may have started with the operative clause because the draft dissent revealed the weakness of the majority's view of the preamble.

Not surprisingly, Justice Stevens in his dissent criticized Scalia for beginning his analysis with the amendment's operative clause, which, he wrote, was not how the Court ordinarily reads text. "Perhaps the Court's approach to the text is acceptable advocacy, but it is surely an un-usual approach for judges to follow." The text, he said, makes no mention of any non-military use of firearms. "If the text were ambiguous, which I don't think it is, the clear statement of purpose in the preamble would provide the basis for resolving any ambiguity."

The amendment's principal draftsman, James Madison—"not those who wrote generations later"—and those who participated in the amendment's enactment, considered and rejected proposals in state constitutions that would have protected an individual right, he added, and that is a "fair analysis of original intent." The majority also misinterpreted the 1939 *Miller* decision, which had been relied on by hundreds of federal judges and countless legislators, to mean that the amendment protects a militia-based right, according to Stevens.

"The regulation of civilian use of firearms raises critically important questions of public policy," he said, which until today's decision had been resolved by the political branches of government. "This is just the first in a series of decisions the Court will be required to make to define the dimensions of the newly discovered right. The Court should stay out of this political thicket. Adherence to a policy of judicial restraint would be far wiser than the bold decision announced today."

In his separate dissent, Justice Breyer wrote that he agreed with Stevens that the amendment protected militia-related, not self-defense-related interests. Assuming for purposes of his dissent that self-defense was the amendment's purpose, Breyer argued the District's law was consistent with the amendment because the regulation, "which focuses upon the presence of handguns in high-crime urban areas, represents a permissible response to a serious, indeed life-threatening, problem."

Breyer argued that in examining the constitutionality of gun regulations, the Court should make an "interest-balancing" inquiry, with interests protected by the amendment on one side, the government's public safety concerns on the other, and "the only question being whether the regulation at issue impermissibly burdens the former in the course of advancing the latter." In conducting that inquiry, Breyer said he found "substantial evidence" to support the District's judgment and little evidence of a burden on interests protected by the amendment.

Breyer, noting the majority had derided his approach as "judge-empowering," countered that although his approach requires judgment, its very nature—"requiring careful identification of the relevant interests and evaluating the law's effect upon them"—limits the judge's choices and reveals the judge's reasoning for all to see. He considered his approach more transparent than the majority's methodology.

"Also important, the majority's decision threatens severely to limit the ability of more knowledgeable, democratically elected officials to deal with gun-related problems," wrote Breyer. "The majority says that it leaves the District 'a variety of tools for combating' such problems. It fails to list even one seemingly adequate replacement for the law it strikes down. I can understand how reasonable individuals can disagree about the merits of strict gun control as a crime-control measure, even in a totally urbanized area. But I cannot understand how one can take from the elected branches of government the right to decide whether to insist upon a handgun-free urban populace in a city now facing a serious crime problem and which, in the future, could well face environmental or other emergencies that threaten the breakdown of law and order."

The Scalia and Breyer opinions laid bare once again the great divide in their constitutional interpretation: the originalist versus the pragmatist.

During that afternoon in his chambers in July 2011, Scalia explained that he considered the *Heller* decision the greatest vindication of originalism "because not only did the majority apply an originalist approach, the dissenters foolishly tried to do the same thing. I thought we just utterly destroyed Justice Stevens's attempt to display the contrary as an originalist matter." But revealing a strong strain of cynicism, he added: "We won't apply that reasoning in the next case. Very disappointing."

Is Stevens an "originalist"? The term is somewhat misleading, he believes. Some people think it is the answer to every question, he said. He, like many judges, always looks to the original evidence, but believes it is not necessarily controlling.

Both Scalia and Stevens were strikingly confident in their views of the scope of the Second Amendment and the evidence they marshaled to support those views, even though historians themselves are divided on the meaning. Where the evidence is in equipoise, Stevens would say there are two powerful tiebreakers: deference to legislators responsible for policy decisions in this area and *stare decisis*. Scalia, however, sees no equipoise. "As far as being demonstrably correct on the history in *Heller*, I don't even think it's a debate," he said.

For Scalia, the decision was not only the triumph of his originalist approach to the Constitution, but it also quieted skeptics who had said he was unable to forge majorities because of that approach. He not only had five votes; none of the five wrote separately to narrow or question any part of his ruling.

Advocates of originalism hailed the first part of Scalia's opinion dealing with the threshold issue of what kind of right the Second Amendment protects. It was a true originalist opinion, they claimed, perhaps the most important and faithful exercise of that approach in modern history.

But some of those same advocates also criticized the latter half of Scalia's opinion in which he approved of several types of gun control, for example, prohibiting possession by convicted felons, permitting gun-free zones in sensitive places such as schools and government buildings, and banning machine guns. They were critical because he offered no historical justification for the exceptions, only saying that will come later. And, they claimed, Scalia, while correct in the result, had provided little historical justification for invalidating the District's handgun ban.

One of those individual right advocates, the Second Amendment legal scholar Nelson Lund of George Mason University School of Law, in a panel discussion during a Federalist Society convention, asked: "So, for instance, why does the Court say that the ban on handguns in Washington, D.C., is constitutionally impermissible but, as the Court suggests, a ban on machine guns would not be? Well, the Court says, '[h]andguns are the most popular weapon chosen by Americans for self-defense in the home, and a complete prohibition of their use is invalid.' Machine guns, by contrast, are 'dangerous and unusual weapons' that are not in common use. But this isn't originalism. It's Living Constitutionalism. Modern conditions and modern preferences shape the scope of the Second Amendment's meaning and protection."[6]

Neily also was disappointed by the gun control exceptions. "He doesn't cite any support for those," he said of Scalia. "It seems like an unreflected bone. The language on sensitive places—you can imagine what a gaping opportunity that is. If you don't like guns, everywhere is a sensitive place, outside of someone's closet." And Neily, of course, was disappointed with the dissents, calling Stevens's view "fairly ludicrous" and Breyer's dissent reducible to "I never needed a gun to defend myself and you'll never need a gun to defend yourself."

The decision also drew surprising criticism from two leading conservative appellate judges: J. Harvie Wilkinson of the U.S. Court of Appeals for the Fourth Circuit and Richard Posner of the Seventh Circuit.

Wilkinson, in a *Virginia Law Review* article, compared *Heller* to the *Roe v. Wade* abortion decision. He wrote: "*Heller* represents a triumph for conservative lawyers. But it also represents a failure—the Court's failure to adhere to a conservative judicial methodology in reaching its decision. In fact, *Heller* encourages Americans to do what conservative jurists warned for years they should not do: bypass the ballot and seek to press their political agenda in the courts." *Heller* and *Roe*, he said, are guilty of the "same sins" in many important ways: "an absence of a commitment to textualism; a willingness to embark on a complex endeavor that will require fine-tuning over many years of litigation; a failure to respect legislative judgments; and a rejection of the principles of federalism."[7]

Richard Posner, in a *New Republic* article, wrote that the decision "is questionable in both method and result, and it is evidence that the Supreme Court, in deciding constitutional cases, exercises a freewheeling discretion strongly flavored with ideology."[8]

But most disappointed obviously was the District's Mayor Fenty and his lawyer, Walter Dellinger. The decision led Dellinger to conclude that the Roberts Court was a "strikingly aggressive" Court. Even if evidence about the meaning of the Second Amendment was ambiguous and conflicting, he said, "Why not defer to the political branches of the government when you have a question settled for seventy years by a Supreme Court precedent, when there is not a great political chance that Congress is going to adopt any significant gun control legislation, and when most states have constitutional provisions that protect the right at least in theory? It takes a very aggressive Court to reach back seventy years and make a new issue out of this. It changed my view of the Court in the sense that it made me think this Court is willing to take very bold steps in the future."

The decision ultimately offered little guidance to lower courts on how to determine whether a particular gun regulation runs afoul of the Second Amendment. When the Court recognizes a right, scholars say, it generally provides a standard of review. But Roberts suggested during oral arguments that it would not announce a standard. The Court, he said, did not have to get entangled in which of the typically three standards should apply in this case. And as Scalia wrote, it was enough for now to define the right protected. But after arguments in the case, during the conference and in the drafting, the justices actually were unable to agree on a standard of review.

Gura and Levy were very happy with the decision. "The decision is lucid, not ambiguous at all, and lays down a lot of useful guidance on a host of issues which of course the other side has no use for," said Gura. "I thank Mayor Fenty every day for petitioning for cert."

As of roughly 10:30 am on that June 26, 2008, the Second Amendment applied only to the District of Columbia. The Second Amendment is part of the Bill of Rights, which was intended to protect citizens from actions by the federal government. Over the years, most of the Bill of Rights has been applied through a judicial process known as "incorporation" to actions by state governments as well as to actions by the federal government. The Second Amendment was one of the few remaining amendments unincorporated.

After the decision was announced and Roberts gaveled the session to a close, Gura, Neily, and Levy left the courtroom and walked downstairs to the clerk's office to get paper copies of the decision. Gura flipped through the opinion and saw Scalia's footnote 23, which said the Court did not reach the question of incorporation of the Second Amendment, but Scalia suggested it might be incorporated under the Court's modern incorporation analysis. As the three men left the building to face television cameras on the plaza, Gura got on his cell phone and called a lawyer in Chicago, David Sigale. He told Sigale simply: "File it."

In April after the arguments in *Heller*, Gura had flown to Chicago and signed Otis McDonald, a seventy-six-year-old South Side Democrat whose home had been broken into three times, as his lead client in a challenge to Chicago's handgun ban. The lawsuit directly raised the question of whether the Second Amendment was incorporated against the states. Phase two of a strategy hatched six years earlier by Levy, Neily, and Gura had begun; but this time, Gura's new case—*McDonald v. City of Chicago*—would move swiftly to the Supreme Court, arriving just one year later, in 2009.

Three weeks after the *Heller* decision, the board of the Village of Morton Grove, Illinois, threatened with legal action by the National Rifle Association, voted 5–1 to repeal its twenty-seven-year-old handgun ban. In 1981, Morton Grove, a residential suburb of Chicago, became the first city or town in the nation to ban handguns. The ban had survived three separate legal challenges, including one that led to the U.S. Supreme Court in 1983.[9]

The village board repealed its ban even though the Roberts Court had yet to decide whether the Second Amendment applied to the states.

Repealing the ban was "just common sense," said Dan Staackmann, village president. "With the economic downturn and what litigation costs, there's no sense having a law on your books that if you go to court, you're going to lose. If there was litigation against the village, I'm looking to spend $50,000 on something I'm going to lose? Ridiculous."[10]

The village's handgun ban, he added, had been "a noble experiment."

PART 3

MONEY

CHAPTER 10

———◆———

"I'm an ultimate Reagan guy. We have a very simple philosophy: we win, you lose."

—David Bossie, president of Citizens United, 2011

At the beginning of August 2008, one month after the Supreme Court ended the national debate over the meaning of the Second Amendment, Barack Obama was just weeks away from his historic nomination as the Democratic candidate for president. GOP senator John McCain of Arizona soon would grasp the Republican nomination that had eluded him in 2000. And a small, conservative activist organization in Washington, D.C., named Citizens United headed into the Supreme Court.

The non-profit Citizens United, operating out of a sparsely decorated Pennsylvania Avenue row house, one Metro stop away from the Court itself, planned to file a challenge that neither it nor anyone else that summer could have foreseen would begin to transform the nation's election landscape.

The justices' final decision in the case would not come until 2010, but when it did, money, the lifeblood of American political campaigns, soon afterwards would erupt like a gusher into congressional and presidential election contests. The Roberts Court's ruling would deepen an open vein of cynicism about the Court in a large segment of the American electorate, a wound first inflicted by the Rehnquist Court's 2000 decision in *Bush v. Gore*, which handed the presidency to George W. Bush.

And as with the Seattle-Louisville school cases, the outcome of this high-stakes challenge would be the result primarily of one critical change in the Court's personnel: Justice Samuel Alito Jr. as successor to Justice Sandra Day O'Connor.

None of that was on the mind of Citizens United president David Bossie on August 14, 2008. On that day, he took his legal battle with the Federal Election Commission (FEC) over ads and a movie that he had produced critical of presidential candidate Hillary Clinton to the next level—the U.S. Supreme Court.

Like the great constitutional clashes involving race and schools, guns and the Second Amendment, and the later titanic one over health care and the commerce clause, the legal architects of this fight were smart conservative lawyers who were particularly attuned to the ways of the conservative-dominated Roberts Court. This time, however, the battle-ground would be the First Amendment.

Citizens United's Bossie is an energetic and gregarious self-described Reaganite, who had earned his own measure of fame in the political environs of Washington, D.C., well before Citizens United's case hit the Supreme Court. He joined Citizens United in 1991 after doing campaign work for Republicans such as Senator Bob Dole. Back then it was essentially a two-man operation. During the 1992 presidential campaign, he and Citizens United's president Floyd Brown (who created the devastating Willie Horton campaign ad against 1988 Democratic presidential candidate Michael Dukakis) went after candidate Bill Clinton in a paperback book entitled *Slick Willie*. After the election, they continuously probed the Clintons, particularly their Whitewater real estate investment, and fed numerous documents and tips to news media and congressional Republicans.

Because of their Whitewater efforts, Bossie said, he landed a position as an investigator for the Senate committee investigating Whitewater in early 1995. When that ended, he moved over to the House Government Reform and Oversight Committee as chief investigator. "I headed up all their investigations—the White House travel office, the Vince Foster suicide," he recalled.[1]

In 1998, House Speaker Newt Gingrich pressured Committee Chairman Dan Burton to fire Bossie because of Bossie's release of selectively edited taped conversations between jailed Whitewater figure Webster Hubbell and his wife about billing irregularities at the law firm where Hubbell and Hillary Clinton had been partners. A statement by Hubbell that Clinton had "no idea" of the billing irregularities had been deleted. Bossie subsequently resigned.[2]

His critics and his fans during those years dubbed Bossie with a variety of positive and mostly negative monikers, including "political mudslinger," "right-wing hitman," "relentless sleuth," and "renowned Republican dirty trickster."

In 2000, Bossie returned to Citizens United as vice president. The organization says its mission is "to reassert the traditional American values of limited government, freedom of enterprise, strong families, and national sovereignty and security." Citizens United started in 1988 and took as its first advocacy project a campaign against statehood for the District of Columbia. The project targeted Jesse Jackson, in particular, who had been elected the city's "shadow senator," accusing him of promoting his "personal left wing, anti-America agenda."[3] When Floyd Brown left to run the Reagan Ranch operation in California, the Citizens United board made Bossie the new president and chairman of the board.

Bossie's right-hand man is vice president and general counsel Michael Boos, a longtime conservative activist. The small board of directors includes Brian Berry, a Texas Republican media strategist; Douglas Ramsey, a Seattle sports marketing executive; Ron Robinson, president of Young America's Foundation, which calls itself the conservative movement's principal outreach organization; Washington State GOP chairman Kirby Wilbur, also head of Americans for Prosperity-Washington, the state chapter of the conservative political advocacy group founded by the Koch brothers; and John Bliss, a Denver attorney who served as chief counsel to former GOP senator Hank Brown.

Citizens United has an annual budget of about $12 million, which is funded mostly by donations from individuals and a small portion by corporations. It also has a lobbying arm—American Sovereignty Project—whose stated goals include complete withdrawal from the United Nations and defeat of the treaty establishing the International Criminal Court; and it has a political action committee (PAC) funded by individual contributions.

The organization's Supreme Court case had its roots in what Bossie describes as a "revelation" that he experienced in the spring of 2004. That May, the Cannes Film Festival awarded its highest prize to Michael Moore's *Fahrenheit 9/11*, a documentary critical of President George W. Bush, the war on terror, and news media coverage. The film became the highest-grossing documentary of all time.

"You had this new film coming out and they launched it at a film festival to take the world by storm," recalled Bossie. "It was an anti-Bush screed trying to influence the election. I woke up and said, 'Why the hell don't we do that?'"

There were at least several reasons: Citizens United did not know how to make a movie, was not sure it could afford it, and did not know anyone in Hollywood.

"We had a list of reasons as long as your arm on why it couldn't be done," he added. "On the other hand, I'm a political guy. When you're running a campaign and your opponent puts up a thirty-second commercial against you, what do you do? Put up a thirty-second response!"

Bossie had not seen the movie, but he had seen the thirty-second commercials promoting it on television. The ads, he believed, were terrific, better than anything that the Democratic presidential candidate John Kerry had offered in his own campaign.

As he and Boos discussed making their own movie and ads, they decided first to go after Moore's ads. In June 2004, they filed a complaint with the Federal Election Commission, charging that Moore's ads violated the federal Bipartisan Campaign Reform Act of 2002, better known as the McCain-Feingold Act, after its two chief sponsors, John McCain of Arizona and Democratic senator Russell Feingold of Wisconsin.

The McCain-Feingold Act represented a long and hard-fought effort by its two named senators and reform groups to regulate and restrict the flow of special interest money into federal elections. Before Congress passed the act, federal law prohibited corporations and unions from spending their general treasury funds on certain election-related activities. Instead, corporations and unions were permitted to create separate political action committees, funded by individual contributions, which were limited in amount, and to spend those monies on election activities.

In the Supreme Court's landmark *Buckley v. Valeo* campaign finance ruling in 1976, the justices said the ban on spending general treasury funds applied only to "express advocacy" by corporations and unions, for example, activities using the magic words "vote for" or "vote against" a particular candidate. But in the 1990s, so-called issue ads began appearing during campaigns. Some were genuine issue ads addressing topics of public concern. Others were sham issue ads clearly designed to influence an election, but they went unregulated because they avoided using the magic words. For example, the ad would express a viewpoint on a political issue and then urge voters to contact Senator X and tell him "what you think of his vote," a vote that opposed the ad's viewpoint. There were no limits on how those advertisements were financed and no disclosure was required. As a result, millions of dollars from corporate and union treasury funds financed campaign advertising through the sham issue ad loophole.

The McCain-Feingold Act tackled that loophole and others. The act contained a provision (Section 203) barring corporations and labor unions from using their general treasury funds to pay for "electioneering communications" during specific periods leading up to primary and general elections. The ban applied to broadcast, cable, or satellite communications that featured a candidate for federal office and could reach 50,000 people thirty days before a primary and sixty days before a general election.

The act also contained two provisions intended to reveal who and how much was behind the funding for electioneering communications. Under the disclosure requirement, any corporation or union that spent more than $10,000 to produce or air these communications had to report to the FEC the names and addresses of those contributing $1,000 or more. And under the disclaimer requirement, the broadcast had to say who was responsible for the content. Corporations and unions could still take the alternative funding route—using their political action committees to pay for these electioneering communications.

In 2003, the Rehnquist Court upheld the constitutionality of key parts of the act, including the electioneering provision, by a 5–4 vote in *McConnell v. Federal Election Commission* (Kentucky GOP senator Mitch McConnell challenged the act). That decision also reaffirmed a 1990 ruling in another case—*Austin v. Michigan Chamber of Commerce*—which had upheld a state ban on independent campaign expenditures by corporations. Justice Sandra Day O'Connor was key to the outcome in the *McConnell* decision. Both the electioneering provision and the 1990 *Austin* decision would play key roles in the ultimate fate of Citizens United's challenge in the Supreme Court.

But that challenge was still four years away as Bossie and Boos examined the 2004 schedule for the airing of Moore's ads for *Fahrenheit 9/11*. When they found that some were listed for the law's blackout periods, they complained to the Federal Election Commission. They charged that the ads would violate the law's prohibition against the broadcast of corporate communications mentioning candidates' names in the sixty days preceding a general election. The movie's distributors responded that ads airing after July 30—thirty days before the Republican National Convention in New York City—and sixty days before Election Day, November 3, would exclude clearly identified presidential or vice-presidential candidates. Instead, the ads would focus primarily on audience and critical reaction to the film.

The FEC rejected Citizens United's complaint, saying it was based on "mere speculation." There was "no reason to believe [Moore] violated the Act because the film, associated trailers and website represented bona fide commercial activity, not 'contributions' or 'expenditures' as defined by the Federal Election Campaign Act."

Bossie, however, viewed the result as a victory because the movie's distributors had decided, in response to the complaint, not to show any presidential or vice-presidential candidates in the ads. "I think they did it because the lawyers at Lionsgate and the Weinsteins—huge, enormous Hollywood entities—they didn't know how to deal with the Federal Election Commission," speculated Bossie. "That tells you what the fear of the federal government can do to even Hollywood powerhouses. . What kind of violation is it? Is it a criminal violation or a civil violation? What are the fines? If you're going to spend $10 million on an ad buy, it could be a $10 million fine."

Bossie and Boos reveled in their "victory." At the same time, they were planning to make their first movie.

Citizens United was preparing a book about Democratic presidential candidate John Kerry and wanted to do a movie on the candidate as well. Bossie and Boos approached the FEC for an advisory opinion on whether they could advertise the movie and the book if the content referred to Kerry or Bush. The commission said no because the film and ads for both the film and the book would be "electioneering communications." It also said that Citizens United could not claim any of the law's exemptions, including a media exemption, because this was its first movie and it did not produce movies in its ordinary course of business, according to Boos.

"So we went out and started making movies," said Boos.[4]

They installed production equipment in the basement of their row house and dipped into the organization's fund for costs. They responded to *Fahrenheit 9/11* with *Celsius 41.11: The Temperature at Which the Brain*

Begins to Die. Next came *Broken Promises*, on the United Nations. And they targeted the American Civil Liberties Union in *ACLU: At War with America* and illegal immigration in *Border War*.

By the time the next presidential election cycle began, Citizens United had made at least four films and had created its own distribution system. It was ready to go back to the FEC, this time for its biggest and most controversial movie.

"By 2007, everybody in America—to quote John McLaughlin with metaphysical certitude—knew Hillary Clinton would be the nominee for president," said Bossie. "The bottom line is we started to put into production a very big, very expensive, long-term investment in a film on and about Hillary Clinton. We did it to go back to the FEC and say, 'You said a couple of years ago why we can't do this. Now why not?' "

Bossie had to raise a substantial amount of money to fund the movie and the advertisements that would promote it. He viewed as an obstacle the law's requirement that he disclose the sources of and the amounts of funds contributed to the project.

"We wanted to do ads," recalled Bossie. "That was the whole premise. As far as Moore's documentary was concerned, yes, the movie was seen by a lot of people, but tens of millions more people saw his ads, and through his ads, the movie entered the popular culture and was used to educate people. Forget the film was full of lies and deceit."

Hillary: The Movie was a brutal takedown of Hillary Clinton as a potential president. Bossie planned to distribute it through theaters, video-on-demand broadcasts, and DVD sales in all of the early presidential primary states. He also had produced three television ads for the movie.

Bossie wanted to use the organization's general treasury funds to pay $1.2 million to a cable television consortium to make his movie available for free download to "on demand" subscribers. He could have used funds contributed to Citizens United's political action committee and avoided problems with the corporate electioneering provision, although he still would have to disclose the sources of those contributions. Instead, he chose to use the organization's general treasury monies, which included some corporate funding. He and Boos feared that the film would violate the law's ban on corporate-funded electioneering communications and that they would be subject to civil and criminal penalties.

The two men decided to file a federal lawsuit arguing that the ban on corporate electioneering communications and the law's disclosure and disclaimer requirements were unconstitutional as applied to the Hillary movie and its three ads. But first they needed to find a lawyer willing to take on the challenge. In 2007, as they worked through their strategy, Bossie recalled, not many lawyers were willing to challenge the federal law which the Supreme Court had upheld just four years earlier. He interviewed several lawyers in his office, he said, including Republican superstar litigator Theodore Olson of *Bush v. Gore* fame.

"I told them my theory and I don't know if they were underwhelmed, but nobody showed a passion," said Bossie. "When you're dealing with a cause-oriented outcome, you want whoever you hire to be passionate about it. When I'm interviewing these people, what I'm looking for is who is going to go hammer and tong for us, who is going to fight every step, every half step, who is going to be forward-leaning, not wishy-washy."

And above all, they wanted to get to the Supreme Court. "That was definitely part of the strategic thinking," he emphasized. "We felt we had a unique twist: the law's application to a movie. This case would have to be decided by the Supreme Court whether on an appeal by us or an appeal by the FEC."

And when the case did get to the Supreme Court, the justices would not be examining or writing on the nearly clean slate that confronted them in the Second Amendment gun case.

The first federal campaign finance law was enacted in 1867, but it was a very narrow law that simply barred federal officials from soliciting contributions from Navy Yard workers. The modern era of campaign finance legislation really began with the Tillman Act of 1907.[5] The law barred direct contributions by corporations and national banks to federal campaigns. The Tillman Act was the point of reference used by President Barack Obama in his 2010 State of the Union address when he criticized the Roberts Court for reversing a "century of law" and opening the "floodgates" to corporate spending in elections because of the justices' ultimate decision in *Citizens United*.

The Tillman Act was sponsored by Senator Benjamin ("Pitchfork Ben") Tillman, a white supremacist and Democrat from South Carolina. His motives were far from pure in proposing the 1907 law. Tillman wanted to punish the Republican Party for imposing Reconstruction on the South. At the same time, however, public support for reform had been growing since the 1896 presidential campaign between Republican William McKinley—the recipient of allegedly unethical corporate contributions—and William Jennings Bryan. There were rumors and charges of bribery in that election. Although a Republican and a beneficiary of corporate contributions, Theodore Roosevelt in 1904 ran for president on a clean government platform. After his election, Roosevelt, with support from the progressive National Publicity Law Association and other grassroots groups, pushed for campaign finance reform, and the result was the Tillman Act.

(In a 2010 speech shortly after the Roberts Court ruling in *Citizens United*, Justice Clarence Thomas defended the ruling by pointing to Tillman's motives. Thomas told a law school audience, "Go back and read why Tillman introduced that legislation. Tillman was from South Carolina, and as I hear the story, he was concerned that the corporations, Republican corporations, were favorable toward blacks and he felt that there was a need to regulate them." Given that history, he added, it is a mistake to consider the regulation of corporate speech as "some sort of beatific action."[6] Of course, Tillman was not the only member of Congress who supported the legislation, and members of Congress often have different motives for the votes they cast. Regardless, as Thomas himself often argues, it is the text of the law that matters.)

As is true of most of the history of campaign finance regulation, loopholes in the Tillman Act were discovered and plumbed. Corporations gave "bonuses" to their employees, who were told that the money was to go to the corporation's chosen candidate. The Tillman Act ban was largely ignored. In 1910 and 1911, Congress also passed campaign disclosure legislation and spending limits for all congressional candidates.

Congress's next attempt at comprehensive reform did not come until 1947. In that year, the Taft-Hartley Act became law and prohibited certain labor union practices. Congress included unions in the ban on direct campaign contributions by corporations and interstate banks, and prohibited all of them from making expenditures to influence federal elections. Nothing much happened on the reform front for the next two decades until the Federal Election Campaign Act of 1971 and its 1974 amendments enacted in the wake of the Nixon-Watergate scandal.

The act and its amendments created the Federal Election Commission to enforce the Federal Election Campaign Act, imposed limits on campaign contributions and spending, and required disclosure of those funds. They also permitted corporations and unions to use treasury funds to establish a separate segregated fund, known as a political action committee, and to solicit voluntary contributions to the PAC. Those funds, whose sources had to be disclosed, could then be used to contribute to federal campaigns.

Despite the ambitious reform attempt, Republican senator James Buckley of New York and Democratic senator Eugene McCarthy of Minnesota almost immediately challenged the constitutionality of key parts of the 1974 amendments. The result of their lawsuit was the 1976 landmark *Buckley v. Valeo*, an unsigned decision of the Supreme Court headed by Chief Justice Warren Burger.

Richard Hasen of the University of California at Irvine—one of the top election law experts in the country—has called *Buckley* "the fountainhead of modern U.S. campaign finance jurisprudence."[7] In *Buckley*, the Court drew a line between campaign contributions and campaign expenditures. It ruled that limits on contributions did not violate the First Amendment, but limits on spending did.

Contribution limits, according to the Court, did appear to restrict a type of political speech, but the limits helped to prevent corruption or the appearance of corruption. The limits "serve[d] the basic governmental interest in safeguarding the integrity of the electoral process without directly impinging upon the rights of individual citizens and candidates to engage in political debate and discussion." Contributions to a candidate posed a greater danger of quid pro quo corruption or the appearance of buying the candidate.

Limits on campaign spending, on the other hand, imposed "direct and substantial restraints" on the amount of political speech, said the Court. The decision rejected arguments that spending limits served the public interest by equalizing the financial resources of candidates and that large independent expenditures posed the same threat of corruption or its appearance. Independent expenditures were not prearranged or coordinated with a candidate, explained the Court, and that alleviated the danger of quid pro quo commitments from candidates.

The battle in *Buckley*, which continues to this day on the Roberts Court, was over how to view money in elections. The *Buckley* majority viewed the spending of money as a form of "speech" because in today's society, money is essential for effective communication in campaigns. However, as Justice Byron White, dissenting in part, wrote: "As an initial matter, the argument that money is speech and that limiting the flow of money to the speaker violates the First Amendment proves entirely too much." Money is not always equivalent to speech or even used for speech in campaigns, he wrote, and Congress, in order to prevent corruption, had as much justification for limiting expenditures as it did for restricting contributions.

After the 1974 amendments to the Federal Election Campaign Act and the Supreme Court's *Buckley* decision, campaign finance reform languished until Senators McCain and Feingold won a five-year-long battle for passage of their Bipartisan Campaign Reform Act of 2002, which the Rehnquist Court largely upheld as constitutional by a 5–4 vote in *McConnell v. FEC* in 2003.

Since the *Buckley* decision in 1976, according to Hasen, the Supreme Court's campaign finance rulings have "swung as a pendulum toward and away from deference" to congressional and legislative regulation as members of the Court changed.[8] With the arrival of Roberts and Alito, who replaced Chief Justice William Rehnquist and Justice Sandra Day O'Connor, the pendulum abruptly swung away from regulation of money in campaigns, he said.

And evidence quickly mounted of another sharp and enduring divide on the Roberts Court, this one over the First Amendment and its relation to campaign finance regulation.

The Roberts Court's experience with campaign finance law began in its first term—the 2005–06 term—when the justices took up a Vermont case in which a state legislative candidate and others challenged Vermont's limits on campaign contributions and spending. In a fractured decision, the Court struck down both limits. The Court's majority found that Vermont's campaign spending limits ran afoul of the landmark *Buckley* decision, which held that expenditure limits violated the First Amendment. And, although *Buckley* had upheld limits on contributions because contributions presented the greater risk of quid pro quo corruption, Vermont's contribution limits violated the First Amendment, wrote Breyer, because the limits were so low that they restricted the ability of candidates to raise funds necessary to run competitive campaigns and the ability of political parties to help their candidates.

Justices Breyer, Roberts, and Alito rejected Vermont's call to revisit *Buckley*'s holding that spending limits violate the First Amendment. Although agreeing with the judgment, or outcome, of the case, two justices—Scalia and Thomas—said they would have overruled *Buckley* entirely in order to end all restrictions on campaign financing. Kennedy agreed only with the outcome and voiced skepticism about the entire field of campaign finance regulation.

Stevens, Souter, and Ginsburg dissented. Stevens, saying money does not equal speech, would have overruled *Buckley*'s rejection of limits on expenditures and upheld all of Vermont's restrictions. Souter and Ginsburg said it was premature to reject Vermont's spending limits and a lower court should study whether the limits were narrowly tailored and justified. As for Vermont's contribution limits, they said, those "are not remarkable departures either from those previously upheld by this Court or from those lately adopted by other States."

The following term offered a clearer picture of where the Roberts Court was headed, as well as the possible fate of Citizens United's case.

Federal Election Commission v. Wisconsin Right to Life (FEC v. WRTL) was actually the second time that the Roberts Court had examined the Wisconsin anti-abortion group's complaint. In 2006, the Court, in an unsigned ruling, held that the group could pursue a lawsuit challenging the McCain-Feingold Act's ban on corporate funding of electioneering communications as it applied to what the group argued was its "grassroots lobbying" ads. The justices, with Justice O'Connor on the bench, did not rule on the merits of the group's complaint, but sent the case back to a lower court for a hearing on whether the group's ads fell within the financing ban.

Wisconsin Right to Life (WRTL) won in the lower court and the Federal Election Commission brought the case back to the Roberts Court. This time, O'Connor was no longer on the Court. And the eventual decision in this case clearly signaled that the Roberts Court was inclined to inflict a major wound on the McCain-Feingold Act.

WRTL had wanted to run ads during the 2004 election campaigns of Senators Russell Feingold and Herb Kohl of Wisconsin to urge voters to tell Feingold and Kohl to oppose the filibuster of President George W. Bush's judicial nominees. In the Supreme Court, WRTL, represented by James Bopp Jr., a lawyer from Terre Haute, Indiana, argued that its ads were true issue ads and were not express advocacy or the "functional equivalent" of express advocacy—the test devised by the Rehnquist Court in its 2003 *McConnell* decision. As bona fide issue ads, Bopp argued, there was no justification for imposing the ban on corporate funding of the ads or for requiring WRTL to pay for the ads through a political action committee. To do so violated First Amendment rights of free speech, free association, and petitioning the government, charged Bopp.

On June 25, 2007, the Court, in a 5–4 ruling, agreed with WRTL and took a major step toward undoing the corporate-union funding ban in McCain-Feingold. Although Chief Justice Roberts wrote a narrow decision holding that the corporate electioneering ban was unconstitutional as applied to these particular ads, he crafted a new test for what kind of advertisements would fall within the law's prohibition on corporate and union funding. And his test broadened the field of ads that would go unregulated.

Roberts said that an advertisement is "the functional equivalent of express advocacy" only if it is "susceptible of no reasonable interpretation other than as an appeal to vote for or against a specific candidate." In applying that test, he said, the advertiser's intent and the advertisement's effects are irrelevant.

Roberts held that WRTL's ads were plainly not the functional equivalent of express advocacy because they focused on a specific legislative issue and did not mention an election, a political party, or a candidate. Unless the ads explicitly urged votes for or against a particular candidate, he explained, imposing the law's ban would be censorship of core political speech protected by the First Amendment.

"Discussion of issues cannot be suppressed simply because the issues may also be pertinent in an election. Where the First Amendment is implicated, the tie goes to the speaker, not the censor," wrote Roberts. His decision concerned only the constitutionality of the electioneering ban as it applied to these particular advertisements. Roberts specifically stated that the case did not present the occasion to reconsider the Court's 2003 decision in *McConnell v. FEC*, upholding the facial constitutionality of the ban.

A word about "facial" attacks on laws: Facial challenges argue that every application of a statute is unconstitutional. Those bringing this type of challenge have a heavy burden of proof and courts generally disfavor such challenges.

Roberts's opinion in *WRTL* was joined in full only by Justice Alito, who, in a separate and almost prescient concurring opinion, noted that if courts or the FEC applied Roberts's test in a way that chilled political speech, "we will presumably be asked in a future case to reconsider the holding" in *McConnell*, the decision upholding the constitutionality of the law's ban.

Scalia, Kennedy, and Thomas agreed with the result—that the ban did not apply to WRTL's ads—but not with Roberts's reasoning. They would have gone much further in undoing the law.

Scalia, Kennedy, and Thomas said that the effect of Roberts's opinion was to overrule the Court's 2003 decision in *McConnell v. FEC* without saying so directly. Scalia, writing for the trio, said that he would have overruled *McConnell* outright, as well as the justices' 1990 decision upholding the constitutionality of the state ban on corporate independent expenditures in *Austin v. Michigan Chamber of Commerce*. He wrote that there was no test that could separate issue speech from election speech with the clarity "that unchilled freedom of political speech demands." Scalia sarcastically accused Roberts of "faux judicial restraint" amounting to "judicial obfuscation."

The four dissenters in the *WRTL* decision agreed only that the majority had effectively overruled *McConnell*. "From early in the 20th century through the decision in *McConnell*, we have acknowledged that the value of democratic integrity justifies a realistic response when corporations and labor organizations commit the concentrated moneys in their treasuries to electioneering," wrote Justice David Souter for the dissenters. As for applying the electioneering ban to WRTL's ads, Souter said, any "alert voters" who saw or read the ads would have understood that WRTL was telling them that Senator Feingold's position on judicial filibusters was reason to vote against his reelection.

Souter noted that WRTL also had a PAC, funded by individual donations, which had been active over the years in elections involving Senator Feingold. Throughout the 2004 election campaign, he said, WRTL "made no secret of its views" about who should win the election and explicitly tied its position to the filibuster issue. Its PAC issued press releases saying, for example, "Send Feingold Packing!" But instead of using its PAC money to fund the television and radio ads at issue in the high court, it chose to use its general treasury boosted by corporate contributions.

Because of the majority's decision, Souter said, the federal law's other ban on direct campaign contributions by corporations and unions also would be easily circumvented. "The ban on contributions will mean nothing much, now that companies and unions can save candidates the expense of advertising directly, simply by running 'issue ads' without express advocacy, or by funneling the money through an independent corporation like WRTL."

Scalia's criticism of Roberts for "faux judicial restraint" was ironic. During the 2006–07 term in which the *WRTL* case was decided, Roberts, Scalia, and their fellow conservatives faced similar criticism from their more liberal colleagues and from a number of academics and advocacy groups who charged that the conservative wing of the Court was engaging in "stealth" overrulings of precedents in other areas. For example, the 5–4 decision upholding the federal partial-birth abortion law in *Gonzales v. Carhart* in 2007 had the practical effect, claimed critics, of overturning the 5–4 decision in *Stenberg v. Carhart* in 2000, striking down a nearly identical Nebraska law. And also in 2007, after the 5–4 ruling in *Hein v. Freedom From Religion Foundation*, little remained of a 1968 decision giving taxpayers the right to challenge government spending that might violate the establishment clause.

Was Roberts in his *WRTL* decision exercising the kind of restraint that he promised in his Senate confirmation hearings? Or, as his critics charged, was he engaged in a step-by-step dismantling of campaign finance limits so as to cushion the "jolt" to the legal system caused by overruling precedents?

Whether "faux judicial restraint" or the "minimalism" that he espoused during his confirmation hearings, Roberts clearly was not ready to deal a death blow to a key section of the McCain-Feingold campaign finance law—at least not yet.

The decision in *FEC v. WRTL* was above all a warning shot to campaign finance reform groups that there were now five potential votes for that end game. And the decision was a door of opportunity for Citizens United.

On the heels of the *WRTL* decision came another blow to the McCain-Feingold Act in the 2007–08 term. Jack Davis, the New York millionaire running for a U.S. House seat, challenged the so-called millionaires' amendment in the law in *Davis v. Federal Election Commission*. Under that provision, when a candidate's spending of his own personal funds exceeded $350,000, his opponent could receive three times the usual limit on individual contributions ($2,100 at the time) and also political party expenditures above the usual limit. Once the opponent exceeded the $350,000 amount, the normal limits would apply. Congress enacted the provision out of concern that candidates of modest means would not be able to compete effectively as elections grew more and more expensive.

Davis argued that the amendment violated the First Amendment because it burdened his political expression and deterred other self-financing candidates from running for Congress by giving benefits to their opponents. A lower court disagreed with Davis and upheld the provision. The Roberts Court reversed in a 5–4 decision.

The chief justice assigned the majority opinion to Justice Alito. In his opinion, Alito rejected the government's argument that the amendment's different financing limits were justified because they "level electoral opportunities for candidates of different personal wealth." Alito said the Court had never recognized that as a legitimate government objective. Preventing corruption or the appearance of corruption, he emphasized, are the only legitimate or compelling government interests for restricting campaign finances that the Court's decisions have recognized.

The millionaires' amendment, Alito wrote, "requires a candidate to choose between the First Amendment right to engage in unfettered political speech and subjection to discriminatory fundraising limitations. Many candidates who can afford to make large personal expenditures to support their campaigns may choose to do so despite [the amendment], but they must shoulder a special and potentially significant burden if they make that choice."

The dissenting justices—Stevens, Souter, Ginsburg, and Breyer—countered that the amendment did not burden or chill any speech. "On the contrary, it does no more than assist the opponent of a self-funding candidate in his attempts to make his voice heard; this amplification in no way mutes the voice of the millionaire, who remains able to speak as loud and as long as he likes in support of his campaign," wrote Stevens.

And, the dissent added, the Court had never said that only the interest in combating corruption or its appearance can justify congressional regulation of campaign financing. Stevens noted, for example, the 1990 decision upholding a law banning corporate independent spending, a ban justified, according to the decision, by the interest in combating "the corrosive and distorting effects of immense aggregations of wealth." What Stevens suspected, but did not yet know with certainty, was that the 1990 decision was on life support.

Six months after the *WRTL* decision, the Federal Election Commission issued a new rule and a 17-page explanation of the meaning of Roberts's new test for electioneering communications covered by the corporate-union financing ban. In the summer and fall of 2008, as the election season ramped up, business and labor groups wasted no time in testing the Roberts test.

The U.S. Chamber of Commerce spent $8.8 million in just five weeks on issue ads that mentioned House and Senate candidates' names in ten states, and the union-backed American Rights at Work spent $2.3 million in one month on broadcast issue ads featuring Senate candidates in five states, according to the Center for Public Integrity, a non-partisan, non-profit investigative news organization.

The three Roberts Court decisions—the Vermont campaign limits challenge, the millionaires' amendment case, and the *WRTL* case—demonstrated the conservative majority's increasing hostility toward and impatience with federal and state regulation of money in elections.

With the *WRTL* victory in particular in mind, Citizens United's Bossie and Boos had made their decision about a lawyer for their lawsuit. They found "true passion," campaign finance expertise, and a winning track record in the successful lawyer for WRTL and the Vermont challengers: James Bopp Jr.

A tall man, with a thinning shock of white hair and blue eyes, Bopp is a familiar face to the justices. During the abortion litigation battles in the 1980s to the early 1990s, Bopp, as general counsel to the National Right to Life Committee, defended anti-abortion laws and restrictions and brought creative lawsuits intended to undermine and eventually overturn the landmark 1973 abortion decision, *Roe v. Wade*. Since the mid-1990s, Bopp, vice chairman of the Republican National Committee, has waged a relentless, often successful war against campaign finance laws and their disclosure requirements. He also has fought state restrictions on campaign speech by judicial candidates through lawsuits filed across the country. In his attacks on campaign finance and judicial speech regulations, his clients frequently are anti-abortion groups.

In 1996, Senator Mitch McConnell (R-KY), also an aggressive opponent of campaign finance regulations, helped Bopp set up the nonprofit James Madison Center for Free Speech, formed in response to the "concerted attack on political speech which is at the core of the First Amendment," according to the center's statement of purpose. The center, funded by conservative donors, supports Bopp's litigation efforts.[9]

Viewed as ultra-conservative even by some in his own party, Bopp was among the GOP lawyers working for George W. Bush in the contentious Florida election in 2000. In 2009, as a member of the Republican National Committee, he proposed a ten-point purity test for Republican candidates. Those candidates would have to agree to eight of the ten principles in order to get financial support. The principles included opposition to federal funding of abortion, to same-sex marriage, and to amnesty for illegal immigrants.

Bopp filed Citizens United's lawsuit in federal district court in Washington, D.C., to begin their road to the Supreme Court.

"We were consumed every single day by the question of whether we would get to the Supreme Court," said Bossie.

The district court subsequently ruled in 2008 that the law's corporate electioneering provision was constitutional as applied to *Hillary: The Movie* because the movie was "susceptible of no other interpretation than to inform the electorate that Senator Clinton is unfit for office, that the United States would be a dangerous place in a President Hillary Clinton world, and that viewers should vote against her." And, although the ads for the movie were not subject to the law's corporate financing ban because they were not express advocacy or its functional equivalent, Citizens United must disclose its funding sources, ruled the court.

With that court's decision, Citizens United's path to the Supreme Court was now clear.

CHAPTER 11

—•—

"The greatest living issue confronting us today is whether the corporations shall control the people or the people shall control the corporations."

—Montana newspaper, 1906

The opening of the October 2008–09 Supreme Court term offered little hint of the drama that would mark the term's ending.

By the time Citizens United had filed its challenge in August 2008, a new crop of law clerks was already deep into preparations with their justices for the first week of arguments and into some of the traditions that lighten their workloads. One very old tradition was the clerks' weekly Happy Hours.

The responsibility for organizing the Happy Hours rotated among the chambers and some justices would occasionally participate. The planning ranged from fairly simple to elaborate. The Summer Olympics had ended shortly before the term's opening and some of the Happy Hours featured improvised Olympic Games. Later in the term, the clerks would hold a New England–style clambake in honor of the justice from New Hampshire—David Souter, whose retirement would contribute to the drama toward the end of the term.

But the term itself appeared to be something of a snooze at the beginning. There were no cases with the potential blockbuster status of the prior term's Second Amendment gun ruling or the Guantánamo Bay detainees' challenge.

Appearances can be deceiving, however, especially at the Supreme Court.

"There are several species of tough and important cases at the Court," said a former clerk from that term. "The high-profile cases—they often are huge when decided, but then they go away. There also are those institutional cases that really might not be high profile immediately, but they have a deeper and wider impact on the [legal] system and their presence is felt more significantly at the Court because they live on."

Two cases fell into that latter category during the 2008–09 term: *Melendez-Diaz v. Massachusetts*, and *Ashcroft v. Iqbal*. In *Melendez-Diaz*, justices crossed the ideological divide to reach the ruling; but in *Ashcroft*, the outcome reflected the traditional ideological divide among them.

The *Melendez-Diaz* case involved the Sixth Amendment's confrontation clause, which guarantees the right of an accused to confront—to cross-examine—the witnesses against him. Luis Melendez-Diaz challenged his drug conviction on grounds that the prosecution violated his confrontation clause right by admitting laboratory test reports without allowing him to cross-examine the analysts who prepared the reports.

This case followed the Court's confrontation clause revolution begun in 2004 with a Scalia-authored opinion in *Crawford v. Washington*. Looking to history and the clause's "original meaning," Scalia in *Crawford* said that "the Framers would not have allowed admission of testimonial statements of a witness who did not appear at trial unless he was unavailable to testify, and the defendant had had a prior opportunity for cross-examination."

The *Crawford* decision in 2004 was unanimous, but the Court has split 5–4 several times since then over what is "testimonial," and the justices' alignments have been unusual. Scalia is usually joined by Thomas and their more liberal colleagues, Ginsburg and until their retirements, Stevens and Souter. And Kennedy regularly leads the dissenters, joined by conservatives Roberts and Alito and the liberal Breyer.

Melendez-Diaz was a 5–4 outcome to require lab analysts to testify about their reports unless the criminal defendant waives his right in some way. The dissenters claimed the majority had "swept away" a century of practice in which scientific analysis could be admitted into evidence without testimony by the analyst. They predicted chaos and delays as states tried to produce analysts for trial, analysts who often conduct hundreds of drug tests per week or month.

The Roberts Court's line of cases involving the confrontation clause fails to grab front-page headlines, but the cases have significant practical impact on the criminal justice system. Scalia and Kennedy battle almost every term over these cases. For Scalia, the cases demand application of his original meaning interpretation of the Constitution. For Kennedy, who is rarely an originalist, they require an examination of history, text, and consequences.

Kennedy looks for cases coming into the Court for opportunities to restrict or narrow what *Crawford* has wrought, and Scalia tries to keep those cases at bay, say former clerks.

"This drives [Kennedy] batty," said one former Kennedy clerk. "He believes this is wrong and this affects every prosecution of most crimes."

Ashcroft v. Iqbal generated greater, early attention on the term's docket, primarily because of its facts. Javaid Iqbal, a Pakistani Muslim living in New York, was among more than 1,000 people swept up in the post-September 11, 2001, arrests and detained by federal officials. He sued, claiming that he was targeted because of his race, religion, or national origin, in violation of the First and Fifth amendments. He also charged that he was detained in harsh and restrictive conditions. Iqbal claimed that Attorney General John Ashcroft and FBI director Robert Mueller knowingly adopted and condoned that unconstitutional policy.

Government lawyers unsuccessfully moved to dismiss the lawsuit. The Roberts Court, in a 5–4 decision by Justice Kennedy, reversed. The majority, which included Roberts, Scalia, Thomas, and Alito, held that Iqbal had failed to plead sufficient facts in his lawsuit to show that Ashcroft and Mueller adopted the arrest policies for the purpose of discriminating on account of race, religion, or national origin.

Suddenly, a potentially fascinating case about the post-September 11 liability of high-ranking government officials had morphed into a rather dry procedural decision. What kind of facts does someone have to put in his lawsuit in order to overcome a motion to dismiss the lawsuit?

For many years, the federal rule had been that a lawsuit—a complaint—had to contain "a short and plain statement of the claim showing that the pleader is entitled to relief." It was a very low hurdle designed essentially to keep lawsuits in court, not out. The lawsuit's merits would be tested later in the process, during the discovery phase or through a trial. *Iqbal* changed the rule, and no party in the case had asked the Court to make that change.

Someone who files a lawsuit must plead sufficient facts for a court to conclude that it is "plausible" that the person suing is entitled to relief, wrote Kennedy, imposing a much higher hurdle on plaintiffs in lawsuits. The decision had huge ramifications for anyone filing a civil lawsuit.

Like the *Melendez-Diaz* decision, the *Iqbal* decision had a forerunner. The Roberts Court had toughened the pleading requirements a year earlier in *Bell Atlantic Corp. v. Twombly*, a case stemming from an antitrust lawsuit brought by consumers. The decision surprised the legal world by overturning a 1957 ruling heavily relied upon by federal courts. At the time, it was not clear whether *Twombly*, a 7–2 decision, applied to all lawsuits or just to the type of lawsuit at issue in that case— an antitrust suit. The *Iqbal* decision made clear that the higher pleading standard applied in all civil cases.

Justice Souter, who actually authored *Twombly*, led the dissenters in *Iqbal* and said the Kennedy majority had misapplied his *Twombly* decision.

Under the *Iqbal* standard, federal courts have much more discretion to dismiss lawsuits at the very beginning of a case if they think the allegations are not plausible—whatever "plausible" means to the particular judge. The decision was considered a boon to corporate defendants, who wasted no time in raising *Iqbal* as a defense to consumer, civil rights, and other lawsuits. Two months after the ruling, federal courts had cited *Iqbal* more than five hundred times in federal cases, according to a *New York Times* report.

Iqbal and *Twombly* would become arrows in the quiver of predominantly liberal special interest groups who had begun building a political case that the Roberts Court was a pro-corporate Supreme Court. But the sharpest arrow was yet to come: the decision in Citizens United's case.

As it was filed at the Court that term, Citizens United's challenge, on the surface, had none of the signs of a potential landmark ruling. Election law experts and others who had followed closely the Roberts Court's few campaign finance decisions, however, saw the potential.

Still, as the University of California's election scholar, Richard Hasen, has noted, the Roberts Court had never openly or formally overruled any prior campaign finance decisions—until *Citizens United*.

And Citizens United initially was not asking the Roberts Court to overrule any campaign finance decisions. James Bopp, its lawyer, intentionally framed a narrow case, explaining, "If you don't make a narrow argument, you're going to lose [the justices]. I think they're quite serious about the Court having restraint."[1]

The strategy never included asking the Court to overrule the 2003 *McConnell* decision upholding the McCain-Feingold Act or the 1990 *Austin* decision's approval of the ban on corporate independent spending, he added.

"But they always had the option as they always did," said Bopp. "We were hoping in *Planned Parenthood v. Casey* that they would overturn *Roe v. Wade*. If they're being asked to apply a precedent, the validity of the precedent is always before the Court."

The disclosure requirements in the McCain-Feingold law were the primary target in the appeal. Bopp had argued that the ads for *Hillary: The Movie* were protected political speech because they did not contain an "appeal to vote" or a clear call for action—the test constructed by the Roberts Court majority in the *Wisconsin Right to Life* case. He also argued that the movie itself could not be treated as "broadcast ads" subject to the law's ban on financing from general treasury funds. A movie, he contended, was "categorically different" from the broadcast ads that influenced Congress in enacting the McCain-Feingold law.

Citizens United's "animating concern was the reporting of their contributors," said Bopp, explaining that Bossie and Boos believed that compelled disclosure of donors to the movie project would subject the donors to retaliation by political opponents.

The Federal Election Commission, represented at the time by Solicitor General Gregory Garre, urged the Roberts Court to dismiss the appeal or to affirm the lower court decision. That decision "rests on a straightforward application of settled legal principles," Garre told the justices. Garre thought there was a chance that the Court would not take Citizens United's appeal because federal law had required disclosure of campaign financing since 1910, and the Supreme Court had upheld the constitutionality of past and present disclosure requirements.

Garre also challenged Citizens United's description of the movie. He said it was clearly "express advocacy" because it attacked candidate Clinton's character and fitness. The law did not exclude such movies from regulation, he said.

But three months after Bopp filed Citizens United's case in the Supreme Court, the justices in November agreed to hear it and scheduled arguments for March 24, 2009. A week after the Court's announcement, Citizens United's David Bossie dumped Bopp.

Earlier in October, Bossie had attended an event at the Capitol Hill Club where former Bush solicitor general Theodore Olson of Gibson, Dunn & Crutcher was being named "Republican Lawyer of the Year" by the Republican National Lawyers Association.

"I'm sitting there, thinking about my case," recalled Bossie. "Every Republican lawyer in town is there. Bill Kilberg of Gibson Dunn gets up to introduce Ted and says Ted Olson has won *X* number of cases and he's the winningest Supreme Court lawyer. I've known Ted forever and I said to myself, 'How is it I am not in Ted Olson's hands?' "

The next day, Bossie went to Mike Boos and suggested replacing Bopp with Olson.

"There was no ill reflection on Jim [Bopp]," he added. "When you change battlefields, you change generals. I wanted to feel we were in the right hands to go forward at that level. It's not about, 'Oh well, Jim got us here; we owe it to him.' Look, if you get to the Super Bowl with your second-string quarterback and your first stringer comes off the injured reserve list, you put him back in. Not that Jim is second string. When you're at the big leagues, you have to make very dispassionate decisions."

After discussing the pros and cons of switching lawyers, Bossie and Boos decided to approach Olson. "I had met with Ted years before and told him my idea for the case; I don't think he took me very seriously," recalled Bossie. However, Olson did now, said Bossie, and he agreed to take the case. Bossie offered Bopp the co-counsel or second chair position; Bopp refused and withdrew from the case.[2]

Olson is indisputably the "dean" of the so-called Supreme Court bar, a growing group of lawyers who appear frequently in cases before the justices. He was the mastermind of the case for George W. Bush in *Bush v. Gore* and Bush appointed him solicitor general—the government's top appellate lawyer—after he took over the Oval Office. Olson also is one of the top appellate lawyers in the nation and commands an hourly rate of more than $1,200. Highly regarded, well liked, and plugged into the Republican establishment, Olson has the kind of stature that has allowed him to survive the scorn of the party's extreme right wing because of his constitutional attack on California's ban on same-sex marriage.[3]

Citizens United's new lawyer also was no stranger to the legal issues surrounding the McCain-Feingold Act. It was Olson, as Bush solicitor general, who led the successful defense of the act's constitutionality in 2003 from the attack brought by a fellow Republican, Senator Mitch McConnell of Kentucky. Now Olson would be the attacker, and the strategy in the Supreme Court would change.

"We sat down and decided you really had to go for the heart of the case, which is the constitutionality of this prohibition itself," recalled Olson. "We wanted to make the narrow arguments too—there were four or five—because we wanted to win the case; but we felt the best, the ultimate way to win the case was to go after the prohibition on its face—in other words, to take the whole thing on."[4]

Olson was aware that Scalia, Thomas, and Kennedy in the *Wisconsin Right to Life* decision had said they would strike down the ban on corporate spending in *McConnell* and the 1990 *Austin* decision. And the reasoning of the majority in the *Austin* decision, he said, was "very mushy."

But there was a problem in pushing the Court to overrule those decisions. Citizens United had dropped the facial challenge from its lawsuit in the lower court. The government never had an opportunity to respond to that challenge, and the court never built a record or made a ruling on it. So the facial constitutionality issue was not before the justices.

The justices generally reject attempts by lawyers to raise new issues after the Court has granted review on a specific issue.

"We had to be careful how we wrote the brief," said Olson. "It took a lot of work to make sure we didn't anger the Court."

There was concern with how far Roberts would be willing to go in terms of overruling the earlier decisions, recalled Boos. "That also was one of Jim Bopp's main concerns. The chief justice had just one year earlier authored the *WRTL* opinion in which they didn't go all the way. By overruling *Austin*, you were essentially taking the *WRTL* opinion and rendering it moot. We wanted options on the table that we could win if it turned out the majority was not prepared to go that far."

In his main brief to the Court, Olson flipped the emphasis in Citizens United's initial appeal from the disclosure requirements to the movie. He attacked the constitutionality of the corporate funding ban as applied to *Hillary: The Movie*.

"Although Senator Clinton's candidacy was the backdrop for the 90-minute documentary, neither the movie's narrator nor any of the individuals interviewed during the movie expressly advocated her election or defeat as President," he argued. "The movie instead presents a critical assessment of Senator Clinton's record as a U.S. Senator and as First Lady in order to educate viewers about her political background."

The interest in preventing quid pro quo corruption and the appearance of corruption, which justifies the electioneering ban, he said, is "categorically inapplicable" to feature-length movies distributed through video on demand. Viewers must affirmatively request those movies, he explained, and so the movies are "far less likely than broadcast advertisements to reach and persuade undecided voters and thereby influence the outcome of an election."

Olson then, in just two paragraphs, attacked the 1990 ruling in *Austin v. Michigan Chamber of Commerce* upholding a state ban on the use of corporate treasury funds for independent spending. That decision, he wrote, which held that the government had a compelling interest in preventing the "corrosive and distorting effects of immense aggregations of wealth that are accumulated with the help of the corporate form," was wrongly decided. It should be overruled, he charged, because it was "flatly at odds with the well-established principle that First Amendment protection does not depend on the identity of the speaker."

Regardless, *Austin*'s reasoning, he added, does not apply to *Hillary: The Movie* because it was funded overwhelmingly by donations from individuals, not corporations.

Finally, he argued that the law's disclosure, reporting, and disclaimer requirements were unconstitutional as applied to the ads for the movie. Because the lower court had found that the ads were not express advocacy or its functional equivalent, the government had no compelling or lesser interest in applying the requirements to the ads.

When the deadline came for the government's response, Barack Obama had won the presidency and Bush solicitor general Gregory Garre had left office. Edwin Kneedler, the highly regarded senior career deputy solicitor general, stepped into the role of acting solicitor general. He and Deputy Solicitor General Malcolm Stewart came out swinging in their response.

From beginning to end, the message of *Hillary: The Movie* is that

"Clinton's character, beliefs, qualifications, and personal history make her unsuited to the office of President of the United States," they told the Court. The film repeatedly impugned her honesty and character, they added, and allegations in the film were tied to her fitness for elective office. There was no question that the movie was "the functional equivalent" of express advocacy and subject to the electioneering communications provision.

Distributing the movie as video on demand did not give it a special status or exemption from the law, the government also argued. Paying a cable group to distribute the movie as video on demand was no different from buying broadcast time for an infomercial as had been done by political candidates for years, it told the Court. And the public's interest in full information about participants in elections was directly implicated by broadcast ads, it added, whether those ads were considered campaign advocacy or not.

Outside the Court, the case was slowly attracting attention. Ten amicus briefs supporting Citizens United were filed by conservative, libertarian, and business organizations, such as the Cato Institute and the U.S. Chamber of Commerce. The government drew support from two: a brief by Senators McCain and Feingold and former Representative Martin Meehan of Massachusetts, and another by the Center for Political Accountability.

While giving the Court a menu of reasons to rule narrowly for his client, Olson had planted the seed for a bolder step, but the question remained whether Roberts and Alito would take it.

As the March 2009 argument date moved closer for Olson and his legal team, the term itself was gaining momentum. Race was back on the docket in two cases, one involving voting rights and one concerning employment discrimination. And there was another campaign finance case, an unusual challenge that would play a small role in Citizens United's case and would inspire John Grisham's novel *The Appeal*.

The campaign finance case involved judges, money, bias, and a bitter battle between competing West Virginia coal companies. Hugh Caperton of Harman Mining Co. won a $50 million jury award in 2002 against Don Blankenship, president of Massey Energy, because of Blankenship's interference with Caperton's coal contracts. Caperton lost his business and almost everything he owned and his employees lost their jobs.[5] (Blankenship and Massey Energy owned the Upper Big Branch mine where an explosion in 2010 killed twenty-nine miners, the worst U.S. coal-mining disaster since 1970.)

Between the jury verdict and Blankenship's appeal in 2006, a closely fought campaign unfolded for a seat on the West Virginia Supreme Court between the incumbent justice and an attorney, Brent Benjamin. Blankenship spent $3 million in that contest, most of which went to an organization known as "And for the Sake of the Kids." The organization's goal was to defeat the incumbent, and about $517,000 of the $3 million was spent in direct support of Benjamin.[6]

The high-stakes contest attracted national and state media attention. And the local media reported Blankenship's contributions and noted his likely appeal of the $50 million jury verdict to the state supreme court. Brent Benjamin was elected and seated in 2004.

When Blankenship's appeal came before the state appellate court, Caperton twice moved to recuse Benjamin because Blankenship's "extraordinary" financial support for Benjamin's campaign created an unacceptable appearance of impropriety. The court denied Caperton's first motion and then voted 3–2, with Benjamin joining the majority, to reverse the $50 million verdict won by Caperton. Caperton made a second recusal motion as part of his request for a rehearing. Benjamin again refused to step aside, and then in the role of acting chief justice because of two other justices' recusals related to Blankenship, appointed two state circuit judges for the rehearing. He and his colleagues again voted 3–2 to reverse the verdict.

Caperton, represented by Olson, appealed to the U.S. Supreme Court.[7] During his argument to the Court, Olson told the justices that the Constitution's guarantee of due process required a fair trial in a fair tribunal. Fairness means not only the absence of actual bias, he added, but the absence of the appearance of bias, the probability of bias, or the likelihood of bias. West Virginia's Justice Benjamin should have stepped aside from Blankenship's appeal because of the probability of bias.

Scalia, Roberts, Kennedy, and others pushed Olson hard for a concrete standard or test for judges' recusals in these situations and questioned whether the issue should be left to the states to handle through their campaign finance laws instead of creating a constitutional standard.

"You really have no test other than probability of bias," said Scalia. "We can't run a system on such a vague standard."

Olson countered, "The circumstance in this case involves the appearance of judges being bought." The Court has repeatedly said actual bias, he added, is impossible to prove. "That's why the appearance of probability of bias is so important to the respect that we need to have for the judicial system."

Scalia, openly hostile to restrictions on money in elections, surprisingly suggested that state limits on spending and contributions to political committees could solve the due process problem. And Roberts wondered if that approach would "constitutionalize McCain-Feingold at the state level."

The case was not about the First Amendment or McCain-Feingold, which figured in Citizens United's appeal, but it was about independent campaign expenditures and the appearance of corruption, or more specifically, bias. Just how the Roberts Court answered the constitutional question, thought those watching it closely, could shed light on what the justices might do in *Citizens United*.

Olson had less than a month between his argument in *Caperton* and the arguments in *Citizens United*, but he again was no stranger to campaign finance law, having led the government's defense of McCain-Feingold in the *McConnell* challenge six years earlier. His interest in that area of the law actually began in the late 1960s when, as a young lawyer, he started getting involved in politics. William French Smith, the senior partner at Olson's law firm and later President Ronald Reagan's first attorney general, would send Olson out to give speeches for Republican candidates.

"It was a whole lot simpler back then," recalled Olson. "Campaign finance is fundamental to how we elect people today. You have this tension between people who want good government and don't like elections being overwhelmed by money. On the other hand, I believe you've got to let the process work. If there is any reason for the First Amendment at all, it isn't about protecting naked dancers but protection for talking about government and who shall lead this country."

Citizens United's case was particularly interesting to him, he added, because it involved the First Amendment and corporations.

Like many lawyers who appear regularly in the Supreme Court, Olson had a routine for getting ready for arguments. He collected binders of all of the relevant cases and binders for the briefs, with a set at his office and a set at his home. He read everything in the binders, took notes in longhand, and prepared a list of questions. Three other lawyers from his firm—part of Olson's team—did the same.

"I had some of the younger lawyers prepare an analysis of each of the justices based on how they might come out, from most likely to least likely to vote for us, and in several pages on how they came to that conclusion," said Olson. "I ultimately have thirty pages of analysis so I can focus on each of [the justices]." And as with all of his Supreme Court cases, he did two to three mock "moot" court arguments to get ready.

On the government's side, Deputy Solicitor General Malcolm Stewart, a former clerk to Justice Harry Blackmun, was handling the argument in defense of the law's corporate financing ban. Stewart, a career attorney in the Office of the Solicitor General, had been promoted to deputy from assistant to the solicitor general shortly before the term began. He had been in the office for sixteen years, twice had received one of the Justice Department's highest honors, and often had argued complex regulatory cases, such as issues involving taxes and the environment. There are four deputies—three career attorneys and one political appointee—and seventeen assistants who appear before the Supreme Court and federal appellate courts. They are generally viewed by other lawyers as the *crème de la crème* of government attorneys.

The office has a two-moot-court rule for its lawyers, which was part of Stewart's own preparation for the *Citizens United* arguments.

The justices also geared up for the arguments, and their routine, not surprisingly, varied by each chamber. Besides mastering the arguments in the briefs and the lower court's decision, the justices are aided by their clerks. Some justices require bench memos about the cases. Ginsburg's clerks typically prepared long memos, but Scalia asked for a maximum of two pages, 14-point font, and the clerk's personal decision on the case. Justice Sonia Sotomayor, who would join the Court later in 2009, required rigorous, detailed memos with a table of contents. Other justices preferred an informal conversation with their clerks. Regardless of their routine, the justices on this Court are exceptionally well prepared and primed for verbal battle with the lawyers before them.

Citizens United's case was the only argument scheduled for the morning of March 24. Bossie, his wife, and Boos took seats in the courtroom about a half hour before the 10 am start time. The courtroom seemed small, thought Bossie as he waited, but as he gazed at the nine empty chairs of the justices and the ornate ceiling which told the history of law, he began to feel overwhelmed by the seriousness of what was about to take place. Olson sat at the lawyers' table in front of the justices' bench and to the left of the lectern that separated the two sides in the case. Stewart, dressed in the formal gray morning coat worn for decades by members of the Office of the Solicitor General, and his colleagues sat to the right of the lectern, the official seat of the government.

After the traditional "Oyez, Oyez" call by the Court's marshal, the justices took their seats and Olson began his argument. In a conversational yet firm tone, Olson told the justices that a ninety-minute documentary, like *Hillary: The Movie*, was not what Congress intended to prohibit in the McCain-Feingold law.

Congress was going after "short, punchy" advertisements that viewers have no choice in seeing, he argued. A ninety-minute documentary offered by a small, ideological corporation to people who choose to view it does not pose any threat of quid pro quo corruption or its appearance. And, he stressed, this movie was not the "functional equivalent of express advocacy," the test for regulation of electioneering communications. Instead, the movie was a long discussion of the record of a public figure—qualifications, history, and conduct—who was running for office.

Three justices—Souter, Breyer, and Ginsburg—pushed back at Olson's characterization of the movie. Souter, quoting the movie and its ads, read in his distinctive New England accent: She will lie about anything. She is deceitful. She is ruthless, cunning, dishonest, do anything for power, will speak dishonestly, reckless, a congenital liar, not qualified as commander in chief. "I mean, this sounds to me like campaign advocacy," he said with a trace of amusement. Breyer said he had seen the movie "and it's not a musical comedy." And Ginsburg added, "If that isn't an appeal to voters, I can't imagine what is."

Scalia rescued Olson at one point by noting that the kind of speech in a serious ninety-minute documentary may be entitled to more constitutional protection than the short, punchy ads, particularly speech that is not only offered to but invited by the listener who will pay for it, as in video on demand. "I agree with that completely," Olson responded, and he then reserved the remainder of his thirty-minute argument time for a rebuttal to the government.

Malcolm Stewart, more formal in style, argued that the functional equivalence test in *Wisconsin Right to Life* did not depend on the length of the advertisement or the medium used. Shortly afterward, Justice Alito launched a series of questions that soon dominated Stewart's argument. Alito, who often sits with chin in hand and a slightly puzzled look on his face, does not ask questions as frequently as some of his colleagues, but when he does, they reflect a sharply analytical mind that zeroes in on an argument's weakness.

Alito asked if the Constitution required Congress to limit, as it did, the corporate financing ban to broadcast and cable communications, or could the ban apply to communications distributed through the Internet, books, or DVDs? Stewart replied that the restrictions could have been applied to additional media to the extent they were constitutional under the Court's *Wisconsin Right to Life* decision.

"That's pretty incredible," said Alito, as an audible gasp slipped from the audience at Stewart's response. "You think that if a book was published, a campaign biography that was the functional equivalent of express advocacy, that could be banned?" Stewart calmly answered, "I'm not saying it could be banned. I'm saying Congress could prohibit the use of corporate treasury funds."

The deputy tried to explain that the statute contained a media exemption, but Alito interjected, "I'm not asking what the statute says. The government's position is that the First Amendment allows the banning of a book if it's published by a corporation?" Stewart gamely responded, "Because the First Amendment refers both to freedom of speech and of the press, there would be a potential argument that media corporations, the institutional press, would have a greater First Amendment right."

At that point, Roberts led Stewart through a series of hypotheticals about Kindles and books, books that mention a candidate's name once, 500-page books that at the very end say, "Vote for *X*." "Our position would be that the corporation could be required to use PAC funds rather than general treasury funds," said Stewart. "And if they didn't, you could ban it?" asked Roberts. "If they didn't, we could prohibit the publication of the book using corporate treasury funds," repeated Stewart.

Breyer stepped in, saying the answer to whether the government can ban labor unions, corporations, or environmentalists from saying they love *A*, *B*, or *C*, is "of course the government can't ban that. The only question is who's paying for it. And they can make a determination of how much money the payors can pay, but you can't ban it." Stewart agreed. "That's correct."

The deputy solicitor general told the justices that what made *Citizens United* an "easy" case was not simply that the movie repeatedly criticized Hillary Clinton's character and integrity. "The clincher is that the film repeatedly links Senator Clinton's purported character flaws to her qualifications for president."

In his rebuttal, Olson immediately picked up on the book-banning exchange with Stewart and said it was clear that the government believed any form of express advocacy by a corporation can be prohibited, whether books, yard signs, newspapers—anything in printed form. But Breyer rejoined, "Of course you can't prohibit all those things. What you do is put limitations on the payment for them. See that there are other ways of paying, say as PACs, and then limit very carefully the media that are affected and the times for which they are affected." Those reforms are in the statute, he added.

Olson replied that five justices in *Wisconsin Right to Life* had said the PAC mechanism was burdensome and expensive, and, he added, it is particularly burdensome on small corporations—the least capable of communicating.

When the hour-long, swiftly paced argument ended, the lingering image in most observers' minds was of the government banning books. Despite Stewart's attempt to apply the language of the law and the Roberts Court's most recent interpretation of it to Citizens United's movie, what emerged from the arguments was a clear indication that five justices might be ready to overturn the 2003 decision upholding the McCain-Feingold law, and by doing that, fundamentally change political campaigns.

"Malcolm Stewart has huge integrity," recalled Bossie. "It certainly didn't sound good for their side when he said they can ban books. It really made us think we could win this thing. All I wanted to do was win something."

"After that it was just a waiting game," said Boos. Bossie added, "And the waiting game was really hard."

Shortly before the arguments in *Citizens United*, a new solicitor general had come into office to represent the government before the Court: Elena Kagan, the forty-nine-year-old dean of Harvard Law School and a former adviser in the Clinton White House's domestic policy office, was tapped by President Obama to head the office. Kagan, the first woman to fill that post, was widely admired for her brilliance and her management of the law school and her ability to bring together colleagues with diverse viewpoints. Her ties to Obama went back to their days in Chicago where she was a tenured professor at the University of Chicago School of Law and he was a part-time lecturer.

Kagan's chief deputy in the office was Principal Deputy Solicitor General Neal Katyal, a highly respected constitutional law scholar at Georgetown University Law Center. Kagan, a former clerk to Justice Thurgood Marshall, not only had never argued before the Supreme Court but had never argued a case in any court. When he moved into the Office of Solicitor General, Katyal, a former Breyer clerk, had made just two Supreme Court arguments, the most important of which was his victory in *Hamdan v. Rumsfeld* during the first term of the Roberts Court. A 5–3 Court struck down the military commissions established by the Bush administration and Congress to try Guantánamo Bay detainees in the war on terror.

One of the brightest lawyers of his generation, the soft-spoken, unflappable Katyal, just thirty-nine at the time, would play a key role in the defense of Obama's Affordable Care Act, a legal battle just one year away.

That spring, the Court itself was on the brink of another transition. In April 2009, rumors that David Souter would retire flew across airwaves and blog posts. The telltale sign? Although Souter was generally among the last of the justices to hire clerks for a new term, he had not begun to interview potential clerks by mid-April for the coming term. The eccentric Souter, a Yankee Republican who wrote with a fountain pen, worked by natural light until forced to turn on a lamp, and eschewed computers, never grew to like Washington even after nearly two decades on the Court, and he never hid his desire to return eventually to his home in New Hampshire.

Souter's official retirement announcement would not come until

May 1. Before that, however, he and his colleagues had the term's final round of arguments to hear, and on that April calendar were two of the term's biggest cases once again raising questions involving race discrimination.

The city of New Haven, Connecticut, administered promotion exams in 2003 to eligible firefighters. When the test results came back, they showed dramatic racial disparities. The pass rate of black candidates on exams for captain and lieutenant was about one half the pass rate of white candidates, and out of nineteen possible candidates for promotion to the fifteen available positions, no black firefighter scored high enough to qualify.

If it certified the test results, the city worried it could be sued by black firefighters for so-called disparate impact discrimination, which occurs when a policy or practice—neutral on its face—adversely affects a protected class of people. The city held several days of public hearings on whether to certify. At the end of the hearings, the city's civil service board voted 2–2, which left the results uncertified. Soon afterwards, a group of white and one Hispanic firefighter sued the city, charging that its refusal to certify the results discriminated against them on the basis of race in violation of the Fourteenth Amendment's equal protection clause and the ban on disparate treatment (intentional) discrimination in the nation's major job bias law: Title VII.

The backdrop to the case, *Ricci v. DeStefano*, was a long history of racial discrimination in the hiring and promotions of firefighters across the country. That discrimination had proven to be more difficult to eliminate than in any other public or private sector employment, according to briefs filed by civil rights groups in the case.

"The case involving the firefighters was terribly difficult," recalled one justice, adding it was harder than the Seattle and Louisville school cases.

The difficulty for the Court was that the *Ricci* case pitted two critical prohibitions in Title VII against each other: the bans on disparate impact and on disparate treatment discrimination on the basis of race, color, gender, religion, and national origin. New Haven believed it would be sued whatever it did with the test results.

During the *Ricci* argument, Justice Souter summed up the dilemma for employers by saying it was a "damned if you do, damned if you don't situation."

The case also was difficult because it cracked open again the divide among the justices on how to view racial classifications. John Roberts had come to the Court deeply skeptical of all such classifications, and by the time he wrote his opinion in the Seattle and Louisville school cases in 2007, his skepticism had changed to overt hostility.

Roberts pressed the city's lawyer on why the city's failure to certify the test results was not intentional discrimination. "There are particular individuals here and they say they didn't get their jobs because of intentional racial action by the city," said the chief justice.

The city, supported by the United States, argued that it was trying to comply with Title VII and that declining to use the results of a flawed test was a race-neutral decision. In the end, no one was promoted. That decision, the United States also agreed, was not equivalent to prohibited racial balancing or imposing quotas.

However, the white firefighters' lawyer countered that specific individuals had earned their promotions, "and then the city says too many non-minorities passed this test, and we are going to scuttle these results based on identifiable individuals who have passed and not based on anything approaching a demonstration that there is actually any disparate impact liability." More is needed from the city than simply saying it was acting in good faith, he said.

The *Ricci* case and its final decision would take on even greater prominence later that summer during the Senate Judiciary Committee's hearings on President Obama's nomination of Judge Sonia Sotomayor to succeed Souter. Sotomayor sat on the three-judge appellate panel that ruled against the white firefighters, who then took their appeal to the

Supreme Court. Her role in the case would become a target for Senate Republicans and others opposing her nomination.

On the term's final day of arguments, the justices took up the second race-related case, a potential blockbuster involving race in a very different context. Chief Justice Roberts would lead the Court's decision, and that decision may well have been the unusual precursor to Roberts's ruling in the landmark health care case in 2012.

The Voting Rights Act of 1965 took center stage in *Northwest Austin Municipal Utility District No. 1 v. Holder*, commonly called *NAMUDNO*. By 1965, violence and other acts of terrorism had injured and taken the lives of voting rights activists in southern states hostile to giving black Americans the full enjoyment of their rights under the Fifteenth Amendment. The U.S. Department of Justice was making little headway in fighting discriminatory voting practices on a case-by-case basis in those states because as soon as it won a case against one particular discriminatory practice, a new practice would emerge to replace it.[8]

President Lyndon Johnson and Congress decided that tougher, more effective anti-discrimination laws were needed. The result was the Voting Rights Act, considered the nation's most effective civil rights law. The act has two critical provisions, one permanent—Section 2—and the other temporary but periodically reauthorized by Congress—Section 5.

The act's Section 2 bans racial discrimination in voting nationwide. Section 5 requires certain state and local jurisdictions with a history of voting discrimination to obtain federal approval (known as "preclearance") of proposed changes in their voting or election procedures. Those so-called covered jurisdictions (nine states and portions of seven others) must demonstrate either to the Justice Department or the federal district court in Washington, D.C., that the proposed change does not have the purpose or effect of denying the right to vote on account of race, color, or language-minority status. Covered jurisdictions could bail out by showing they had not run afoul of the act for the past five years. Section 5 is widely regarded as the heart of the Voting Rights Act.

By 2009, when the justices took up the *NAMUDNO* case, Congress had reauthorized the act five times, most recently in 2006 when the House and Senate, by an overwhelmingly bipartisan vote, extended its provisions for an additional twenty-five years. Congress acted after holding twenty hearings and collecting more than 17,000 pages of testimony documenting the continued need for the act.

Ten days after the 2006 extension was signed by President George W. Bush, the Northwest Austin Municipal Utility District No. 1, a small water district within Austin and Travis counties in Texas (a covered jurisdiction), challenged the act in federal district court. Edward Blum, head of the one-man, conservative activist organization the Project on Fair Representation, recruited the water district in order to make the constitutional challenge to Section 5.

Blum, a non-lawyer, is a longtime opponent of race-based laws, who raises funds and finds lawyers to bring lawsuits against racial classifications by public entities. He is the moving force behind the affirmative action challenge to the University of Texas's admissions policy scheduled for argument and decision in the 2012–13 Supreme Court term, as well as another Section 5 voting rights challenge to be decided in that same term.[9]

Blum's contact with the water district came via the late Gregory Coleman, a former Clarence Thomas clerk, a former Texas solicitor general, and a formidable appellate attorney. Coleman, who represented the white New Haven firefighters in the *Ricci* case, knew the head of the water district and suggested him to Blum when Blum was looking for a plaintiff to bring the Section 5 lawsuit.

The water district wanted to move its elections from private homes and garages to a school or another public place, but it chafed under the federal law's preclearance requirement for making election changes. In its lawsuit, it sought to use the bailout provision in the Voting Rights Act, arguing that the district had never discriminated in voting and had always received approval for its election changes. Failing that option, it argued that Section 5 was unconstitutional. The federal court ruled against the water district on both claims and the district appealed to the Supreme Court.

During the April 29 arguments, the justices again appeared to split into two camps. Justices Breyer, Ginsburg, and Souter challenged Coleman, representing the water district, on his basic argument that times have changed significantly since enactment of the Voting Rights Act and that Congress could not justify its 2006 extension of the act using the formula and outdated evidence that it relied upon. The three justices pointed to statistical evidence in the congressional record of enforcement actions by the Justice Department that, they said, showed some improvement in voting practices in covered jurisdictions but not enough to justify abandoning Section 5.

However, Coleman countered that Congress failed to compare covered and non-covered jurisdictions to see where problem locations exist today. "Preclearance once again is based on the results—well, whether there was a [discriminatory voting] test or device in the 1960s and the results of the 1964, 1968, and 1972 presidential elections," he said.

His opponent, Principal Deputy Solicitor General Neal Katyal, told the Court, "After 16,000 pages of testimony, 21 different hearings over 10 months, Congress looked at the evidence and determined that their work was not done." Katyal soon faced tough questioning, primarily from Roberts and Kennedy.

Roberts noted that one twentieth of 1 percent of requests for preclearance of election changes are rejected. "That, to me, suggests that they are sweeping far more broadly than they need to, to address the intentional discrimination under the Fifteenth Amendment," said Roberts. But Katyal said the numbers suggest Section 5 is working well and is a deterrent. To which Roberts rejoined, "Well, that's like the old— you know, it's the elephant whistle. You know, 'I have this whistle to keep away the elephants.' You know, well, that's silly. Well, there are no elephants, so it must work."

Roberts also questioned the repeated extensions of Section 5 by Congress since 1965. At some point, he said, it begins to look like it will go on forever. And Kennedy, pointing to the small number of bailouts approved by the government, called bailout an "illusion," which gave him pause as to Section 5's constitutionality.

By the end of the arguments, Section 5's constitutionality appeared in serious trouble with five justices inclined to strike it down. The high stakes in the case were reflected in dozens of amicus briefs filed by a range of organizations, scholars, and public figures, remarkably similar to the outpouring in the Seattle-Louisville school cases.

When a term's arguments end in April, the entire building seems to breathe a collective sigh of relief. Although the justices had been writing and issuing decisions throughout the term, the heaviest writing begins as the arguments end. However, relief this term was short-lived. Two days after arguments in the voting rights case, the White House officially announced Justice Souter's retirement. The justice would not stay until his successor was confirmed, as O'Connor did, but said his last day would be the term's last day. The Court was heading into its third transition in just four years.

Speculation about Souter's successor did not last long. President Obama made his choice known less than a month later: fifty-four-year-old Judge Sonia Sotomayor of the U.S. Court of Appeals for the Second Circuit, the federal appellate court whose territory includes New York, Connecticut, and Vermont. Obama, according to later reports, apparently had focused on the Hispanic American, Bronx-born Sotomayor during his own transition to the presidency some six months earlier in discussions about potential Supreme Court candidates. Sotomayor and Harvard Law dean Elena Kagan topped his list. A questionnaire that Sotomayor completed for the Senate Judiciary Committee before her confirmation hearings began showed that White House lawyers actually contacted her about the potential nomination on April 27—four days before National Public Radio broke the first news report of Souter's retirement.

After the May 26 announcement of Sotomayor's selection, attention shifted again to the Court while the Senate Judiciary Committee, the

White House, and outside advocacy groups prepared for the July 13 confirmation hearings.

In early June, the Court issued the decision in the West Virginia coal mine case—*Caperton v. A.T. Massey Coal Co.* A 5–4 majority, led by Kennedy, held that the constitutional guarantee of due process—here of a fair tribunal—required the judge who was elected with financial support from Don Blankenship to step aside from hearing Blankenship's appeal of a $50 million jury award.

"We conclude that there is a serious risk of actual bias—based on objective and reasonable perceptions—when a person with a personal stake in a particular case had a significant and disproportionate influence in placing the judge on the case by raising funds or directing the judge's election campaign when the case was pending or imminent," wrote Kennedy.

The key factors to consider, he explained, were the contribution's relative size in comparison to the total amount of money contributed to the campaign; the total amount spent in the election; and the apparent effect the contribution had on the election's outcome.

Chief Justice Roberts, joined by Scalia, Thomas, and Alito, disagreed. Roberts said the majority's new rule—that due process requires judges to step aside when there is a "probability of bias"—offered no real guidance to judges and litigants because it was too vague. "This will inevitably lead to an increase in allegations that judges are biased, however groundless those charges may be," he wrote. "The end result will do far more to erode public confidence in judicial impartiality than an isolated failure to recuse in a particular case." Roberts then listed forty questions that judges and litigants will have to grapple with as a result of the majority's decision.

Although Kennedy said the case presented an extraordinary situation, his analysis that large independent expenditures had the potential to influence—corrupt—a judge's judgment would later feed criticisms of his final decision in *Citizens United*. How could those independent expenditures be "corrupting" in that judicial election, but not corrupting or giving the appearance of corruption in other political campaigns?

In June, Citizens United's Bossie and Boos started going to the Court every day on which decisions were scheduled for release. The Court will announce—usually one week ahead—what days will be decision days, but it never reveals the names of the cases.

"We waited and waited and waited," recalled Bossie. "We were thinking if the decision came in the last week or two, it must be controversial. As it came down to the last week and then the last day, we were in sheer panic. How big could this be?"

On June 29, the last day, four cases remained: *Citizens United*; the New Haven firefighters' challenge; the Texas voting rights case; and a case involving the New York attorney general's fight with the U.S. Office of the Comptroller of the Currency over the attorney general's authority to continue an investigation into predatory lending practices by national banks.

Before Bossie, Boos, and Olson took their seats that morning, the clerk of the Court, William Suter, approached Olson and said that he needed to speak with him as soon as the session ended. "I thought, 'What in the world have I done?'" recalled Olson.

Solicitor General Elena Kagan and her principal deputy, Neal Katyal, also were in the courtroom. "And Suter comes up to us and says, 'I need to tell you something very unusual is going to happen,'" remembered Katyal. "And then we said, 'Okay, what?' He says, 'I can't tell you, but you need to know something very unusual is going to happen.' We were, like, what's going to happen? Are we going to have an argument next week or what?" He chuckled in amazement.

The clerk left the three lawyers in suspense as the justices opened their final session. By tradition, a justice who has the majority opinion in a case reads a brief summary from the bench. A dissenting justice also may occasionally read a summary, and that usually signals strong disagreement. The justices read their opinions according to seniority, with the chief justice always last.

Kennedy started off with the decision in *Ricci*, the firefighters' case. Joined by Roberts, Scalia, Thomas, and Alito, Kennedy held that the white firefighters were discriminated against because of their race when the city refused to certify promotion test results because black firefighters had scored so poorly. Although the city had argued it acted in good faith because it feared a disparate impact suit by the black firefighters, Kennedy said, "Fear of litigation cannot justify an employer's reliance on race to the detriment of individuals who passed the examinations and qualified for promotions."

The Kennedy majority said the city had to have "a strong basis in evidence" that it faced a disparate impact lawsuit if it certified the results, and there was no evidence in this case. The majority had created a new standard to apply in these types of disputes, but instead of sending the case back to the lower court to see if the city could meet the new standard—the usual course—the majority ruled outright for the white firefighters.

Leading the four dissenters, Ginsburg also read a summary of her dissent. She noted the long history of discrimination against minorities in municipal fire departments. The majority, she said, ignored "substantial" evidence that the New Haven test was flawed. "By order of this Court, New Haven, a city in which African-Americans and Hispanics account for nearly 60 percent of the population, must today be served— as it was in the days of undisguised discrimination—by a fire department in which members of racial and ethnic minorities are rarely seen in command positions," she said.

The dissent would have ruled that an employer who jettisons a selection device when its disproportionate racial impact becomes apparent does not violate Title VII's disparate treatment bar automatically or at all if the employer has good cause to believe it could not defend the test as job-related.

The decision disappointed both civil rights groups and employers, the former because it appeared to make it harder to weed out the more difficult and subtle form of race discrimination—disparate impact— and the latter because the new standard was rather muddy and likely to trigger more lawsuits. The majority's decision, however, was more restrained than it could have been. The Roberts Court had decided the case under the federal statute, Title VII, and had avoided a more sweeping ruling by deciding whether the city's action violated the Constitution's equal protection clause.

Nevertheless, two dramatically different worldviews had collided again in the Court. In the Seattle-Louisville school cases, the Court's conservative majority said the school districts' use of race as a tiebreaker in assigning students in order to preserve integration was an unconstitutional racial classification just as were those racial classifications that once segregated students. The dissenting liberals viewed the use of race by the school districts as exactly the opposite of those historically used to demean or subject black Americans. And, in *Ricci*, the same majority found that the city violated Title VII's ban on intentional discrimination when it made the race-conscious decision to discard the test results in order to avoid Title VII's ban on disparate impact discrimination. The same dissenters said a race-conscious decision to discard the test because of reasonable doubts about its reliability could not be considered discrimination "because of race."

From Seattle to New Haven, Roberts and his conservative colleagues continued a march toward zero tolerance of government's use of race classifications for any purpose.

After *Ricci*, Justice Scalia had the opinion in the bank case. In an unusual alignment with the Court's four more liberal justices, Scalia held that state attorneys general could enforce their state fair lending laws against national banks. Chief Justice Roberts then announced that he had the opinion in the Texas water district's challenge to Section 5 of the Voting Rights Act.

Defying predictions and speculation after the arguments, Roberts, with only Thomas dissenting, interpreted the law in a way that avoided the constitutional question.

"Our usual practice is to avoid the unnecessary resolution of constitutional questions," wrote Roberts. "We agree that the district is eligible under the Act to seek bailout. We therefore reverse, and do not reach the constitutionality of Section 5."

Roberts, quoting a 1927 high court decision, noted that judging the constitutionality of an act of Congress is "the gravest and most delicate duty that this Court is called on to perform." And while the Court will not "shirk its duty," he added, there is a well-established principle that the Court will not decide a constitutional question if there is some other ground on which to dispose of the case. In the water district's case, that other ground was its argument that it was entitled to bail out of the pre-clearance requirements.

Thomas, dissenting, said he would strike down Section 5 as exceeding Congress's power to enact laws under the Fifteenth Amendment.

Some experts and scholars later would see in Roberts's decision upholding the Obama administration's health care law, where he found an interpretation that saved the statute, traces of this approach in *NAMUDNO*.

Even though the Roberts majority saved for another day the battle over the heart of the Voting Rights Act, the chief justice devoted considerable time in his opinion to explaining why Section 5 raised serious constitutional problems. It was a virtual road map for Congress to act if it wanted to avoid a showdown with the Court. And that showdown was definitely coming. Challenges to Section 5, including one backed by Blum, the same man behind *NAMUDNO*, were already moving through the lower court pipeline. Blum's case, *Shelby County, Ala. v. Holder*, reached the Supreme Court in July 2012, and the justices in November of that year agreed once again to decide the constitutionality of Section 5.

After reading his summary, Roberts calmly announced that *Citizens United* was being held for reargument.

He then read a letter to David Souter from his colleagues in which they expressed "a profound sense of loss" over his retirement, but understood his desire, in the words of the poet Robert Frost, to " 'trade white marble for White Mountains, and return to your land 'of easy wind and downy flake.' " Souter then said he too had a letter to read and told his colleagues, "We have agreed or contended with each other over those things that matter to decent people in a civil society. For nineteen terms, I have lived that life with you, all of us sharing our own best years with one another, working side by side as fellow servants and friends."

Shortly afterwards, Roberts gaveled the session to a close.

In the audience, Bossie turned to Boos and asked, "What the hell just happened?" Boos replied that they were getting a rehearing. "Which instantly means dollar signs to me," said Bossie. "That's the harsh reality to me. The first thing was how much is this going to cost? We don't have unlimited resources. We had to do this for the right reason and we were, but it's a complicated thing."

Olson told the two men that he would meet them outside after he saw the clerk of the Court. He emerged from the building with the reargument order in hand. The order directed Citizens United and the government to answer whether the justices should overrule either or both of two major campaign finance decisions: the 1990 *Austin v. Michigan Chamber of Commerce*, which upheld a state ban on corporate independent expenditures, and that part of the 2003 decision in *McConnell v. FEC* upholding the prohibition on the use of corporate or union general treasury funds for electioneering communications. Reargument was set for September 9, just nine weeks away, and almost six years to the day from when the *McConnell* case itself was argued.

Olson explained the order as the three men stood on the steps of the Court, and he asked them if they wanted to go forward again. "I said, 'Absolutely. Let's go,' " said Bossie. As they left the Court, one question still lingered in their minds, the minds of the government's lawyers, and of those closely following the case: What had happened to trigger the reargument?

The conventional wisdom that day and to this day was that reargument was ordered because the justices realized the breadth of the government's argument and its consequences for political speech when Alito and Roberts questioned Deputy Solicitor General Malcolm Stewart about book banning. The sequence began with Alito asking whether there was a constitutional difference between distribution of Citizens United's video-on-demand movie and providing the same thing in a book. Stewart answered that the electioneering restrictions could have been applied to other media.

His answer led inevitably to Alito's memorable question of whether the government could ban a corporate- or union-sponsored book, and Roberts's follow-up to that, if the book had just one sentence at the end urging a vote for a candidate? Although Stewart was precise in his answer that the law and the government did not ban books or any political speech, only the use of corporate or union general treasury funds for such a book, some justices refused to see the distinction. For those justices, the bottom line was that the book, in effect, might not get published if there were no PAC or other source of funds to publish it.

"Malcolm is such a straight shooter and a great advocate," said a former colleague. "He is not a weaver and a dodger. He sees this as the logical implication of the government's position." Indeed, the Federal Election Commission and the lower district court had found that *Hillary: The Movie* was an electioneering communication and so a book with the same purpose or similar language advocating a vote would fall within the funding restrictions as well. Stewart's answer was based on the law as it stood at the time. To have answered otherwise would have forced him to explain, in answer to the justices' next inevitable question, why the Constitution places a higher value on speech in a book than in a movie.

Despite the conventional wisdom that Stewart's concession triggered the reargument order, a number of justices in later interviews said that the conventional wisdom was wrong.

"There was an intense debate within the Court that I don't think was heavily influenced by what the solicitor general said," recalled one justice. Another justice agreed, saying, "The reargument issue had nothing to do with that, at least not for me. It's a tough thing to hang on Malcolm Stewart." And a third opined that the ultimate decision in the case was never in doubt after the first conference vote.

The key reasons for the reargument order were Kennedy and Souter, longtime opponents on the battleground of campaign finance regulation and the First Amendment. Kennedy had written a draft majority opinion that went beyond what Citizens United had sought from the Court. The opinion achieved what Kennedy and Scalia had long sought: the overruling of the Court's 1990 decision upholding a state ban on corporate independent expenditures, and the undoing of McCain-Feingold's restrictions on electioneering communications funded by corporate or union treasury funds.

Not surprisingly, the Court's liberal wing disagreed with Kennedy. Stevens assigned the dissent to Souter who, in strong words, tore into Kennedy's legal analysis. But his strongest words he saved for the procedural flaws in the way the majority was deciding the case: it was moving aggressively to decide issues that not only had been abandoned by Citizens United in the lower district court but had not been fully briefed and argued before the justices themselves.

Respect for prior decisions and caution in overruling them had been a particular concern of Souter's throughout his nearly two decades on the Court. In the 1992 abortion case, *Planned Parenthood v. Casey*, the plurality opinion, which reaffirmed the landmark *Roe v. Wade*, was written by three justices: O'Connor, Kennedy, and Souter. On the day the decision was issued, each read out a portion of the opinion from the bench. Souter's summary emphasized the importance of respect for precedents.

After his retirement, one of his former clerks said, "None of us really knows to this day what he thinks of *Roe v. Wade* and how he would have voted if it came before him on a clean slate. But the respect for prior decisions and continuity on the Court were extremely important to him. I think he deeply believed the law and important constitutional principles were not things that should vary back and forth depending on new appointments to the Court."

Roberts was ready to put out the Kennedy opinion which had responded to Souter's dissent. Souter went to Roberts to emphasize his point that this was not the way—the right procedure—for the Court to handle the case. Although the justices may write harsh comments about each other's analysis in their decisions, the comments are rarely taken personally or have lasting effect. However, there is what one former clerk from the term called a "protect the institution" button that is pushed when a justice believes the Court is ignoring practices or procedures that protect the institution's credibility and standing. When pushed, it can make all of the justices feel uncomfortable, and perhaps no one gives it more weight than Roberts. Souter pushed the button very hard.

With the end of the term fast approaching, the justices met in conference to discuss the *Citizens United* opinion. There was "intense debate" about what to do. When that debate ended, the justices had reached a consensus that, as Souter and also Stevens had suggested, *Citizens United* should be reargued and the lawyers directed to address whether *Austin* and part of the 2003 *McConnell v. FEC* decision should be overruled. The opinions by Kennedy and Souter were put aside because the case was starting anew and there would be new opinions based on the new arguments. Souter, of course, was leaving the Court and would not be participating in the reargument.

Roberts and the other justices knew the outcome would be no different, but by ordering reargument, the procedural accusation would be put to rest.

"This was really to give the lawyers a shot at answering the question that the Court had raised," said one justice who had joined Souter's draft dissent. Another who was in the draft majority agreed, saying, "Once you decide the issue is implicated, we could have just sailed ahead, but instead we made the decision, no, we're going to take this slowly and make sure we've all given serious thought to what it is."

CHAPTER 12

—◆—

"The most misguided, naive, uninformed, egregious decision of the
United States Supreme Court, I think, in the twenty-first century."
—Senator John McCain on *Citizens United v. FEC*, 2012

Race, guns, and money dominated Supreme Court news over the summer, not in cases being argued and decided, but under the glare of television cameras in a large, crowded hearing room where one of the fundamental exercises under the Constitution was about to unfold.

On July 13, 2009, about a block away from the Court, the Senate Judiciary Committee opened hearings on the nomination of Judge Sonia Sotomayor to succeed Justice David Souter on the Supreme Court. She was no "stealth" nominee in the sense that Souter was when he was nominated. She had the proverbial paper trail, having spent eleven years as an appellate judge on the U.S. Court of Appeals for the Second Circuit, and before that, six years as a trial judge.

Although confirmation hearings in the last two decades had taken on the air of gladiatorial encounters, with special interest groups battling each other more than a contest between the actual nominee and the senators, there was very little for Republicans to use against Sotomayor. Her thousands of opinions as a judge reflected a careful attention to the facts and often narrow, workmanlike applications of law to those facts. And Republicans had good reason to proceed cautiously: her nomination was historic—the first Hispanic American nominated to the high court. Her background exemplified the American dream as she rose from a Bronx housing project to an Ivy League education to one of the country's most important courts, and a popular president in his first term made her his first Supreme Court nominee.

In the month before the hearings began, White House and Justice Department lawyers put Sotomayor through a series of mock hearings in which they played the role of Judiciary Committee members and asked questions based on her record and speeches and statements made earlier about her by senators. The White House also took a page from the prior Republican administration by arranging conference calls with reporters, special interest groups, and political leaders in an effort to shape the message about the nominee.

When the hearings opened in the Senate Hart Office Building, the nation saw a nominee who appeared much as she is today in her approach to legal questions. As she does on the bench, Sotomayor spoke in a careful, deliberate manner, using her hands to emphasize and elaborate. During breaks in the hearing sessions, she seemed to relax as she left her seat and passed senators on her way out of the room. She would stop to chat with both Republicans and Democrats, leaning in close to hear them, touching a shoulder or arm, and giving a quick smile or laugh.

"It was no secret coming into those hearings what the attack was going to be on her," recalled a committee staffer who worked on the nomination. "That also helps frame what the positive case is going to be. It helps to refute or preempt what the negative case is going to be."

The "big" issues for the Republicans were guns, race, and Sotomayor's by-then-famous comment about "a wise Latina" in a speech that she gave in 2001. The gun issue arose because of a decision in which she, and two other judges, held that New York's ban on a martial arts weapon—nunchaku—did not violate a man's Second Amendment rights.[1] Although the Supreme Court in 2008 had ruled that the amendment protected an individual right to possess a weapon in the home for self-defense, the three-judge panel said correctly that the Supreme Court decision only applied to the federal government and it was up to the Supreme Court whether to apply it to the states. Gun rights activists accused Sotomayor of being hostile to gun rights. The National Rifle Association, which publicly rates the votes of members of Congress on bills favorable or unfavorable to the organization, later said it would score a vote supporting her confirmation against the senator casting the vote—the first time it had ever scored a Supreme Court confirmation vote.[2]

During the hearings, Sotomayor continued to defend her panel's decision. However, to repeated questions probing her views on guns, she said she considered the Supreme Court's 2008 decision in *District of Columbia v. Heller* to be settled law and would go no further, explaining that other gun-related issues could come before her if she were confirmed. In fact, those other issues, such as challenges to state laws on concealed weapons and bans on campus weapons, were being pressed in lawsuits around the country, which was why senators on both sides of the aisle, gun control advocates, and the NRA cared so much.

The race issue also stemmed from an appellate panel ruling in which Sotomayor participated. The case was the New Haven white firefighters' challenge before it got to the Supreme Court. The panel, in a one-paragraph decision, affirmed the trial court's ruling against the white firefighters, and she later voted against having the full appellate court review the panel's decision. By the time she faced the senators, the Supreme Court had reversed her panel's decision in *Ricci v. DeStefano*.

Republican committee members criticized her panel's decision for spending only one paragraph on a case raising difficult and sensitive questions about job discrimination; but Sotomayor countered that the panel based its decision on a "very thoughtful, very thorough" 78-page opinion by the trial court. In reaching its own decision, the panel, she said, applied the law as it stood in her circuit, which allowed the city to discard the test results. The Supreme Court, she acknowledged, had now changed the law.

Sotomayor kept her composure even as committee Republicans brought into the hearings Frank Ricci and eleven other New Haven firefighters in blue dress uniforms who took seats behind her witness table. But the GOP senators made little headway against her confirmation with that tactic. When Ricci later testified about how hard he worked to pass the promotion exam, he was asked by Democratic senator Arlen Specter of Pennsylvania: "Do you think Judge Sotomayor acted in anything other than good faith in trying to reach a fair decision in the case?" Ricci replied: "That's beyond my legal expertise. I simply welcome an invitation by the United States Senate to come here today."

Even before she went before the committee, much ink and airtime had been spent on the "wise Latina" comment. It became the basis of opponents' claims that she would be an activist, even racist, justice. In her 2001 speech about how a judge's ethnicity and gender may affect her judging, Sotomayor had questioned a statement by former Justice Sandra Day O'Connor that a wise old man and a wise old woman would reach the same decision in deciding cases. She said in her speech: "I would hope that a wise Latina woman with the richness of her experiences would more often than not reach a better conclusion than a white male who hasn't lived that life."

To senators' questions, she explained that the words were a "rhetorical flourish" that did not work. What she meant by them was that "Life experiences have to influence you," she said. "We're not robots who listen to evidence and don't have feelings. We have to recognize those feelings, and put them aside."[3]

She repeated, almost like a mantra, that her judicial philosophy was "to apply the law to the facts," a mantra that frustrated senators on both sides as well as outside groups and observers for how little it revealed of her approach to fundamental constitutional questions. In the end, however, there was little doubt that Sonia Sotomayor would take her place on the highest court in the land, and she would get there in time to sit during the reargument of *Citizens United*.

As Sotomayor endured the Senate ritual, lawyers for Citizens United and the federal government shifted to warp speed in the face of a brutal, Court-ordered schedule for filing briefs on the Court's reargument questions. Olson's legal team had to cancel an Alaskan fishing trip in August because of the upcoming argument.

"When you know for sure the whole ball game is up for grabs, you take it very seriously," said Ted Olson. "I suspect I spent every bit of time that I spent on the first argument, if not more, getting ready. Even if you think you've got the odds going in your direction because of the way the Court's order read, it always could come out the other way and lots of things could happen."

When a law passed by Congress is struck down or its constitutionality is at stake, the solicitor general of the United States personally takes on the defense. Solicitor General Elena Kagan, on the job just shy of four months, also prepared for the September 9 arguments. The *Citizens United* showdown would be the former Harvard Law dean's first appellate argument in any court.

Perhaps because she was aware of her own lack of experience compared to the career deputies and line attorneys in her office, or perhaps because she has unshakable self-confidence, Kagan immediately became a hands-on solicitor general (or "SG," as it is commonly known), who worked as hard if not harder than anyone in her office, according to lawyers there.

"She took one day off the entire time she was SG," said one former attorney in the office. "She was in every weekend, every Saturday, every Sunday. She is an extremely demanding person and thinks everyone should work as hard as she works, and nobody frankly can. There isn't another human being who can. She just lived it and breathed it."

On her first day in office, the government had a reply brief due in a case. Kagan took the brief, which had been written by one of the office's best writers, and turned it around the same day with more words of hers in it than of the original attorney, recalled the former attorney. "Those first few months were tough on some people," he said. "It wasn't that she was just rewriting briefs. She was just better. It's shocking for people who believe law is about experience. She is really just such a good writer and strategist."

Ted Olson, the Supreme Court veteran, had his routine for preparing an argument. Kagan now had to find her own. She turned for advice to her principal deputy, Neal Katyal, who, like Olson, prepares binders with every case cited in the briefs by the government and the other side. He reads the cases and takes notes. Kagan asked him to prepare the binders. They later began discussions about the issues and the shape of the argument. Kagan also followed the office's two-moot-court rule. Her attorneys and attorneys from the Federal Election Commission held the two mock arguments in which she practiced her arguments. Afterwards, she brainstormed the issues with only the lawyers who had worked on the initial case.

The Court's reargument order had ratcheted up the stakes in what had been essentially a narrow campaign finance challenge, and the implications of that order resounded in the media and the blogosphere. Forty-two amicus briefs attempting to persuade the justices to adopt their viewpoints were submitted to the Court by business, labor, good government groups, conservative, libertarian and liberal advocacy organizations, media outlets, members of Congress and states.

One amicus brief came from the Michigan Chamber of Commerce, which told the justices that the Court was wrong in 1990 in *Austin v. Michigan Chamber of Commerce* when it upheld the state ban on corporate independent expenditures, and the time had come to right that wrong. The chamber's brief was written by the same lawyer who had argued and lost the case nineteen years earlier.

Like the District of Columbia gun challenge, the Michigan Chamber's challenge back in 1990 stemmed from an entirely manufactured case in which the chamber's vice president and its legal counsel chose to stretch the boundaries of campaign finance law. They decided to use the chamber's general treasury funds to support a candidate in a 1985 special election. Although state law prohibited the use of those funds, they picked a candidate, drafted an ad supporting him to run in the *Grand Rapids Press*, and then went into federal court to get an injunction against the law so they would not be charged with a felony for violating it.[4]

The chamber was optimistic about its chances nearly twenty years ago because the Supreme Court, shortly after the landmark campaign finance decision in *Buckley v. Valeo* in 1976, had ruled in favor of corporate political speech in two cases. In the 1978 *First National Bank of Boston v. Bellotti*, a 5–4 majority of the Burger Court struck down a Massachusetts law that banned corporations from spending money to influence a public referendum that did not concern the corporation's business. The majority said the value of speech in terms of its ability to inform the public does not depend on its source. And in a 1986 decision, *FEC v. Massachusetts Citizens for Life*, the justices held that the Federal Election Campaign Act's ban on corporate expenditures was unconstitutional as it applied to a narrowly defined type of non-profit corporation.

Dissenting in both cases was, surprisingly, conservative Justice William H. Rehnquist, who wrote in the 1986 case, "Congress expressed its judgment in [the federal law] that the threat posed by corporate political activity warrants a prophylactic measure applicable to all groups that organize in the corporate form. Our previous cases have expressed a reluctance to fine-tune such judgments; I would adhere to that counsel here."

Despite those two rulings, when the chamber's *Austin* case reached the Supreme Court, a 6–3 majority found support in its campaign finance decisions for upholding Michigan's corporate spending ban. Justice Thurgood Marshall, writing for the majority, said Michigan's regulation was aimed at a different type of corruption from the typical quid pro quo. It was aimed at "the corrosive and distorting effects of immense aggregations of wealth that are accumulated with the help of the corporate form and that have little or no correlation to the public's support for the corporation's political ideas."

He emphasized that "the mere fact that corporations may accumulate large amounts of wealth is not the justification for [the state law];

rather, the unique state-conferred corporate structure that facilitates the amassing of large treasuries warrants the limit on independent expenditures. Corporate wealth can unfairly influence elections when it is deployed in the form of independent expenditures, just as it can when it assumes the guise of political contributions."

Kennedy wrote a dissenting opinion that was joined by Scalia and O'Connor, and Scalia also wrote a caustic dissent, insisting, as he still does today, that speech is speech and the more speech the better. O'Connor later would shift her position toward greater regulation of campaign finances and vote in 2003 to reaffirm Marshall's decision in *Austin*. Kennedy, however, has remained steadfast in his position that the First Amendment and the Court's decisions draw a line between campaign contributions and expenditures, and independent expenditures are entitled to more protection than campaign contributions.

In late July, as the government and Olson and his team continued their argument preparations, Olson received a phone call from Senate GOP leader Mitch McConnell of Kentucky. McConnell, who had filed an amicus brief supporting Citizens United, told Olson that he wanted his lawyer—the renowned First Amendment expert Floyd Abrams—to share Olson's thirty minutes before the justices. Abrams had represented McConnell in the 2003 *McConnell v. FEC* case. Olson told him that the decision had to come from David Bossie, head of Citizens United. Olson then called Bossie and said he needed every second of his thirty minutes and to not give any of it to McConnell. Within minutes, McConnell called Bossie and repeated his request. Bossie told him that he had to consult with Olson, but he was not inclined to give away any argument time. Bossie then called Olson and instructed him to call Abrams with Bossie's decision against divided argument time.

A few days later, Abrams called Bossie and asked if he would object to McConnell filing a motion with the Court seeking argument time. Bossie said he could not stop him and Abrams filed the motion. Olson urged the Court to reject the motion, saying, "While Senator McConnell doubtless has familiarity with the case bearing his name, he does not have any specific familiarity with the record of this case." The government, on the other hand, had consented to participation in the argument on its side by a lawyer for Senators John McCain and Russell Feingold.

The Court ultimately resolved the squabble by granting ten extra minutes to Abrams and ten extra minutes on the government's side to the lawyer for McCain and Feingold, former Clinton solicitor general Seth Waxman. The reargument was scheduled for eighty minutes—twenty more than the usual one hour.

Inside the Court, the changeover of clerks for the approaching new term had taken place, but the new clerks soon were consumed with old business: *Citizens United*. And the Court also was preparing for a new justice. On August 6, the Senate, after nearly twenty hours of debate, voted 68–31 to confirm Sonia Sotomayor. Only nine Republicans voted for her. Two days later, she took the judicial oath, which was administered by Chief Justice Roberts. On September 8, the Court held a ceremonial investiture ceremony in the courtroom where, as her mother, friends, pop star Ricky Martin, Vice President Joseph Biden, and others looked on, Sotomayor repeated the oath and took her seat at the far end of the justices' bench. Shortly afterwards, escorted by Roberts, she took the traditional walk down the front steps of the building to the plaza, where a battery of press and their photographers stood behind a roped-off area for the usual photo op. With a final "Bye, guys," she disappeared inside the marble halls of justice.

The next morning, September 9, the justices gathered again in the courtroom for the start of reargument in *Citizens United* and whether the justices should overrule the 1990 *Austin* decision's ban on corporate independent expenditures and the McCain-Feingold law's prohibition on using corporate general treasury funds for electioneering communications.

Bossie and his wife had waited for seats in the public line outside the Court, but once inside, they were seated in the front of the public section. The courtroom was packed with visitors, including some members of Congress and many leaders of campaign finance reform groups and opposing groups. Directly across from Bossie, about ten to fifteen feet away, sat the two authors of the McCain-Feingold law.

The solicitor general has her own office in the Court as well as in the Justice Department. The court office was under renovation that morning, as was the lawyers' lounge. All of the lawyers in the case ended up sharing space in the clerk's office on the ground level of the building. Although it was Kagan's first argument, she showed no trace of nerves or anxiety. Instead, she spent the waiting time cracking silly jokes for the captive audience.

The government knew that the reargument order was bad news and believed it had been triggered by the book-banning admission. As its lawyers headed into the reargument, they had two challenges: responding to the book-banning concern and defending *Austin*. They felt that if they could take the book concern off the table, they might be able to steer the Court toward upholding the McCain-Feingold electioneering provision. *Austin* was more troublesome. The conservatives on the Court clearly were hostile to the *Austin* decision. It was a Thurgood Marshall opinion. And even though *Austin* was reaffirmed in 2003 by the Court in *McConnell v. FEC*, the Court's membership had changed since then. Should Kagan rely on *Austin* or try a different rationale for upholding the ban on corporate spending?

"What we were trying to do was count to five [justices] and realizing we probably weren't going to get to five, but to the extent there was any chance at all, we wanted to take that chance," said a former lawyer in the office at the time. "But we were not under any illusions."

Olson, first at the podium, opened his argument with a direct attack on *Austin*, which, he said, stood for a "radical concept" that would authorize the government to ban books and signs. Ginsburg soon triggered a series of questions about whether Olson believed there was any difference in the First Amendment rights of individuals and corporations for purposes of campaign finance. "A corporation, after all, is not endowed by its creator with inalienable rights," said Ginsburg. Olson replied that the Court has said "over and over again" that corporations are persons entitled to First Amendment protection. But what about megacorporations, she asked, and megacorporations with foreign investors? Olson said the First Amendment applies and Congress would have to identify some compelling government interest to justify any spending restrictions.

Sotomayor told Olson that although he was making "impassioned" arguments about why current campaign finance regulations and decisions were bad, "there is no record that I am reviewing that actually goes into the very question that you're arguing exists, which is a patchwork of regulatory and jurisprudential guidelines that are so unclear." But he rejoined that it was the government's burden to produce a record justifying its speech restrictions and it had not done so.

Olson had coordinated earlier with Floyd Abrams on how to spend his time most effectively. When Abrams next took his turn, he urged the justices not to rule narrowly as the case was first presented but to decide the constitutional questions now instead of waiting for the next case like *Citizens United* and the next case and the next case, all of which would have some special wrinkle setting them apart from the last one. Ginsburg and Stevens sparred with him on respect for the *Austin* and *McConnell* decisions and noted that their rationales for limiting corporate expenditures went back a half century or longer and should not be so easily discarded.

Sotomayor told Abrams that state and federal lawmakers had worked hard for the last one hundred years to find the right balance between the First Amendment and protection of the election system. A broad ruling, she said, might cut off that future democratic process. And then, in a comment that surprised the audience, she suggested she might be rethinking the basic underlying premise of protection for corporations. She told Abrams, "What you are suggesting is that the courts, who created corporations as persons, gave birth to corporations as persons, and there could be an argument made that that was the Court's error to start with, not *Austin* or *McConnell*, but the fact that the Court imbued a creature of State law with human characteristics."

Olson, seated at the counsel's table, was startled by Sotomayor's comment: "I thought surely they're not going to say corporations are not protected under the First Amendment or the Constitution generally. I thought that was pretty interesting that she would say that." He was pleased with Abrams's argument and responses. "Floyd Abrams is a First Amendment icon and yet he is a liberal," said Olson. "For him to be there and to say, 'Wait a minute; this is about fundamental free speech,' I can say that but I'm not a First Amendment icon. He added a lot of credibility to our side."

Kagan, in a confident yet conversational style, began her argument by saying that the Court for one hundred years had left in place limits on contributions and then limits on expenditures, which were specifically approved in *Austin*. Roberts soon cut to the heart of the government's defense of *Austin* and asked Kagan if she was relying on *Austin*'s justification for the ban on corporate spending: "the corrosive and distorting effects of immense aggregations of wealth."

Kagan said the government's position was similar and that it was relying on the distortion of the electoral process that occurs when corporations use the money of shareholders who may not agree with the political policies that the corporation is pursuing with their money. She also cited the concern with quid pro quo corruption. Roberts pointedly told her that the government was grounding *Austin* on interests that the Court had never recognized as justifying restrictions on independent expenditures.

Justice Alito jumped into the crossfire to note that more than half the states permit corporate expenditures in elections and, he asked, "Have they all been overwhelmed by corruption?" Kagan fought back, saying the experience of half the states cannot be more important than the hundred-year-old judgment of Congress that these expenditures would corrupt federal elections.

Justice Scalia's hostility toward Congress suddenly surfaced as he interjected that Congress has a self-interest and he doubted that a body of incumbents could draw restrictions that did not favor incumbents. Kagan, bluntly but politely, told Scalia that he was wrong. "In fact, corporate and union money go overwhelmingly to incumbents," she rejoined. "This may be the single most self-denying thing that Congress has ever done."

The book-banning question did not come until the very end of Kagan's argument, when Ginsburg asked for the government's position. Kagan responded, "The government's answer has changed," and laughter erupted in the courtroom. Although part of the law extended to full-length books, she said, there would be a good-as-applied challenge to any attempt to apply the corporate treasury ban to books. She added that the FEC had never applied it to books and a book had never been an issue for sixty years. Roberts leaned forward with sudden intensity, saying, "We don't put our First Amendment rights in the hands of FEC bureaucrats."

Seth Waxman stood up after Kagan and stressed one point: if the Court wanted to reexamine the basis for the rulings in *Austin* and *McConnell*, it should do it in a case where the issue had been squarely presented and litigated in the lower court so the justices had a complete record on which to make a decision, just as it had in *McConnell* in 2003 and in other cases. The Court did not have such a record in *Citizens United*.

Olson took five minutes for rebuttal, and then the argument, which had grown from eighty minutes to ninety-four minutes, ended.

After Roberts announced that the case was over, the justices left the bench and the Supreme Court police began to release the audience row by row. As Bossie moved to leave his aisle seat, he met, directly across the aisle from him, McCain and Feingold. They did not know Bossie, but he recognized the two senators and he overheard McCain say to Feingold, "Russ, I don't know how we win this thing." Feingold answered, "This is an uphill battle."

Neither they nor anyone else in the courtroom that morning, except for the nine justices, knew that the battle had been lost months earlier.

The *Citizens United* reargument on that September morning closed out the Roberts Court's fourth term. Although a final decision would not come until the new term, whose start was just weeks away, the case would be officially a part of the October 2008–09 term.

The term that was ending looked something akin to the childhood game of "Simon Says." There had been a giant step to the right with *Citizens United*, which almost everyone expected after the reargument would lift restrictions on corporate and union spending in elections. There had been two small steps back from the brink of major rulings in two race cases. And there had been small but significant steps to the right in three other areas: criminal justice, age discrimination, and the environment.

In that latter category of smaller steps to the right, Roberts led a 5–4 majority of his conservative colleagues in a decision that relaxed the so-called exclusionary rule that requires courts to exclude evidence obtained from an illegal search or arrest. In *Herring v. United States*, police made an arrest based on erroneous information supplied by a police clerk. Roberts and the majority, which had been gradually narrowing the application of the exclusionary rule, said, for the first time, that the rule did not apply "when police mistakes are the result of negligence such as that described here, rather than systemic error or reckless disregard of constitutional requirements." The decision was potentially a broader application of the "good faith" exception to the exclusionary rule.

And in *Montejo v. Louisiana*, Alito led the conservative majority which, in overruling a twenty-three-year-old decision, pared back a criminal suspect's right to a lawyer before police interrogation. But there was a notable liberal victory in *Graham v. Florida*, when a 6–3 majority ruled that the Constitution forbade a sentence of life in prison without parole for juveniles who committed crimes other than murder. Roberts agreed with the outcome but wrote separately to say that he disagreed with a categorical ban on the sentence and, instead, said that judges should take a case-by-case look at whether the sentence should be applied. Scalia, Thomas, and Alito dissented.

Thomas led the 5–4 conservative majority in *Gross v. FBL Financial Services* where, even though no party in the case had raised the issue or sought Thomas's outcome, the majority aggressively moved to impose a higher burden of proof on people bringing job-related age discrimination claims than is required for proving race and gender discrimination under Title VII.

And it was considered the worst term ever for environmental advocates, who lost all five of their cases in the term even though they had prevailed in the lower courts.

After four years of the Roberts Court, Justice Kennedy—as he had since O'Connor's departure—continued to hold the key to outcomes in cases that divided the justices along ideological lines; but he was much more closely aligned with the conservative wing than she had been in her later years on the Court.

The Roberts Court also had shown a willingness to reach out for issues that were not in dispute in the cases brought to them and to move the law in a more conservative direction in decisions such as *Gross v. FBL Financial Services* (greater burden of proof on people bringing job-related age discrimination cases), *Ashcroft v. Iqbal* (a higher bar on people seeking to bring cases in federal courts), and *Montejo v. Louisiana* (overruling a 1985 precedent on an accused person's waiver of the right to counsel during police interrogations).

And despite his commitment to narrow rulings and a modest role for the Court in public policy debates, Roberts had delivered two major "jolts" to the legal system in the Seattle-Louisville school cases and the District of Columbia gun case. The biggest, and perhaps most unpopular jolt since the 2000 *Bush v. Gore* decision, was still to come.

As September eased into October and the start of a new term, Citizens United's Bossie and Boos once again waited and waited. They planned their schedules around the days on which the Court was sitting because when their decision did come down, they had to be ready to respond to media requests for reaction. Olson was in California, where he, along with David Boies, who had represented Al Gore in *Bush v. Gore*, was leading the legal challenge to California's ban on same-sex marriage—Proposition 8—a case that would reach the Court in 2012. As for Kagan and her office, well, this was a new term with cases for the government to pursue.

Guns and the Second Amendment were back on the docket in *McDonald v. City of Chicago*, undoubtedly the blockbuster of the term, regardless of its outcome. Alan Gura, the aggressive young lawyer who won the District of Columbia gun case just one year earlier, had filed the *McDonald* case on the day of that landmark victory. He was now asking the justices to go a step further and apply the Second Amendment's individual right guarantee to all states and local jurisdictions.

The Roberts Court also was continuing its fascination with the First Amendment. Although nearly every term for years had held a healthy number of First Amendment cases, the justices would decide a remarkable five, in addition to *Citizens United*, in its October 2009–10 term. The five cases implicated speech, association, and religious rights protected by the amendment.

Anthony Kennedy is the closest to an absolutist on the First Amendment since Justice Hugo Black, appointed by President Franklin Roosevelt, served on the Court from 1937 to 1971. Black believed the Court should enforce constitutional rights literally, especially the freedom of speech in the First Amendment. On that amendment's command that Congress "shall make no law . . . abridging the freedom of speech," Black thundered, "No law means no law!" The First Amendment in his view was the cornerstone of liberty and freedom of speech was its heart.

Kennedy, however, is no absolutist or literalist; in fact, he has always said he has no particular judicial philosophy, unlike his colleagues, Scalia and Breyer. Instead, his personal views of what liberty and democracy mean, and, in particular, his respect for individual dignity have animated his most important rulings since taking his seat on the Court in 1988.

Those three concepts—liberty, democracy, and individual dignity—lead him to be especially skeptical of government regulation of speech because, as he wrote in the 2002 First Amendment case, *Ashcroft v. Free Speech Coalition*, "The right to think is the beginning of freedom, and speech must be protected from the government because speech is the beginning of thought."

Kennedy is the most reliable First Amendment vote on the Roberts Court, said one of his colleagues, even more than Roberts, who has written a number of stirring decisions protective of particularly offensive speech. But Kennedy has been less protective of some types of speech, his critics and First Amendment scholars note, and that shows a lack of fidelity to the principles he claims to espouse. One example was the 2006 ruling in *Garcetti v. Ceballos*, where he led the Roberts Court's conservative wing to hold that public employees cannot claim the First Amendment's protection for statements they make in the course of their public duties. Richard Ceballos was a deputy district attorney who discovered false statements by a sheriff in a search warrant affidavit. He informed his supervisors, but when they decided to go forward with the case anyway, he spoke to defense counsel about the false statements and was subpoenaed to testify. He subsequently was demoted and barred from working on murder cases. Ceballos sued, claiming retaliation for his cooperation with the defense, which, he said, was protected by the First Amendment. Kennedy basically said government employees who speak in the context of their employment are not speaking as citizens.

Since O'Connor's departure in 2006, Kennedy has been the so-called swing vote in cases that divide the justices by ideology, a position of power that some of his colleagues believe he enjoys. However, the one area of the First Amendment in which Kennedy has been unfailingly consistent is the government's regulation of campaign finances. And it was not surprising, given his vehement dissents in *Austin* in 1990 and *McConnell* in 2003, that he would lead the effort to overturn both decisions in *Citizens United*.

From the fall into the winter of 2009, impatience among campaign finance reformers, speech advocates, news media, and others for the decision in *Citizens United* was building to a crescendo. Editorialists, columnists, and bloggers erupted in headlines: "Supreme Court about to Gut Campaign Finance Laws . . . and Democracy?" "Still no decision on Bombshell Supreme Court Finance Case," "Corporations Aren't People Yet."

On Wednesday, January 20, 2010, a lawyer who worked with Olson on the case phoned Bossie to say the Court clerk's office had called. The Court would be sitting the next day—an unusual Thursday session— and probably would release a decision. When the Thursday session was announced, word spread like tweets on steroids that the reason must be the decision in *Citizens United*.

At 10:01 am that morning, in a packed courtroom, Kennedy ended the suspense by reading in his slightly nasal, stern fashion that a five-justice majority had eliminated the limits on corporate spending in federal elections. The decision also was assumed to apply to independent expenditures by unions and would undoubtedly result in the demise of state law prohibitions as well.

The decision had taken nearly five months since reargument in the case; the likely reason was the time taken to produce the five opinions totaling 176 pages by a bitterly divided Court. Kennedy, Roberts, Scalia, and Thomas all wrote separate opinions, with Kennedy's the lead. Stevens, joined by Ginsburg, Breyer, and Sotomayor, wrote a passionate 90-page dissent.

In opening his majority opinion, Kennedy ironically said, "In this case we are asked to reconsider *Austin* and in effect *McConnell*," ironic because it was the Court, not the parties, that had posed the question. Kennedy, who stumbled and lost his place at times during his reading, said the 1990 *Austin* decision and the 2003 *McConnell* ruling, both of which imposed restrictions on corporate expenditures in elections, were "outliers" in the Court's First Amendment campaign finance rulings. By overruling both, he said the Court was returning to the principle established in its landmark 1976 campaign finance *Buckley* decision that the government may not suppress political speech on the basis of the speaker's identity.

The government could not identify a sufficient reason to justify limits on the political speech of non-profit or for-profit corporations, he wrote. The censorship imposed by *Austin* and *McConnell*, he dramatically intoned, was "vast in its reach."

However, the Court's decision did more than simply return to *Buckley*'s essential principle. Significantly, it narrowed the definition of corruption, the government's justification for regulating campaign money.

In the past, the Court had said that the hallmark of corruption is the financial quid pro quo—dollars for political favors, said Kennedy. But by definition, an independent expenditure is political speech that is not coordinated with a candidate, he said, adding, "The fact that speakers may have influence over or access to elected officials does not mean that these officials are corrupt. The appearance of influence or access, furthermore, will not cause the electorate to lose faith in our democracy."

Stevens called out Kennedy on his view of corruption and independent expenditures by reminding him of the Court's recent decision in the West Virginia mine company case—Caperton—where the justices held that a state judge must step aside from an appeal brought by a man who had made large expenditures to get the judge elected. In that decision, Stevens said, the Court had accepted the premise that, at least in some circumstances, independent expenditures will raise "an intolerable specter of quid pro quo corruption." One consequence of the *Citizens United* decision, he added, would be to unleash "the floodgates of corporate and union general treasury spending" in judicial races. Kennedy parried with just one unconvincing paragraph that *Caperton*'s holding was limited to the rule that the judge must be recused, "not that the litigant's political speech could be banned."

Kennedy also rejected the argument that the law was not banning corporate speech because corporations could speak through their political action committees. He called PACs burdensome, expensive to administer, and subject to extensive regulation. The Federal Election Commission, he added, had created a regulatory regime analogous to a prior restraint of speech because of its ambiguous, multi-factor tests for determining electioneering communications. Thomas wrote separately, saying that the majority had not gone far enough. He said the disclosure, disclaimer, and reporting requirements in McCain-Feingold were unconstitutional as well. No one joined Thomas's opinion.

Scalia butted heads with Stevens over the "original understanding" of the First Amendment and the Framers' views of corporations. Stevens argued that the Framers considered it a given that corporations could be regulated for the public welfare and they had little difficulty distinguishing between corporations and human beings when they wrote the First Amendment. "It was the free speech of individual Americans that they had in mind," he insisted. Scalia countered that the amendment was written in terms of "speech," not speakers.

Roberts too wrote separately and, not surprisingly, devoted his opinion to judicial restraint and *stare decisis*, principles to which he had expressed a strong commitment during his confirmation hearings. He said the majority was correct to reject narrower grounds for ruling in Citizens United's favor because "we cannot embrace a narrow ground of decision simply because it is narrow; it must also be right." After moving step by step through the analysis for deciding whether a prior decision should be respected, Roberts concluded that continued adherence to *Austin* threatened the principled development of the Court's First Amendment case law.

Justice Stevens, eighty-nine, haltingly read his dissent's summary for twenty minutes and had difficulty pronouncing similar-sounding words, such as "corporations" and "corruption." (He later said his performance that morning was a factor in his decision to retire from the Court that term.) He had assigned to himself the *Citizens United* dissent after Souter left the Court, and it owed so much to Souter's own draft dissent that Stevens had included a footnote thanking him. He was later persuaded by colleagues to remove the footnote. Despite his trouble reading that morning, his message in his dissent was clear. Corporations are not human beings, he insisted, and have no consciences or desires. "They are not themselves members of 'We the People' by whom and for whom our Constitution was established."

He emphasized that the Court had improperly reached out for the question it was now answering and reargument did not cure that fundamental problem. The Court could have found narrower grounds on which to rule for Citizens United, and it failed to respect its precedents.

"Essentially, five Justices were unhappy with the limited nature of the case before us, so they changed the case to give themselves an opportunity to change the law," he said. He warned that the ruling "threatens to undermine the integrity of elected institutions around the country."

Lost in the rush of overwhelmingly negative public reaction to the Court's decision was the fact that corporations still were prohibited from making direct contributions to candidates. However, scholars, lawmakers, and others realized immediately that the *Citizens United* decision, resting on the principle that political speech cannot be suppressed on the basis of the speaker's identity, threatened the prohibition on direct contributions, as well as the McCain-Feingold law's central ban on so-called soft money contributions to political parties. In fact, lawsuits challenging those prohibitions were filed soon after.

Six days later, President Obama denounced the decision during his State of the Union address to Congress. Six justices, including the chief justice, sat in front as the president said, "With all due deference to separation of powers, last week the Supreme Court reversed a century of law that I believe will open the floodgates for special interests, including foreign corporations, to spend without limit in our elections." Alito was caught on camera shaking his head and mouthing the words, "Not true," an image later replayed countless times. Roberts pushed back gently in a later speech, saying, "The image of having the members of one branch of government standing up, literally surrounding the Supreme Court, cheering and hollering while the court—according to the requirements of protocol—has to sit there expressionless, I think is very troubling."

Obama's comments in the speech were solely the work of the White House. At the time, Principal Deputy Solicitor General Neal Katyal was concerned that the Court, with which the solicitor general's office has a special relationship of trust, might think his office had participated in the speech decision. Katyal, who once worked with Roberts when both were in private practice, went to see the chief justice to tell him that the office had nothing to do with the speech.

There was speculation that Roberts would not attend the State of the Union the following year, but in a display of statesmanship and courage, he did attend with several other justices. Justice Alito had a prior commitment: a speech in Hawaii.

Some justices in the majority in *Citizens United* were surprised and puzzled by the intense criticism of the decision. "*Citizens United* just restored *Buckley v. Valeo*. That's all it did," said Scalia one afternoon in his chambers. "It had been effectively overruled in *Austin*. There's all this hullabaloo that the Court is upsetting prior jurisprudence. It upset prior jurisprudence which had upset prior jurisprudence which everybody had thought was the law for forty years."[5]

A dissenting justice was not surprised by the public reaction, but instead, "I was surprised by my colleagues' reaction after the O'Connor-Stevens opinion in *McConnell* [2003 decision reaffirming the corporate spending ban]. I thought that [decision] might have lasted a little longer."

There are, said another justice who was in dissent, "tremendous psychological temptations to overrule things. You think, 'This is going to be my only chance.' But it's somebody just like me who ruled. You have a lot of temptations and my advice is to resist them. Keep your predilections in line."

But for the most part, justices who were in the majority remain convinced that they were right and were surprised that the public reaction was not more balanced; after all, this was the First Amendment and at stake was the political speech not just of big for-profit corporations but also newspapers, book publishers, and non-profit corporations.

They showed their steadfastness in 2012 when the state of Montana tried to save its hundred-year-old ban on corporate campaign expenditures by asking the justices to either affirm its own state supreme court, which had upheld the ban, or reconsider *Citizens United* as it applied to state elections. In an unsigned decision that June, the Court summarily reversed the Montana Supreme Court with a cursory statement that *Citizens United* applied. Breyer—writing separately for himself and Justices Ginsburg, Sotomayor, and Kagan—said the four would have voted to hear Montana's case if there had been any indication that the other five justices were open to reconsidering the basis for *Citizens United* in view of the huge influx of money in the congressional and presidential campaigns that year.

Despite the claim by Scalia and others that *Citizens United* simply restored the state of the law to 1976's *Buckley v. Valeo*, which prohibited limits on independent expenditures, the decision by the Roberts Court majority did more. Supreme Court decisions have consequences, and not just for the parties involved in the case.

Citizens United's direct effect was to free corporations and unions to use their treasury funds to air political ads advocating the election or defeat of federal and state candidates. They no longer were required to use the vehicle of a PAC, financed through individual contributions that were limited by law. However, roughly a month after the Court ruled, a federal appellate court in Washington, D.C., relying on the *Citizens United* decision, held that if limits on independent expenditures were unconstitutional, then contributions to PACs that make only independent expenditures (not coordinated with a candidate) could not be constitutionally restricted. That combination of *Citizens United* and the ruling in *SpeechNow.org v. FEC* gave birth to the "Super PACs" that dominated the 2012 election season. These Super PACs can raise and spend unlimited amounts as long as they do it independent of any candidate.

Whether Super PACs are really independent of candidates is debatable because a number of former campaign aides moved to create them and then used their funds on behalf of their former bosses. Federal law requires Super PACs to disclose their donors, and the Roberts Court, all except Justice Thomas, affirmed the constitutionality and wisdom of such disclosure and reporting requirements.

However, campaign donors can evade those reporting requirements—and they do—by channeling their money through a 501(c)(4) entity, a tax-exempt, non-profit organization which, under the tax law, must show that its primary purpose is to promote social welfare, not to engage in political campaigning. Those groups include, for example, the Republican Crossroads GPS, a 501(c)(4) entity, and the Super PAC American Crossroads.

By August 5, 2012, 718 groups organized as Super PACs reported total receipts of $319,137,071 and total independent expenditures of $181,176,796 in the 2012 election cycle, according to the non-partisan Center for Responsive Politics.

Together, the *Citizens United* and *SpeechNow* decisions created a dual system of financing campaigns. Individuals may contribute directly to candidates, but they are limited to donating a total of $5,000 in an election cycle in order, as the landmark *Buckley v. Valeo* said, to avoid quid pro quo corruption or the appearance of corruption. And yet, unlimited money may be contributed to Super PACs, and by mid-August 2012, a small group of the wealthiest Americans was dominating Super PAC donations.

Citizens United also contributed to a new dynamic among candidates—whether incumbents or neophytes—running for Congress, said the longtime congressional scholar Norman Ornstein of the American Enterprise Institute, author with Thomas Mann of *It's Even Worse Than It Looks: How the American Constitutional System Collided with the New Politics of Extremism*. Candidates tell Ornstein that they now have to raise money not only for their own campaigns and the "team" (their political party) but even more funds to try to counteract the anonymous Super PAC that may parachute into their district to spend unlimited funds to oppose them.[6]

"Now, I'm all for everybody having a voice in campaigns, but a campaign, if it is a market where voters are consumers and they are trying to make a choice, the core of the dialogue should be between the candidates and those who are making a choice," added Ornstein, a self-described "raging moderate." If candidates are drowned out because others have superior monetary resources, he explained, "it's like saying, 'Everybody can speak but I'm going to put a gag on you, candidate, and give you a megaphone large enough that you can shatter everybody's eardrums. Oh, and by the way, you're both equal.' That's what Justice Kennedy helped to bring about in this case. I think it's troubling, to say the least."

Ornstein, who was present at the difficult birth of the 2002 McCain-Feingold campaign finance law, argues that what partly motivates the Roberts Court is "an enormously high level of naïveté" based on lack of experience in the real world. "I mean Kennedy as much as anybody," he added. "He is one of these guys who goes to cocktail parties and dinners around town. He likes to be a part of the Washington fabric."

With the departure of O'Connor, a former state legislator and elected state judge, Ornstein noted, the Court now has justices who have never been involved in politics. "They don't know anything about the real world of campaigns. Never been involved in the legislative process. They don't have any sense of the kind of pressures that exist in campaigns."

The *Citizens United* decision, however, changed "every facet of our existence," from greater name recognition to more donors, said David Bossie, the organization's president. "We won bigger than we went for. At the end of the day, we got more than we ever hoped to accomplish by going to the Supreme Court. It's so hard to get to the Supreme Court and so hard to get them to take your case, much less decide it. From about June 2004 up until January 21, 2010, we worked every day to get to that moment."

Citizens United quickly became the Roberts Court's most unpopular decision and the centerpiece of critics' continuing claims that the Court was pro-business. It ranked with the Court's Seattle-Louisville school decision and Second Amendment gun ruling as the most aggressive decisions yet of the conservative Court. It also would be a major focus in the confirmation hearings of the next nominee to the Court.

The Roberts Court, however, was not done with campaign finance limits after *Citizens United*. Before the term ended, the justices, in an aggressive and widely criticized act, temporarily blocked Arizona's public campaign finance system until they could decide whether to hear a constitutional challenge to that system. The Court's action came in the middle of an election in which a number of candidates for state offices were anticipating the system's matching funds.

The Court would agree to hear the challenge in the following term. When that time came, it would not be Kennedy locking horns with Stevens on the First Amendment, but Roberts and the Court's newest justice in what one scholar called "a doctrinal death match between two incompatible world views."[7]

PART 4

—◆—

HEALTH CARE

CHAPTER 13

———

"From day one, we always had the Supreme Court in the back of our minds. We didn't want to get waylaid and some other case gets to the Supreme Court first."

—Former Florida attorney general Bill McCollum, 2012

An exuberant crowd of about three hundred supporters filled the East Room of the White House shortly before noon on March 23, 2010. Just two months after the Roberts Court had jolted the political world with *Citizens United*, its blockbuster campaign finance ruling, the stakes in the upcoming midterm elections and beyond were about to soar again.

As Democratic congressional leaders, cabinet members, and friends hovered around him, President Barack Obama, using twenty-two different pens, signed into law the signature success of his domestic agenda—a success that many of his predecessors going back to Teddy Roosevelt had failed to achieve. The Patient Protection and Affordable Care Act (ACA for short, or Obamacare to its critics) had survived a contentious partisan battle in Congress to offer the hope of health insurance to 50 million uninsured Americans.

Seven minutes after Obama put down his pen, a lawyer in the office of Florida Republican attorney general Bill McCollum electronically filed the first lawsuit challenging the new law's constitutionality in a federal district court in Pensacola, Florida.[1] By the 5 pm close of business that day, three additional challenges had been lodged with federal courts in Richmond, Virginia; Lynchburg, Virginia; and Detroit, Michigan. They had discharged the opening volley in a fierce legal and political battle over the most sweeping social legislation in decades.

Besides their legal arguments, those separate lawsuits shared a common pedigree: the architects of the four challenges were some of the most conservative members of the Republican Party and associated organizations.

There was McCollum, leading ten other Republican state attorneys general whose numbers eventually would swell to twenty-six; Tea Party favorite Ken Cuccinelli, the attorney general of Virginia; Liberty University, founded by the evangelical fundamentalist Jerry Falwell and run by his son, Jerry Falwell Jr.; and the Thomas More Law Center, a conservative Christian legal organization created in 1999 by a prominent Roman Catholic and the founder of Domino Pizza, Tom Monaghan.

Regardless of the courts in which the lawsuits were filed, all four had one ultimate, planned destination—the U.S. Supreme Court—and one time frame: as fast as possible. Although the lawsuits raised similar constitutional challenges, each of their leaders, anticipating a historic showdown with the White House, wanted to have the case that the justices would review. However, conventional wisdom favored the suit by the Republican attorneys general because of its broad attack on the law; and this time, conventional wisdom was right.

Before becoming Florida's top legal officer, Bill McCollum served in the U.S. House of Representatives for twenty years. He held a number of Republican leadership positions while representing much of Orlando, and he was one of the House managers of President Bill Clinton's impeachment trial in the Senate. In 2006, he was elected Florida's attorney general. Slight in stature and with a calm, soft-spoken manner, McCollum jumped into the health care fight while the legislation was working its way through Congress. He was part of a working group of about twelve state attorneys general, led by South Carolina Republican attorney general Henry McMaster, who were outraged by the so-called Cornhusker kickback amendment, a proposal to give Nebraska $100 million to help pay for the bill's Medicaid expansion.[2] The amendment never made it into the final health care bill.

In September 2009, six months before health care reform became law, McCollum spotted an op-ed column in the *Wall Street Journal* by his former law firm partner, David Rivkin, and another lawyer, Lee Casey, both of whom were partners in a Washington, D.C., law firm. Rivkin and Casey had served in the administrations of Ronald Reagan and George H. W. Bush. Rivkin already was advising the Cornhusker group of state attorneys general when he and Casey wrote the *Wall Street Journal* article.

The op-ed piece targeted the proposed requirement that eligible Americans purchase health insurance—the so-called individual mandate.[3] Although the mandate was a "hardy perennial" in health care reform proposals dating back to Hillary Clinton's reform effort in the 1990s, it was unconstitutional back then and "profoundly unconstitutional" now, they argued. The two men had published an article in 1993 raising similar questions about the Clinton proposal. Setting up what would be key arguments in the coming attacks on the Obama administration's health care law, they said the mandate could not be justified as an exercise of Congress's power to regulate economic activity because there was no activity here to regulate.

"Simply being an American would trigger [the mandate]," they contended. And even though the Senate version of health care labeled the mandate a "tax," it could not be based on Congress's taxing power, they added, because the mandate was really a penalty beyond Congress's taxing authority.

McCollum took the article and gave it to his legal staff with instructions to research the constitutional issues to see if there was a legitimate argument that the health care proposal was unconstitutional. "These are career people whose judgment I respect," recalled McCollum. "I don't know whether they're Democrats or Republicans. And they said, 'Yeah, we think he's got a really good point about this, and here's why, and secondly, we think there are other problems, like the Medicaid issue.'

Medicaid was a huge issue for us." McCollum and other Republican attorneys general and governors believed the expansion of Medicaid coverage to low-income parents and other adults would impose a heavy financial burden on state budgets even though the Congressional Budget Office estimated that the federal government would cover nearly 93 percent of the cost during the first nine years and never less than 90 percent permanently.

In November of that year, McCollum, armed with his staff's research, went to the Cornhusker group of attorneys general and proposed a lawsuit challenging the health care act if it became law. And McCollum wanted to take the lead. Most of the group said they would join in such a lawsuit. McCollum then began approaching other state attorneys general around the country.

"Most of the time was spent on trying to corral as many attorneys general as we could," he recalled. "I actually thought we were going to get several Democrats at that point. We ended up getting one who later switched to Republican. I think I know the political pressure they felt." He also brought Rivkin and Casey on board to help with the drafting of a lawsuit.

Rivkin has a "personal passion" for constitutional issues, said McCollum. Rivkin and Casey, friends since 1987, have written about or been involved in numerous constitutional cases and issues since their days in the Reagan and Bush administrations. They confess to "eating, drinking, and breathing" those issues whenever they are not handling their regular law practices. Rivkin, at first glance, appears to be something of a dandy, or at least eccentric, dressed in a purple-striped shirt, purple tie, red suspenders, and purple and green socks. His law office is crammed with antiques on his desk, shelves, and table; an antique rug warms the floor and old maps cover the walls. A chiming clock makes its presence known intermittently. However, he is neither dandy nor fool.

Accepting McCollum's invitation, he and Casey tackled the first, immediate hurdle to bringing a lawsuit in federal court—what is known as standing to sue. A person filing a federal lawsuit must show that he or she has suffered an injury that the court can remedy in order to get into the front door. Although the state attorneys general could argue that the health care law injured them in their sovereign capacities as states, Rivkin and Casey wanted to be sure they had more than that to fight back an inevitable standing challenge by the federal government which, if successful, would kick them out of court.

And so they went hunting for individuals who could claim to be injured by the mandate to buy health insurance, and they also wanted to bring in some organization that could claim standing because its members would be injured by the mandate.

"We had to look for the best possible plaintiffs," recalled Rivkin. "You need to find people genuinely injured, but you also need presentable people, people who look okay and, if need be, can go through a deposition. And then you need an association with sufficient language in its articles of incorporation and bylaws so [the lawsuit] will be germane to its purposes. This is not exciting, but it's necessary."[4]

They found their plaintiffs in two private individuals: Mary Brown, who owned a small auto repair business in Florida; and Kaj Ahlburg, a retired New York investment banker living in Washington State, as well as the National Federation of Independent Business, a small business association.

The question of where to file their lawsuit when the time came also topped their list of strategic issues. They looked for which federal circuit offered the best opportunity for success not only at the district—trial—court level, but also at the appellate level because someone was going to lose and file an appeal.

"There was a considerable amount of thinking on the front end about this," recalled Rivkin. "But the Eleventh Circuit was really the one." That circuit includes federal courts in Alabama, Florida, and Georgia, and its court of appeals is considered one of the most conservative courts in the country.

Because McCollum was the lead state attorney general, Florida became the venue; and the most logical district court was just down the street from his office in Tallahassee. However, logic does not always dictate legal strategy. The lawyers, instead, decided that the court in Pensacola—nearly two hundred miles away—would be their starting point.

"You look at the bench. You look at their opinions and the caseload," explained Rivkin. "You go to the southern district [of Florida] and they've got all the drugs and thug cases and you get stuck there for a long time. And the idea was to punch through quickly." Casey agreed, saying, "Pensacola did not have that caseload and it would be done quickly." And, perhaps most important, they liked the bench: the three federal judges in Pensacola, they noted, were Reagan-Bush appointees.

"So much of the time between the moment this all got started and the time we filed the lawsuit was really developing strategy and trying to build the appropriate parties to the lawsuit," said McCollum. "From day one, we always had the Supreme Court in the back of our minds. We didn't want to get waylaid and some other case gets to the Supreme Court first."

As McCollum increased his efforts to bring more state attorneys general to the lawsuit and held weekly conference calls with those already committed to it, two other key events occurred to support the coming legal challenges. The Tea Party movement, a loosely formed coalition of conservatives and libertarians angry over bank bailouts, rising budget deficits, stimulus spending, and big government in general, emerged seemingly overnight. It successfully backed Republican Scott Brown in the Massachusetts U.S. Senate primary race that November, and his subsequent election dramatically changed the vote calculus for health care legislation in the Senate. Brown won the seat of the late Senator Ted Kennedy, which reduced the Democratic majority in the Senate by one critical vote. Defeating the president's health care proposal soon became the Tea Party's primary goal.[5]

The second key event occurred early that December. The Heritage Foundation, the conservative think tank that in 1989 proposed a health insurance individual mandate but later changed its position, published a "Legal Memorandum" on why the mandate was "unprecedented and unconstitutional." The article was written by three lawyers: Randy Barnett, the libertarian law professor at Georgetown University Law Center; Nathaniel Stewart of the White & Case law firm; and Todd Gaziano of the Heritage Foundation.[6]

Barnett, who would rise to national prominence with his dogged campaign against the health care law, and the two other lawyers carefully laid out their arguments, complete with "talking points," on why the mandate exceeded Congress's powers to regulate interstate commerce and to tax for the general welfare. They created what would become the core argument against the mandate—an "activity-inactivity" distinction: Congress may regulate economic activity pursuant to its lawmaking powers under the Constitution's commerce clause, but an individual's decision to forgo health insurance was both inactivity and non-economic.

Barnett and other academics who supported his legal theory kept up a steady stream of posts on widely read and influential Internet legal blogs, primarily the conservative Volokh blog, in which they attacked the constitutional basis for the health care proposal before and after it became law. They faced pushback from liberal and progressive blogs, such as Balkinization and the American Constitution Society. The debate soon spread to other blogs and the arguments were picked up by journalists in their coverage of the health care legislation, and later by members of Congress and even by the federal courts ruling on the legal challenges to the law.

Barnett, who also was among those advocating the individual right view on guns and the Second Amendment in law review articles and elsewhere at least a decade before, became the public face of the expert opposition to the health care law, appearing on news shows, talking on radio, and engaging in debates. He frequently faced off with Walter Dellinger, acting solicitor general in the Clinton administration and the lawyer who defended the District of Columbia's handgun ban in the Roberts Court's landmark Second Amendment case. Dellinger, a constitutional law scholar, entered the fray on behalf of the Obama White House and did a better job defending and explaining the health care law to the public than anyone in the White House itself.

And yet, until the federal courts began ruling in the health care lawsuits, the arguments by Barnett, Rivkin, and McCollum were considered outside the mainstream or "off the wall," not just by liberals and progressives supporting the law but even by a number of conservative scholars and Republican lawmakers. Former Reagan solicitor general Charles Fried of Harvard Law School, for example, famously promised in an appearance on Fox News to eat his Kangaroo leather hat on camera if the Supreme Court struck down the law, so certain was he of its constitutionality.

"As this developed, we faced considerable resistance by colleagues on the right who again had this mind-set that, well, if it involves economics, then Congress can do it," said Casey. "You found that on both sides of the aisle [in Congress]." His partner, Rivkin, agreed, adding, "Nobody took it seriously. We got slammed and ridiculed a bit."

And there were good reasons for skepticism of their arguments, reasons related to the Supreme Court and its history of interpreting the commerce clause. No Supreme Court in history had ever recognized an "activity-inactivity" distinction in analyzing Congress's power under the commerce clause.

The meaning and scope of the commerce clause, which is inextricably linked to the development of the nation's economy and its ability to address problems national in scope, has been debated for more than a century.

The Articles of Confederation, the precursor to the Constitution, left the regulation of commerce to the states, and that was not working well for the fledgling nation. The states were acting to protect and enhance their own economies in ways that often thwarted the national interest. The Framers' response to the problem was the commerce clause which, as James Madison, the father of the Constitution, explained in an 1829 letter "grew out of the abuse of the power by the importing States in taxing the non-importing, and was intended as a negative and preventive provision against injustice among the States themselves, rather than as a power to be used for the positive purposes of the General Government, in which alone, however, the remedial power could be lodged."[7]

The Constitution creates a national government of limited powers. Congress's powers are enumerated in Article I, Section 8. In clause 3 of Section 8, the so-called commerce clause, Congress is given the authority "To regulate Commerce with foreign Nations, and among the several States, and with the Indian Tribes." Congress is also given the power "To make all Laws which shall be necessary and proper for carrying into Execution" the commerce power—the so-called necessary and proper clause, also in Article I, Section 8, as clause 18. Over time, the Supreme Court has interpreted those two clauses to allow Congress to regulate: the channels of interstate commerce, such as roads and waterways; the instrumentalities of interstate commerce, for example, cars and ships, as well as persons or things in it; and other economic activities that "substantially affect" interstate commerce. Justice Thomas, even before the health care case came to the Court, had never accepted that third category, arguing that it is inconsistent with original understanding of Congress's powers.

The Supreme Court's commerce clause rulings, like its campaign finance decisions, have swung like a pendulum over time, from granting Congress wide latitude to deal with the needs of the national government to restricting its authority and back again. The case that set the stage for broad congressional power over national issues was the justices' 1824 ruling in *Gibbons v. Ogden*, a dispute involving rival steamboat ferries on the Hudson River. Chief Justice John Marshall, known as the "Great Chief Justice" and someone whom Chief Justice John Roberts Jr. has sometimes embraced as a model, interpreted the commerce clause for the first time, giving meaning to its words. He also read Congress's commerce clause power as broadly as possible, writing: "It is the power to regulate; that is, to prescribe the rule by which commerce is to be governed. This power, like all others vested in Congress, is complete in itself, may be exercised to its utmost extent, and acknowledges no limitations, other than are prescribed in the Constitution."

By the end of the nineteenth century, however, the pendulum had swung to the other extreme and the Court began limiting Congress's authority, a period that became known as the Lochner era and that endured for nearly forty years. That era was marked by the Court's protection of economic rights, rights of contract and property. The justices wielded a heavy ax, striking down state and federal regulations of working conditions. The era was named for the now widely discredited 1905 decision in *Lochner v. New York*. In that case, the justices invalidated the New York Bakeshop Act, which prohibited bakers from working more than ten hours per day or sixty hours per week, because the act interfered with the right of contract between employer and employee. And in 1918 in *Hammer v. Dagenhardt*, the Court struck down a federal law designed to end child labor by prohibiting the movement in interstate commerce of any good made by children under the age of fourteen.

The Court's restrictive approach to Congress's commerce clause power brought the justices into a major confrontation with President Franklin Roosevelt, who was dealing with the nation's crippling crisis, the Great Depression, by seeking creative legislative initiatives to get the country back on its economic feet. The Court's laissez-faire approach to the economy ran headlong into Roosevelt's hands-on approach. The Court, not easily dissuaded from its narrow view of Congress's commerce power, struck down the Farm Bankruptcy Act of 1934, the National Industrial Recovery Act of 1935, and a tax on agricultural processors in the Agricultural Adjustment Act of 1933. A frustrated Roosevelt threatened to pack the Court with justices who would approve his initiatives, a threat that badly backfired with the general public.

In 1937, the Lochner era ended when the Court, ruling 5–4 in *National Labor Relations Board v. Jones & Laughlin Steel Corp.*, upheld the National Labor Relations Act of 1935. The board had charged the steel company with discriminating against workers who were union members. The New Deal Court abandoned its view that labor relations had only an indirect effect on commerce and, for the first time, held that Congress could regulate intrastate employment activities that had "a close and substantial relation to interstate commerce."

The pendulum swung even farther toward broader commerce power in 1942 in a case that would loom large in the legal battle over the health care law. Roscoe Filburn was an Ohio farmer who raised dairy cattle and poultry and planted winter wheat, part of which he sold and the rest he kept for use on his farm. The new Agricultural Adjustment Act imposed an acreage allotment on wheat farmers in order to keep wheat prices from crashing. Filburn's wheat harvest violated his allotment and he was penalized 49 cents per bushel. The farmer sued, arguing that the wheat grown over the allotment stayed at home and did not enter commerce. When his case reached the Supreme Court, Justice Robert Jackson ruled for the government, writing in *Wickard v. Filburn*: "But even if [Filburn's] activity be local, and though it may not be regarded as commerce, it may still, whatever its nature, be reached by Congress if it exerts a substantial economic effect on interstate commerce, and this irrespective of whether such effect is what might at some earlier time have been defined as 'direct' or 'indirect.' " The decision is viewed by some as a turning point or a "high-water mark" in the Court's commerce clause jurisprudence.[8]

If Congress could use its commerce clause power to reach Roscoe Filburn's home use of wheat with its minimal connection to interstate commerce, how could it not use the same power to reach individuals who do not buy health insurance but free-ride off of those who do, increasing costs in one of the largest interstate markets today? the Obama administration and supporters would argue later in the health care case.

For the next nearly sixty years, Congress's commerce power grew in scope and became the basis for federal regulation of the environment, food and drugs, securities, and other areas. Racial discrimination had a substantial effect on interstate commerce, the Court ruled, when it upheld the landmark Civil Rights Act of 1964 which banned discrimination in public places, such as motels and restaurants.

However, the pendulum swung back in 1995 when the Rehnquist Court struck down the federal Gun-Free School Zone Act, which banned possession of a firearm near a school zone, because Congress had exceeded its commerce clause authority. The decision, *United States v. Lopez*, was part of the Rehnquist Court's "federalism revolution" in which five justices—Rehnquist, O'Connor, Kennedy, Scalia, and Thomas—prevailed in a series of bitterly fought cases cutting back Congress's lawmaking powers under both the commerce clause and Section 5 of the Fourteenth Amendment while enhancing the rights of states. *Lopez* was followed in 2000 by *United States v. Morrison*, in which the same five justices invalidated the civil damages remedy for victims in the federal Violence Against Women Act. In both *Lopez* and *Morrison*, the majority held that the laws' connection to interstate commerce was too insubstantial. Congress "may not regulate noneconomic . . . conduct based solely on that conduct's aggregate effect on interstate commerce," wrote Chief Justice Rehnquist in *Morrison*.

The Court had not struck down a federal law on commerce clause grounds in nearly sixty years, and the two rulings shocked the political and legal establishments. However, the ground under Congress soon shifted again. Five years later, in *Gonzales v. Raich*, the Rehnquist Court held that Congress did have authority under the commerce clause to prohibit the local cultivation and local use of homegrown marijuana for medical purposes even where it complied with state law. The difference this time was Justice Scalia, who switched sides, joining the Court's liberal wing—Stevens, Souter, Ginsburg, and Breyer. The case of that old Ohio farmer, Roscoe Filburn, played a key role in the decision. Whether it is marijuana or wheat, Stevens wrote, production of a commodity meant only for home use can have a substantial effect on the national market for that commodity. Congress had a rational basis to believe that failure to regulate that type of marijuana would affect the price and demand for marijuana in the national market and leave a huge hole in federal enforcement of the Controlled Substances Act, concluded Stevens.

Scalia, in a concurring opinion, explained why he believed the situation in *Raich* differed from those in *Lopez* and *Morrison*. In *Raich*, he explained, Congress was regulating purely intrastate activity—home use of marijuana—in order to control the interstate market in marijuana. Neither *Lopez* nor *Morrison*, he wrote, involved "control over intrastate activities in connection with a more comprehensive scheme of regulation."

Randy Barnett, who was leading the debate against the health care legislation, had argued and lost the *Raich* case in 2005; it was a defeat not easily accepted. "My interest in the commerce clause came about because of the Raich case," he recalled. "In the late 1990s, I started working first with the Open Cannabis Buyers Club and their commerce clause challenge to the Controlled Substances Act. Then two other lawyers and myself brought the Raich case on behalf of Angel Raich. That was how I started to learn a lot about it."[9]

Lopez and *Morrison*, restricting Congress's commerce power, would become weapons in the arsenal of those challenging the new health care law. *Wickard* and *Raich*, with their broader view of Congress's authority, would be claimed by the law's supporters.

The Roberts Court had little experience with commerce clause cases in its first four terms. However, coincidentally, a month before the health care law was enacted, the justices heard arguments in a case whose decision later that May encouraged White House and Justice Department lawyers and other health care supporters about their future chances before the justices. In *United States v. Comstock*, the justices were asked to decide whether Congress had exceeded its power when it enacted a law authorizing federal courts to order the civil commitment of sexually dangerous prisoners after they had served their prison sentences. A 7–2 majority, led by Breyer, said Congress was within its authority. Breyer relied on the necessary and proper clause, which, he wrote, "makes clear that the Constitution's grants of specific federal legislative authority are accompanied by broad power to enact laws that are 'convenient, or useful' or 'conducive' to the authority's 'beneficial exercise.'" The civil commitment law, he explained, was a necessary and proper means of exercising the authority that Congress has to create federal criminal laws, to punish their violation, to imprison violators, and to protect the public.

Only Justices Thomas and Scalia dissented, with Thomas writing that the necessary and proper clause empowers Congress to enact only those laws that "carry into execution" one of the enumerated powers in the Constitution. There was no such link between the civil commitment law and the legislative powers enumerated in Article I, Section 8, he said.

White House and Justice Department lawyers believed the *Comstock* decision bolstered one of their defenses of the health care law: the individual mandate was a necessary and proper means of accomplishing the comprehensive market reforms in the law, and those reforms clearly fell within Congress's enumerated power to regulate interstate commerce. Roberts had joined the *Comstock* majority and that suggested he might be open to the government's necessary and proper clause argument. And if Scalia remained faithful to his concurrence in *Raich*, the medical marijuana case, they thought, he might seriously entertain their argument that the individual mandate was an integral part of a comprehensive scheme of economic regulation just as medical marijuana fell within the government's comprehensive regulation of the market for controlled substances.

With the signing of the Affordable Care Act and the filing of the lawsuits, the race to the Supreme Court was on. The White House immediately started holding strategy meetings, and so did the Justice Department, with close communication between the two. That closeness was unusual but not surprising, given the high stakes and significance of the massive health care program. The White House wanted to know what was being done.

In another unusual step, Attorney General Eric Holder contacted Robert Weiner, a partner in the Washington law firm of Arnold &

Porter, and asked him to join the department to oversee the defense of the health care law. Weiner, a former senior counsel in the Clinton White House and former Thurgood Marshall clerk, had broad experience in dealing with complex litigation and public policy issues, such as global warming, financial reform, and national security. He agreed to take on the new job as the associate deputy attorney general, and he was as passionate about the health care law's constitutionality as David Rivkin and Bill McCollum were about its unconstitutionality.

"My view from the beginning was if the courts applied the law as it stood, we would win," he recalled. "Whether courts would apply the law at each level was not as clear." The decision by the Republican state attorneys general to file their challenge in the federal court in Pensacola—which had no real connection to the case—was not accidental, he added.[10]

The Justice Department assembled a broad group of its lawyers with trial and appellate experience to participate in weekly strategy sessions. The department's Office of Federal Programs, headed by Ira Gershengorn, took the lead on defense of the law at the first level of courts: the district court.

Like their opponents, the department lawyers faced some early, important procedural questions and two particularly crucial substantive ones. The first substantive question involved the Anti-Injunction Act (AIA), an 1867 law that bars lawsuits that try to block the assessment or collection of any federal tax. Taxpayers who object to a tax can have their day in court after they pay the tax by suing for a refund. The theory behind the law is that without the lawsuit prohibition, the government would be tied up in court fighting tax challenges and never be able to collect the revenue it needs to operate. If the AIA applied, the courts would not be able to consider any challenges to the health care law until the penalty for not having health insurance—enforced by the Internal Revenue Service—showed up on income tax returns in 2015.

Lawyers in the department's tax division pushed to have the government argue that the AIA applied, not because they wanted to delay court action on the health care lawsuits, but because they needed to protect the fundamental purpose of the AIA and not risk having it undermined. "They said that they had a very strong institutional interest in making [AIA] arguments in a variety of contexts and they should be made," said a lawyer close to the discussions.

The second crucial issue in the defense of the law was whether to raise Congress's power to tax as a basis for the individual mandate. Another group in the strategy sessions pushed to include the argument that the individual mandate was a constitutional exercise of Congress's power to tax and spend for the public welfare as well of its commerce power. "The theory was that two arrows in your quiver are better than one," recalled the lawyer. "That faced a lot of pushback given what the president had said about a tax." He was referring to the Obama administration's public, and very political, position that the mandate was not a tax but a penalty, and that the new law did not increase taxes.

Despite pushback from the White House, the department decided to make both the AIA and the tax power arguments in the district courts—the first front in the fast-approaching battle.

At the time, another high-ranking administration lawyer involved in the discussions recalled thinking, "What we should expect is there are going to be district judges who rule for us and district judges who rule against us. And, in part, that was probable because of the [challengers'] ability to forum-shop [search for the most potentially favorable court in which to file the lawsuit], which the other side did effectively.

"Then I thought there would probably be some split decisions in the courts of appeals because there were multiple cases going on," he added. "I wasn't surprised. There's a narrative out there—how the other side was able to take its legal position from the fringe to the mainstream. I think that's a fair characterization of it. You could see that happening; it was distressing."

As the lawyers on both sides prepared to head into district court on health care, a Supreme Court justice, the longest serving among the nine and the unassuming but effective leader of the liberal side of the bench, was preparing to leave. On April 9, 2010, Senior Associate Justice John Paul Stevens informed President Obama that he intended to retire on the day after the Court ended the term for its summer recess. The Court was now facing its fourth vacancy in five years.

Although Stevens's successor would be a Democratic appointee and like Souter's replacement by Sotomayor would not change the ideological balance on the Court, his departure would be felt acutely in a number of ways. The only justice on the Roberts Court with active duty military experience, having served in the U.S. Navy during World War II, Stevens brought a realistic view of government power to the George W. Bush administration's exercise of that power in the war on terror. As senior associate justice, Stevens had the power to assign majority decisions whenever he was in the majority and the chief justice was in dissent. He either wrote or assigned the majority opinions in a series of terrorism-related cases, and those decisions reined in broad assertions of power by the president and Congress, imposed due process— fairness—in the government's detention of alleged enemy combatants, and reinforced the importance of the Great Writ of habeas corpus and the role of the federal courts in the constitutional scheme.

"Unconstrained Executive detention for the purpose of investigating and preventing subversive activity is the hallmark of the Star Chamber,"* Stevens wrote in *Rumsfeld v. Padilla*, the 2004 case involving the American "shoe bomber" Jose Padilla, who was being detained by U.S. officials. "For if this Nation is to remain true to the ideals symbolized by its flag, it must not wield the tools of tyrants even to resist an assault by the forces of tyranny."

He succeeded in those and other 5–4 decisions often because he was able to find common ground with Kennedy, and before Kennedy with Sandra Day O'Connor in other areas of the law, such as affirmative action and civil and consumer rights. He did no face-to-face persuasion of his colleagues in the privacy of their chambers, as Justice William

---

* An early, secretive English court that became a symbol of the abuse of power.

Brennan Jr. often did, recalled some justices, but won their support through the strength of his draft opinions and memos and his accumulated experiences in life and the law.

Stevens also led a "revolution" in criminal sentencing. A concern for due process—or fairness—undergirded his opinions in this area as well as other issues within the criminal justice system, such as the death penalty and the Sixth Amendment right to counsel. In an unusual coalition with Scalia and Thomas, Stevens dismantled the mandatory nature of federal sentencing guidelines that judges were required to follow and reinvigorated the role of the jury in sentencing matters.

During the course of his three decades on the Court, he also made a remarkable journey in his thinking about the death penalty. In 1976, Stevens co-authored with Justices Potter Stewart and Lewis F. Powell Jr. a trio of decisions reinstating the death penalty in Georgia, Texas, and Florida, after it had been struck down by the Court in 1972. Although supporting capital punishment, he sought to constrain its use to the most egregious of crimes and offenders. He wrote majority opinions narrowing the eligibility for the penalty by striking down capital punishment for those under age fifteen and for mentally retarded persons. He also is credited with being particularly influential in the 2005 decision, written by Kennedy, barring the penalty for juveniles under eighteen.

Stevens, in a concurrence to a decision upholding Kentucky's procedures for administering lethal injection, finally concluded in 2008 that the death penalty "with such negligible returns to the state" was unconstitutional.[11] It was the same conclusion reached earlier by two of his former colleagues who voted with him in that 1976 decision reinstating the capital punishment—Powell and Harry Blackmun.

When appointed by President Gerald Ford, Stevens, a federal appellate judge at the time, was known as a moderate Republican. He seemed an unlikely heir to the mantle of "leader of the left" or master strategist of the Court's liberal wing, as some called him. Early in his tenure on the high court he was a maverick, often writing sole dissents or concurrences on issues in cases that failed to move or intrigue his colleagues and were difficult to label as consistently liberal or conservative. He rejected claims by the media and others that he had evolved or become liberal as the years passed. In several interviews before and after his retirement, he explained that it was the Court that had moved much more to the right.

"The makeup of the Court has changed dramatically," Stevens said in a 2009 interview with *USA Today*. "If you use the term 'conservative' the way a lot of people use it, since I joined the Court, every new appointee has been more conservative than his or her predecessor. You can go right down the line," with the exception of Ruth Bader Ginsburg, who succeeded Byron White.[12]

Perhaps one of his most memorable lines in an opinion came in his dissent in *Bush v. Gore* when he wrote: "Although we may never know with complete certainty the identity of the winner of this year's presidential election, the identity of the loser is perfectly clear. It is the nation's confidence in the judge as an impartial guardian of the rule of law."

After his retirement, Stevens said in an interview that he believed the Roberts Court's Second Amendment decision in *District of Columbia v. Heller*, finding an individual right to own a gun, and the Rehnquist Court's states' rights rulings involving sovereign immunity and the Eleventh Amendment, were among the Supreme Court's worst decisions. Ironically, his last opinion for the Court would be a dissent in the sequel to the *Heller* gun decision, a case asking whether the Second Amendment should be applied to the states.

Who among the justices was likely to fill Stevens's role on the left? No one seemed obvious, but then, neither had Stevens after Brennan and Blackmun left the bench. Going forward, when the Court's five conservatives stood firm, Justice Ruth Bader Ginsburg, as senior justice in the minority, would have the power to assign dissents. Appointed in 1993, Ginsburg had carved a niche in two areas: civil rights, particularly those involving the nation's job bias laws; and the often arcane world of civil procedure—rules for conducting litigation in the federal courts. Her diminutive size and solemn speaking style on the bench belied a steely resolve. How she would wield the assigning power, one of the few ways an individual justice could try to control the course of an opinion, when given the opportunity was as yet unknown.

As he had with the Sotomayor nomination, President Obama wasted no time in tapping a nominee to succeed Stevens. A month after Stevens's announcement, Obama named the other person who had been at the top of his list of potential high court appointments even before he took the oath of office. Solicitor General Elena Kagan, who only eight months earlier made her first appellate argument ever in *Citizens United*, got the nod on May 10, and the Court and the country once again prepared for the Senate's exercise of its constitutional advice and consent duties.

At the same time, the Roberts Court was starting its busiest part of the 2009–10 term—the final lap. The *Citizens United* decision, the announced retirement of Stevens, and the nomination of Kagan would have been enough to mark the term as one of the most important since Roberts became chief justice. But there was more to come.

From early spring until the end of June, the justices decided the bulk of their docket. Roberts, Scalia, and Kennedy separately led the Court in four of the five First Amendment cases to be decided. Roberts, in an 8–1 decision in *United States v. Stevens*, held that a federal law criminalizing the creation, sale, or possession of certain portrayals of animal cruelty violated the First Amendment because the law was "substantially overbroad." The law focused on so-called crush videos, which often depict women slowly crushing small animals to death "with their bare feet or while wearing high heeled shoes," sometimes while "talking to the animals in a kind of dominatrix patter." But the case focused on the law's application to videos of dogs fighting with each other or different animals.

Roberts said the law's text applied to any depiction in which "a living animal is intentionally maimed, mutilated, tortured, wounded, or killed." While the terms "maimed, mutilated and tortured" convey cruelty, he wrote, "wounded or killed" do not, and the law could be read to apply to depictions of hunters and slaughterhouses. Although the government argued that it interpreted the law to apply only to acts of "extreme cruelty," Roberts was not persuaded, saying, "We would not uphold an unconstitutional statute merely because the Government promised to use it responsibly."

Justice Alito, who statistically has had the highest rate of voting agreement with Roberts than any other pair of justices, disagreed this time with the chief. He disputed the majority's concern that the law could be applied to hunting and other legal activities, noting that nearly all the states that prohibited animal cruelty expressly exclude wildlife or exempt hunters. The federal law, he argued, could be applied constitutionally to illegal animal crush videos and dog-fighting videos and so was not so broad as to be unconstitutional on its face.

Kennedy soon followed with a 5–4 decision holding that Congress acted properly to resolve a First Amendment violation by transferring land in the Mojave Desert National Preserve, on which a five-foot cross stood, to the Veterans of Foreign Wars. Stevens led the dissenting liberal wing, saying the land swap was an obvious attempt to keep the cross in place and still had the unconstitutional effect of advancing religion.

Seven of the nine justices wrote opinions in *Doe v. Reed*, a decision in which an 8–1 majority led by Roberts held that the disclosure of signatures on a referendum petition generally does not violate the First Amendment. The names and addresses of petition signers were accessible under Washington's Public Records Act. Roberts said the disclosure was sufficiently related to the state's interest in ferreting out invalid signatures and combating fraud. Only Justice Thomas dissented, saying the state had narrower ways of protecting the integrity of the petition process and warning that the Court's decision would chill citizen participation.

The Court, however, departed from its strong speech protection in *Holder v. Humanitarian Law Project*, where speech collided with the war

on terror. A 6–3 majority, led by Roberts, ruled that the federal government could prosecute those who train foreign terrorist organizations
to use peaceful means to resolve disputes for violating the federal law
against material support to those organizations. Even seemingly benign
support bolsters the activities of those organizations, wrote Roberts,
who garnered one vote from the left—that of Stevens. Breyer, expressing his strong disagreement by summarizing his dissent from the bench,
countered that while charitable contributions might free up funds in
those organizations to buy more weapons, the teaching of human rights
law would not.

On June 28, 2010, the term's final day, no one expected Ginsburg
to take her seat on the bench. Her husband, who, she later said, had
been her "chief cheerleader" in life, had died the day before from cancer.
However, Ginsburg had written the 5–4 majority opinion in the last of
the First Amendment cases—*Christian Legal Society v. Martinez*—and
she showed up to read her summary. One of her colleagues later said,
"It was so hard, but Ruth is just so strong." Writing for her liberal colleagues and Kennedy, she said a university's policy that university recognition of student groups required those groups to accept "all comers"
did not violate the First Amendment rights of the Christian Legal Society. The society required prospective members to swear allegiance to
the Bible and Jesus Christ and to disavow gay and premarital sex. Alito
led the dissenters and called the ruling a "serious setback for freedom of
expression."

The decision in the term's second marquee case—the return of the
gun battle—also came on that final day. Repeating the same ideological division that marked the District of Columbia gun ruling in 2008,
a 5–4 majority, this time led by Alito, applied the Second Amendment
and its guarantee of an individual right to own a gun to the states. The
dissenters were again led by Stevens and Breyer, and they were joined
for the first time by Sotomayor, who insisted that the 2008 gun case was
wrongly decided. But even accepting the premise that the amendment
protects an individual right, Stevens said, its obvious purpose was to

prevent elimination of the militia. "It is directed at preserving the autonomy of the sovereign States, and its logic therefore 'resists' incorporation by a federal court against the States," he concluded.

It was Stevens's last major dissent and his last day on the Supreme Court. In a 2002 interview on National Public Radio, Ginsburg had said, "Dissents speak to a future age. It's not simply to say, 'My colleagues are wrong and I would do it this way.' But the greatest dissents do become court opinions and gradually over time their views become the dominant view. So that's the dissenter's hope: that they are writing not for today but for tomorrow." [13]

The majority once again did not decide what kind of scrutiny—the most searching or something less—to give to gun restrictions to see if they violate the amendment. Despite that uncertainty, like the aftermath of *Citizens United* in which political activists attempted to use the decision to topple local campaign funding limits, the ruling in *McDonald v. City of Chicago* triggered a wave of lawsuits in which the National Rifle Association, criminal defendants, and others launched challenges to state and local gun restrictions around the country.

And once again, a term had ended in which Justice Anthony Kennedy dominated the cases that divided the Court most closely. There were sixteen 5–4 decisions out of seventy-three cases, and Kennedy was in the majority in eleven. Of the eleven in which the Court split along ideological lines, Kennedy voted with the conservatives in eight and the liberal justices in three. And once again, as they had for most of the five years of the Roberts Court, the media, legal scholars, and others declared it the "Kennedy Court."

CHAPTER 14

"If I wanted to sponsor a bill and it said, 'Americans, you have to eat three vegetables and three fruits every day,' and I got it through Congress, and it's now the law of the land, got to do it, does that violate the commerce clause?"

—Senator Thomas Coburn (R-OK), 2010

The last day of the term was the first day of the Senate hearings on the nomination of Elena Kagan to the seat formerly held by John Paul Stevens. The hearings were striking not because anything revealing was learned about the nominee, but because they appeared to be the first time in years that Republican and Democratic members of the Judiciary Committee had coherent and consistent messages to convey.

"When [Joseph Biden] was chair, he made no effort to coordinate the message; he left it up to everybody," recalled a former committee lawyer. "The next chairman is [Patrick] Leahy and he made it a priority. It was something Leahy felt was very, very important and he wanted to do that."

While the confirmation hearings for Justice Sonia Sotomayor focused on guns, property rights, the "wise Latina" speech, and the New Haven firefighters case, the Kagan hearings were, for the Republicans, about the health care law, and for the Democrats, the pro-business Roberts Court in general and *Citizens United* in particular.

That the Republican members had health care on their minds was evident in questions, for example, by Senator Thomas Coburn of Oklahoma, who asked Kagan if Congress could pass and the president sign a law requiring Americans to eat a certain number of vegetables a day—a veiled reference to the broccoli mandate that challengers to the health care law were using to undermine the law's constitutionality.[1]

Besides that being a "dumb law," Kagan responded, "I think that there are limits on the commerce clause . . . which are the ones that were articulated by the court in *Morrison* and in *Lopez*, which are primarily about non-economic activity and Congress not being able to regulate non-economic activity.

"I guess the second point I would make is I would look to *Gibbons v. Ogden*, where Chief Justice [John] Marshall did, in the first case about these issues, essentially read that clause broadly and provide real deference to legislatures and provide real deference to Congress about the scope of that clause, not that the clause doesn't have any limits, but that deference should be provided to Congress with respect to matters affecting interstate commerce."

Coburn later asked her directly, "Was there any time [when] you were asked in your present position to express an opinion on the merits of the health care bill?"

Kagan replied: "There was not." Her answer would never satisfy certain special interest groups, who later lobbied hard to get Kagan to recuse from the health care challenge when it got to the Supreme Court.

Besides health care, the Republican message was that Kagan was more the product of politics than law. She had less practical legal experience than any nominee in at least fifty years, they said. Her background was more extensive in policy and politics. She had worked in the Clinton White House, and she admired and had associated with such liberal activist judges as Abner Mikva and Thurgood Marshall. In one of the more bizarre parts of the hearings, some Republican members even tried to make Marshall, dead for nearly twenty years and a civil rights hero, an issue in Kagan's nomination. They also hammered away at her enforcement as Harvard Law dean of a policy prohibiting mili-

tary recruiters from contacting students directly through school channels because the federal ban against gays serving in the military violated
Harvard's non-discrimination policy.

On the Democratic side, more than a few senators believed the Roberts Court was "overly pro-business and *Citizens United* was an illustra-
tion of that," recalled a committee staffer.

"One reason why *Citizens United* became as much of a focus as it did
was not all the Democrats' doing," he explained. "I actually think it was
a central target of the Republicans." He explained that the Republicans
had targeted the ruling for several reasons:

"It was a loss that Kagan had in one of her arguments and they could
use her experience against her—she lost the biggest case she argued," he
said. "Second, the criticism was she maintained, as did the dissenters, in
that case, a judicial activist position—trying to deviate from precedent
and disregard the First Amendment. It became a target of a source of
her ideology. Third, it might have been to suggest Kagan, as solicitor
general, was going to be tied into all sorts of things, like health care, that
she wouldn't recuse herself from."

However, only Republican senator Orrin Hatch of Utah offered a
spirited defense of *Citizens United*. Committee Democrats went on the
attack, speaking primarily to the public audience and expecting little
or no response from Kagan. For example, Senator Al Franken of Minnesota clearly had "briefed" his case against the Court and its decision:

"In the early 1960s, car companies knew that they could avoid a large
number of fatalities by installing seat belts in every vehicle, but they
didn't want to. They said safety doesn't sell. But Congress didn't listen
to the car companies. And so in 1966, Congress passed a law requiring
that all passenger cars have seat belts. Since then, the fatality rate from
car accidents has dropped by 71 percent.

"Here's another story. Around the same time that we passed the seat
belt law, people started to realize that leaded gasoline that cars ran on
was poisoning our air. But oil companies didn't want to take the lead
out of gasoline because altering their refineries was going to be, in the

words of the *Wall Street Journal*, a multi-billion-dollar headache. But in 1970, Congress passed the Clean Air Act anyway, and thanks in part to that law, by 1995 the percentage of children with elevated levels of lead in their blood had dropped by 84 percent.

"Along with the Clean Water Act of 1972, the Clean Air Act of 1970 and the Motor Vehicle Act are three pillars of the modern consumer safety and environmental laws. And here's something else they have in common: They were all passed around 60 days before an election.

"Do you think those laws would have stood a chance if Standard Oil and G.M. could have spent millions of dollars advertising against vulnerable congressmen, by name, in the last months before their elections? I don't.

"So here is my point, General Kagan. *Citizens United* isn't just about election law. It isn't just about campaign finance law. It's about seat belts. It's about clean air and clean water. It's about energy policy and the rights of workers and investors. It's about health care. It's about our ability to pass laws that protect the American people even if it hurts the corporate bottom line."

Other Democratic senators made a broader attack on the Court's five conservative justices, accusing them of ignoring or overruling precedents and making law in cases such as the Second Amendment gun ruling, *Citizens United*, the Seattle-Louisville school race cases, a key antitrust decision that overturned a ninety-six-year-old precedent, and wage and age discrimination rulings.

The charge that the Roberts Court is a corporate or pro-business Court—a charge that has sometimes included the Court's moderate-liberal justices as well as its conservatives—began early in the life of the Roberts Court and is fed by the continuing success before the Court of an active and aggressive U.S. Chamber of Commerce. In fact, in the 2011–12 term that produced the health care decision, the chamber's litigating arm had a perfect winning record.[2]

The liberal Constitutional Accountability Center in Washington, D.C., has named Roberts and Alito as the chamber's greatest allies and has reported that since 2005—the beginning of the Roberts Court—the Court has voted for U.S. Chamber of Commerce positions 68 percent of the time.

However, despite that success and a number of serious losses by consumers, the corporate or pro-business label does not stick consistently; and like the justices' views of race, the history of the Second Amendment, and campaign finance and the First Amendment, there are often different reasons for their votes.

For example, limits on punitive damages awards would seem to be a surefire winner for business before a conservative-dominated Supreme Court. And yet, two of the Court's toughest conservatives—Antonin Scalia and Clarence Thomas—oppose those limits because they believe nothing in the Constitution supports them.

Left-leaning special interest groups and some academics raised the pro-business alarms during the first full term of the Roberts Court, the 2006–07 term. It was a tremendously successful term for the business community, and a number of the business-related decisions seemed to bear out those groups' concerns about Roberts and Alito during their confirmation hearings.

Roberts and Alito cut their teeth in the Reagan Justice Department, where department leaders emphasized the importance of technical doctrines that could shut down lawsuits: for example, challenges to opponents' standing to sue or to the ripeness of an opponent's claim; assertions of sovereign immunity from suit; and other defenses. Rigorous or stringent application of those doctrines can narrow dramatically the kinds of cases that can get through the courthouse door.

The first decision of the Roberts Court to capture the public's attention and ire came in the 2006–07 term and involved Lilly Ledbetter, the only female supervisor at a Goodyear Tire & Rubber plant in Gadsen, Alabama. She did not know until shortly before her retirement, after nineteen years with the company, that she was being underpaid compared to the male supervisors. She discovered the discrimination after an anonymous note with the information was slipped into her mailbox.

A jury found that her employer had discriminated against her and it awarded her more than $3.5 million.

A 5–4 Supreme Court ruling in 2007, written by Alito, found against her, saying that her discrimination lawsuit had not been timely filed. Alito wrote that the federal law required a suit to be filed within 180 days of the initial act of alleged discrimination. However, Ledbetter did not know about the discrimination when it first occurred; she argued that each paycheck was a new violation of the law.

"We apply the statute as written, and this means that any unlawful employment practice, including those involving compensation, must be presented within the period prescribed by the statute," wrote Alito. Although Alito, along with Roberts, Scalia, Kennedy, and Thomas, was faithful to the text of the law, they were not faithful to Congress's clear intent, echoed in numerous earlier Supreme Court decisions, that the nation's civil rights laws—remedial statutes—are to be interpreted and enforced broadly in order to avoid unfair and incongruous results.

The decision provoked a strong dissent by Ginsburg, joined by Stevens, Souter, and Breyer. Reading a summary from the bench, she said, "In our view, the court does not comprehend, or is indifferent to, the insidious way in which women can be victims of pay discrimination. Pay disparities often occur, as they did in Ledbetter's case, in small increments; only over time is there strong cause to suspect that discrimination is at work." She called on Congress to reverse the decision for future cases, which it did with the Lilly Ledbetter Fair Pay Act of 2009—the first bill signed into law by newly elected President Barack Obama.

Other decisions that term using those technical or procedural hurdles included *Bell Atlantic v. Twombly*, a large antitrust class action brought by consumers against regional "Baby Bell" telephone companies. A 7–2 majority, led by Souter, raised the bar on what consumer-plaintiffs had to put into their complaints in order to keep their lawsuits from being dismissed early in the court process. In reaching its decision, the majority essentially overruled a seminal decision that for fifty years had held that plaintiffs were not required to set out in detail the facts on which their lawsuits were based. Stevens and Ginsburg dissented. Souter, however, did caution lower courts not to read the ruling too broadly.

Two years later, a different majority raised the bar even higher in *Ashcroft v. Iqbal*. Kennedy led a 5–4 majority to hold that *Twombly* applied to all civil lawsuits, not just antitrust cases. Souter and Breyer joined Ginsburg and Stevens in dissent, charging that the majority had misread the *Twombly* ruling.

Despite the liberal wing's unhappiness with the duo of *Twombly* and *Iqbal,* Ginsburg led an 8–1 majority in *Tellabs v. Makor* to impose a higher burden on those bringing securities fraud lawsuits under the Private Securities Litigation Reform Act of 1995. That law, Ginsburg said, was intended "to curb frivolous, lawyer-driven litigation." Scalia and Alito, concurring, would have made it even harder for plaintiffs to survive early in the proceedings. Stevens, advocating a friendlier plaintiff standard, dissented.

In the wake of those business victories, one veteran Supreme Court litigator suggested at the time, "some people say the Court is angry at the plaintiffs' bar. That's not quite the way I would put it. I would say the Court had come to the conclusion the civil justice system has gotten out of balance. It has become too burdensome, too expensive, too unpredictable, even erroneous in results in cases. *Twombly* is Exhibit A for that."

Despite those concerns by the justices, a unanimous Roberts Court in 2011, led by the chief justice, handed a hugely significant victory to shareholders and others bringing securities class actions. The Court refused to impose a heavy burden of proof on shareholder-plaintiffs before they could go forward with their class actions. In *Erica P. John Fund v. Halliburton*, shareholders had accused Halliburton of hiding the magnitude of the company's asbestos liability from them.

There have been other cases in which technical doctrines favored by the Reagan Justice Department have been used by the Roberts Court to limit access to the courts, and not just in business-related cases. In *Hein v. Freedom From Religion Foundation*, the Court split ideologically in narrowing to the point of non-existence the standing of taxpayers to challenge the federal government's funding of religious activities. And in *Bowles v. Russell*, a 5–4 conservative majority, led by Clarence Thomas, refused to allow an appeals court to consider a convicted murderer's appeal because it was untimely filed. The prisoner had filed his appeal according to the time frame ordered by his trial court, but that court had made a mistake about the deadline. Although the prisoner had urged the Court to apply the doctrine of "unique circumstances" to his situation, Thomas said, the "Court has no authority to create equitable exceptions to jurisdictional requirements." He and the majority then overruled two earlier precedents that appeared to authorize such an exception to the jurisdictional rule. Souter, in a dissent joined by Stevens, Ginsburg, and Breyer, wrote: "[i]t is intolerable for the judicial system to treat people this way, and there is not even a technical justification for condoning this bait and switch."

One of the most important legal doctrines for business is federal preemption. If Congress expressly states that federal law is supreme, then any state laws on the subject will be preempted or displaced. Where Congress has not made that intent clear, the Court must look at whether a state law on the same subject conflicts with the federal law or whether Congress has legislated so broadly that the federal law "occupies the field" and there is no room for state regulation. Business generally favors federal preemption because it prefers to operate under one, uniform federal law instead of trying to comply with fifty different state laws. However, business also prefers federal law because it perceives federal courts to be more hospitable than state courts and juries when it is sued, usually by consumers who want, where state law provides it, to hold businesses to a tougher standard. A concerted effort was launched by the George W. Bush administration to insert preemption clauses in newly adopted federal regulations.

There is a long-standing judicial presumption against preemption, but it is fast disappearing in the Roberts Court. The business community has been quite successful in arguing for preemption of state lawsuits alleging personal injuries in a number of areas: against claims of defective design, labeling, and manufacturing of medical devices; state-law securities class action lawsuits by holders of securities; state inspection and registration requirements for bank subsidiaries; state-law product liability lawsuits against vaccine makers; failure to warn and defective design of locomotive parts; and even state requirements for the humane treatment in slaughterhouses of pigs that cannot walk.

However, despite those business successes, a number of which were won with large Court majorities, there have been some preemption defeats for business, though not as many as the victories. In the 2008–09 term, a 6–3 majority found no preemption of a state-law claim that drug manufacturers put an inadequate warning label on a drug that led to the amputation of a musician's arm. In a case involving the marketing of "light" cigarettes, a 5–4 Court allowed a state-law fraud suit to go forward despite the Federal Cigarette Labeling and Advertising Act. And in 2011, a unanimous Court held that federal auto safety standards did not preempt state personal injury suits on whether car manufacturers should have installed lap-shoulder belts instead of simply lap belts on the rear inner seats of Mazda minivans.

Business suffered a major preemption defeat in 2011 in a case actually brought by the U.S. Chamber of Commerce. In *U.S. Chamber of Commerce v. Whiting*, the chamber challenged an Arizona anti-immigration law that severely penalized businesses that hired illegal aliens. The chamber argued unsuccessfully that the law was preempted by federal immigration law. The 5–3 decision in favor of Arizona was written by Roberts and joined by Scalia, Kennedy, Thomas, and Alito.

That the results in preemption cases are so often unpredictable and sometimes involve unusual alignments of justices is not surprising. Underlying preemption cases are difficult and divisive questions about federalism—the relationship between the national and state governments—and the different ways in which individual justices interpret the text of statutes, legislative history, and congressional intent. Some justices, such as Thomas, stop at the text.

Two other areas of the law have figured into the charges that the Roberts Court is pro-business: arbitration and job discrimination. Long before the Roberts Court, a pro-arbitration view dominated the Supreme Court. Arbitration is largely a private process before a neutral arbiter. Its advocates contend it is a more cost-efficient and timely resolution of disputes than court litigation. Much of its shine has dulled in recent years, however, as academic and other studies revealed that the process does not always take place on an even playing field and the arbiter is not always so neutral.

For some time, few if any justices on the Roberts Court were seriously skeptical of arbitration as are many consumer organizations today. Through a series of rulings, the justices have strictly enforced arbitration clauses demanded by business, including prohibiting class actions in consumer contracts and removing civil rights claims by employees from court review. Whether recent pushback by the Court's liberal wing will continue is too early to tell.

The U.S. Chamber of Commerce likes to point to its losses in job discrimination cases in the Roberts Court as evidence that the Court is not pro-business or pro-chamber. But as with preemption, the results are mixed. Business has suffered the most losses in cases involving claims of retaliation by employers against employees who claim discrimination or witnesses who report discrimination. The justices, often unanimously, broadly read the protections from retaliation in the nation's job-bias laws. In one sense, critics claim, those are easy cases for the justices because the retaliation provisions themselves are broadly written and even the most conservative justice would be offended by a boss who retaliates against a worker asserting a right to be free from discrimination. However, those defeats for business are significant because retaliation claims are the fastest growing category of discrimination claims today and employers risk substantial damages if they violate the law.

Other business defeats have not been as significant and often involve interpretations of technical words in the statutes. Civil rights groups are more concerned about business victories, such as in the *Ledbetter* decision, reflecting a cramped view of Congress's intent that civil rights laws be read broadly, and again in a 2009 decision in *Gross v. FBL Financial Services*. In *Gross*, a sharply divided Court, led by Thomas, essentially made it much more difficult for workers to prove age discrimination under the federal Age Discrimination in Employment Act. The conservative majority, in its decision, ignored the issue that the Court initially agreed to decide and that was briefed and argued by the parties. Instead, the majority adopted a new, more rigorous proof standard never sought by the parties. The Court's dissenters, led by Justice Stevens, accused the majority of "unnecessary lawmaking" as well as a wrong interpretation of the discrimination law.

Standing, preemption, burdens of proof, time limits, arbitration— unlikely headline-grabbers, but keys to the courthouse doors. So what to make of the accusations that the Roberts Court is pro-business in the face of often mixed results? In a series of interviews, a number of justices across the ideological spectrum rejected the pro-business label as a superficial analysis of their rulings, and politically motivated.

"The Court decides cases in a way that corporations tend to win, no doubt, and it's a pro-defendant Court," said one justice, explaining that for many of them, the issue is more a concern with costly litigation, which is considered a potential burden on the economy. This justice hastened to add, "But I think its decisions are the result of analyzing issues in a fair way."

Another justice was more forceful in disputing the label. "Go through our opinions. We've come out on the side against corporations— I haven't counted the cases, but as far as I know, as much the other way. That's nonsense, political nonsense. Some of it is lawyers are just more resourceful. There are more organized causes. Public Citizen raised a lot of this dust. That's one factor."

Some disagreements in the business cases run deeper than others, and arbitration is emerging as an area of potentially deeper divisions in the future. As one justice noted, "Some cases it is very difficult to see how my colleagues see things. One of them, *AT&T Mobility v. Concepcion*." (In that decision, involving consumers' attempts to bring a class action over cell phone charges, a 5–4 majority said federal law preempted a California law that held waivers of class actions in arbitration agreements were unenforceable.)

"Here was the Federal Arbitration Act trumping whatever rule the state had about contracts," said the justice. "The FAA started out as a means to solve disputes less expensively, more swiftly. The initial tug against it was judges who thought it was encroaching on their turf, so there was resistance to arbitration. Using the Arbitration Act to disadvantage consumers is not an inevitable interpretation of the act."

Another justice initially thought the pro-corporate charge was the result of "some law professor doing a poor research job." However, "Then I read [Judge Richard] Posner and thought, 'I see there's a point here.' I don't know to what extent it is, but too much is made of it because there are so many different cases. It's easy to beat the Court with."

This justice was referring to a 2010 study by the leading conservative federal appellate judge Richard Posner of Chicago; the political scientist and law professor Lee Epstein of the University of Southern California; and the economist William Landes of the University of Chicago. They analyzed more than 1,400 "economic activity" decisions from 1953 to 2009 to determine whether the Roberts Court was pro-business. Those cases involved antitrust, mergers, bankruptcy, regulation of public utilities, federal/state consumer protection, labor arbitration, and employment discrimination.

Comparing the last five years of the Rehnquist Court, which ended in 2005, to the first five years of the Roberts Court, the study found that the Roberts Court ruled for business 61 percent of the time to 46 percent for the Rehnquist Court, and to 42 percent for all Supreme Courts since 1953—a "statistically significant" difference. The study also found that of the top five most pro-business terms since 1953, two were in the Roberts Court.[3]

Robin Conrad, head of the U.S. Chamber of Commerce's litigating arm, challenges claims that the success of business and the chamber in the Roberts Court is the result of the Court's pro-business bias.

"Two key values that seem to influence the outcomes of business cases are the preference for a uniform set of legal rules, and for laws and regulations that produce predictable results," she wrote in 2009. "The business community regularly advances these values in its amicus briefs. Another possible explanation for the degree of consensus among the Justices is that most business cases involve questions of statutory interpretation, which are less controversial than culturally-charged constitutional cases."[4]

• Numbers only tell part of a story that is more complex than appears on the surface. However, Senate Judiciary Democrats successfully painted a portrait of the Roberts Court as pro-business with some staying power during the Kagan hearings that summer of 2010, and the Court itself helped them with its ruling in *Citizens United*.

For her part, Kagan sailed through her confirmation hearings, handling more than seven hundred questions with what was fast becoming a trademark sense of humor and few insights into how she would rule. She did, however, distance herself somewhat from the chief justice in her view of a judge's role. Roberts captured media and public attention with his comparison of the judge to baseball's umpire: someone who just calls balls and strikes. Kagan agreed with the metaphor's suggestions that judges should be neutral and that while they have an important role, it is a limited one because it is the people and their elected representatives who make the fundamental decisions for the nation.

"I suppose the way in which I think that the metaphor does have its limits was that the metaphor might suggest to some people that law is a kind of robotic enterprise, that there's a kind of automatic quality to it, that it's easy, that we just sort of stand there and, you know, we go ball and strike, and everything is clear-cut, and that there is no judgment in the process," she said. "And I do think that that's not right. And it's especially not right at the Supreme Court level where the hardest cases go and the cases that have been the subject of most dispute go.

"And as to that, I think that judges do, in many of these cases, have to exercise judgment. They're not easy calls. That doesn't mean that they're doing anything other than applying law. But we do know that not every case is decided 9–0, and that's not because anybody's acting in bad faith. It's because those legal judgments are ones in which reasonable people can reasonably disagree sometimes. And so in that sense, law does require a kind of judgment, a kind of wisdom."

On August 5, 2010, the Senate confirmed Kagan by a vote of 63–37; one Democrat voted no and five Republicans voted yes. On the first Monday in October of that year, she took her seat as the third female justice on the bench—a historic milestone.

Like Sotomayor, Kagan took to the bench like a veteran. In the words of one of their colleagues, "Neither of them is a shrinking violet." Both women are more vocal during arguments than the justices whom they succeeded, and they have energized the moderate-liberal side of the bench.

Kagan's questions during arguments on her first day were concise, direct, and delivered in a pleasant tone. She also showed a deftness in picking up on her colleagues' questions if they had gone unanswered. She seemed to know intuitively that oral arguments are as much a conversation between justices as between justices and the lawyers arguing the case.

However, it was not as easy as it looked. Unlike Sotomayor and the rest of the justices, Kagan had never been a judge and she had to learn the mechanics of being a judge—from the totally mundane to the more important. For example, when should the briefs in a case be read? Two weeks before the argument, or the night before? How should the four clerks be used? Should they write first drafts of opinions? Should they work off an outline provided by her? Should they all be brought into the discussion on all cases, or just the clerk assigned to a particular case?

318 — THE ROBERTS COURT

318 — THE ROBERTS COURT

After a period of experimentation, Kagan found her comfort level. She runs a collective type of shop in which she talks with all four clerks before and after arguments and sometimes at other times, but one clerk takes the lead on each case. The lead clerk on a case writes a bench memo for Kagan in which she asks the clerk how he (or she) would deal with the case if he were a judge. The memo is shared with all of the clerks so all can participate in the case discussions. For opinion writing, Kagan has the lead clerk prepare an outline, which she revises, a draft opinion, and a notebook with all of the cases mentioned in the draft opinion. She then puts the draft opinion on one computer screen, opens a new document on another, and completely rewrites the draft. As with Chief Justice Roberts, whose clerks also write a first draft, the final opinion is all Kagan. The first opinion of the junior justice is rarely a major one, and Kagan's first—a bankruptcy decision—was no different. But she soon would show a very distinctive style.

The 2010–11 term was, in a sense, a term overshadowed by anticipation for those who closely followed the Court: anticipation of health care's arrival. The term had barely begun that October when a federal district judge in Michigan issued the first decision in one of four key challenges: *Thomas More Law Center v. Obama*. Judge George Steeh, a Clinton appointee, upheld the law. In November, one of the two Virginia challenges was decided—*Liberty University v. Geithner*—another victory for the Obama administration. That was followed in December and January 2011 by two defeats: *Virginia v. Sebelius* and *State of Florida v. U.S. Department of Health and Human Services*, respectively.

From day one, the health care law was a politically charged issue, but it became even more so in the public's mind because of the political pedigree of the four district court judges who ruled between October and January. Two Democratic-appointed judges had upheld the law, and two Republican-appointed judges had struck it down. Appeals to the next level—federal appellate courts—were inevitable, although Virginia attorney general Ken Cuccinelli tried (unsuccessfully) to leapfrog the pack by going directly to the Supreme Court. The justices would wait for the appeals court rulings.

All bets were still on the Florida challenge, brought by the Republican attorneys general (AGs), as the vehicle for Supreme Court review. Now that the district courts had ruled and appeals were planned, the Obama administration and the state AGs decided it was time to bring in appellate specialists in preparation for the ultimate showdown in the Supreme Court.

Kagan's principal deputy, Neal Katyal, had become acting solicitor general. Obama had nominated Donald Verrilli Jr., a veteran appellate lawyer who had been monitoring the health care litigation while in the White House Counsel's Office, to be the new solicitor general, but his confirmation was months away. Attorney General Eric Holder asked Katyal to handle the appeals court cases.

Florida attorney general Bill McCollum, who had launched the AG challenge, also had left office for what would be an unsuccessful run for governor. His Republican successor, Pam Bondi, took control of the litigation. When the state AGs initially filed their health care lawsuit, they had been joined by the National Federation of Independent Business, but that organization was preparing to split off and continue with its own lawyer, Michael Carvin of Jones Day, a veteran of the Reagan Justice Department who specializes in constitutional, civil rights, and civil litigation against the government. Carvin, at the time, also was handling a lawsuit challenging the heart of the Voting Rights Act of 1965, a suit that was expected to go eventually to the Supreme Court.

Two weeks after winning in the district court, Bondi and her legal team flew from Tallahassee to Washington, D.C., to interview potential lawyers who could represent the state AGs in the appeals court and eventually the Supreme Court. She was about to engage in a familiar ritual known as the "beauty contest," in which appellate and Supreme Court practitioners make their arguments as to why they should be hired for a particular case.

Bondi, with an eye on the Supreme Court, had three of the nation's top Supreme Court practitioners on her list: Miguel Estrada of Gibson, Dunn & Crutcher, a Republican and Federalist Society favorite; Gregory Garre, head of the appellate and Supreme Court practice at Latham & Watkins and a former George W. Bush administration solicitor general; and his predecessor, Paul Clement of the Bancroft law firm, who had argued the Seattle-Louisville school cases and the District of Columbia gun case for the Bush administration. Estrada's partner, Theodore Olson, perhaps the dean of Supreme Court practitioners, would have been at the top of anyone's wish list, but some state AGs deemed Olson unacceptable because he, along with David Boies, who represented Al Gore in *Bush v. Gore*, was challenging California's ban on same-sex marriage.

Bondi met separately with each of the lawyers in a conference room at Cadwalader, Wickersham & Taft where her brother practiced law. She and her team settled on Clement, whom they found passionate, humble, brilliant, and—well—affordable. Reportedly for a flat rate of $250,000, they would be getting a lawyer considered by many to be the premier Supreme Court advocate of his generation. At forty-five, he had argued more than fifty cases before the justices, and since leaving government service, he had become the singular choice of conservatives to handle their hot-button causes. Clement was representing House GOP leaders in defense of the federal Defense of Marriage Act; the state of Arizona in defending its tough anti-immigration law; Texas, whose congressional redistricting plan was challenged as discriminating against Latinos; and South Carolina, whose voter identification law faced a discrimination challenge by the Obama administration.

With Katyal and Clement in place for the next round in this constitutional power struggle, both sides faced decisions about their legal arguments that would affect the case when the Supreme Court became involved. The government's Anti-Injunction Act argument, which would have blocked any challenges to the health care law until 2015, had been a loser in the district courts. Despite that lack of success, some administration officials wanted to continue to make the argument because it would put off a decision on the law's constitutionality until after the November presidential election. On the other hand, the Internal Revenue Service was spending millions of dollars in preparation for implementing the penalty for not having health insurance. The Department of Health and Human Services was moving forward with creating health insurance exchanges. And the insurance community was implementing some of the law now and planning to implement other parts later, and it worried about its losses if the process were halted. There were strong policy reasons for getting an answer about the health care law as soon as possible. The Anti-Injunction Act itself and how it applied to the health care law presented a very complicated statutory argument, and it had gone nowhere.[5]

Katyal made the call to abandon the Anti-Injunction Act argument. However, despite continued opposition from some in the administration, he would not abandon the argument that the health care law was a constitutional exercise of Congress's power to tax and spend for the general welfare.

"I thought the tax argument was important to have in our arsenal," said Katyal. He recalled that the Yale Law School constitutional law scholar Akhil Amar called him and urged him to use in the government's appeal a 2009 decision by Chief Justice Roberts in which the chief avoided the constitutional issue in a voting rights challenge by finding another way to read the voting rights law.[6]

In *NAMUDNO v. Holder*, Roberts, quoting an earlier Supreme Court decision, said, " '[i]t is a well-established principle governing the prudent exercise of this Court's jurisdiction that normally the Court will not decide a constitutional question if there is some other ground upon which to dispose of the case.' " Instead of deciding whether Section 5 of the Voting Rights Act was constitutional, the 8–1 majority interpreted another provision in the law to resolve the utility district's problem with the Voting Rights Act.

"[Amar] said, 'You should really cite the *NAMUDNO* case,' and we did because, he said, 'If you can construe this as a tax, if there's a way to do so, the chief's opinion in that case is the way to do it.'

"It's the precedent which basically drives what the chief justice did," explained Katyal. "It's rewriting the statute in a way to make it constitutional, what the chief calls a saving construction. I thought Akhil's suggestion was very smart, to basically say, you could see it as a tax, you might not, but *NAMUDNO* tells you your duty is to save the statute by construing it as a tax. I didn't think, honestly, at the time, the *NAMUDNO* saving construction idea was going to be the thing that won, but you know, it turns out to be."

And there was the government's basic commerce clause argument: the individual mandate regulates the way people pay for health care services, which is a type of economic activity that substantially affects interstate commerce.

For his part, Paul Clement took his side's commerce clause arguments and, in his trademark style, boiled them down to a clear and simply framed argument: Congress has substantial power to regulate interstate commerce, but it may not compel individuals to enter into commerce so that Congress may better regulate them. Upholding the law would mean there is no meaningful limit on Congress's power.

Unlike Clement, who would argue health care in one appellate court, Katyal would make the government's argument in four appellate courts while managing his office's caseload in the Supreme Court. Because of the high stakes in the health care case, he departed from the office's tradition of two mock- or "moot"-court arguments per case and did four; and he took one other unusual step.

"I also went to all the agencies and listened—Treasury and the IRS, HHS, the White House, to understand the different policy concerns," he said. "Normally as SG, everyone comes to you. But I really wanted to go there and learn what concerned them. You don't often get that by who they send to you. If you go there, there are twenty people talking to you. If they come to you, there's one person."

A tenured professor at Georgetown University Law Center, Katyal had taught constitutional law numerous times and was comfortable with the legal arguments in the case, "but all of the facts and what the Affordable Care Act did, the 2,400 pages—all of that, it was huge and required a massive amount of time for preparation."

As the health care cases moved through the appellate courts that spring, the Supreme Court prepared to put the 2010–11 term to bed.

In some ways, the last day of the term was a mini-portrait of the entire term. There were more Court-imposed obstacles for injured persons trying to hold companies accountable, more protection of repugnant speech, and a freshman who wielded words like a swordsman.

The most surprising, headline-grabbing case of the term turned out to be a civil procedure case—a very big one, involving federal court rules for certification of class action lawsuits. The case was *Wal-Mart v. Dukes*, the largest gender discrimination class action in history. A lower court had certified a class of 1.5 million female Wal-Mart employees who claimed they were paid less than men in comparable positions and received fewer promotions to management positions. The class was later reduced to 500,000.

The justices agreed to answer two questions, one of their own making. The women had won class certification under a rule provision intended to apply to classes seeking injunctions or declarations as relief, and not money damages. However, these women were seeking monetary relief, such as back pay and front pay. Were they properly certified as a class under that particular rule? The second question was whether this class met the basic requirements for class action certification, particularly so-called commonality—questions of law or fact common to the class.

The Court had little problem answering the first question. The justices unanimously agreed that the class was improperly certified under a provision excluding class actions for damages. However, they divided 5–4 on the second and more crucial question. Justice Scalia, writing for the conservative majority, said these class members were too dissimilar, in their jobs, their supervisors, their store locations and store policies. "They have little in common but their sex and the lawsuit," he wrote. The majority also said the women had failed to show that Wal-Mart had a general policy of discrimination, and it rejected expert testimony that the company's policy of delegation of discretion to supervisors over pay and promotions could itself lead to discriminatory results.

Justice Ginsburg, joined by Breyer, Sotomayor, and Kagan, strongly dissented, accusing the majority of imposing a more stringent commonality test on the women, one that disqualified classes "at the starting gate."

The case was one of three closely followed by the U.S. Chamber of Commerce. The chamber won all three. The second was *American Electric Power Co. v. Connecticut*, in which eight states and New York City sued five power companies and the federal Tennessee Valley Authority, claiming their greenhouse gas emissions created a public nuisance. The Court, led by Ginsburg, unanimously agreed that the Clean Air Act and proposed federal rulemaking to limit greenhouse gas emissions displaced any public nuisance action by the states and the city. The third case, involving arbitration clauses in cell phone contracts, was the 5–4 ruling by the conservative majority in *AT&T Mobility v. Concepcion*, preempting a California law prohibiting waivers of class action lawsuits in contracts. However, the chamber lost its own case challenging on preemption grounds an Arizona law penalizing employers who hire illegal immigrants.

The Court also turned again to an area of law fast becoming identified with the Roberts Court: the First Amendment. The justices decided four important cases, prompting one constitutional scholar to label the Roberts Court "the most consistently and strongly protective free speech Court in history."

The Court, as it did in the previous term when it struck down a federal law banning animal crush videos, refused to carve out of the First Amendment's protection hateful speech by the Westboro Baptist

Church, a fringe group that pickets funerals of military servicemembers with anti-gay and other hate signs and chants. The church was sued by the father of a serviceman whose funeral the church picketed. He claimed intentional infliction of emotional distress.

Roberts wrote for the 8–1 majority in *Snyder v. Phelps* that "Given that Westboro's speech was at a public place on a matter of public concern, that speech is entitled to 'special protection' under the First Amendment. Such speech cannot be restricted simply because it is upsetting or arouses contempt." Alito, as he was in the animal crush video case, was the lone dissenter. He said the tort of intentional infliction of emotional distress was narrow, with rigorous requirements for recovery. "When grave injury is intentionally inflicted by means of an attack like the one at issue here, the First Amendment should not interfere with recovery," he countered.

In *Brown v. Entertainment Merchants Association*, Scalia led a 7–2 majority in striking down a California law that banned the sale or rental of violent video games to minors. "As a means of protecting children from portrayals of violence, the legislation is seriously underinclusive, not only because it excludes portrayals other than video games, but also because it permits a parental or avuncular veto," he wrote. "And as a means of assisting concerned parents it is seriously overinclusive because it abridges the First Amendment rights of young people whose parents (and aunts and uncles) think violent video games are a harmless pastime."

A surprising dissenter was Stephen Breyer, who called the law a "modest" speech restriction, justified by a compelling interest in assisting parents in protecting children from harmful and violent interactive games. He noted that under the Court's precedents, states can prohibit the sale of nude depictions to minors. "But what sense does it make to forbid selling to a 13-year-old boy a magazine with an image of a nude woman, while protecting a sale to that 13-year-old of an interactive video game in which he actively, but virtually, binds and gags the woman, then tortures and kills her?" he asked. "What kind of First Amendment would permit the government to protect children by restricting sales of that extremely violent video game only when the woman—bound, gagged, tortured, and killed—is also topless?"

Thomas also dissented, reiterating his originalist view that there is no right to speak to minors, or a right of minors to access speech without going through their parents or guardians.

Although they agreed with the majority that the law was unconstitutional, Alito and Roberts took a different, narrower approach. Alito said the Court should move cautiously when applying constitutional principles to new, evolving technology. Unlike the majority, he was not sure violent video games were harmless. He and Roberts said the law did not define violent video games or minors with the kind of specificity the First Amendment demands, and because the definition was vague, the law did not give constitutionally required fair notice to whom it applies. "And I would go no further," wrote Alito. "I would not express any view on whether a properly drawn statute would or would not survive First Amendment scrutiny. We should address that question only if and when it is necessary to do so." Alito and Roberts took the more restrained path and would have given the state the opportunity to redraft the law.

The bottom line: four different views crossing ideological lines.

A third First Amendment case drew less media attention but had potentially greater implications. In *Sorrell v. IMS Health*, a 6–3 majority, led by Kennedy, invalidated Vermont's law prohibiting pharmacies from selling doctors' prescribing information to drug companies and companies that data-mine—extract information from a data set to spot buying trends and for other uses. The Supreme Court historically has given less First Amendment protection to commercial speech. Vermont argued its law safeguarded medical privacy and protected against the marketing of drugs that might not be in the patient's best interest.

The majority analyzed the law under "heightened" scrutiny—a tough, but not the toughest type of scrutiny for a law to survive. Kennedy wrote: "The State gives possessors of the information broad discretion and wide latitude in disclosing the information, while at the same time restricting the information's use by some speakers and for some purposes, even while the State itself can use the information to counter the speech it seeks to suppress. Privacy is a concept too integral to the person and a right too essential to freedom to allow its manipulation to support just those ideas the government prefers."

Breyer, joined by Ginsburg and Kagan, saw it very differently. The Vermont law, he explained, affects speech in only one way—by depriving data-mining and drug companies of data that could help drug companies create better sales messages. "In my view, this effect on expression is inextricably related to a lawful governmental effort to regulate a commercial enterprise," he wrote. "The First Amendment does not require courts to apply a special 'heightened' standard of review when reviewing such an effort."

The potential implications of the majority's approach were captured by the dissenters, who said the Court had never applied heightened scrutiny to commercial speech, and warned that the majority's view "threatens to return us to a happily bygone era when judges scrutinized legislation for its interference with economic liberty. History shows that the power was much abused and resulted in the constitutionalization of economic theories preferred by individual jurists." Breyer was referring to the much discredited era of *Lochner v. New York*.

Campaign finance moved to the fore once again in *Arizona Free Enterprise Club v. Bennett*, and on the way, it revealed a new justice with analytical and writing chops.

The Court at the end of the prior term had intervened aggressively in Arizona's primary election by temporarily blocking the use of the state's decade-old public financing system until it decided a constitutional challenge to the matching fund mechanism. The challenge had come from a conservative organization and some self-financed candidates. Under the state system, candidates who agreed to limit their personal spending received an initial amount of public financing, which subsequently was increased, up to a certain limit, based on spending by their privately financed opponents and independent spending groups supporting them.

On the merits of the constitutional challenge, Roberts, writing for the same majority that decided *Citizens United*, said the matching fund system burdened the speech of self-financed candidates and the independent groups supporting them, and was an unconstitutional attempt to level the playing field—a justification the Court had rejected in prior campaign finance rulings.

"The whole point of the First Amendment is to protect speakers against unjustified government restrictions on speech," wrote Roberts.

Kagan, joined by Ginsburg, Breyer, and Sotomayor, strongly disagreed, saying all the law does is fund more speech. "What the law does, all the law does is fund more speech," wrote Kagan. She said of the challengers to the law, "So they are making a novel argument: that Arizona violated their First Amendment rights by disbursing funds to other speakers even though they could have received (but chose to spurn) the same financial assistance. Some people might call that chutzpah."

Ginsburg assigned the dissent to Kagan, a plum assignment for a freshman even though a dissent, and a reflection of Ginsburg's confidence in Kagan's ability to duel analytically with the brilliant chief justice.

The Arizona decision marked the third time in four years that the Roberts Court's conservative majority had struck down a campaign finance reform law. The Arizona law was passed by voters in a ballot initiative in 1998 in response to a wave of election-related corruption cases.

Ginsburg assigned Kagan a second major dissent in *Arizona Christian School Tuition Organization v. Winn*, another 5–4 decision in which Kagan crossed words, this time with Kennedy. In that case, Kennedy wrote that taxpayers who challenged a state tax credit for contributions to student tuition organizations that primarily funded religious schools had no standing to bring their suit. The taxpayers claimed the tax credit violated the establishment clause and they had standing under a doctrine that allows taxpayers to challenge government spending for religious purposes.

Kennedy held that a challenge to a tax credit was different from a challenge to government spending. Kagan did not buy the difference. Using a technique that would become typical of her writing, she offered a piercing hypothetical to counter Kennedy:

"[A]ssume a State wishes to subsidize the ownership of crucifixes. It could purchase the religious symbols in bulk and distribute them to all takers. Or it could mail a reimbursement check to any individual who buys her own and submits a receipt for the purchase. Or it could authorize that person to claim a tax credit equal to the price she paid. Now, really—do taxpayers have less reason to complain if the State selects the last of these three options? The Court today says they do, but that is wrong."

Kagan's years as a law teacher appear to influence her approach to writing opinions. Her hypotheticals, peppered throughout the opinions, are used to communicate her arguments in a vivid way that is clear, simple, and likely to stick with her audience. Although both opinions were dissents, she showed a style and substance that reflected a new force to be reckoned with on the Court.

The term also revealed more about Sotomayor, who is increasingly making her voice heard in criminal cases, particularly in defense of criminal defendants' *Miranda* rights—the right to remain silent during police questioning, the right to consult a lawyer and to have the lawyer present during questioning, and the right to have a lawyer appointed if the suspect is indigent. Kennedy assigned her the 5–4 majority opinion in *J.D.B. v. North Carolina* in which the Court held for the first time that a suspect's age (here a juvenile)—should be a factor in determining whether he or she is in custody and must receive *Miranda* warnings.

Sotomayor said that considering age was a "commonsense" approach to the *Miranda* question, but Alito, who led the dissenting Roberts, Scalia, and Thomas, said police would find it too difficult to apply, and called the decision the beginning of the end of the clarity and ease of application that had long been the chief justification for *Miranda*. Both Sotomayor and Alito are former prosecutors, but Alito is a very pro-government vote in criminal cases, while Sotomayor is less easily pigeonholed.

The *J.D.B.* decision, said one Court expert, continued the "constitutional transformation" of the criminal justice system for juveniles that the Supreme Court, led by Kennedy, began when it prohibited capital punishment for juveniles under eighteen in 2005, and in 2010, life in prison without parole for juveniles who commit non-homicides.

In the cases that divided the Court most sharply, the 5–4 decisions, Anthony Kennedy continued to be the justice most often holding the key. In the 2010–11 term, the Court split 5–4 in sixteen of its eighty-two cases, or 20 percent, according to statistics kept by the non-partisan SCOTUSblog, for an average of 22 percent over six terms. Kennedy joined the majority in fourteen of the sixteen 5–4 splits, siding with the conservative wing in ten and with the liberal wing in just four.

Although the Court remained closely divided in such areas as campaign finance, preemption, and criminal justice, Roberts appeared to have had considerable success during the term in forging greater consensus—a goal he espoused in his confirmation hearings. The Court issued unanimous, 8–1, or 7–2 decisions in sixty of its eighty-two rulings. Of course, one term is not predictive of the next.

Two days after the Court wrapped up the term's business, the first appellate court ruling in one of the four major health care challenges was handed down, and it was a surprising and huge victory for the Obama administration. For the first time, a Republican-appointed judge had voted to uphold the law, and it was not just any Republican-appointed judge.

Judge Jeffrey Sutton of the U.S. Court of Appeals for the Sixth Circuit in Cincinnati was widely respected by conservatives. In a 2009 public appearance, Scalia called Sutton "One of my former clerks whom I am the most proud of" and "one of the very best law clerks I ever had."

In *Thomas More Law Center v. Obama*, Sutton, in a 2–1 ruling, said the challengers had raised plausible and serious arguments. The critical question, he said, was whether the commerce clause contained an activity-inactivity distinction that limited Congress's power, as the challengers claimed. Sutton answered, "No."[7]

Acting Solicitor General Katyal, who reported to the attorney general after each appellate court argument, had told General Holder after the Sixth Circuit arguments that based on the lines of questioning, he believed the government had lost, but it did not. "Sutton was just so tough and the follow-ups were so good," he recalled.

The government's euphoria was short-lived. Less than two months later, the Eleventh Circuit weighed in on the Republican state attorneys general suit. In a 2–1 decision, the judges struck down the individual mandate, but upheld the Medicaid expansion.[8] The two Virginia appeals were decided in early September. A 2–1 panel in *Liberty University v. Geithner* held that the Anti-Injunction Act applied to bar the health care challenge even though the government had abandoned the argument, and in *Virginia v. Sebelius*, the panel said the state lacked standing to sue and ordered the dismissal of the lawsuit.[9]

In just eighteen months, the challengers to Obama's signature achievement had carved a path through the lower federal courts to the Supreme Court. The stage was set for the most important term in the brief history of the Roberts Court.

CHAPTER 15

————◆————

"I don't think the Court is going to be influenced one bit by the politics or the election. They'll feel free to accept valid constitutional arguments, particularly because the law is so unpopular with people. I just think they're going to call it the way they see it."

—Randy Barnett, counsel to the National Federation
of Independent Business, November 2011

Each Supreme Court term is a story in itself, and as each story unfolds, an unpredictable twist or turn almost always surprises the conventional view of the nation's highest court.

Witness the stunning trio of authors who in 1992 reaffirmed—saved—the landmark abortion decision, *Roe v. Wade*, while also weakening it. The unprecedented intervention in, and decisive end to, the 2000 presidential election. The path-breaking gay rights ruling in *Lawrence v. Texas*. And the emotion-laden battle among the justices over the meaning of *Brown v. Board of Education* in the Seattle-Louisville public school decision.

Despite the nearly inevitable twist or turn, the challengers to the fledgling health care law had reason to be optimistic about their chances as they filed their appeals with the Roberts Court throughout the fall of 2011. They had taken an off-the-wall constitutional argument about the commerce clause containing an activity-inactivity distinction and had persuaded veteran appellate judges to consider it seriously, and in some cases, to accept it. With that argument, they had dictated the terms of the legal fight with their government opponents as well as the debate over the law in the media and with the public. And they had a conservative majority on the Roberts Court, not always solidly conservative, but fairly reliably so.

The law's supporters also were optimistic. In the 230-year history of the commerce clause, the Supreme Court had never found an activity-inactivity dichotomy to limit Congress's authority under the clause. The Court also had never struck down as unconstitutionally coercive a federally imposed condition on the states for receiving federal funds, the argument being used by the state attorneys general to attack the health care law's expansion of Medicaid coverage for the nation's poor and disabled. And fairly recent commerce clause–related rulings by Scalia and Roberts offered hope that those justices might be more open to the government's arguments.

However, just as everyone knew who had followed the Roberts Court since Sandra Day O'Connor's departure in 2006, both sides realized there was one, probably determinative, wild card: Justice Anthony Kennedy. They could not underestimate how pivotal Kennedy's vote might be. He had been the key to 5–4 victories in the school race cases, the death penalty, abortion, gun rights, and terrorism-related cases, among others, since the beginning of the Roberts Court.

For its part, the Roberts Court was facing the most politically charged term since its beginning in 2005. In August 2011, Arizona's governor, Jan Brewer, asked the justices to decide whether federal immigration law preempted certain parts of her state's tough anti-immigration law. A lower federal court had temporarily blocked the law from taking effect after the Obama Justice Department filed suit. The political and legal stakes were high. Immigration already was a front-burner issue in the coming presidential election, and a number of states and localities had enacted laws and ordinances modeled after the Arizona statute.

In September, the solicitor general of the United States lodged with the Court the government's appeal of its defeat in the health care challenge brought by the Republican state attorneys general, whose numbers had grown to twenty-six. The state AGs would file their own petition stemming from their loss in Florida on the Medicaid issue. And the National Federation of Independent Business (NFIB), whose legal team now included Randy Barnett, one of the first to articulate the activity-inactivity argument, had split off from the states' challenge to make its own arguments in the Supreme Court.

The state of Texas brought a redistricting appeal to the justices in November. Redistricting—the drawing of congressional district lines after the census—is the most contested task undertaken by state legislatures. Because of its history of voting discrimination, Texas was required to get approval—preclearance—of its redistricting plan from a federal court in Washington, D.C., or from the Justice Department. Texas went to the federal court. When it became clear that the court would not rule before the approaching 2012 primary election in Texas, the D.C. court asked the federal court in Texas to draft an interim plan, and it did. Texas then asked the Supreme Court whether a federal court had authority to issue its own interim redistricting plan when the state's plan was pending approval. The Justice Department and certain groups had argued that the Texas plan deliberately sought to reduce the influence of Hispanic votes and to strengthen state Republican candidates' chances.

The Texas, Arizona, and Florida challenges were all being handled by one lawyer: former Bush solicitor general Paul Clement. And all three had the potential to sharply divide the justices.

The new term also would see the return of the *Citizens United* campaign finance decision, which eliminated restrictions on independent expenditures by corporations and unions. The state of Montana and its supreme court said *Citizens United* did not apply to the state's century-old ban on corporate independent spending in that state's elections. The man who brought *Citizens United* to the Supreme Court—James Bopp Jr.—was now representing the corporations asking the justices to overrule the Montana Supreme Court.

Immigration, redistricting, health care, and campaign finance were

not, like abortion, gay marriage, and affirmative action, the kind of issues that aroused heated passions at the dinner table or water cooler.
They were structural issues, raising fundamental questions about the
roles and relationships among three branches of the national government, as well as between the national government and state governments. On a broader, non-legal plain, they also raised questions about
the type of nation and government its citizens wanted.

In the U.S. Supreme Court, however, the immediate focus is on the
legal. The Senate had confirmed a new solicitor general, Donald Verrilli Jr. Before joining the Obama administration, Verrilli was head of
the appellate and Supreme Court practice at the national law firm of
Jenner & Block. Tall and thin, with salt-and-pepper hair and bushy
mustache, Verrilli is widely liked and respected by his colleagues across
the ideological spectrum.

No one doubted that the justices would agree to hear the health care
cases. A federal appellate court in the state attorneys general challenge
had struck down a law enacted by Congress and the solicitor general
was seeking Supreme Court review—one of the primary grounds for
granting review. Though the opposition had sought it from the beginning, the Roberts Court was not acting aggressively or reaching out for
the case, as it did in the school race cases, the Second Amendment challenge, and *Citizens United*. Boldness and aggressiveness would not be
at the front end this time, but at the back end, and in a most surprising way.

On November 14, the Court granted review to the case that experts
had predicted from the beginning would be the ultimate vehicle for
determining the health care law's constitutionality. The case, initially
brought by the Republican attorneys general, was now three cases on
the justices' docket because the government, the state AGs, and the National Federation of Independent Business had each sought review of
key issues addressed by the lower appellate court.

The justices took from the three cases four questions to decide:

First, did the Court even have jurisdiction to review the health care law because of the Anti-Injunction Act's bar against review of pre-enforcement tax challenges?

Second, was the individual mandate a constitutional exercise of Congress's powers under Article I of the Constitution?

Third, if the mandate were unconstitutional, could it be severed from the law or must the entire law be struck down?

Fourth, did the Medicaid expansion unconstitutionally coerce the states into participating because of the threat that they would lose their federal Medicaid funds if they did not participate in the federal-state program?

The Court subsequently scheduled six hours of argument over three days—not an unprecedented amount of time, but rarely experienced in modern times.

In the Justice Department, many hands had been in the health care brew since the litigation began. Now that the case was in the Supreme Court, Solicitor General Verrilli worked with a core group that included Associate Deputy Attorney General Rob Weiner, who had been overseeing the litigation for more than a year; acting Assistant Attorney General Stuart Delery of the civil division; Ira Gershengorn, who had argued for the government in the district courts; Chad Golder, a young department attorney; and three veterans in Verrilli's own office: senior career Deputy Solicitor General Ed Kneedler and Assistants to the Solicitor General Leondra Krueger, who would shoulder work on the Medicaid and severability issues, and Joseph Palmore. Verrilli would turn to Kneedler to make the government's argument on severability of the individual mandate if it were struck down. Verrilli himself would make the government's arguments on the Anti-Injunction Act issue, the individual mandate, and the Medicaid expansion.

Although these lawyers were confident that the government would win, they thought the case was harder than some people inside and outside of the government thought, and consequently, they had no illusions that winning would be easy. What those seasoned lawyers realized was that although there was a body of case law that stood for certain principles that should favor the government, there was no single controlling precedent for the health care case. That meant that at the end of the day, the justices would have room to make a judgment.[1]

Even before making their arguments to the Supreme Court, Verrilli's team had to decide again what to do about that old Anti-Injunction Act. The federal appellate panel in the Virginia health care lawsuit had resurrected it to bar that lawsuit even though the government had abandoned the argument. The lawyers knew that telling the justices that the Anti-Injunction Act did not apply because the law imposed a penalty, not a tax, for failing to have health insurance weakened one of their central arguments—that the mandate was constitutional under Congress's taxing power. However, they risked damaging their credibility with the Court by switching positions again and so chose to make the best of their arguments on both issues.

In the normal course of their work, solicitors general do not have the time to focus on one case for an extended period or even become heavily involved in the brief writing. Even if they prefer to be hands-on, the workload is too great and court deadlines are always pressing. But the health care case was different. The stakes were enormous; the issues were complex. Verrilli immersed himself in the case. He read every government brief and line-edited them, and consulted as well with experts outside the department on a regular basis.

His opponent, former Solicitor General Paul Clement, had been more of a hands-on solicitor general, said a former colleague from that office. Since leaving the solicitor general's office in June 2008, Clement, a former clerk to Justice Scalia and conservative D.C. Circuit judge Laurence Silberman, had become the go-to lawyer for conservative legal causes. A native of Wisconsin and a graduate of Harvard Law School, he had argued more than sixty cases in the Supreme Court, including the Seattle-Louisville school race cases and the Second Amendment case, *McDonald v. City of Chicago*. With a quick wit and confident argument style, Clement enjoyed an easy rapport with the justices during arguments. His mind often seemed to be racing ahead of their questions and he was never rattled or at a loss for words. He was now working at a small, thirteen-lawyer firm, and treated the case in small-firm style, according to his associate Erin Murphy. "There wasn't any war room or anything like that," she said in an interview with *The National Law Journal*. "Paul is very self-sufficient." Murphy, a former law clerk to Chief Justice Roberts, wrote first drafts of all the health care briefs, but the final products were Clement's work.[2] She would be Clement's second chair at the argument. Clement planned to argue for the state AGs on the individual mandate, severability, and Medicaid.

Michael Carvin, representing the National Federation of Independent Business, had big firm resources at Jones Day, but his closest team member was partner Gregory Katsas. The two men coordinated efforts with Clement. "Obviously the states have their interests," said Carvin shortly before the arguments in the case. "We generally worked through Paul and we understand he has a number of clients. Since we're both moving in the same direction in terms of a goal, it hasn't presented any serious issues."[3]

Katsas was the designated hitter on the Anti-Injunction Act, while Carvin was to share argument time with Clement on the individual mandate.

The Court itself added two additional lawyers to the argument mix. Because none of the parties argued for the Anti-Injunction Act to apply, the justices appointed a veteran appellate lawyer with no connection to the case—Robert Long of D.C.'s Covington & Burling—to make that argument. On the severability question, Clement and Carvin wanted the entire law to fall if the mandate were found unconstitutional. The government, however, said the mandate was crucial to provisions guaranteeing coverage of preexisting conditions and prohibiting premium increases for people with those conditions. If the mandate was struck, it should be severed along with those two provisions, according to the government.

The Court wanted to hear an argument that only the mandate should be severed from the law and appointed another veteran Supreme Court lawyer, H. Bartow Farr of D.C.'s Farr & Taranto, to make that case.

The time, place, and players were set for an extraordinary and historical debate in late March 2012 over the nature and scope of Congress's powers under the Constitution. However, as many justices have said over the years, Supreme Court cases are rarely won or lost because of oral arguments. Instead, the most important factor is the legal brief.

Not surprisingly, lawyers often write briefs with certain justices in mind. In hopes of attracting as many votes as possible, they will glean decisions—whether majority, concurring, or dissenting opinions—by the justices for arguments that might bolster their own cases.

The government's main health care brief clearly hoped to reach three justices in order to get to the five votes needed to win: Scalia, Kennedy, and Roberts. It drew on Scalia's concurring opinion in the medical marijuana commerce clause case, *Gonzales v. Raich*, in which the justice noted that marijuana grown at home for personal use is "never more than an instant from the interstate market." The same principle applied to health care, said the government, because "we are all potentially never more than an instant from the 'point of consumption' of health care."[4]

The brief also tried to show Kennedy that the law was on the constitutional side of the line that he drew in his commerce clause opinions in the gun-free school zone case, *United States v. Lopez*, and the case involving civil commitment of sexually dangerous prisoners, *United States v. Comstock*. The mandate, the government argued, was necessary to achieve the law's comprehensive insurance market reforms, and was itself an economic regulation of the timing and manner of paying for health insurance, and so its links to interstate commerce were "tangible, direct and strong."

Also emphasized throughout the brief was a principle that Roberts had espoused during his confirmation hearings: respect for the democratically accountable branches of government.

Finally, and most importantly, although not widely recognized at the time, Verrilli strengthened in the main brief and the reply brief the government's argument that the mandate was a constitutional exercise of Congress's tax power.

Paul Clement's brief for the state AGs was considered powerful and direct. Throughout, he stressed that the mandate represented an "unprecedented and unbounded" claim of federal power.[5] In what could only have been a direct appeal to Kennedy, the brief argued that the mandate was a threat to individual liberty—the concern for individual liberty is the principle animating much of Kennedy's jurisprudence. And the power to compel an individual to engage in commerce, the brief charged, is "a revolution in the relationship between the central government and the governed." Kennedy would use almost the identical language in a question to Verrilli during the oral arguments.

Michael Carvin's trademark hard-charging style was evident in his brief's arguments against the mandate, which emphasized how the law "commanded," "compelled," and "forced" people into interstate commerce. He, too, framed the argument around the threat to individual liberty and challenged the government's factual and economic justifications for the law as well as its legal ones.[6]

Outside of the Court, some liberal and conservative special interest groups waged an unsuccessful effort to force the recusal of Kagan and Thomas from the case. Those conservative groups, including some Republican members of Congress, would not accept the Justice Department's insistence that Justice Kagan, as solicitor general, had never worked on the health care litigation. And the liberal groups argued that Justice Thomas had a conflict of interest, or at least the appearance of one, because of his wife's lobbying activities against passage of the health care law.[7]

The two justices never commented on the recusal demands, but it was clear from their silence when the Court granted review in the health care cases that they were in them to stay.

The demands came during a year in which several justices were criticized by the media and good government organizations for being too close to partisan politics. Scalia was targeted for delivering a lecture on the Constitution to the House Tea Party Caucus. Alito drew fire for attending the conservative *American Spectator*'s annual fund-raising dinner, where he previously had been the keynote speaker. There were questions about Thomas's relationship with the Texas real estate magnate Harlan Crow, a major supporter of conservative causes. And both Scalia and Thomas were criticized for appearing at separate meetings hosted by Republican mega-donors, the billionaire Koch brothers.[8]

The recusal demands and ethical questions surrounding Scalia, Thomas, Kagan, and Alito mixed into the hyper-partisan atmosphere choking Congress and the executive branch, and resulted in a political minefield for a Court whose justices' ideologies were now aligned with the politics of their appointing presidents.

Special interest groups also conducted an unprecedented amicus effort in the health care case. More than 150 friend of the court briefs were filed by medical associations, insurers, conservative and liberal civil rights and social welfare organizations, law professors, health professionals, and others.

Before the health care arguments in March, the justices avoided one potential mine. The Court, in an unsigned opinion, sent the Texas redistricting case back to the federal judge who drafted the interim redistricting plan. It vacated the interim plan because it was not clear that the judge had applied the correct standards in drafting the plan, including giving appropriate consideration to the Texas legislature's own map.

Concerns never materialized that the Court would use the Texas case to confront the constitutionality of the Voting Rights Act's provision requiring preclearance of voting changes by states with histories of voting discrimination.

Although the Court's marble-laden home has a remarkable insulating effect, figuratively and literally, the justices were acutely aware of the politically charged atmosphere surrounding the term, and the health care case in particular.

The weekend before the health care decision was issued, Ruth Bader Ginsburg delivered remarks at the annual convention of a liberal legal advocacy organization, the American Constitution Society. She noted that "No contest since the Court invited new briefs and argument in *Citizens United* has attracted more attention in the press, the academy and the ticket line outside the Supreme Court, a line that formed three days before the oral arguments commenced."

And another justice confided the day before the health care ruling that he had felt the political tensions surrounding the term more than in prior terms. "I felt it more this term," said the justice, adding, "I don't know why. Perhaps it was the many difficult issues [on the docket] and the political atmosphere coming together."

On the first day of the health care arguments, Monday, March 26, 2012, the action outside the Court was more energized than the arguments inside. Old-fashioned protests, complete with signs and chants, unfolded in front of the Supreme Court Building, and a long line of hopeful observers snaked around the corner. The Anti-Injunction Act of 1867 was the issue of the day, and it quickly became clear that the justices did not see that act as a bar to their reviewing the constitutionality of the health care law.

When Donald Verrilli stood up to make the government's argument that the act did not apply, he faced little pushback. Although not evident at the time, the Court's relatively low-key questioning left Verrilli with extra time to fill, which he seized effectively by laying the groundwork for the government's argument on Congress's tax power. Justice Sotomayor provided the opening by asking if there were any collateral consequences of not having health insurance. Verrilli spent considerable

time explaining how the penalty—tax—for not having insurance operated. That explanation, it would be seen later, had a keen impact on the
chief justice.

Tuesday, March 27, the second day, was the main event—the constitutionality of the individual mandate. Outside, a near-circuslike atmosphere prevailed: demonstrators, music, even a belly dancer occupied
the sidewalk below the building's plaza. Inside, the lawyers would play
to a packed house. More than a dozen members of Congress from both
sides of the aisle took seats in the courtroom, as did a number of Obama
administration cabinet members, including the attorney general and the
secretary of Health and Human Services. Bill McCollum, the former
Florida attorney general who had spearheaded the health care lawsuit,
had a special seat in the justices' guest section. The chief justice's wife,
who works as a legal headhunter, had recruited him for the law firm
where he then worked, and she gave him her seat since she was out of
town that day. McCollum found himself sitting between two of the chief
justice's physicians.

Verrilli was first at the podium and immediately encountered a
freakish problem. Slightly hoarse with a frog in his throat, he struggled
to begin his argument, took a sip of water, failed to clear his throat,
and tried again. Roberts, looking concerned yet unsure what to do,
leaned forward as if to say something, but Verrilli found his voice and
started again. After that, his argument seemed disjointed and weak.
Later, he was harshly criticized as having blown the most important
argument of the century.

Various factors led to that criticism. Verrilli, according to a recent
study of the arguments, was interrupted 180 times—an average of every
twenty-two seconds—during his fifty-six minutes at the podium by
questions primarily from the Court's conservative wing. He was able
to speak roughly ten or fewer seconds more than 40 percent of the time
before being interrupted. By contrast, his main opponent, Clement,
was interrupted thirty-three times in thirty minutes and spoke for one
minute or longer before being interrupted. He and Carvin faced far

fewer questions from the conservative justices, even though they were the challengers.[9]

Verrilli, Clement, and Carvin also have dramatically different styles. The solicitor general is soft-spoken and deliberate. Clement, standing with no papers to aid him, is quick, confident, and at ease with light bantering with the justices. Carvin is aggressive and tenacious. The Court's conservative justices, frankly, also are better questioners than their colleagues on the left, although that is slowly changing as Kagan and Sotomayor gain experience.

In the end, scholars and others who closely followed the mandate arguments agreed that Verrilli made the points that he needed to make. Working off of Judge Jeffrey Sutton's opinion in the Sixth Circuit, Verrilli stressed the unique features of the health insurance market. Because everyone would enter the market but there is no control over when, an insurance requirement in advance of the point of sale was justified. It was an application of the commerce clause, not an extension of it. Based on their later questions to Clement, both Roberts and Kennedy understood the government's argument, if not persuaded by it. Verrilli also reinforced the tax power argument from the previous day.

There was no question that it was a bad day for the government. There also was a surprising partisan overtone to some of the questions by Scalia and Alito. Scalia in particular seemed to be repeating the opponents' talking points and was the first to raise the broccoli argument against the individual mandate (if the government could force individuals to buy health insurance, it also could require them to buy broccoli). He later also referred to the so-called Cornhusker kickback amendment as if he believed it was still in the law, even though it had been removed two years earlier. And he startled the audience when, after Verrilli explained that we as a society had obligated ourselves to care for the uninsured when they showed up in emergency rooms for care, the justice leaned forward to retort, "Well, don't obligate yourself to that!"

The third and last day was not a good one either for the government. At least four justices seemed inclined to strike down the entire law if the mandate was unconstitutional, and the states' challenge to the Medicaid expansion appeared to make headway with a number of the justices—a remarkable reaction given the fact that the Supreme Court had never found a federal funding condition to be coercive and the federal government was covering the cost of the Medicaid expansion at 100 percent in the first three years and never less than 90 percent permanently.

The arguments ended on Wednesday, March 28, and the justices met the following Friday to vote on the issues.

The rest of the term might have seemed anti-climactic after the health care arguments, but the justices had other difficult issues to wrestle with and ultimately they did so with a surprising degree of consensus.

They unanimously recognized a "ministerial exception" to the nation's job-bias laws for religious employers sued for discrimination by employees who act as ministers for their churches. They also agreed that attaching a GPS unit to a vehicle and then using it to monitor a suspect's movements is a search under the Fourth Amendment. The earlier Texas redistricting decision had been unanimous. The justices also found common ground in two other cases that many expected to divide the Court: defining a fundamental question of what is patentable subject matter, and permitting judicial review of environmental compliance orders under the Clean Water Act.

However, they divided 5–4, in an opinion by Kennedy, that jail officials can conduct strip searches of prisoners to be released into the general jail population without the reasonable suspicion usually required by the Fourth Amendment. Roberts, Scalia, Thomas, and Alito joined Kennedy. And Kennedy joined his liberal colleagues in a 5–4 decision banning life in prison without parole for juvenile murders. As senior justice in the majority, he assigned the opinion to Elena Kagan, her most important opinion since joining the Court.

In one of the term's most aggressive rulings, Alito led a divided court in *Knox v. Service Employees International Union*. The case asked the justices if a union was required to send a notice to non-union members before deducting certain fees from their paychecks in a special assessment to challenge two state ballot referenda. The Court, voting 7–2, held that the union failed to give proper notice. That should have been the end of the case; but Alito, in a second ruling for the five conservative justices, overruled a long-standing precedent which had held that the First Amendment required unions to give non-union employees covered by union contracts the opportunity to opt out of special fees. The majority held that the union cannot require non-members to pay unless those members affirmatively opt in: a blow to unions' ability to raise money.

Late in the term, the Court's conservative majority quickly disposed of Montana's effort to preserve its century-old ban on corporate independent expenditures despite the *Citizens United* ruling striking down a similar federal ban in 2010.

In an unsigned decision, the same majority in *Citizens United* said, "The question presented in this case is whether the holding of *Citizens United* applies to the Montana state law. There can be no serious doubt that it does. Montana's arguments in support of the judgment below either were already rejected in *Citizens United*, or fail to meaningfully distinguish that case." [10]

Justice Breyer, writing for Ginsburg and Sotomayor, reiterated disagreement with *Citizens United* (as did Kagan for the first time) and added that "Montana's experience, like considerable experience elsewhere since the Court's decision in *Citizens United*, casts grave doubt on the Court's supposition that independent expenditures do not corrupt or appear to do so."

Despite important 5–4 ideological splits, there also was noticeably more "fluidity" among the justices, the breaking up of the usual ideological alignments. That was dramatically evident in the final two major decisions of the term: the immigration challenge, *Arizona v. United States*, and the health care ruling, *NFIB v. Sebelius*.

In the *Arizona* case, a 5–3 majority (Kagan recused) found that most of the state's controversial immigration provisions were preempted by federal immigration law. Roberts joined Kennedy, Ginsburg, Breyer, and Sotomayor in what was a major victory for the Obama administration and Verrilli, who argued the case for the administration.

Between the March arguments in the health care case and close to the end of the term, considerable chatter filled political and legal blogs over what was happening inside the Court. Reports that Chief Justice Roberts was "wobbly" on finding the mandate unconstitutional came from some sources. Accusations flew from right to left and back that certain commentators, even U.S. senators, were trying to intimidate the justices, particularly Roberts, with dire public warnings in essays and speeches of harm to the Court's institutional credibility if it became the first Supreme Court in more than seventy years to strike down a president's signature program. The blogging on the right, primarily by law professors such as Randy Barnett, exhibited a sort of controlled frenzy about the pending decision.

On June 28, 2012, the term's last day, the courtroom again was filled to capacity. The spouses of some of the justices came, as did retired Justice John Paul Stevens. At 10 am, the justices emerged from behind the maroon velvet drapes that separate the courtroom from their chambers and stood at their chairs as the marshal of the Court gave the traditional "Oyez, Oyez" call. Absent were the usual smiles and nods by the justices to the audience that marked the end of the term. Sotomayor and Kagan, bookends on the bench, appeared exhausted. Scalia, Thomas, and Alito looked grim and leaned back in their chairs. Only Breyer looked, well, content.

After disposing of two cases, only health care—the most important decision in the history of the Roberts Court—remained. Not surprisingly, Roberts announced that he had the opinion. And then Chief Justice Roberts, clear-eyed and in matter-of-fact voice, delivered the most remarkable opinion of his career.

He began by restating the government's argument that the individual mandate was a proper exercise of Congress's power to regulate commerce and to tax. Roberts said that he and Justices Scalia, Kennedy, Thomas, and Alito had concluded that the individual mandate was an unconstitutional exercise of Congress's commerce power. That power only allows Congress to regulate activity, not inactivity. "The individual mandate, however, does not regulate existing commercial activity," he wrote. "It instead compels individuals to become active in commerce by purchasing a product, on the ground that their failure to do so affects interstate commerce. Construing the Commerce Clause to permit Congress to regulate individuals precisely because they are doing nothing would open a new and potentially vast domain to congressional authority. Every day individuals do not do an infinite number of things."

The mandate also could not be upheld under the necessary and proper clause, added the chief justice, because even if it were necessary to achieve the act's insurance reforms, the expansion of federal power is not a "proper" means for making the reforms effective.

Roberts then turned to the government's second argument: the tax power. He noted the "well established" judicial principle "that if a statute has two possible meanings, one of which violates the Constitution, courts should adopt the meaning that does not do so." Roberts, joined by Ginsburg, Breyer, Sotomayor, and Kagan, held that the mandate was a constitutional exercise of Congress's power to tax. Although the act calls the payment for not having insurance a "penalty" and not a "tax," Roberts said the label does not determine whether it falls within the tax power. What is determinative is how it functions, he explained, and this penalty functions like a tax in many respects. For example, it is paid into the Treasury by taxpayers when they file their tax returns, he said. The requirement to pay is in the Internal Revenue Code and is enforced by the Internal Revenue Service. The amount is determined by such familiar factors as taxable income, number of dependents, and joint filing status, and it produces some revenue for the government. He added, "Because the Constitution permits such a tax, it is not our role to forbid it, or to pass upon its wisdom or fairness."

On the Medicaid issue, all of the justices except Ginsburg and Sotomayor agreed that the expanded program exceeded Congress's authority under the spending clause. Congress unconstitutionally coerced the states to adopt the changes by threatening to withhold all of the states' Medicaid grants. Roberts called the threat "a gun to the head." The surprise here was the agreement by Breyer and Kagan, who had been particularly skeptical of the challengers' arguments.

However, Roberts, joined only by Ginsburg, Breyer, Sotomayor, and Kagan, held that the constitutional violation could be remedied by invalidating the unconstitutional condition—the threat to withhold all existing Medicaid funds for failure to comply—and not the entire program. States now have a real choice, he said, adding, "We are confident that Congress would have wanted to preserve the rest of the act."

An emotional Kennedy next summarized an unusual joint dissent written, he said, by himself, Scalia, Thomas, and Alito. "In our view, the Act before us is invalid in its entirety." They agreed that the mandate could not be justified as an exercise of the commerce power, but they also did not see it as a proper exercise of the tax power. Congress, he said, went to great lengths to structure the mandate as a penalty, not a tax, and he accused the majority of "judicial tax-writing."

The Medicaid expansion, he said, could not be saved by the majority's remedy because that is "rewriting the statute" and there is no judicial authority to do so. Finally, he concluded that the mandate and the Medicaid expansion were central to the law's design and operation, and the act's other provisions would not have been enacted without them. "It must follow that the entire statute is linked together, and without the mandate and Medicaid expansion, the entire Act is inoperative," he said.

Amazingly, Kennedy, the center of power on the Roberts Court for six years, had lost the most important case on power in more than sixty years.

Ginsburg, in her trademark straightforward and calm manner, summarized perhaps her most thorough, clear, and persuasive opinion in her long career. Joined by Breyer, Sotomayor, and Kagan, she "emphatically" disagreed with the commerce clause ruling. She compared Congress's enactment of the Affordable Care Act in 2010 to its enactment of Social Security in 1930. The commerce clause ruling, she said, "harks back to the era, ended 75 years ago, when the Court routinely thwarted legislative efforts to regulate the economy in the interest of those who labor to sustain it. It is a stunning step back that should not have staying power." Her reference was to the long-repudiated *Lochner* era. And she, joined only by Sotomayor, explained how the Court went wrong in its view of the Medicaid expansion.

Roberts's decision was remarkable in that it gave the law's opponents a new limit on Congress's commerce clause power—the activity-inactivity distinction—as well as a new opportunity for states to challenge federal conditions on funding or regulations that they deem coercive. And yet, he upheld the mandate for the law's supporters and saved the Medicaid expansion. The decision also avoided an ideological split that would have made the Court vulnerable to charges of partisan politics since he and the liberal wing agreed on the tax power, and Kagan and Breyer joined the conservative wing on the Medicaid issue.

The boldest, most aggressive decision in the case, however, came from the four joint dissenters who would have struck down the entire, 2,700-page law, including many provisions that had nothing to do with the insurance reforms, such as amendments to the Black Lung Benefits Act that evened the playing field for dying coal miners or their widows seeking benefits from coal companies.

Just days after the decision, a CBS News correspondent reported that sources with specific knowledge of the deliberations had told her that Roberts initially voted to strike down the mandate but later switched his position.[11] The leaks told of how hard the conservatives tried to win Roberts back and, upon failing, they decided to have nothing more to do with him. The rift in the Court, she reported, was "deep and personal."

Suddenly, Roberts was being attacked by some opponents of the mandate as not a true conservative, unprincipled and political, motivated less by law and more by the desire to remove the Court from the eye of a political storm.

For example, in an interview with *National Review*, Randy Barnett, the leading opponent of the health care law who previously had said the Court would not be influenced "one bit by politics or the election," said after the ruling: "The fact that this decision was apparently political, rather than legal, completely undermines its legitimacy as a precedent. Its result can be reversed by the people in November, and its weak-tax-power holding reversed by any future Court without pause."[12]

The government's tax power argument had been rejected in the lower federal courts, but it was not considered a weak argument by some leading constitutional scholars and tax law experts, who wrote articles and amicus briefs advocating it from the beginning of the litigation through the Supreme Court. The Justice Department never waivered in raising the tax argument from the outset. Roberts himself mentioned that the penalty looked like a tax on the opening day of the health care arguments.

While the mandate's opponents were tearing down John Roberts, its supporters were comparing him to John Marshall, the Great Chief Justice, and how Marshall deftly avoided a constitutional showdown with President Thomas Jefferson. And, they suggested, Roberts was the modern Felix Frankfurter, a leading proponent of judicial restraint.

Justices change their minds, or make up their minds, even after they vote in the privacy of their conferences, after they exchange draft opinions with back-and-forth comments, after they find that an opinion "just doesn't write." As Ginsburg said in a late summer interview, "It ain't over 'til it's over."

The leak, perhaps the most significant breach of the Court's confidentiality in modern times, also said the health care dissenters' unhappiness with Roberts was "deep and personal," with potentially long-lasting effect.

In public comments later that summer and fall, Scalia and Kennedy denied the existence of a rift with Roberts. Other justices, in interviews with this author, acknowledged the high tensions and emotions at the term's end, but were confident that emotions would ease over the summer, just as they had after the Seattle-Louisville decision in 2007 and *Bush v. Gore* in 2000.

The end of the term was "certainly hard," said one justice. Another justice explained, "The term always starts friendly and relaxed, and gets tense at the end when the most difficult cases pile up. It's still collegial, but there is an overlay of frustration."

Despite sharp, often passionate disagreements, the Roberts and Rehnquist Courts have been among the most collegial Supreme Courts in history.

"When you arrive, it's apparent they're all friends," said one justice. "They disagree passionately sometimes, but don't take it personally. And when you're put in that environment, you tend to behave the same way. I can't imagine the Court when William O. Douglas and Felix Frankfurter were on it and they wouldn't speak to each other."

Another justice asked, "Who on the Court is the sort of person who is going to carry a grudge? Nino Scalia isn't going to carry a grudge. Clarence Thomas is going to pat you on the back and give you a hearty laugh all the time. That's a big part of it."

In general, one justice explained, "There's a lot of mutual esteem and mutual affection. There have been times on the Court when that hasn't been true, but I don't find it surprising that it is true now when I think about it. We have to live with each other for a long time. It's a lot more enjoyable if you like the people you work with, and this is a likable set of people."

The job of a justice is unusual in the sense that there is almost nothing like it, said another justice. "We all do the same thing. We read the same briefs; we go to the same arguments; we sit in the same conferences; we write the same decisions. It's easy to bond in a special way.

There are only eight people in the world I can talk to about politics, about a lot of things. So you do tend to share a lot and you do know everybody suffers under the same disability. To a large extent on a large number of subjects, we are the only choice of friends we have, so you find a way to get along."

All of which makes the possibility of long-term fallout among the justices because of the Affordable Care Act decision difficult to believe.

The leak report also said, "Some people say you would have to go back nearly 70 years to see this kind of tension, and almost bitterness, that now exists among the justices." Seventy years ago is a return to the Court of Douglas, Frankfurter, Robert Jackson, and Hugo Black. In his book *Scorpions*, Noah Feldblum describes those years as a time of bitter rivalries and invective among those justices.

When the term ended, several justices traveled overseas to teach and others left the city for favorite summer vacation spots. One justice predicted that the fall of 2012 would bring cooler temperatures inside the Court as well as outside.

"Everyone here does have the sense the institution is so much more important than the nine who are here at any point in time and we should not do anything to leave it in worse shape than it was in when we came on board," said the justice. "My guess is we'll come back in the fall and have the opening conference and it will be almost the same. I would be very surprised if it's otherwise." [13]

The justice appeared to be right when the new term opened on October 1, 2012. The justices seemed to be engaged in business as usual and there was no visible sign of the tensions that marked the end of the prior term. However, the new term once again threatened to expose deep divisions and to trigger high emotions.

Unlike the health care term, in which the justices struggled with structural issues concerning the roles and powers of the national and state governments under the Constitution, the new term raised issues of equality that would play out in challenges involving affirmative action, same-sex marriage, voting rights, and perhaps even abortion before the final day.

And those issues in the new term again present a challenge for Chief Justice Roberts, who had espoused consensus, humility, and modesty in making decisions during his confirmation hearings.

Roberts's upholding of the individual mandate in the health care law was the first time he had joined the Court's liberal wing in a 5–4 decision since becoming chief justice. Despite criticism by bitter and disappointed opponents of the law who questioned his conservative credentials, Roberts is no liberal, not even close. However, he is the chief justice of the United States, and as one justice, referring to the justices' alignments last term in the health care and the Arizona immigration decisions, noted: "The institution [Supreme Court] moves you, and perhaps even more a chief justice."

That is not to say that Roberts's decision was unprincipled.

Read his decision, Justice David Souter would say. What is not clear yet is the long-term significance of the commerce clause and Medicaid rulings. Roberts and the Court's four other conservatives approved a new limit on Congress's lawmaking power under the commerce clause, perhaps ultimately the most important limit in more than seventy years. How that will affect Congress's ability to address national problems, for example, a health crisis requiring mass inoculations, is yet unknown. And because of the Medicaid ruling, seven justices opened to potential challenges numerous federal programs that place conditions on states in return for federal funding.

Seven years before Roberts faced the most challenging case of his career, he sat in a Senate hearing room, a stone's throw from the Court to which he had just been nominated. A Democratic senator, not expecting an answer, asked: "What kind of justice will John Roberts be? Will you be a truly modest, temperate, careful judge in the tradition of Harlan, Jackson, Frankfurter and Friendly?"

Those four judges were practitioners of judicial restraint, long the mantra of the conservative legal community. It emphasizes deference to legislative bodies and respect for past precedents. Roberts claims that tradition when, in his health care opinion, he quotes an earlier Court, saying, " 'Proper respect for a co-ordinate branch of the government' requires that we strike down an Act of Congress only if 'the lack of constitutional authority to pass [the] act in question is clearly demonstrated.' "

In the health care battle, ironically, the liberal legal community, often accused of promoting judicial activism, was urging judicial restraint, and many in the conservative legal community, pushing a novel and "off the wall" commerce clause theory, were seeking judicial activism.

Roberts's decision and the joint dissent by Kennedy, Scalia, Thomas, and Alito also reflected two different views of what judicial restraint should have dictated that the Court do. For Roberts, it was the view of Harlan, Frankfurter, Jackson, and Friendly: If there is a reasonable construction of the law, save it. For the joint dissenters, judicial restraint meant: Strike down the law in order to enforce or protect the Constitution's limits on federal power.

Before the health care ruling, the constitutional law scholar and former acting solicitor general Neal Katyal, in a question-and-answer article in *The Washington Post*, said he thought "one of the hardest things about constitutional law is that there aren't clear answers to questions. There's some room for discretion on the part of judges."[14]

As the health care litigation in the lower courts and in the Supreme Court showed, reasonable judges and justices have different ways of finding the answers, and often in ways that defy ideology and politics.

In the years since the senator asked what kind of justice Roberts would be, Roberts has acted with a boldness that angered those on the left on issues of race, guns, and campaign finance, and with restraint and modesty at times that frustrated those on the right. Each term is a story in itself. With the health care decision, the Kennedy Court faded into the background and the Roberts Court firmly emerged.

There are many more stories to be told. With same-sex marriage, affirmative action, and voting rights on the docket in the 2012–13 term, a story dramatically different from the prior term may unfold. But at least for the one term that will be known always for its historic, landmark health care decision, Roberts could answer that senator's long ago question about whether he would be a moderate, temperate judge like Harlan, Jackson, Frankfurter, and Friendly, with a simple "Yes."

ACKNOWLEDGMENTS

The U.S. Supreme Court is one of the best and one of the strangest beats for a journalist. It is one of the best because there is constant variety in the cases that the justices hear and constant challenges in understanding the legal issues at the core of those cases. Behind even the dullest or most complex tax or ERISA case there often is a very human story waiting to be told. And the Supreme Court correspondent gets a number of opportunities as well to be a witness to history from Senate confirmation hearings to decisions that dramatically affect the nation.

The beat is also one of the strangest for a reporter because there is so little direct contact with the primary sources of the news—the justices. The reporter cannot call up the justice who wrote a majority opinion and ask, "Now what exactly did you mean by the fourth paragraph on page twenty-seven of your opinion?" The justices are notoriously, and unfortunately, reluctant to grant on-the-record interviews. Supreme Court reporters learn about the Court and the justices themselves through the justices' opinions and by observing them during oral arguments.

We also look to some of the brightest and most dedicated lawyers and law professors across the political spectrum who have spent years practicing before the Court and studying their decisions and the development of the law. As a reporter for *The National Law Journal*, I have benefited tremendously over the years in my work in general and in this book in particular from their willingness to give generously of their time and knowledge. There are too many to mention by name. I owe much to Rick Hasen of the University of California Irvine School of Law and Brad Smith of Capital University Law School for always responding to questions about campaign finance laws. Walter Dellinger of O'Melveny & Myers and Ted Olson of Gibson, Dunn & Crutcher, two of the busiest and finest appellate court practitioners, have shared their expertise with me not just for this book but for countless articles that I have written in the last twenty-five years, and I am truly grateful because there is always something new to learn about the Supreme Court, and they are superb teachers.

I owe a special thanks to Paul Smith of Jenner & Block and Greg Garre of Latham & Watkins. Both men head their firm's Supreme Court and appellate practices. They shared their experiences as practitioners and "students" of the Court during the early stages of this book and gave me invaluable context as I started on this journey.

This book simply would not have been possible without the support of David Brown, the editor in chief of *The National Law Journal*. From day one, he backed the project, juggled my schedule, exuded confidence in me, listened and offered suggestions when I got stuck in the writing, and made the impossible possible. "Thank you" just doesn't seem enough, David, but it is heartfelt. My colleague, Tony Mauro, generously bore more than his share of our newspaper duties when I took time to write. Without his willingness to do so, my task would have been much harder. I hope to return the favor some day. Another longtime colleague, Joan Biskupic, author of two books, one on Justice Sandra Day O'Connor and the other on Justice Antonin Scalia, was a valuable sounding board, offering advice when asked and encouragement when needed.

My cousin Paula Russo gave up many of her summer evenings to reading draft chapters. What a trouper! She gave excellent, detailed suggestions for clarifying legalese and explanations of decisions. Her input was invaluable and I am indebted to her. Thanks also go to Doug Kmiec of Pepperdine University School of Law for being a reader when I asked.

The entire team at Simon & Schuster impressed me from the beginning with their professionalism and commitment. The publisher,

Jonathan Karp, and my editor, Alice Mayhew, never wavered in their enthusiasm for the project. Before meeting her, I had heard of Alice Mayhew's reputation as one of the best editors in publishing. It was an honor to work with her and I was humbled by her confidence in and patience with a first-time book writer. Her assistant, Jonathan Cox, kept me on schedule, handled many details associated with producing a book, and always answered my questions swiftly and thoroughly. I could not have had better support throughout the process. My agent, Rafe Sagalyn, was my window into this new world of book publishing and provided sage advice and support. He was never intrusive but I always knew he was there if and when needed.

I also am very grateful to my entire family, not just my immediate family, for their interest and support along the way. No one could ask for better cheerleaders. My most indefatigable cheerleader, my mother, died shortly before the book was finished, and with her death went the certainty of at least one glowing review, and so much more.

Finally, this book is for the many people who have written to and e-mailed me over the years, often after my appearances on *PBS News-Hour*, because they were eager to know more about this institution that is so critical a player in our democracy. The late Justice Harry Blackmun, after being interviewed on C-SPAN many years ago, told me that he did not think the Supreme Court should be a great mystery to the American people. I hope this book makes it less mysterious to all who read it.

NOTES

The author conducted interviews with current and retired justices and former clerks from June 2011 through July 2012. Those interviews were on background, meaning that their comments could be used but without their names. In certain instances, Justices Antonin Scalia and John Paul Stevens agreed to have portions of their interviews on the record.

INTRODUCTION

1. H. Jefferson Powell, *A Community Built on Words: The Constitution in History and Politics.* University of Chicago Press, 2002, rev. ed. 2005, p. 6.
2. Morgan Smith, "One Man Standing Against Race-Based Laws," *Texas Tribune* (republished in *New York Times*, Feb. 23, 2012).
3. Greg Stohr, "Roberts Supreme Court's Partisan Split Shows New Justices Are Predictable," Bloomberg News, quoting Barbara Perry of University of Virginia's Miller Center of Public Affairs, July 1, 2011.
4. Joan Biskupic, "Justice Ginsburg Reflects on Term, Leadership Roles," *USA Today*, July 2, 2011.
5. Author interview with Theodore Olson, July 2011.
6. Jack Balkin, "High Politics and Judicial Decisionmaking," Balkinization, May 4, 2003.
7. Associate Justice Antonin Scalia, *Fox News Sunday*, July 29, 2012.
8. Associate Justice Stephen G. Breyer, "The Work of the Supreme Court," *Amer. Acad. of Arts & Sci.*, September–October 1998, p. 47.
9. "A Conversation with David Souter: How Does the Constitution Keep Up with the Times?" New Hampshire Supreme Court Society, Sept. 14, 2012.

PART 1: RACE
CHAPTER 1

1. Author telephone interview with James Ho, former clerk to Justice Clarence Thomas, September 2011.
2. "Gold Stripes: Chief Justice Rehnquist's Final Interview," NBC News, Sept. 4, 2005.
3. Author's interview with Justice Antonin Scalia, July 2011.

4. Author's interviews with justices, June 2011–July 2012.
5. Alex Markel, "Why Miers withdrew as Supreme Court nominee," National Public Radio, quoting conservative leaders on their opposition to Harriet Miers, Oct. 27, 2005.
6. George W. Bush, *Decision Points* (Crown, 2010), p. 98.
7. Senate Judiciary Committee Hearing on the Nomination of John Roberts Jr., Sept. 12–15, 2005; first session, p. 170.
8. Ibid., p. 144.
9. Ibid., p. 454.
10. Hope Yen, "Roberts Seeks Greater Consensus on Court," *Washington Post*, May 21, 2006, speech to Georgetown University Law Center graduates.

CHAPTER 2

1. Author's telephone interview with David Engle, May 2011.
2. Author's interview with Kathleen Brose, head of Parents Involved in Community Schools, February 2011.
3. Magnolia Chamber of Commerce, 2000 Census figures.
4. Douglas Judge, "Housing, Race and Schooling in Seattle: Context for the Supreme Court Decision," *Western Washington University Journal of Educational Controversy*, vol. 2, Winter 2007.
5. Author's interview with Joseph Olchefske, former superintendent of Seattle public schools, May 2011.
6. *Parents Involved in Community Schools v. Seattle School District No. 1*, 426 F.3d 1162 (CA9 2005).
7. Nina Totenberg, "Supreme Court to Weigh Schools' Racial Plans," National Public Radio, Dec. 4, 2006.
8. *Meredith v. Jefferson County Board of Education*, Brief for respondent on the writ of certiorari.
9. Press conference statement by Crystal Meredith, June 28, 2007.
10. James E. Ryan, "The Supreme Court and Voluntary Integration," *Harv. L. Rev.*, 131 (2007), p. 121.
11. Ibid., p. 140.
12. Michael Klarman, "Has the Supreme Court Been Mainly a Friend or a Foe to African Americans?" Symposium on Race and the Supreme Court, scotusblog, Feb. 1, 2010.

CHAPTER 3

1. Author's interview with Kathleen Brose, February 2011.
2. Mark Tushnet, *A Court Divided: The Rehnquist Court and the Future of Constitutional Law* (W. W. Norton, 2005), pp. 40–41.
3. Author's interview with Harry Korrell of Davis Wright Tremaine, February 2011.
4. Author's telephone interview with Sharon Browne of the Pacific Legal Foundation, March 2011.

5. Keith Ervin, "Parents Challenge Seattle District on Racial 'Tiebreaker,' " *Seattle Times*, July 19, 2000.
6. Author's interview with Michael Madden of Bennett Bigelow & Leedom, February 2011.
7. Jenni Laidman, "Order from the Court," *Louisville Magazine*, March 2009, p. 52.
8. Ibid., p. 55.

CHAPTER 4

1. *Comfort v. Lynn School Committee*, 418 F.3d 1 (CA1 2005).
2. Author's interview with Sharon Browne of the Pacific Legal Foundation, March 2011.
3. Author's interview with Michael Madden, February 2011.
4. Senate Judiciary Committee Hearing on the Nomination of Samuel Alito Jr., Jan. 9–13, 2006, p. 40.
5. Adam Liptak, "Few Glimmers of How Conservative Judge Alito Is," *New York Times*, Jan. 13, 2006.
6. George W. Bush, *Decision Points*, Crown, 2010, p. 102.
7. Author's interview with Walter Dellinger of O'Melveny & Myers, May 2011.
8. Author's interview with Michael Madden, February 2011.
9. Jessica Blanchard, "Supreme Court to Hear Seattle Schools Race Case," *Seattle Post-Intelligencer*, June 5, 2006.
10. National Review Online, June 6, 2006.
11. A Conversation with Justice Ruth Bader Ginsburg, Ohio State University Moritz College of Law, symposium on the Jurisprudence of Justice Ruth Bader Ginsburg, April 10, 2009.
12. Analyses of 2005–06 voting patterns of justices by Thomas Goldstein, scotusblog.

CHAPTER 5

1. Author's interview with Michael Madden, February 2011.
2. *Scribes Journal of Legal Writing* (2010), interviews with the justices.
3. Ibid.
4. Author's interview with Harry Korrell, February 2011.
5. Author's interview with Sharon Browne, March 2011.
6. Author's interview with Theodore Olson, July 2011.
7. Seth Waxman, Solicitor General of the United States, "Presenting the Case of the United States as It Should Be: The Solicitor General in Historical Context," Address to the Supreme Court Historical Society, June 1, 1998.
8. Author's interviews with former Department of Justice attorneys.
9. Author's interview with Michael Madden, February 2011.
10. Jeffrey Toobin, "After Stevens," *New Yorker*, March 22, 2010.
11. Author's interviews with justices.
12. Author's interview with Justice Antonin Scalia, July 2011.

CHAPTER 6

1. *Ledbetter v. Goodyear Tire & Rubber Co.*, rejecting the long-standing policy of the Equal Employment Opportunity Commission, held that Title VII's statute of limitation period (180 or 300 days) for filing a pay bias charge begins to run when "each allegedly discriminatory pay decision was made and communicated" to the employee and does not start over with each later paycheck;

   Hein v. Freedom From Religion Foundation: An old precedent permitting limited taxpayer standing to challenge government expenditures in violation of the First Amendment's establishment clause does not allow challenges to the Bush administration's use of federal funds to support its Office of Faith-Based and Community Initiatives program.

   National Association of Home Builders v. Defenders of Wildlife: The consultation requirement in the Endangered Species Act does not apply to the Environmental Protection Agency's transfer of water permitting authority to states under the Clean Water Act.
2. *Morse v. Frederick*, 551 U.S. 393 (2007), Thomas concurring.
3. *Ayers v. Belmontes*, 127 S.Ct. 469 (2006), Scalia, joined by Thomas, concurring.
4. Author's interview with John Payton, February 2011.
5. Adam Liptak, "The Same Words, but Differing Views," *New York Times*, June 29, 2007.
6. *Fisher v. University of Texas-Austin*, No. 11-345, argued Oct. 10, 2012.
7. Marcia Coyle, "Prevailing Winds: In the First Full Term with Alito, Court Took Marked Conservative Turn," *National Law Journal*, Aug. 1, 2007.

PART 2: GUNS
CHAPTER 7

1. *U.S. v. Emerson*, 270 F.3d 203 (CA5 2001).
2. *U.S. v. Miller*, 307 U.S. 174 (1939).
3. John Ashcroft, Attorney General of the United States, Letter to James Jay Baker, executive director, National Rifle Association, Institute for Legal Action, May 17, 2001.
4. John Ashcroft, Memorandum to All United States' Attorneys, Nov. 9, 2001.
5. Author's interview with Clark Neily, September 2010.
6. Author's interview with Robert Levy, September 2010.
7. Author's telephone interview with David Lehman, September 2010.
8. Author's interview with Alan Gura, September 2010.
9. Author's telephone interview with Stephen Halbrook, September 2010.
10. Author's telephone interview with Dennis Henigan, September 2010.
11. *Parker v. District of Columbia*, 311 F. Supp. 2d 163 (2004).
12. *Parker v. District of Columbia*, 478 F.3d 370 (CA D.C. 2007).
13. Author's telephone interviews with Dick Heller and Dan Von Breichenruchardt, November 2010.

14. David Nakamura and Robert Barnes, "Appeals Court Guts Strict D.C. Handgun Law," *Washington Post*, Feb. 11, 2007.
15. Christine Hauser, "Virginia Tech Shooting Leaves 33 Dead," *New York Times*, April 16, 2007.

CHAPTER 8

1. Antonin Scalia, *A Matter of Interpretation* (Princeton: 1997), pp. 136–137, note 13.
2. Author's interview with Alan Morrison, September 2010.
3. *District of Columbia v. Dick Anthony Heller*, Petition for a writ of certiorari, 07-290.
4. *District of Columbia v. Dick Anthony Heller*, Brief in response to petition for writ of certiorari, 07-290.
5. *Hamdi v. Rumsfeld*, 543 U.S. 507 (2004); *Rumsfeld v. Padilla*, 542 U.S. 426 (2004); *Rasul v. Bush/Al Odah v. U.S.*, 542 U.S. 466 (2004); *Hamdan v. Rumsfeld*, 548 U.S. 557 (2006).
6. Robert Barnes, "Administration Rankles Some with Silence in Handgun Case," *Washington Post*, Jan. 20, 2008.
7. Dick Cheney, *In My Time* (Simon & Schuster, 2011), p. 495.
8. Author's telephone interview with Peter Nickles, September 2010.
9. Author's interview with Walter Dellinger, September 2010.
10. Paul Collins Jr., *Friends of the Supreme Court: Interest Groups and Judicial Decisionmaking*, New York: Oxford University Press, 2008; Marcia Coyle, "Amicus Briefs are Ammo for Gun Case," *National Law Journal*, interview with Paul Collins Jr., March 10, 2008.

CHAPTER 9

1. Author's interview with Justice Antonin Scalia, July 2011.
2. Randy Barnett, "Scalia's Infidelity: A Critique of Faint-Hearted Originalism," William Howard Taft Lecture at the University of Cincinnati College of Law, Feb. 2, 2006.
3. Stephen Breyer, *Making Our Democracy Work* (Random House, 2011), pp. 80–81.
4. *Scribes Journal of Legal Writing* (2010).
5. "Notebook: Alito Is a Springsteen Fan," Associated Press, Jan. 9, 2006.
6. "Civil Rights: The Heller Case." Minutes from a Convention of the Federalist Society, Nov. 20, 2008.
7. J. Harvie Wilkinson III, "Of Guns, Abortions, and the Unraveling Rule of Law," *Va. L. Rev.* 95, no. 2, April 2009.
8. Richard A. Posner, "In Defense of Looseness: The Supreme Court and Gun Control," *New Republic*, Aug. 27, 2008.
9. Village of Morton Grove Handgun Ordinance, Morton Grove Public Library, July 29, 2008, www.webrary.org/ref/handgun.html.
10. Author's telephone interview with Dan Staackmann, Morton Grove Village president, August 2011.

PART 3: MONEY
CHAPTER 10

1. Author's interviews with David Bossie, April and May 2011.
2. George Lardner Jr. and Juliet Eilperin, "Burton Apologizes to GOP," *Washington Post*, May 7, 1998.
3. Glen Elsasser, "And the Last Shall Be 51st," *Chicago Tribune*, November 22, 1993.
4. Author's interviews with Michael Boos, April and May 2011.
5. Federal Election Campaign Laws: A Short History, www.fec.gov/info/app four.gov.
6. Adam Liptak, "Justice Defends Ruling on Finance," *New York Times*, Feb. 4, 2010.
7. Richard L. Hasen, "Citizens United and the Illusion of Coherence," Richard L. Hasen, 109 *Mich. L. Rev.*, 581 (2011).
8. Ibid.
9. Eric Lichtblau, "Long Battle by Foes of Campaign Finance Rules Shifts Landscape," *New York Times*, Oct. 15, 2010.

CHAPTER 11

1. Author's interview with James Bopp Jr., May 2011.
2. Author's interviews with David Bossie, April and May 2011, and with James Bopp Jr., May 2011.
3. California's Proposition 8, also known as the California Marriage Protection Act, was a ballot initiative approved by voters in 2008 that amended the state constitution to prohibit same-sex marriage.
4. Author's telephone interview with Theodore B. Olson, July 2011.
5. Barry Meier, "A New Round in a Long Coal Battle," *New York Times*, Nov. 9, 2010.
6. Marcia Coyle, "High Court Review Sought on Judicial Recusals," *National Law Journal*, Aug. 4, 2008.
7. *Caperton v. A.T. Massey Coal Co.*, Petition for a writ of certiorari, No. 08-22.
8. The Voting Rights Act of 1965, History of Federal Voting Rights Laws, U.S. Department of Justice, Civil Rights Division.
9. The two cases backed by Edward Blum in the 2012–13 Supreme Court term are *Fisher v. University of Texas-Austin* and *Shelby County, Ala. v. Holder*.

CHAPTER 12

1. The decision was *Maloney v. Cuomo*, a ruling by a three-judge panel of the U.S. Court of Appeals for the Second Circuit. Sotomayor was on the panel that rejected a man's claim that a New York ban on the martial arts weapon, nunchaku, violated the Second Amendment.
2. David Savage and James Oliphant, "Senate Set to Begin Sotomayor Debate; NRA is urging senators to vote against the Supreme Court nominee," *Los Angeles Times*, Aug. 4, 2009.

3. Warren Richey, "Sotomayor: 'Wise Latina' a bad choice of words," *Christian Science Monitor*, July 14, 2009.

4. Marcia Coyle, "The Case at the Center of Citizens United," *National Law Journal*, Aug. 3, 2009.

5. Author's interview with Justice Antonin Scalia, July 2011.

6. Author's interview with Norman Ornstein, American Enterprise Institute, September 2011.

7. Heather Gerken, Yale Law School, "Campaign Finance and the Doctrinal Death Match," Balkinization, balkin.blogspot.com/2011/06/campaign-finance -and-doctrinal-death.html.

PART 4: HEALTH CARE
CHAPTER 13

1. Author's interview with former Florida attorney general Bill McCollum, June 2012.

2. Jordan Fabian, "State Ags request Reid, Pelosi drop Nebraska Medicaid funds from health bill," *The Hill*, Dec. 30, 2009.

3. David Rivkin and Lee A. Casey, "Mandatory Insurance Is Unconstitutional," *Wall Street Journal*, Sept. 18, 2009.

4. Author's interviews with David Rivkin and Lee Casey, May 2012.

5. "Tea Party Activists Make Last Stand Against Health Care Vote," Foxnews .com, March 20, 2010.

6. Randy Barnett, Nathaniel Stewart, and Todd Gaziano, "Why the Personal Mandate to Buy Health Insurance Is Unprecedented and Unconstitutional," Heritage Foundation Legal Memorandum, No. 49, Dec. 9, 2009.

7. Letter from James Madison to J. C. Cabell, Feb. 13, 1829, The Constitutional Sources Project, www.consource.org/document/james-madison-to-j-c-cabell -1829-7-1-2/.

8. Jim Chen, "The Story of *Wickard v. Filburn*," University of Louisville Law School Legal Studies Research Paper Series, No. 2008-40 (available at http:// ssrn.com/abstract=1268162).

9. Marcia Coyle, "Supreme RX: The health care law's pro-and-con spin doctors," *National Law Journal*, Nov. 9, 2011.

10. Author's interview with Robert Weiner, June 2012.

11. Although Justice Stevens concluded that the death penalty was unconstitutional in *Baze v. Rees*, he concurred in the decision upholding Kentucky's lethal injection procedures out of respect for the Court's precedents on the death penalty. He explained: "The conclusion that I have reached with regard to the constitutionality of the death penalty itself makes my decision in this case particularly difficult. It does not, however, justify a refusal to respect precedents that remain a part of our law. This Court has held that the death penalty is constitutional, and has established a framework for evaluating the constitutionality of particular methods of execution. Under those precedents, whether

as interpreted by The Chief Justice or Justice Ginsburg, I am persuaded that the evidence adduced by petitioners fails to prove that Kentucky's lethal injection protocol violates the Eighth Amendment. Accordingly, I join the Court's judgment."

12. Biskupic, Joan, "Justice Stevens Keeps Cards Close to Robe," *USA Today*, March 12, 2010.

13. National Public Radio interview with Justice Ruth Bader Ginsburg, May 2, 2002.

CHAPTER 14

1. Senate Judiciary Committee Hearing on Nomination of Elena Kagan to Be an Associate Justice of the Supreme Court of the United States, June 28–30 and July 1, 2010 (available at: http://purl.fdlp.gov/GPO/gpo12385).

2. Tony Mauro, "A Strong Supreme Court Term for Business," *National Law Journal*, Aug. 1, 2012.

3. Lee Epstein, William M. Landes, and Richard A. Posner, "Is the Roberts Court Pro-Business?" at http://epstein.usc.edu/research/RobertsBusiness.pdf, Dec. 17, 2010.

4. Robin Conrad, "The Roberts Court and the Myth of a Pro-Business Bias," *Santa Clara L. Rev.* 49, no. 4, Jan. 1, 2009.

5. Author's interviews with Obama administration and Department of Justice lawyers, July–August 2012.

6. Author's interview with Neal Katyal of Hogan Lovells, June 2012.

7. *Thomas More Law Center v. Obama*, 651 F.3d 529 (CA6 2011).

8. *State of Florida v. U.S. Department of Health and Human Services*, 648 F.3d 1235 (CA11 2011).

9. *Liberty University v. Geithner*, 671 F.3d 391 (CA4 2011); *Commonwealth of Virginia v. Sebelius*, 656 F.3d 253 (CA4 2011).

CHAPTER 15

1. Author's interviews with Department of Justice attorneys, July–August 2012.

2. Tony Mauro, "Paul Clement's Second Chair," *National Law Journal*, April 2, 2012.

3. Marcia Coyle, "On Deck to Argue Against the Mandate: Carvin," *National Law Journal*, March 14, 2012.

4. *U.S. Department of Health and Human Services v. State of Florida*, No. 11-398, Brief for Petitioners on the Minimum Coverage Provision (available at acalitigationblog.blogspot.com/).

5. *U.S. Department of Health and Human Services v. State of Florida*, No. 11-398, Brief for State Respondents on the Minimum Coverage Provision (available at acalitigationblog.blogspot.com/).

6. *U.S. Department of Health and Human Services v. State of Florida*, No. 11-398,

Brief for Private Respondents on the Individual Mandate (available at acalitiga tionblog.blogspot.com/).

7. Joan Biskupic, "Calls for Recusal Intensify in Health Care Case," *USA Today*, Nov. 20, 2011; Robert Barnes, "Health-care Case Brings Fight Over Which Supreme Court Justices Should Decide It," *Washington Post*, Nov. 27, 2011.

8. Jeff Shesol, "Should Justices Keep Their Opinions to Themselves?" *New York Times*, June 28, 2011.

9. Ryan Malphurs and L. Hailey Drescher, " 'That's Enough Frivolity': A Not So Funny Countdown of the Supreme Court's Affordable Care Act Oral Arguments," June 6, 2012. "We studied the justices' interactions within oral arguments across the four cases, and disappointingly learned the justices took a less than fair approach when questioning parties" (available at SSRN: http:// ssrn.com/abstract=2079136, or http://dx.doi.org/10.2139/ssrn.2079136).

10. *American Tradition Partnership v. Bullock*, No. 11-1179, per curiam, decided June 25, 2012; Breyer, Ginsburg, Sotomayor, and Kagan, dissenting.

11. Jan Crawford, "Roberts Switched Views to Uphold Health Care Law," CBS News, July 1, 2012.

12. Fund, John, "The Flip That Will Flop?" National Review Online, July 2, 2012.

13. Marcia Coyle and Tony Mauro, "Justices Say Any Rifts Are Temporary," *National Law Journal*, July 16, 2012.

14. Sarah Kiff, "Neal Katyal on Defending Obamacare," *Washington Post*, March 28, 2012.

BIBLIOGRAPHY

BOOKS

Bailey, Michael A. and Forrest Maltzman. *The Constrained Court*. Princeton University Press, 2011.

Biskupic, Joan. *American Original*. Farrar, Straus & Giroux, 2009.

Breyer, Stephen. *Active Liberty: Interpreting Our Democratic Constitution*. Knopf, 2005.

———. *Making Our Democracy Work*. Knopf, 2010.

Burns, James MacGregor. *Packing the Court*. Penguin, 2009.

The Cato Institute. *Cato Supreme Court Review 2009–10*. 2010.

Greenburg, Jan Crawford. *Supreme Conflict*. Penguin, 2007.

Klarman, Michael J. *From Jim Crow to Civil Rights: The Supreme Court and the Struggle for Racial Equality*. Oxford University Press, 2004.

Powe Jr., Lucas A. *The Supreme Court and the American Elite*. Harvard University Press, 2009.

Rehnquist, William H. *The Supreme Court*. Knopf, 2001.

Rosen, Jeffrey. *The Supreme Court: The Personalities and Rivalries that Defined America*. Holt, 2007.

Savage, David G. *Turning Right: The Making of the Rehnquist Supreme Court*. John Wiley, 1993.

Scalia, Antonin. *A Matter of Interpretation: Federal Courts and the Law*. Princeton University Press, 1997.

Schwartz, Bernard. *A History of the Supreme Court*. Oxford University Press, 1993.

Stevens, John Paul. *Five Chiefs*. Little, Brown, 2011.

Toobin, Jeffrey. *The Nine*. Doubleday, 2007.

Tushnet, Mark. *A Court Divided*. Norton, 2005.

ARTICLES

"Civil Rights: The Heller Case," 4 NYU J.L. & Liberty 293 (Minutes from a Convention of the Federalist Society, 11-20-08)

Balkin, Jack M., and Sanford Levinson. "Understanding the Constitutional Revolution," 87 *Va. L. Rev.* 1045 (2001)

Barnett, Randy E. "Scalia's Infidelity: A Critique of Faint-Hearted Originalism," 75 *U. Cin. L. Rev.* 7 (2006)

————, Don B. Kates, "Under Fire: The New Consensus on the Second Amendment," 45 *Emory L.J.* 1139 (1995)

Biskupic, Joan. "The Alito/O'Connor Switch," 35 *Pepp. L. Rev.* 5 (2008)

Charles, Patrick J. "The Right of Self-Preservation and Resistance: A True Legal and Historical Understanding of the Anglo-American Right to Arms," *Cardozo Law Review De Novo*, Vol. 18, 2010

Chen, Jim. "The Story of *Wickard v. Filburn:* Agriculture, Aggregation, and Commerce," *Constitutional Law Stories* (Michael C. Dorf ed., 2d ed., Foundation Press, 2009)

Conrad, Robin S. "The Roberts Court and the Myth of a Pro-Business Bias," 49 *Santa Clara L. Rev.* 997 (2009)

Cornell, Saul "Originalism on Trial: The Use and Abuse of History in District of Columbia v. Heller," 69 *Ohio St. L. J.* 625 (2008)

Epstein, Lee, William M. Landes, Richard A. Posner. "Is the Roberts Court Pro-Business?" Dec. 17, 2010, at: http://epstein.usc.edu/research/Roberts Business.pdf

Gerken, Heather K. "Justice Kennedy and the Domains of Equal Protection," 121 *Harv. L. Rev.* 104 (2007)

Goldstein, Joel K. "Not Hearing History: A Critique of Chief Justice Roberts's Reinterpretation of Brown," 69 *Ohio St. L.J.* 791 (2008)

Hasen, Richard L. "Citizens United and the Illusion of Coherence," 109 *Mich. L. Rev.* 581 (2011)

————. "No Exit? The Roberts Court and the Future of Election Law," 57 *S. C. L. Rev.* 669 (2006)

Howell, Larry. "Once Upon a Time in the West: Citizens United, Caperton, and the War of the Copper Kings," 73 *Mont. L. Rev.* 25 (2012)

Moses, Margaret L. "Beyond Judicial Activism: When the Supreme Court is No Longer a Court," 14 *U. Pa. J. Const. L.* 161 (2011)

Ryan, James E. "The Supreme Court and Voluntary Integration," 121 *Harv. L. Rev.* 131 (2007)

Siegel, Neil S. "Umpires at Bat: On Integration and Legitimation," 24 *Constitutional Commentary* 701 (2008)

Siegel, Reva B. "Dead Or Alive: Originalism As Popular Constitutionalism in *Heller*," 122 *Harv. L. Rev.* 191 (2008)

———. "*Heller* & Originalism's Dead Hand—In Theory and Practice," 56 *U.C.L.A. L. Rev.* 1399 (2009)

Wilkinson III, J. Harvie. "Of Guns, Abortions, and the Unraveling Rule of Law," 95 *Va. L. Rev.* 253 (2009)

KEY ROBERTS COURT DECISIONS

The following decisions raised the most controversial and significant issues during the first seven terms of the Roberts Court.

Ayotte v. Planned Parenthood of Northern New England (2006): 9–0 decision by Justice Sandra Day O'Connor. A New Hampshire law requiring parental notification when minors seek abortions was ruled unconstitutional because it lacked an exception for the health of the mother, but the entire law did not have to be struck down; lower courts may be able to find a narrower remedy.

League of United Latin American Citizens (LULAC) v. Perry (2006): 5–4 decision by Justice Anthony Kennedy. The Texas Legislature's redistricting plan did not violate the Constitution, but part of the plan that diluted Latinos' votes violated the Voting Rights Act of 1965. Majority: Kennedy, Stevens, Souter, Ginsburg, Breyer; Dissent: Roberts, Scalia, Thomas, Alito.

Hudson v. Michigan (2006): 5–4 decision by Justice Antonin Scalia. The Fourth Amendment does not require the exclusion of evidence when police violate the "knock and announce" rule before executing a search warrant. Majority: Roberts, Scalia, Kennedy, Thomas, Alito; Dissent: Stevens, Souter, Ginsburg, Breyer.

Garcetti v. Ceballos (2006): 5–4 decision by Justice Anthony Kennedy. Public employees have no First Amendment protection for statements made in the course of their official duties. Majority: Roberts, Scalia, Kennedy, Thomas, Alito; Dissent: Stevens, Souter, Ginsburg, Breyer.

Kansas v. Marsh (2006): 5–4 decision by Justice Clarence Thomas. Kansas law that imposes the death penalty when mitigating and aggravating circumstances are equally balanced does not violate the Eighth Amendment. Majority: Roberts, Scalia, Kennedy, Thomas, Alito; Dissent: Stevens, Souter, Ginsburg, Breyer.

Hamdan v. Rumsfeld (2006): 5–3 decision by Justice John Paul Stevens. Military commissions established by the George W. Bush administration violate the Uniform Code of Military Justice and the Geneva Conventions. Majority: Stevens, Kennedy, Souter, Ginsburg, Breyer; Dissent: Scalia, Thomas, Alito. (Roberts recused).

Parents Involved in Community Schools v. Seattle School District; Meredith v. Jefferson County Board of Education (2007): 5–4 decision by Chief Justice John Roberts Jr. The use of race in the assignment of students to public schools violates the 14th Amendment. Majority: Roberts, Scalia, Kennedy, Thomas, Alito; Dissent: Stevens, Souter, Ginsburg, Breyer.

Gonzales v. Carhart (2007): 5–4 decision by Justice Anthony Kennedy. The federal Partial-Birth Abortion Ban Act of 2003 is not unconstitutional because it lacks an exception to protect the health of the woman. Majority: Roberts, Scalia, Kennedy, Thomas, Alito; Dissent: Stevens, Souter, Ginsburg, Breyer.

Massachusetts v. Environmental Protection Agency (2007): 5–4 decision by Justice John Paul Stevens. The Environmental Protection Agency has authority under the federal Clean Air Act to regulate carbon dioxide and other greenhouse gases. Majority: Stevens, Kennedy, Souter, Ginsburg, Breyer; Dissent: Roberts, Scalia, Thomas, Alito.

Ledbetter v. Goodyear Tire & Rubber Co. (2007): 5–4 decision by Justice Samuel Alito Jr. Workers bringing Title VII pay discrimination claims must file a complaint with the Equal Employment Opportunity Commission within 180 days of the discriminatory pay-setting decision or be time-barred, even if they were unaware of the discrimination at that time or the effects continued to the present. Majority: Roberts, Scalia, Kennedy, Thomas, Alito; Dissent: Stevens, Souter, Ginsburg, Breyer.

Hein v. Freedom from Religion Foundation (2007): 5–4 decision by Justice Samuel Alito Jr. Citizens do not have standing as taxpayers to bring establishment clause challenges to Executive Branch religious-related programs if they are funded by general appropriations instead of by specific congressional grants. Majority: Roberts, Scalia, Kennedy, Thomas, Alito; Dissent: Stevens, Souter, Ginsburg, Breyer.

Federal Election Commission v. Wisconsin Right to Life (2007): 5–4 decision by Chief Justice John Roberts Jr. The Bipartisan Campaign Reform Act's ban on the use of corporate treasury funds for political advertisements in the sixty days before an election is unconstitutional as applied to ads that do not explicitly endorse or oppose a candidate. Majority: Roberts, Scalia, Kennedy, Thomas, Alito; Dissent: Stevens, Souter, Ginsburg, Breyer.

Morse v. Frederick (2007): 5–4 decision by Chief Justice John Roberts Jr. School officials do not violate the First Amendment when they prohibit pro-drug messages, such as a student sign saying Bong Hits for Jesus at a school-supervised event. Majority: Roberts, Scalia, Kennedy, Thomas, Alito; Dissent: Stevens, Souter, Ginsburg, Breyer.

Bell Atlantic Corp. v. Twombly (2007): 7–2 decision by Justice David Souter. An antitrust lawsuit alleging a violation of Section 1 of the Sherman Act must allege facts that plausibly suggest an illegal conspiracy.

Majority: Roberts, Scalia, Kennedy, Souter, Thomas, Breyer, Alito; Dissent: Stevens, Ginsburg.

Bowles v. Russell (2007): 5–4 decision by Justice Clarence Thomas. A judge's error on the time for the filing of an appeal by a criminal defendant does not excuse the late filing of the appeal. Majority: Roberts, Scalia, Kennedy, Thomas, Alito; Dissent: Stevens, Souter, Ginsburg, Breyer.

Boumediene v. Bush (2008): 5–4 decision by Justice Anthony Kennedy. The Military Commissions Act of 2006 violates the Suspension Clause of the Constitution. Majority: Stevens, Kennedy, Souter, Ginsburg, Breyer. Dissent: Roberts, Scalia, Thomas, Alito.

Kennedy v. Louisiana (2008): 5–4 decision by Justice Anthony Kennedy. The Eighth Amendment bars states from imposing the death penalty for the rape of a child where the crime does not result in death. Majority: Stevens, Kennedy, Souter, Ginsburg, Breyer; Dissent: Roberts, Scalia, Thomas, Alito.

Davis v. Federal Election Commission (2008): 5–4 decision by Justice Samuel Alito Jr. The "millionaire's amendment" to the 2002 Bipartisan Campaign Finance Act, which raised the contribution limit for candidates running against self-financed candidates, violates the First Amendment. Majority: Roberts, Scalia, Kennedy, Thomas, Alito; Dissent: Stevens, Souter, Ginsburg, Breyer.

District of Columbia v. Heller (2008): 5–4 decision by Justice Antonin Scalia. The Second Amendment guarantees an individual right to possess a gun in the home for self-defense. Majority: Roberts, Scalia, Kennedy, Thomas, Alito; Dissent: Stevens, Souter, Ginsburg, Breyer.

Melendez-Diaz v. Massachusetts (2009): 5–4 decision by Justice Antonin Scalia. A criminal defendant has a Sixth Amendment right to confront the lab analyst who prepared a laboratory report intended for use at trial. Majority: Stevens, Scalia, Souter, Thomas, Ginsburg; Dissent: Roberts, Kennedy, Breyer, Alito.

Ashcroft v. Iqbal (2009): 5–4 decision by Justice Anthony Kennedy. An Arab Muslim man arrested after the September 11 terrorist attacks and later released did not plead sufficient facts in his lawsuit charging high-ranking government officials with discrimination. Majority: Roberts, Scalia, Kennedy, Thomas, Alito; Dissent: Stevens, Souter, Ginsburg, Breyer.

Caperton v. A.T. Massey Coal Co. (2009): 5–4 decision by Justice Anthony Kennedy. Due process requires a judge to recuse himself from a case in which one of the parties contributed $3 million to the judge's election campaign. Majority: Stevens, Kennedy, Souter, Ginsburg, Breyer; Dissent: Roberts, Scalia, Thomas, Alito.

Ricci v. DeStefano (2009): 5–4 decision by Justice Anthony Kennedy. Employers must have a "strong basis in evidence" to believe they will be sued for disparate impact discrimination before engaging in intentional discrimination to avoid such a lawsuit. Majority: Roberts, Scalia, Kennedy, Thomas, Alito; Dissent: Stevens, Souter, Ginsburg, Breyer.

Northwest Austin Municipal Utility District No. 1 v. Holder (2009): 8–1 decision by Chief Justice John Roberts Jr. The Voting Rights Act permits all political subdivisions of a "covered" jurisdiction to seek "bail out" from the requirement that they get preclearance of any changes in their voting practices. Majority: Roberts, Stevens, Scalia, Kennedy, Souter, Ginsburg, Breyer, Alito; Dissent: Thomas.

Gross v. FBL Financial Services (2009): 5–4 decision by Justice Clarence Thomas. Workers in an age job discrimination suit must prove by a "preponderance of the evidence" that age was the "but-for" cause of the employer's action. Majority: Roberts, Scalia, Kennedy, Thomas, Alito; Dissent: Stevens, Souter, Ginsburg, Breyer.

Citizens United v. Federal Election Commission (2010): 5–4 decision by Justice Anthony Kennedy. The federal ban on corporations and unions using their treasury funds for independent campaign spending violates the First Amendment. Majority: Roberts, Scalia, Kennedy, Thomas, Alito; Dissent: Stevens, Souter, Ginsburg, Breyer.

Graham v. Florida (2010): 6–3 decision by Justice Anthony Kennedy. The Eighth Amendment bars the imposition of a sentence of life in prison without parole on juveniles who commit non-homicide crimes. Majority: Roberts, Stevens, Kennedy, Ginsburg, Breyer, Sotomayor. Dissent: Scalia, Thomas, Alito.

McDonald v. City of Chicago (2010): 5–4 decision by Justice Samuel Alito. The Second Amendment guarantee of an individual right to possess a gun in the home applies to the states. Majority: Roberts, Scalia, Kennedy, Thomas, Alito; Dissent: Stevens, Ginsburg, Breyer, Sotomayor.

U.S. v. Comstock (2010): 7–2 decision by Justice Stephen Breyer. Congress had authority under the necessary and proper clause to enact a law providing for the civil commitment of dangerous sexual offenders who had completed their criminal sentences. Majority: Roberts, Stevens, Kennedy, Ginsburg, Breyer, Alito, Sotomayor; Dissent: Scalia, Thomas.

U.S. v. Stevens (2010): 8–1 decision by Chief Justice John Roberts Jr. A federal law prohibiting the knowing selling of depictions of animal cruelty was overbroad and violated the First Amendment. Majority: Roberts, Stevens, Scalia, Kennedy, Thomas, Ginsburg, Breyer, Sotomayor. Dissent: Alito.

Doe v. Reed (2010): 8–1 decision by Chief Justice John Roberts Jr. A law requiring public disclosure of the identity of petition signers does not generally violate the First Amendment. Majority: Roberts, Stevens, Scalia, Kennedy, Ginsburg, Breyer, Sotomayor, Alito. Dissent: Thomas.

Holder v. Humanitarian Law Project (2010): 6–3 decision by Chief Justice John Roberts Jr. A federal law prohibiting material support of terrorist-designated foreign organizations is not unconstitutionally vague as applied to a group seeking to teach and advocate peaceful resolution of conflicts to two such designated organizations. Majority: Roberts, Stevens, Scalia, Kennedy, Thomas, Alito; Dissent: Ginsburg, Breyer, Sotomayor.

Chamber of Commerce v. Whiting (2011): 5–3 decision by Chief Justice John Roberts Jr. Federal immigration law does not preempt an Arizona law requiring employers to check the immigration status of potential employees and revoking the business license of those who hire illegal immigrants. Majority: Roberts, Scalia, Kennedy, Thomas, Alito; Dissent: Ginsburg, Breyer, Sotomayor. (Kagan recused).

AT&T Mobility v. Concepcion (2011): 5–4 decision by Justice Antonin Scalia. Federal arbitration law preempts state-law rules prohibiting contracts with clauses that bar class actions. Majority: Roberts, Scalia, Kennedy, Thomas, Alito; Dissent: Ginsburg, Breyer, Sotomayor, Kagan.

Wal-Mart v. Dukes (2011): 5–4 decision by Justice Antonin Scalia. A nationwide class of female employees suing Wal-Mart for discrimination in pay and promotions failed to have common questions of law or fact in order to qualify as a class action under federal rules. Majority: Roberts, Scalia, Kennedy, Thomas, Alito; Dissent: Ginsburg, Breyer, Sotomayor, Kagan.

American Electric Power v. Connecticut (2011): 8–0 decision by Justice Ruth Bader Ginsburg. States cannot use common-law nuisance lawsuits in an attempt to limit greenhouse gases. Majority: Roberts, Scalia, Kennedy, Thomas, Ginsburg, Breyer, Alito, Kagan. (Sotomayor recused).

Snyder v. Phelps (2011): 8–1 decision by Chief Justice John Roberts Jr. The First Amendment protects protests by the Westboro Baptist Church at military funerals from state tort liability, including lawsuits for intentional infliction of emotional distress. Majority: Roberts, Scalia, Kennedy, Thomas, Ginsburg, Breyer, Sotomayor, Kagan. Dissent: Alito.

Brown v. Entertainment Merchants Assn. (2011): 7–2 decision by Justice Antonin Scalia. A state law prohibiting the sale or rental to minors of violent video games violates the First Amendment. Majority: Roberts, Scalia, Kennedy, Ginsburg, Sotomayor, Kagan, Alito. Dissent: Thomas, Breyer.

Sorrell v. IMS Health (2011): 6–3 decision by Justice Anthony Kennedy. A Vermont law banning the sale of doctors' prescribing information to drug and data mining companies violates the First Amendment. Majority: Roberts, Scalia, Kennedy, Thomas, Alito, Sotomayor; Dissent: Ginsburg, Breyer, Kagan.

Arizona Free Enterprise Club v. Bennett (2011): 5–4 decision by Chief Justice John Roberts Jr. The matching funds mechanism in an Arizona campaign finance law violates the First Amendment. Majority: Roberts, Scalia, Kennedy, Thomas, Alito; Dissent: Ginsburg, Breyer, Sotomayor, Kagan.

J.D.B. v. North Carolina (2011): 5–4 decision by Justice Sonia Sotomayor. A juvenile's age is a factor in determining whether Miranda warnings are required. Majority: Kennedy, Ginsburg, Breyer, Sotomayor, Kagan; Dissent: Roberts, Scalia, Thomas, Alito.

Arizona Christian School Tuition Organization v. Winn (2011): 5–4 decision by Justice Anthony Kennedy. Arizona taxpayer group does not have standing to challenge a tuition tax credit that largely goes to private religious schools. Majority: Roberts, Scalia, Kennedy, Thomas, Alito; Dissent: Ginsburg, Breyer, Sotomayor, Kagan.

Arizona v. U.S. (2012): 5–3 decision by Justice Anthony Kennedy. Federal immigration law preempts most of Arizona's anti-immigration law. Majority: Roberts, Kennedy, Ginsburg, Breyer, Sotomayor; Dissent: Scalia, Thomas, Alito. (Kagan recused).

Miller v. Alabama (2012): 5–4 decision by Justice Elena Kagan. The Eighth Amendment bars the sentence of life in prison without parole for juvenile murderers. Majority: Kennedy, Ginsburg, Breyer, Sotomayor, Kagan; Dissent: Roberts, Scalia, Thomas, Alito.

Knox v. Service Employees International Union (2012): 7–2 decision by Justice Samuel Alito Jr. The First Amendment is violated when a union imposes a special assessment without the affirmative consent of non-members. Majority: Roberts, Scalia, Kennedy, Thomas, Ginsburg, Alito, Sotomayor; Dissent: Breyer, Kagan.

National Federation of Independent Business v. Sebelius (2012): 5–4 decision by Chief Justice John Roberts Jr. The Affordable Care Act's requirement that individuals purchase health insurance or pay a penalty is a constitutional exercise of Congress's authority to levy taxes. Majority: Roberts, Ginsburg, Breyer, Sotomayor, Kagan; Dissent: Scalia, Kennedy, Thomas, Alito.

PHOTO CREDITS

INDEX